THE TALE
OF
A LITVAK

BALTIC
SEA

RIGA

LATVIA

ZAGER

.TELZSH   .SHAVEL

.MEMEL
(KLAIPEDAS)

PONIEVEZH

LITHUANIA
1920 - 1940

.KEIDAN

GERMANY

KOVNO
(KAUNAS)

SLABODKA .

KIBART.   .VILKOVISK   .PREN
VIRBALON.   .TROKI
MARIVAMPOLE   BALBIRISHOK   .STOKLISHOK
KALVARI.   .ALYTA
        SIMNA .
LAZDEI.   .SEREI (SEIRIJAI)
   VISHEI.   .MERETZ
SUVALK   SEINI   .LEIPUN
              KOPCHEVE
              .DRUZGENIK
              .SOPOTKIN
              .HALINKE
YAGUSTOV
(AUGUSTOW)

VILNA (VILNIUS)

WHITE RUSSIA

MINSK
WOLOZHIN.

POLAND

RAIGROD.   GRODNO   .LIDA
GRAIEWO.   .SKIDEL   .MIR
      .SUCHOVOLIA
STUCHIN .
(SCZUCZYN)   .SOKOLKA
   .LOMZA

BIALYSTOK   .SLONIN

BOANSK.

.SEMIATICH

WARSAW

BREST   PINSK

MAP of FAMILIAR PLACES IN LITHUANIA & POLAND

THE TALE
OF
A LITVAK

by

Morris S. Schulzinger

Philosophical Library
New York

Library of Congress Cataloging in Publication Data

Schulzinger, Morris S. (Morris Simcho), 1900-
    The tale of a Litvak.

    1. Schulzinger, Morris S. (Morris Simcho),
1900- . 2. Physicians—United States—Biography.
3. Physicians, Jewish—United States—Biography.
4. Jews—United States—Biography. I. Title.
R154.S3537A34   1984   610'.92'4 [B]   84-7693
ISBN 0-8022-2454-7

Published 1985 by Philosophical Library, Inc.
200 West 57th Street, New York, New York 10019.
Copyright 1985 by Morris S. Schulzinger.

Manufactured in the United States of America.

Table of Contents

List of Illustrations

FOREWORD

The vast majority of American Jews came to the United States from Eastern Europe during a mass exodus from Czarist Russia. It began with the Kiev Pogroms of 1881 and continued for forty years until the gates of America were closed to mass immigration in 1921. During these fateful decades three million Jews poured onto the hospitable shores of America. They were forced to uproot from the lands of their birth by the vicious persecutions of anti-Semitic governments instigated or condoned by the Church.

Most of these immigrants arrived in steerage, penniless and exhausted from the long journey. Along with their meager belongings they bore the deep scars of poverty and terror. But they also brought with them a rich heritage of learning, social idealism, a deep yearning for democracy, and a fantastic drive to succeed. The emergence of American Jewry from its humble beginnings to the most affluent, influential and cultured Jewry in history is undoubtedly one of the great sagas in the annals of peoples.

With minor variations of time, place and circumstance, my background in Russia and my experiences in the United States parallel the background and experiences of many American Jews. My lifespan, which coincides with the span of this century, and my involvement in the struggles of the era make me privy to nuances which may be of interest to concerned readers. Most of the older American Jews and their children will readily identify with my story. Their offspring, who are by now largely ignorant of their roots though increasingly eager to learn, will hopefully say, "This is what my parents have told me or have tried to tell me." In the substance and minutiae of my story, which is set against the important events of the times, they may find significant clues to their own roots.

I wrote this account at the age of eighty for my family, with hopes of a wider interested audience. The narrative is based on my own recollections and writings and on the recollections and writings of my parents, who spent nearly equal thirds of their long lives in Europe, the United States and Israel.

I was born in 1900 in a remote corner of Czarist Russia in the village of Serei, Lithuania, in the Government of Suvalk near East Prussia and the Baltic Sea. In 1921, at the age of twenty, I emigrated to the United States and made my home in Cincinnati, Ohio. The world in which I was born was rural, primitive, stagnant, superstitious and sharply divided into two camps— illiterate, deeply religious Christians and deeply religious Jews. Our only common bonds were economic necessity and Czarist oppression. My adopted country, conversely, was a bustling land of opportunity and culture. I discovered the meaning of religious freedom and political equality and was amazed at the democratic spirit, the decency and the fairness of the American people. The bigotry and the ugliness that marred the idyllic American scene during the Twenties and Thirties fade into insignificance by comparison with the brutal world I left behind.

My European education was traditional and began in the home. By the time I entered heder (Hebrew school) at the age of four, I could read in the prayer book and knew a great deal about the Jewish holidays and customs. At the age of five I was enrolled in a modern Hebrew school founded by my mother, and from ages eight to fourteen I studied the Talmud, mostly in *Yeshivoth* (Talmudic academies). As a teenager, I spent World War I dodging artillery shells, watching the advances and retreats of the opposing armies, avoiding the Russian and German forced-labor battalions, getting to know the Karaites of Troki, and feasting on German literature and on old and modern Jewish culture as a war refugee in Vilna.

As a child of seven I nearly lost my life in an acute attack of scarlet fever and learned much about folk medicine and the occult. Near the end of the war I witnessed the revolt of the German Army against the Kaiser and was exposed to the winds of change. In 1918, at the beginning of the Bolshevik Revolution, I narrowly escaped a firing squad when I was arrested and tried by a revolutionary tribunal—thus learning early what Communism was all about. During my last two years in Europe I received a college preparatory education at the first Hebrew gymnasium of the newly liberated Lithuania. I also met my 'Pupi' (Doll) whom I married five years later in Cincinnati.

I came to the United States with firmly set goals and a tremendous drive to succeed. My aims were to pursue knowledge through science; to marry my Pupi and establish a Jewish home; to contribute to leadership in the Jewish community; and to help redress the wrongs against my people through Zionist activities.

During my first seven years in the U.S. I earned a Master's degree in medical research and obtained my M.D. degree. In 1926 I married my high school sweetheart and began raising a family—a daring move at a time when most physicians did not marry until much later in life. In 1928 I was awarded the highest research fellowship by the University of Cincinnati, but my career as a research scientist was cut short by the Great Depression. During the next fifty-five years I was busily engaged in the practice of medicine while leading a very active social and public life and maintaining a lively interest in the tours and detours of the political and scientific developments of the times.

Following in the European Jewish tradition, I became active in Jewish community affairs, and over a period of twenty-five years I founded and led a number of Jewish organizations in Cincinnati. In the course of these activities I got to know many of the Jewish intellectual, religious and public leaders of the U.S. and nearly all of the future leaders of Israel. Many of these personalities were guests at our home, over which my Pupi presided with grace and beauty. The years of World War II were spent ministering to industrial casualties in Cincinnati. After the war, I embarked on a twenty-year study of accident causation and prevention which brought me great personal and professional satisfaction, as well as national and world reknown.

With the end of World War II came the shocking news about the Holocaust, in which one-third of the Jewish people perished. Among the victims were Pupi's mother and a large part of her family, my own sister and her family, and many relatives in Lithuania and Poland. The unspeakable cruelties perpetrated by the Nazis against six million Jews shook the conscience of the world and left the Jewish people dazed and in agony. The repercussions of these crimes against humanity will continue to plague the world for centuries to come. The widespread anti-Semitism and the indifference of most of the world toward the plight of the Jews prevented the saving of millions of Jewish lives, and a world poisoned by hatred reaped a bitter harvest. A personal tragedy still closer to home occurred with the death of our gifted son. These are the permanent scars.

As partial compensation for the Holocaust—if such be possible—came the rebirth of the State of Israel and with it a new era of hope for the Jewish people. I visited Israel on numerous occasions as a guest of the government and on my own, and have contributed modestly to its development. My friendship with Golda Meir, which extended over a period of fifty-five years, was capped by a lengthy, emotional visit to her home during the last year of her life.

I have described the Jewish festivals in Serei with particular fidelity as a memorial to that beautiful Jewish world—the world of our forebears—that is no more. I have also tried to render word portraits and sketches of some of the personalities and leaders I was priviledged to know. I have endeavored to balance biographical and historical events, believing with Emerson that there is properly no history—only biography.

In my journey from Serei to Cincinnati I have witnessed mammoth upheavals—monarchies overthrown, Fascism discredited, democracy perverted, socialism collapsed, capitalism bankrupt, faith discarded, humanity violated, and a confused world sans ideals, wisdom or direction, groping in the dark. Yet, I believe that in time the world will right itself somehow. It is said that "Hope is a better companion than fear" and there is always a chance that there is something better beyond the horizon.

Morris Simcho Schulzinger
June 1983

I wish to acknowledge with deep gratitude the help of my daughter Penina Frankel, who has drawn all the maps and researched the family trees, and who painstakingly typed and proofread the entire manuscript. I also wish to thank my niece Chana Rosen and my daughters Judith Lucas and Penina Frankel for valuable suggestions and for other help, and the publishers for their fine cooperation.

The Hebrew words and idioms used in the shtetl have been transliterated in their Yiddish forms whereas the Hebrew words and expressions used in the narrative sections were transliterated according to modern day spoken Hebrew (Sephardic).

Morris S. Schulzinger

PART ONE

LITHUANIA 1900-1920

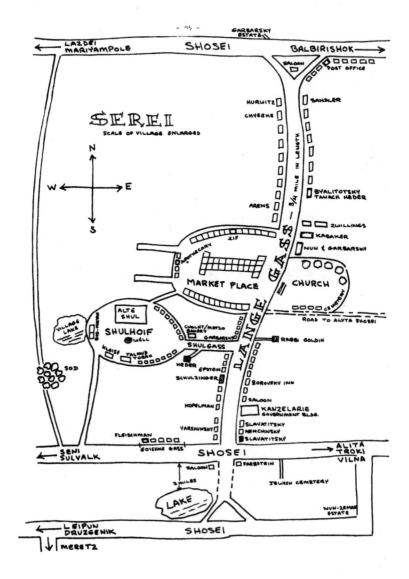

SEREI

SCALE OF VILLAGE ENLARGED

CHAPTER ONE

Early Memories

> "Backward turn, backward,
> O Time, in your flight,
> Make me a child again
> Just for tonight."
> (E.A. Allen)

It was a pleasant, quiet and peaceful place, that little corner of the Old World which I called home. The Napoleonic Wars, which transformed the map of Europe and brought a glimmer of hope to oppressed humanity were still being vividly recalled. Fitful changes in the courts of the Czars occasionally brought rays of hope or new despair. The Cultural Renaissance, the Scientific Revolution, the Industrial Revolution and the American Revolution wrought important changes in the outside world. Yet life in the shtetlach (Jewish villages or townlets) of Lithuania remained almost unchanged for hundreds of years. Most people lived a lifetime without ever leaving their shtetl. Some would occasionally visit a neighboring community, while only a privileged few would travel as far as the regional capital or beyond. The

3

Haskala (Jewish Enlightenment Movement) had been stirring a new ferment in the major Jewish centers for over a century. The shtetlach were bypassed, however, and if there were changes they were imperceptible.

In the rural setting in which we lived, new ways were suspect and deviation from traditional norms was unthinkable. There were few paved roads, the dirt roads were often impassable, and neither were they always safe. Without railroads, automobiles, telephones, telegraph, radio or newspapers, our isolation was nearly complete. Our social and cultural situation was not much better as there was no library, public school, financial institution or any judicial system to speak of. Such basic rights as freedom of speech, political rights or equality before the law were mere abstractions for us. News from the outside world would often reach us in a distorted manner by way of itinerant rabbis, magidim (preachers), m'shulachim (solicitors for institutional or private causes), and other such casual visitors to our village. The rumblings of revolution left us untouched like the attenuated sound of thunder in the distance. While the love of Zion was indigenous to our region, even the Zionist Movement passed us by.

I was born on a slushy, bustling market day—Tuesday, December 19, 1900, and the news spread rapidly that Basheva had given birth to a son. The birth of a male heir was a great event—especially when preceded by three girls. Unknowingly, I was the beneficiary of some choice perquisites, namely: As the youngest child I was the pampered "muzhenik"; as the only son I was the "kaddish" who was to bring joy to my parents in the hereafter by reciting the prayer for the dead; and as the inheritor of the family name I was expected to carry on the family tradition of learning. It was reliably reported that Serei had not seen such a simha (celebration) in a long time as on the day of my brith (ritual of circumcision). During the nearest Sabbath service my father was called up to the Torah at the shul (synagogue) and I was named Moshe Simcho, after my paternal grandfather.

My earliest memories go back to the age of two and relate to weaning, toilet training, dreams, nightmares, Mother's songs, lullabies and Bible stories. The breast feeding of infants was universal and no substitutes were known. Gradually cow's milk and table foods were added, but actual weaning did not take place until the age of two or three, or when it became impractical. In my own case, I recall Mother saying to me one day: "It does not become a big boy to be breast fed"—and that was that. I distinctly recall that the admonition was preceded by tooth-marks. Toilet training came with a sound spanking as I was disgracefully pulled out of my highchair screaming. The highchair was nothing special. It was table high and rigid, with entry and exit from the top. It was custom built of hard wood and was varnished.

My mother was my greatest and best teacher. She taught me to recite the broches (benedictions) as soon as I learned to speak. This was followed by learning to recite the 'Yehi Ratzon'—a confessional for children on retiring for the night in which we entrusted our souls to God for safe-keeping until the morning. I also learned the morning prayer for children (Mode Ani) in which I thanked God for returning my soul to me pure and unblemished. As I grew older, though still a toddler seated on Mother's lap, I learned all about our patriarchs Abraham, Isaac and Jacob and our matriarchs Sarah, Rivka, Leah and Rachel. I also heard stories about Joseph and his brothers; about Moses, Aaron, King David and his son King Solomon; about the Prophets, and many stories about the greatness of our people in our ancient land; the destruction of the Temple in Jerusalem and our long exile because of our sins; and the hope that the Messiah would come someday soon and return us to our ancient land and glory. Then the whole world would pay homage to our God, we would no longer be oppressed, all peoples would live together in peace and brotherhood and life would be an everlasting, glorious Sabbath.

Mother used to sing to me a great deal—many lullabies, religious songs, Hassidic songs, Zionist and national songs, and songs extolling the virtues of learning and labor. Mother had a songbook in which these songs were recorded longhand. A few of her favorite songs are illustrative of the times:

Lullaby

Shlof mein kind mein kaddish meiner
Shlof mein zunenu
Shlof zshe, shlof, shlof l'eis ato
Shlof zshe, lu-le-lu.
In Amerike der tate deiner zunenu
Shlof zshe, shlof, shlof l'eis ato
lu-le-lu, lu lu....

Sleep my child, my kaddish,
Sleep dear son
Sleep, sleep, sleep for now
Sleep, lu-le-lu.
In America is thy father, dear son
Sleep, sleep, sleep for now
lu-le-lu, lu lu....

With many fathers having gone to America to help support their families and to eventually bring them to the U.S. this song was timely and very popular.

Song Extolling Labor

In der soche ligt di mazal broche
Dos vare glick fun leben
Kein zach in yir nit felt
Es kumt on der frimorgen
Men darf nit layen borgen
Eer meiach darf nit zorgen
Vu nemt men oif shabbes gelt.

There is merit in the plow
Real happiness in life
And no real want;
On arising
One need not rush to borrow
And need not have to worry—
Whence the Sabbath meal.

This song reflects the sense of frustration with the struggle to eke out a meager existence from penny trade in a hostile environment. It was also intended as a clarion call to return to our ancient land in Eretz Yisroel and to rebuild our lives on a sound economic basis through toil.

Hassidic Song

Der rebbe is a mufleg
Der rebbe is a godel
Er shlept adruch an elefant
Duch a lechel fun a nodel
Hakores hoben kinder
Fun dem rebben's a broche
Gebensht zol zein der rebbe
Mit zein gantzer mishpoche.

The rebbe is a scholar
The rebbe is outstanding

He can pull an elephant
Through the eye of a needle
Barren women conceive
Through a blessing from the rebbe
Blessed be the rebbe
And all of his family.

The Jews of Lithuania were mostly misnagdim (opposed to Hassidism) and this song is a parody or a tongue-in-cheek praise of the Hassidic Rebbe. Yet the catchy melody and the religious fervor and excitement it evokes elevated us to a tacit acceptance and admiration of the joy and spirited faith in the rebbe of the true Hassidism.

A Modern Song

Unter die grininke beimelach
Shpielen zich Meishelach, Shleimelach,
Sorelach, Rivkelach, Leahlach—
Yidelach frish fun die heielach.

Under the little green trees
Absorbed in play are they
Little Moishes and Shlomos
Soras, Rivkas and Leahs—
Grown little Jews are they.

We were truly adult-like little Jews by the time we started our formal education in the heder.

There was also a somber side to my informal education, for in addition to songs and beautiful stories, I heard gruesome stories about pogroms against Jews by drunken mobs instigated by the Czar's police. Although we had only rarely experienced a pogrom in Serei, or for that matter in Lithuania, the cruelty and the injustices perpetrated against our people evoked in us resentment against our tormentors and a determination to become better and more dedicated Jews.

I also heard a great deal about the dangers of travel at night through our primordial forests where murder lurked at the hands of highway robbers and perdition—or gehenem—at the hands of Satan, Lillith and the hosts of demons in the nether world. I knew, of course, that we had guardian angels to protect us from these and other evils. Our guardian angels Mihoel, Gabriel,

Refoel and Uriel were always strong and ready to defend us if we would only invoke their help. And, in case of dire need, God himself stood ready to intervene on our behalf. I recall a hair-raising story my father told me about being confronted by a group of dancing demons as he was traversing a forest in the darkness of the night. They stopped the horses in their tracks and they tried to induce Father to join them in their blasphemous proceedings. But my father, being well prepared for such a dire occasion, evoked God's name and the demons vanished in an instant. My father never wavered about the accuracy of this sequence of events even after many years in the United States.

My dreams were many and they revolved mainly around the contents of the days' stories and events, but the nightmares most frequently dealt with demons who were trying to do me physical or spiritual harm. Although I knew that if I evoked the name of the Almighty the evil spirits would vanish, my vocal cords became paralyzed and I could not utter the holy name and I would awake in a sweat. When starting on the shortest journey we would recite a T'filah laderech (a journeyman's prayer)—a special prayer evoking the Patriarchs, the angels, and the Holy-One-Blessed-Be-He to guard us against the perils of the road. Some of our people would even travel wrapped in their taleisim (prayer shawls) and t'filin (phylacteries) as a safety measure.

My first recollection of a major event dates back to the summer of 1904. The word had spread that Theodore Herzl, the world Zionist leader, had died suddenly on July 3rd. Since he was regarded by then as a Messiah who would lead us out of our miserable existence in the Galut (exile) into the Promised Land, the entire Jewish world, especially in Eastern Europe, was cast in deep mourning. On the thirtieth day of mourning (shloshim) a memorial service was held in the synagogue, to which I was taken by my father. The sanctuary was packed with men and children to overflowing and the women packed the galleries. With lit candles being held, the crying, lamenting and wailing was heart-rending. The unrestrained display of deep personal sorrow and irreperable loss etched itself forever into my memory. The mood was a combination of the sense of awe on Yom Kippur at Kol Nidre, the sense of tragic national loss on Tisha B'av (Destruction of the Temple), and the heartache felt at the loss of a close member of the family.

Another early memory is the Russo-Japanese War which began in early 1905 and was a lively topic of conversation in our home and in the shul. I remember heated discussions about the merits and demerits of the strategies of opposing generals, the humiliating losses sustained by the Czar's forces, and our own indifference toward the entire affair. Especially memorable is the way some of the back-benchers in the synagogue would use the palms of their hands as a map to illustrate their points. The two deep creases of the palm supposedly represented the front lines or trenches of the opposing armies and the heated debates revolved about how one army or the other could be surrounded if.... The cogent points were emphasized with the aid of the index finger and thumb of the opposite hand.

The First Russian Revolution of 1905 was triggered by the shock of the humiliating defeat of the Czar's armies by the Japanese. The festering environment of oppression, inept and corrupt government, great suffering and the feeling of hopelessness made the attempted upheaval inevitable. The revolution of 1905 was drowned in blood in the Massacre at St. Petersburg and a wave of pogroms in the Jewish Pale of Settlements (the provinces where Jews were permitted to live) as a diversionary tactic by the Russian Government. There was talk in Serei that Cossacks were descending on neighboring shtetlach and that they were arresting Jewish "revolutionaries". One Saturday afternoon I noticed smoke from a neighbor's chimney across the street. I rushed to attract Mother's attention to the unusual sight of smoke from a Jewish chimney on a summer Sabbath day and demanded an explanation. "Oh!" said Mother. "They are probably burning forbidden papers before the coming of the Cossacks." Without saying a word, I found Mother's songbook and hid it in the chicken coop. Later, after sunset, I threw it in the fire. I always regretted this rash act, especially since very little happened in Serei as a result of the visit by the Cossacks.

At the age of four or five, an event transpired which greatly enhanced my education about the devious ways which occasionally surround public or communal affairs. For many years Serei basked in the glory of Rabbi Pinhas, who was also known as Der Tiktiner Rov (the Rabbi from Tiktin). He was famous far beyond the confines of our area because of his wisdom, his worldliness and his great learning. People came to seek his advice from far and wide and he was in great demand as an arbitrator in important business disputes. When Rabbi Pinhas was offered a more prestigious position as the Rabbi of Slonim, he found it difficult to resist the enhanced opportunities of the new position, and the search for a new rabbi began.

In accordance with long-established custom, the selection of a rabbi was the prerogative of the most learned members of the community. As soon as Rabbi Pinhas left for his new post, candidates for the vacated position began to arrive. Each candidate would arrive on Thursday and lead a discourse in Talmud before the Hevra Shas (Talmud Study Group) on Friday and Saturday mornings. He would then deliver a sermon on the Torah portion of the week (sedra) to the entire congregation before the minha (afternoon prayers) service. If the rabbi was not asked to stay and given a contract, he would leave town on Sunday. Serei found it difficult to find a replacement who would measure up to the standards of Rabbi Pinhas and so many rabbis came and left without the position being filled—until the arrival of Rabbi Yisroel Goldin. It became immediately clear that here was a no-nonsense man. He arrived on Monday three days earlier than the rest. He took up lodging with the Borowskys, whose hostelry was across the street from us, and he let it be known that he would like to meet as many people as possible. A stream of visitors began to call on the rabbi, but for some unknown reason they were mostly the shusters (cobblers), shneiders (tailors), balegoles (wagoners) and others from among the poor. It was also strange that none of the learned men of the community were among the callers. The air became charged, and when Rabbi Yisroel finished his Sabbath sermon a chorus of voices began to chant in unison—"Mir villen horav Yisroel!" "We want Rabbi Yisroel!" Whether the revolutionary mood prevailing in the country at that time had anything to do with it or not I do not know, but to the chagrin of the learned elite, a rabbi was elected by an organized rabble who had never been consulted about anything important before. I know nothing about the rabbi's erudition in the Talmud, but it seems that he served the community well for more than two decades before he and his large family emigrated to the United States some-time in the mid-Twenties.

Among the people in Serei that I was extremely fond of and clearly remember was a woman named Chyeshe. She was a good friend of my mother and a close collaborator of Mother in helping the needy without their knowl-edge. I remember vaguely that Chyeshe was a widow and that she had a small store at the lower end of Lange Gass (Long Street). She was always cheerful and ever on the alert for people who might be in need but too proud or too timid to ask for help. She was the epitome of selflessness, doing her work quietly and effectively, a veritable one-woman institution. This was especially remarkable since her own means were modest and she needed all the outside help she could muster to be effective. A visit by Chyeshe to our home on a certain Friday night after the Sabbath meal became a memorable experience. Chyeshe and Mother were leisurely sipping one glass of hot tea with a lump of sugar after another, meanwhile discussing some urgent community problems. After what had seemed to me like an interminable number of hours, Chyeshe rose to take leave and Mother promptly offered to accompany her home.

It was a moonlit summer night and the two women walked arm in arm down the street with me in tow, all the while continuing where they had left off while they were sipping their tea. I was too young to understand what they were talking about, but I do recall that as we reached Chyeshe's home she turned to Mother and said: "Basheva leben (My dear Basheva), I cannot let you walk home by yourself at this late hour. Let me accompany you part way home."

Mother faintly protested, then agreed and the conversation resumed and continued until they were back at our doorstep. At this point Mother said to Chyeshe: "Chyeshe leben (My dear Chyeshe), I cannot let you walk back all by yourself at this late hour, let me accompany you at least part of the way back." The two women thus kept accompanying each other back and forth until at one point, as we reached Chyeshe's home for the nth time, Mother and Chyeshe put their heads together and agreed on a compromise—Chyeshe would accompany Mother back home exactly half way up the street, where they would part. Chyeshe remains enshrined in my memory as one of the taiere neshomes (saintly souls) I have known.

There are very few of my contemporaries in Serei that I remember. One whose face etched itself into my memory was a year or so older than myself. His father was in America and his mother had a small store in the market-place. One day at the minha service in the synagogue, a slender, frail, dark-complected boy was placed on a chair to recite the Kaddish Yosem (Orphan's Memorial Prayer for the Dead). The family had learned that day that the boy's father had died. There he stood, forlorn, reciting the Kaddish in a broken voice with tears streaming down his long melancholy face, a picture of utter dejection. I noticed that he had black hair down to his neck and unusually long fingernails, most likely related to some vow taken by his mother. Shortly thereafter, the family left for America. The boy's name was Steinberg and his father was an uncle of Rabbi Milton Steinberg, author of *"As a Driven Leaf"*, "Basic Judaism" and of the famous address "Mein Shtetele Serei" which he delivered at the Annual Convention of Hadassah in 1946. In this address, Rabbi Steinberg eulogized Eastern European Jewry, depicting Serei as the prototype of the thousands of shtetlach in Eastern Europe that were destroyed in the Holocaust.

Like most children I loved to watch the cows as they were being let out to pasture in the morning and upon their return at dusk in a cloud of dust. I was especially fascinated when mother bottle-fed a newborn calf whose mother's milk was inadequate. I also loved to drive our water tank to the spring and return with a tank full of fresh water. One day I secretly took our horse across the street to our neighbor's field and mounted the horse in an attempt to ride him. Since I had never ridden a horse before and our horse had never experienced a rider, the foredoomed happened—I was not only thrown ig-nominiously into the mud, but was kicked by the horse with one of his hind legs square in the face. The horse returned riderless to his stall and I was carried unconscious into the house and remained in a coma for several hours. Fortunately, recovery was prompt and without after-effects once I regained consciousness. Some twenty-five years later in Cincinnati I remembered this episode when I won my first blue ribbon in horsemanship on a powerful horse that had taken an inexperienced woman rider to her fall straight across a parked automobile.

Another traumatic experience occurred when I was returning home one night from heder with lantern in hand. As I was passing Finkel's Saloon someone, evidently drunk, jumped on me and beat me up. By the light of the lantern I recognized the assailant as the son of the town's carcass skinner, one of the lowliest occupations in Serei. My assailant, who was a few years my senior, emigrated to the United States, and I have known this man in Cincinnati for nearly sixty years as a quiet, decent businessman with a fine family. I have never mentioned the incident to him, although we belong to the same congregation.

Other early memories revolve largely around ethical and religious teachings in the home. Our gratitude to God was constantly being acknowledged through special benedictions (brahot) on every conceivable occasion. There were benedictions on observing beauty in nature or in man; on tasting new fruit or new produce in season; on observing blossoming trees and shrubs; on smelling the fragrance of plants; on seeing the new moon, lofty mountains or the ocean; on observing such natural phenomena as lightning, thunder, blizzards, earthquakes, tornadoes or volcanic eruptions; on seeing a rainbow, a falling star or a solar or lunar eclipse; on seeing a giant or a dwarf, a beautiful tree, a beautiful person or a powerful beast; on meeting an unusual person such as a person of great wisdom, learning and piety, or a ruler; at the beginning of a journey and at the end of a journey; on hearing good or bad tidings; before and after the enjoyment of food, the fruit of the vine, and other pleasures of life; at birth and at journey's end.

These benedictions brought in God as a partner in our daily lives and sanctified our daily activities. The benedictions also gave us a sense of joyful appreciation, enchantment and exaltation, or a sense of awe towards the world we live in. We learned most of these benedictions by heart from our parents at a very tender age and we conceived of them as sincere expressions of thanksgiving, reverence, humility and resignation to the will of God. We were also taught by our parents some very important ethical and moral values to guide us through life. Above all were we taught to respect all of God's creatures and creations and that we were not alone in this world but under the guidance of an All-Powerful Providence—the Creator of heaven and earth.

The author's parents, Chaim and Basheva Schulzinger, wedding picture, 1893.

CHAPTER TWO

Family Background

> "People will not look forward to posterity
> who never look backward to their ancestors."
> (Burke)

My parents came to Serei in 1896 from the village of Halinke near Grodno where they met and were married in 1893. My mother was the youngest of five daughters born to Avrom Sereisky, (affectionately called Avremel) and his first cousin, Chana Dunsky. Nearly everybody in Halinke was a Sereisky or a Dunsky. The baubi (grandmother) Chana was one of many children born to Yudel Dunsky, who was a wealthy landowner who cultivated his land with the help of serfs who dwelt on his land. I do not recall meeting my Baubi Chana, but I was told that she was known for her wisdom, her wit, and her very clever tongue. Some said that she fought fiercely for what she considered just and was therefore thought by some to have had a mean streak, an accusation which her daughters did not share. She died at the age of sixty-five and left many namesakes.

My grandfather, Avremel Sereisky, was a tall, broad-shouldered, powerful man and a tanner by trade. He was born in Halinke in 1820 and died in our

14

Zeide (Grandfather) Avremel Sereisky, at ninety.

Baubi (Grandmother) Chana Dunsky Sereisky.

home in Serei in 1917. He owned a two-family home which was situated a few hundred yards from the shosei (paved highway) leading to Grodno on the west and to Yagustov and Suvalk on the east. In the back of his house was a shop with large vats and other facilities for fabricating rawhide into all kinds of finished and unfinished leather products. By the time I got to know my grandfather he was already in his eighties. He was an honest, humble, pious, hardworking man with a ready smile, a love for people (especially children), and a passion to do good. He never bore a grudge and he readily forgave slights or hurts. Whenever Zeide (Grandfather) Avremel would appear in neigboring Sopotkin, the children would immediately clamber aboard his wagon for the fun of a free ride, though most men would speed up their horse and leave the kids behind in a cloud of dust. Zeide Avremel, also known as Avremel Der Garber (the Tanner), was not a learned man but he had a deep respect for people of learning. He therefore considered himself a very lucky man when he realized his fondest hopes and married off his five daughters to men of learning. Grandfather grew evermore kind and endearing as he grew old and he was dubbed by all who knew him as a tzadik (a saintly man), a "mentsh ohn a gall"—a sweet man devoid of rancor, or a "lamed vovnik"—

one of the thirty-six secret righteous men in the world who, according to Jewish lore, bring succor and comfort to the needy and help soften the Lord's harsh decrees through personal intercedence. These righteous men are, of course, unknown to themselves or to others and are recognized only through their deeds.

My father was born in Semyatich, Poland in about 1869 and died in Herzilya, Israel in 1963. My paternal grandparents were Moshe Simcho Schulzinger and Gitel Bash. My father was the second of five children. The oldest, Eli Dovid, emigrated to Palestine together with his wife and eleven children in 1921 and died in Petach Tikva at the age of ninety-seven with seventy-five members of his immediate family at his funeral. Father's younger brother, Yakov Leib, came to Cincinnati in 1905 and died in 1939. His children are Maurice and Edward who reside in Cincinnati, and the late Max, Harry, and Marcia. There was another brother of my father, Yitzhak, who remained in Semyatich; his son, David Singer, lived in Cincinnati and his daughter, Goldie, married my cousin Moshe Meir Dunsky in Cincinnati. They were the parents of Dr. Irvin Dunsky and Abe Dunsky of Cincinnati and Bessie Rothman of New York. My father's only sister, Rivka, remained in Semyatich. A son, Reuven Gafni, an attorney in New York and Tel Aviv, was the author of an authoritative volume on the historical legal rights of the Jewish people to Eretz Yisroel. He was also a prominent leader in the Hapoel Hamizrahi Religious Labor Zionist Organization.

The people of my father's hometown were extremely poor and many men would come home only for major holidays. Most of the time they would be wandering from shtetl to shtetl raising money for various institutions and for themselves. They thus fulfilled the injunction of our sages, who said: "B'nai Yisroel! L'hu v'isparnesu ze mi ze" (Children of Israel! Go forth and support each other.) My paternal grandfather died very young and very little is known about him except that he was known by the Rabbinic title Horav (Rabbi). My paternal grandmother Gitel was a petite woman from a large family named Bash. One brother emigrated to St. Joseph, Missouri in 1867 and became a wealthy businessman. He later became a major factor in the laundry business in St. Louis, where he was known as Mr. Stone. Another brother came to Cincinnati a few years later, where he served as a shohet (kosher slaughterer) and was known as Mr. Barlow. He was a friend and landsman of Elias Rubel, the founder of the Rubel Baking Company.

Abraham Stone helped bring my father and my Uncle Yakov Leib to Cincinnati with Mr. Barlow as the intermediary. My father's uncle (Mr. Barlow) had two daughters, one of whom married a Mr. Friedman who had a furniture store in Paris, Kentucky. Their children intermarried. A niece of my grandmother also came to St. Joseph, Missouri, and her offspring were Miriam Kranitz and Rose Goldman. Miriam was a very friendly person and she used to write to me long letters with the minutest details about every member of her family in St. Joseph. Her husband, Louis Kranitz, was also a fine and genteel person. He was a prominent attorney and served for many years as national president of The Second District of B'nai B'rith. Another brother of my grandmother emigrated to Jerusalem in 1867. There are some Bashes in Israel but I have not researched the relationship.

A curious incident about my grandmother I learned from my cousin Moshe Meir Dunsky, who spent a short time in Semyatich while attending a yeshiva and boarding with Grandmother. According to my cousin, Grandmother had a small food store in which the staple items were herring and potatoes. These humble products frequently constituted a whole meal, but people were so poor that they could not afford even the lowly herring. They would buy the brine of the herring to eat with potatoes or bread. My cousin noticed that Grandmother was ladling out brine from the same barrel during the entire winter without diminishing its contents. When he called Grandmother's attention to the apparent miracle, she became upset and admonished him for casting an evil spell on her good fortune which was bound to spoil everything.

At the age of twenty, my father was mobilized to serve four years in the Czar's army, and in the course of time he came to the Grodno border garrison which was situated near Halinke. The town's people were always on the lookout for Jewish soldiers whom they could provide with kosher food and other amenities. When they learned that father had spent all his life in yeshivoth (Talmudic academies) they arranged, at some cost to the community, that he be given time off Sabbaths and holidays so that he could spend those days among Jews. One day Father was late returning from his Sabbath leave and he had to report to his superiors. As my father stood at attention the officer looked at him and said: "You know, Ravin (Rabbi), I will have to punish you for being late in order to maintain discipline, but I will give you a light punishment—you will report immediately to guard the regimental brothel for an hour." Father related the episode with a chuckle—how he stood stiffly, in full military regalia, in front of the brothel—the heavy, bayonetted Russian rifle at his side extending beyond his head—and how he recited Psalms all the while to ward off evil thoughts.

My father was short of stature and rather fragile. He had a serious mien and he was a truly dedicated and diligent student of the Talmud. Thus he came to spend a great deal of his spare time studying in the synagogue in Halinke. He caught the Rabbi's attention, who alerted my grandfather Avremel that it would be a wonderful match for his youngest daughter, Basheva. Soon after

Father was released from the army my parents were married. In accordance with established custom, my parents remained in Halinke for three years, boarding with Grandfather while Father continued his studies, and eventually began making plans for the future.

When the time came to go out on their own, my parents decided to settle in Serei and to go into the soft-drink business. As I learned later, Serei and several of the surrounding shtetlach lacked this type of facility and there was apparently a need for this product. My parents produced lemonade, *kwas*, and seltzer and sold it wholesale to saloonkeepers and retail at our place of business and on market days from the rear of our wagon. In addition to selling our product in Serei we also sold it in the two neighboring shtetlach of Leipun and Lazdei. The work was hard and tedious and it provided only a meager livelihood. Father became disenchanted with the prospects for a better future, especially since the long hours and the hard work left him little time to pursue his studies. So he decided in 1905, with Mother's approval, to seek his fortune in America.

During his first trip to America father remained in Cincinnati four years until he decided to return to his family in Serei in 1909. He had worked just as hard in Cincinnati as in Serei, making a living as a customer peddler and sending some money to his family, especially before the holidays. Because of the frequent financial panics in the United States saving came hard and was achieved mainly through penny-pinching. In Father's case five men shared one room, they bought cheap and half-spoiled food in the market, and they employed all sorts of ingenious devices to avoid spending money. Neither Father nor any of his roommates knew anything about housekeeping and so they were all equally miserable. Father, however, disliked America mainly because most Jews had to work on the Sabbath to survive, and because of the wholesale discarding of Jewish religious practices. Yet the freedom, the tolerance, and the lack of persecution got into his blood and he missed life in America when he returned to Serei. Once back home Father again plunged into the soft-drink business which Mother had successfully maintained during his absence, and he found it even more distasteful than before. He then decided to invest the money he had saved in Cincinnati in the forestry business. The fact that he knew next to nothing about this business meant nothing to him. He was confident that his erudition in the Talmud was sufficient preparation for anything he would undertake. A childhood dream of becoming a successful businessman also may have played a part. The felling of trees in a virgin forest far from paved roads or other means of transportation proved a costly enterprise way beyond the few thousand dollars that he had brought with him from America. When a bottle in the soft-drink shop broke and a fragment of flying glass cut and blinded Father's left eye, it was the last straw and Father left again for America in 1911, a totally disillusioned man.

I remember Father's return from America in 1909 only vaguely, perhaps out of a repressed resentment for his long absence or anger at his sudden return. During Father's absence I had gotten accustomed to being treated as the man of the house in ritual matters such as reciting the kiddush (benedictions on the wine), the Hamotze (benediction on the bread) and the Havdalah (benediction at the end of the Sabbath)—as well as conducting the Seder on Pesach (Passover ceremonial), leading the Chanukah candle-lighting ritual, and performing many other chores that were customarily performed by the man of the household. What I do remember clearly is that Father brought me two presents—an inexpensive child's watch and a purse for small change. Both of these items promptly disappeared as I was showing them off to some of my playmates, so that all I had left of the deal was a good cry.

Soon after Father left for America in 1905, Tante (Aunt) Toibe—Mother's older sister—came to live with us. She soon became my second mother and the best friend a child, or for that matter anyone, could ever hope to have. She was a model of goodness and kindness and, despite her tragic and troubled life and her great physical suffering, she was always concerned about the welfare of others and was never known to complain. Tante Toibe was a dark-complected, slender, attractive young woman of medium height who favored her mother, Baubi Chana, physically. But in demeanor and character she was a true descendant of her father, Zeide Avremel. In my gallery of taiere neshomes (precious souls) she occupies the top position alongside the memory of my grandfather Avremel Sereisky. Unlike her younger and older sisters who had all married learned men from other shtetlach, Tante Toibe married a cousin, Hatzkel Dunsky, from nearby Sopotkin. Soon after her marriage she gave birth to a son, Moshe Meir, and two years later she had another son, Yitzhak. I do not know exactly what caused the breakup of the marriage, but from bits and pieces I learned that her husband Hatzkel was a stubborn and contrary type of person who was held under a tight leash by a cruel and domineering father known by his nickname as Der Minister (The Brain). After their separation, Hatzkel emigrated to Rochester, New York, and her two sons left for America in 1904 at the ages of sixteen and fourteen respectively. They lived at first with their father in Rochester, but in 1906 they settled permanently in Cincinnati to be near my father. Cousin Yitzhak Dunsky married Jenny Brown and their only daughter, Ethel, married Dr. Leo Davis of Camden, New Jersey.

As far back as I can remember, Tante Toibe never failed to come up with the right kind of goodies or a hug and kisses to soothe my injured feelings. She remained an integral part of our household, sharing in the chores and especially in the operation of the shop for nearly twenty years. Sometime during her early years in Serei, Tante Toibe began to suffer from bronchial asthma which gradually progressed to severe bronchiectasis. I soon began to hear her soft voice calling me by name in the night. I would rush to her bedside, finding this dear angel fighting for breath, coughing spasmodically, and struggling to bring up phlegm. I never felt so helpless in all my life as I used to feel at her bedside, ready to do almost anything to help her but there being nothing I could do since there were no doctors and no drugs at that time for this harrowing disease—not even any folk remedies. I would place cold towels to her forehead, she would put her head on my shoulder, and I would utter some loving words which seemed to bring a measure of relief. In addition to seasonal exacerbations, there were spasmodic attacks which were brought about by various stresses relating to her life situation. I remember how I used to suffer with her during these nightly episodes while feeling at the same time a sense of pride that my ministrations were of some help. As a physician I now realize that the psychological help she received and especially the love I gave her were precisely what she needed—which is why they worked so miraculously during those dark melancholy hours of the night. A few years later she learned of a powder that when ignited and the smoke was inhaled would stop the spasmodic coughing. This smoke apparently produced bronchial dilation and it had the same effect as aminophyllin or some of the mist inhalations we use today. Tante Toibe received her *get* (divorce) from her husband in Rochester by a special religious messenger. It brought tears and sadness to her beautiful face. They lingered for a while and then nothing more was said about it. Her sons in America wrote occasionally and asked her to join them but she steadfastly refused to go. Once or twice she even returned the steamship tickets which her children had sent her.

Mother was the real manager of the household even when Father was not in America, and she seemed to do it with the greatest of ease. In addition to operating our bottling works and distributing the products, there was the ice house that needed to be filled annually and used judiciously; the horse, cows, and calves had to be fed and managed; occasionally a cow had to be helped with a difficult delivery; the wagon and horse-drawn water tank had to be greased and kept in good repair; the vegetable garden had to be plowed, fertilized, planted, weeded, and harvested; and the garden produce had to be properly stored, dried, or pickled for future use. We also owned a few acres of land on the outskirts, just off the road to the village lake, where we grew oats and fodder for our own needs.

On one part of our land was a lime kiln and twice a year we would gather lime stones from the surrounding fields and produce enough lime for our own needs and for sale to others. The operation of the kiln required special knowledge and expertise. The secret to success lay in skillfully arranging the stones so as to produce an adequate draft when the kiln was fired. The firing lasted three days and the cooling about a week. The dry lime was then placed in a pit in our backyard for future use. When mixed with concentrated sulfuric acid in the shop's machinery, it yielded carbon dioxide for our soft drinks. Another large pit near the barn was used to store viscid lime which was used for plastering and whitewashing. Watching the arranging of the limestones, the firing of the kiln, and then the reopening of the kiln after several days under tremendous heat are among the pleasant memories of my childhood.

The entire household was involved in the operation of the bottling works since everything was done by hand under primitive conditions. The bottles had to be washed and then filled with syrup, of which there were two flavors, lemonade and *kwas*. The carbonated water was produced by mixing well water and carbon dioxide in a sealed metal container with the aid of a huge wheel which was turned continuously by hand. There was no belt line and each bottle was filled individually with carbonated water at the end of a faucet and then corked with a plunger at the end of the faucet. The corking was a dangerous procedure for occasionally a bottle would shatter and cause injury. After one such accident blinded Father's left eye, we attached an improvised wire screen around the corking end of the machine. This slowed down the operation but it prevented further injuries.

A serious problem was the use of saccharin as a sweetener. Sugar was a Government monopoly and it became too expensive and uneconomical for our purpose. Saccharin was cheap but its use was made illegal so as not to interfere with the Government's lucrative source of revenue from sugar. In practice it meant that the police had to be paid off, which was a common practice, and that a few bottles of drink made with sugar had to be kept on hand for any sudden inspection. The police would dutifully notify us when the inspector was due to arrive. In preparation we would thoroughly clean and scrub the shop and its facilities. A legal product would be handed the inspector on his arrival and everybody was happy. Once, when a mix-up occurred and the inspector received a bottle of lemonade made with saccharin, our senior police officer retrieved the wrong bottle for us at the cost of an extra fifth of vodka.

To prevent competition from the neighboring town of Alyta, Mother resorted to personal friendship and diplomacy. The fact that our would-be competitor was a decent God-fearing "Hassid" who would not dream of competing with a woman who had a family to support, also helped. The distribution of our product to neighboring communities was a tricky, tedious, and back-breaking chore. The bottles both full and empty had to be skillfully packed in burlap bags with ample amounts of straw between each bottle. The bags were then hoisted into the wagon and properly positioned to prevent breakage. This seldom happened, but its prevention involved a prodigious amount of work.

Dealing with the saloonkeepers, who sold our product, was not always pleasant. Since dealing with rough and unpleasant situations was their daily fare, they were not the gentlest of people. Although most of them were fair and considerate, there were some in every shtetl who were not adverse to cheating, dragging out payments, or attempting to take unfair advantage of a woman who could not respond in kind. It required a combination of innate wisdom, resourcefulness, shrewdness, adaptability, and fast-thinking to be able to survive—and Mother, fortunately, was blessed with these qualities in full measure. As I grew older I tried to help, when not in school, with anything I could in the shop, the barn, or in the field. I also accompanied Mother to fairs and helped with the delivery of our products in Serei and in the neighboring communities. Our busy season was naturally during the summer months. On the basis of sales on one hot Sunday, I once attempted to project our sales for the rest of the summer providing the weather was favorable. This amused my sisters to no end and they never forgot to tease me about it.

It was not customary for girls in the shtetlach to receive formal education, yet both of my sisters went to heder and my oldest sister Sheine was even sent for a short time to Sopotkin to receive a secular education from a private tutor. With encouragement from Mother, both of my sisters learned to read Hebrew, Russian and German, and they did a great deal of reading on their own. Sheine was five years my senior. She had a dark complexion and she favored Father in appearance. Rivka was two and one-half years my senior and she looked more like Mother, blonde and very pretty. Both Sheine and Rivka had a serious mien and both participated to the fullest in the numerous household chores as well as in managing our economy. I did not get to know my sisters too well during my childhood since the long school hours from 9 A.M. to 9 P.M. made it impossible, and it was not customary for boys and girls to play together. Our happiest time together was during the Sabbath and holiday meals when we would join together to sing the beautiful Z'miroth (Sabbath songs) in our lusty youthful voices. I would also watch them at times during the long winter nights as they would join Mother and Tante Toibe in the perennial sewing, mending, knitting, and preserving.

The womenfolk made their own dresses and there were many discussions as to style, fabric, trim, or decor. Since it was customary for girls to begin working on their wedding trousseau at an early age, this was a perennial enterprise. It included the accumulation of linen, bedding, tableware, and other assorted items. One of the family projects that I remember clearly, and which took two years to complete, was the making of a crocheted tablecloth of intricate and colorful design. The project began with the knitting of a sturdy net about three yards long and half as wide, which was then dyed to pitch black. With the net completed, long discussions ensued on the details of the design and the color scheme. Wool yarn was obtained and dyed in a variety of colors including several shades of red, green, and blue. Each of the four women then took one corner and proceeded to crochet according to design until they met the central design. The center of the tablecloth had a large floral design which harmonized in color and pattern with the color scheme and design of the corners and the borders. Occasionally, an error was made which required several days to correct, at times arguments arose which were settled amicably. The remarkable thing to me was that they never consulted any kind of pattern or design. From beginning to end it was a product of their own ingenuity and imagination. The tablecloth became the most cherished possession of the household and was frequently displayed with a great deal of pride. A few years later, during World War I, a German officer offered Mother a large sum of money for the tablecloth but she refused to part with it. I never succeeded in learning from Mother or my sister Sheine what happened to this beautiful family relic.

I always cherished my visits to Halinke to see my Zeide Avremel. It began with a long eight- or nine-hour ride by a freight wagon which went from Serei to Grodno twice a week. Getting into the massive vehicle, drawn by two strong horses, was quite a problem for women and the older travelers and they would have to be hoisted into their seats by sturdy hands. The seats were comfortable enough with tightly packed sacks of straw in back and below, but the constant jerking over the rough potholed roads was enough to wear down the hardiest of travelers. We would usually leave Serei at about two or three o'clock in the afternoon and would reach Sopotkin by midnight after brief stopovers along the way. The wagon would remain in Sopotkin three hours to feed and rest the horses, drivers, and the passengers, and then proceed on to Grodno.

We would usually get off in Sopotkin and proceed to the home of our friends and relatives, Alte and Leibe Dulsky (Doll), who lived a few houses from the inn in a narrow, two-story brick building which could be entered from the small store in front or from the side. There were five children—Chyene Rochel (Kaplan), Ben Zion (Doll), Simmie (Burgin), Grune (Shapiro), and Yitzhak (Doll). The oldest was about five years my senior and the youngest, Yitzhak, was three years my junior. Despite the late hour we were always received eagerly and treated as honored guests, and Alte never ceased to inquire as to our wishes and comfort. Leibe, who was my mother's cousin, was a hard-working frugal man who considered the waste of time as sinful as the waste of money. Before settling permanently in Cincinnati, he returned three or four times to Sopotkin with the same disastrous results as my father's return to Serei.

Alte, whose family name was Bialystotzky and who hailed from Bialystok, had a nobility of character not unlike that of Tante Toibe and Chyeshe. The Dulsky (Doll) family prospered in the small two-by-four store with its meager amount of merchandise, largely because of the trust and esteem in which they were held. But as far as I could observe, a large part of the traffic consisted of people who came either to ask for a gemilas hesed (free loan) or to repay one. Others came for advice or to share their happiness or misfortune, and like Chyeshe in Serei, Alte was concerned with everybody's well-being and happiness and was always ready with a helping hand. Alte had lost several children in their infancy and she was therefore overly solicitous about the health of her living children. As soon as we arrived a tasty meal was hastily prepared, and I was then put to bed together with Yitzhak, who slept in a daybed. She would tuck us under a heavy down cover and would appear several times during the night to make sure we were not uncovered. In 1920 we were in a position to reciprocate when the entire Dulsky family came to Serei to escape Polish persecution and to await their visas to the United States. They lived with us for six months and we remained close friends in Cincinnati over the decades.

My Zeide Avremel was in his eighties when I first got to know him, but he was an extremely vigorous man and he still worked daily in his tannery. He married his second wife, Breine, about a decade before I was born and they lived happily together. My visits with Zeide were joyful and rewarding occasions. He would take me along wherever he went and would show me off as we went along. I in turn was greatly impressed by the love and respect in which he was held. His wife Breine was always extremely friendly and solicitous about my well-being and she would prepare all kinds of tasty dishes. One thing that troubled me was why Zeide Avremel's right index finger was amputated at the base. Upon questioning, I was told that the finger was lost when it was mangled in a bark grinder. Only much later did I learn the true story. During the reign of Czar Nicholas I, young Jewish boys, six to eight years old, would be kidnapped from their homes for a fee by hapers (kidnappers) and they would be turned over to the authorities to be exiled deep in Russia, where they would be raised as Christians. When these boys grew up they would then be mustered into the Czar's army to serve twenty-five years. Despite the long estrangement from their people, most of these boys remained true to their faith on the basis of their childhood memories. But their harrowing experience left its mark on these unfortunates and it set them apart. They were known all their lives as Nikolayevske Soldaten (Soldiers of Czar Nicholas). The amputation of the right index finger was a favorite device to escape this horrible fate. This device was also used later during more liberal regimes even though the length of service was shortened to four years. The rigors, the deprivations, the cruelty, and the anti-Semitism that prevailed in the Russian armed services were too horrible for many to contemplate.

The happiest home in Halinke was undoubtly that of Hatzkel Sereisky, who was a cousin to grandfather. There were about eight or ten children in the house, all teenagers and most of them girls. The singing, the mirth, and the laughter could be heard for blocks away with windows wide open in the summertime. The place was a beehive of activity with all kinds of sewing, weaving, needlework, and other handiwork. The several visits to this home have left an imprint on my mind as an embodiment of family bliss. Many years later I met some members of this family, now known as Sayer, during family gatherings in Detroit. The twinkle in their eyes and their ready smiles always brought back my childhood memories of their home in Halinke. Most members of this family met an uncertain fate in Communist Russia.

I loved to accompany Zeide Avremel on his Friday afternoon visits to the homes of the villagers to collect their weekly offerings. After a friendly greeting Zeide would stretch out his arm with the alms box in hand and he would turn his head away so as not to shame anyone into giving too much or too little. Those who were in dire need would even take a coin or two from the box. The collected funds were used to support the Rabbi, the shul (synagogue), and other communal needs.

On the inside wall near the entrance to Grandfather's home was a medium-sized slate on which Zeide kept a record of his accounts. On one of my visits to Halinke I surprised a villager as he was wiping off a row of figures. The man turned on his heels and left in a huff. When I told Zeide what I saw he rushed to the slate and exclaimed in disbelief: "Oi der ganev (the thief)!" He had wiped off his account.

On another occasion I saw a peasant pull up in front of Zeide's house with a cart full of farm products, his wife and half a dozen children in tow—trudging barefoot in the deep sand. I was puzzled by the sight until the peasant and Zeide began to negotiate about the prices the peasant wanted for each of the items. As they reached an agreement on the first item they shook hands and the peasant turned to his eldest son, Fedenko, and admonished him in his native Chachlatzk (a White Russian dialect) "Trimai trinashchi"—(remember thirteen). Every time they agreed on a price the peasant called on a different child to remember the figure. At the end of the bargaining, the peasant called on each of his children to recall the figures they were charged to remember and the peasant added up the total with the aid of his fingers. The peasants of this region were nearly all illiterate Ruthenians who were only a few decades removed from serfdom. The family walked on foot to and from the village and at times they would help the scrawny, half-starved horse pull the cart through the deep sand of the country lanes.

Across the street from Grandfather lived Sroli der Toker (Sroli the Spindle maker), who was a pious hard-working craftsman, a distant cousin and a Dunsky. On a Friday before Pesach (Passover), according to my mother, the turkey he was fattening for the holiday got sick from eating too many bugs (praisslach) and was about to die. To avoid this catastrophe, Sroli rushed to the shohet (ritual slaughterer) who freed the bird from its misery. That Friday night, in fear of dying from eating the tainted meat, Sroli put on his tahrihim (burial garb), recited the Vidui (Confessional), and stoically sat down to eat. Sroli died of natural causes at a ripe old age—but the legend lived on.

Among Mother's suitors before her engagement to my father was a young Rabbi who was one of her most ardent admirers. On a Sabbath afternoon as the pair strolled through a lane, the young Rabbi plucked a flower and said: "Basheva, you are as beautiful as this flower." Whereupon Mother, with her characteristic forthrightness said: "A rov a mehalel Shabbes ken men nit getroien (A Rabbi who desecrates the Sabbath cannot be trusted)." This young man eventually became a well-known Orthodox Rabbi in New York and one of the most prominent national leaders of American Orthodox Jewry.

The Rabbi of Halinke was the village's most precious possession and he was very much beloved and admired by the community. Rabbi Eliezer Nitzberg— widely known later by his pen name, "Damesek Eliezer"—was a great scholar who spent most of his time in the synagogue studying and writing. He served the tiny congregation for over thirty years, 1880-1911, and the people of Halinke appreciated the fame he had brought them as the author of five respected volumes on the "Hoshen Mishpat—Yoreh Deiah," The Code of Talmudic Law. Rabbi Nitzberg lived in this small out-of-the-way village on starvation wages soley because of the opportunity it afforded him to devote himself to his studies.

As a small child I was taken by my grandfather to the synagogue to meet the Rabbi on every one of my three or four visits to Halinke and I remember finding him always absorbed in his studies. Rabbi Nitzberg and his family lived in Grandfather's spare apartment for many years until Grandfather began to marry off his daughters and he needed the extra apartment to house the newlyweds. By an interesting coincidence, Rabbi Nitzberg was married to the daughter of Rabbi Yitzhak Hirsh Pomerantz, the Rabbi of my father's home town of Semyatich. Rabbi Nitzberg's daughter, Genendel, also married a young Rabbi of Semyatich by the name of Mowshowitz. They later emigrated to the United States, where their son, Rabbi Israel Mowshowitz of New York, is a prominent Rabbi and a nationally known leader, and their two daughters, Frieda and Rose, are professionals in New York and Hartford, Connecticut. Genendel was one of two trusted girlfriends my mother had in Halinke and she never tired of reminding my niece Chana how she fondled me as an infant. Unfortunately, I never got to know this lovely lady. A recent telephone call from Rabbi Chaim Simcha Gibber of Baltimore, a grandson of Genendel and a great grandson of Rabbi Nitzberg of Halinke, made me feel very good about my efforts to chronicle these events.

Mother's other girlfriend in Halinke was Merche (Miriam) Sereisky, a second cousin. She, like Genendel, was pretty and vivacious and she too emigrated to New York after her marriage to a Mr. Levin from Sidri. Mother and Merche were inseparable and they vowed that one would not get married unless the other did. I met Merche and her husband some fifty years later in Cincinnati when they came to visit their daughter and son-in-law, Ann and Sol Luckman. I remembered more about Halinke than Merche did, but Mother and Merche had a very happy reunion. They had corresponded for many years before their first reunion in New York sometime in the mid-Twenties.

Of great interest to me was Mother's account of two family councils of moment in which all five sisters participated. After duly mourning Grandmother's passing for more than a year, Grandfather wanted to marry a young woman in order to sire a kaddish (male heir)—as they called a son in those days. Although Grandfather was in his seventies there was no problem finding a suitable young woman who would consent to a shiddach (arranged marriage). But the five daughters intervened and decided that it would be best for Zeide to marry an older woman who could take care of him in his old age. Zeide Avremel was not the kind of person to put up a fight or even to do anything that would upset his loving daughters, and so he married Breine, a fine woman some ten or fifteen years his junior who guarded him as her most precious possession. She often expressed her concern lest she die first and he be left alone without anyone to care for her dear Avremel in his declining years. As it turned out, he outlived her by some five years.

Another time the five sisters gathered for an important family decision was when Mirke (the next-to-youngest sister) decided to join her young husband, Rabbi Meir Levy, in the United States. Tante Mirke, following the dictates of her heart, was determined to join her husband in America and she disregarded her sisters' advice that she urge her husband to return to Europe. The counsel of the sisters was motivated by their reluctance to see permanent estrangement in the family and their fear for the quality of her Judaism that emigrating to America evoked in those days. Another name for America in this context was the Treifene Medina—the Non-Kosher land.

Tante Mirke was married in Halinke in 1891. Her first child died in infancy in Europe. After joining her husband in America in 1892 with an infant in arms, the couple lived for a while in Rochester, New York, where Rabbi Levy was engaged in the coal business. After one of the frequent financial panics Rabbi Levy and his family moved to Detroit, where he engaged in the insurance business and then to Toronto, Canada, where he returned to the Rabbinate and served his congregation with great distinction for over forty years. Uncle and Aunt Levy had five daughters and two sons, all of whom prospered and raised fine families. Three daughters—Sarah (Miller), Ida (Goldfine) and Ann (Shiller) lived in Montreal; two daughters—Lottie (Weiss) and Belle (James) lived in Toronto; one son—Nathan Levy, lived in Philadelphia and one son—Jules Levy, lived in New York.

A trip to Grodno as a very young child left an indelible impression on me. It was the first large city I had ever visited. I enjoyed the hustle and bustle of the marketplace where the storekeepers from the shtetlach came to replenish their merchandise. The marketplace was a beehive of activity with haggling and bargaining over prices all around in loud voices. I was especially impressed with the prodigious amounts of merchandise on display—each wholesaler specializing in one or two products. I was also impressed by the prevailing good humor since at the end of the shrewd bargaining there was invariably a hearty handshake and a happy parting between buyer and seller. On arriving in Grodno we stopped at a hostelry (inn) called "Bashevke's" after the name of the proprietress. Many of the wagons from the shtetlach would remain there for twenty-four hours while the merchandise was bought and loaded, to prepare for the twelve- to fourteen-hour return trip. I learned all about the crude language of the balegoles (wagoners) and their taste in eating, drinking, and recreation. These were mostly men on the loose, away from home, and they would permit themselves liberties which they would not dare at home. Yet these were all observant Jews and the first thing in the morning they would all participate in the morning services, wearing their talit and t'filin (prayer shawl and phylacteries), and they would always stop in the evening for the minha and maariv services.

Once, while traveling with Tante Toibe from Halinke to Grodno in a peasant's cart, we got lost in the dark of night in a dense forest. For a while we moved around in circles, then the horse stopped in his tracks and we had no choice but to stay in the wagon, cold and scared, through the remainder of the night, awaiting the dawn. Increasing our misery was the fear of wild beasts or highway robbers, about which there were so many gruesome stories in circulation. The simpleton peasant driver was not much comfort. The heavy stillness of the night was broken only by the wailing of the wind and the occasional shriek of a wild beast—all the while Tante Toibe and I huddled in the wagon for warmth. At times during the night I would conjure up the image of the dancing goblins that my father had told me about, but as soon as it seemed real I evoked the most potent name of the Almighty and the apparition vanished. Six years later, in the first months of World War I, an entire Russian army of three hundred thousand men was trapped in this same forest and was annihilated as a fighting force. It was this event, along with an identical massacre near the Masure Lakes in East Prussia, that shook the very foundations of the Russian Empire and marked the beginning of the end of Czarist Russia.

CHAPTER THREE

My Education—The Old and the New

> "Train up a child in the way he should go
> and when he is old
> he will never depart from it."
> (Bible)

The year 1905 was a memorable year for me because of two important events—my father left for America and I began my formal education in heder (religious elementary school). One day Mother casually suggested that it would be a good idea if I joined my sisters in heder. Though I was not quite five years old, I looked much older and it seemed like a good idea. The heder was located on Shulgass (Synagogue Street) in the home of the rebbe (teacher). It was a delapidated log cabin—a two-room dwelling with a low ceiling, a few small windows, and a pressed clay floor. It also housed the rebbe's family of several small children, a number of chickens on the loose and a goat. I was greeted by a friendly bearded man and was seated at the end of a bench at one of two plain long wooden tables in the living room around which other small boys and a few girls were seated. As soon as I was seated the rebbe tested my reading ability in the Sidur (Prayer Book) and, "because you were such a good boy," an angel dropped a groshen (small Russian coin) on my sidur as a reward. My eyes were quicker than the rebbe's hand and I saw where the money came from, but I asked no questions and kept the pretense and everyone was happy.

I remained in this heder for about a year studying Humash (Pentateuch) and the daily and holiday prayers by rote. Except for the Sabbath and the holidays, we studied the year round, five days a week from 9 A.M. to 9 P.M.—except on Fridays, when we quit at noon in time to prepare for the Sabbath. In wintertime, spring and fall, we carried kerosene lanterns to heder to light our way back home at night. There was no play time and rest periods were few; these were used mainly to attend to personal needs and to eat a warm meal at home during the noon hour. Discipline was maintained by pulling the offender's ears or by flogging him with a strap while he was stretched across the rebbe's lap. Many years later as I was teaching in religious schools in Cincinnati, and afterwards as an active lay leader in Jewish education, I often reflected on the amount of Jewish knowledge I had acquired at Mother's knee and on Father's lap before entering heder. Without exaggeration, most of my wards did not know as much by the time they had graduated from the Jewish educational system in Cincinnati, even though it was considered one of the better school systems in the country.

My rebbe, known as a dardeke melamed (infants' teacher), taught beginners at the lowest level and eked out a meager existence from small payments in cash or in kind. It was an exhilarating experience therefore when my wife and I met a daughter of this rebbe at the Orly Airport in Paris in 1953 while waiting for a flight to Israel. It turned out that this charming lady, who was also flying to Israel, was married to a wealthy Chicago businessman and was a girlhood friend of my sister Sheine. We subsequently met in my sister's home in Herzliya and on several occasions in Chicago and reminisced. I was fascinated to note how out of the grinding poverty of Serei there had emerged such a lovely, elegant, fully Americanized lady. Her expensive furs and jewelry and her household furnishings were all in good taste, and she contributed heavily to the United Jewish Appeal and other philanthropic causes. It was amusing, though, that in her vivid imagination our small village became a capitol city and her father, the dardeke melamed, emerged as a professor at the University of Serei. Her husband was a Hungarian Jew but her deep involvement stemmed from Serei. Her brother, who visited with us in Cincinnati, became a successful businessman in Des Moines, Iowa and an important leader of the Jewish community.

My mother apparently got caught up with the Haskala (Enlightenment)

Movement which, since its inception in the late part of the eighteenth century, had achieved a measure of cultural progress in the Diaspora. Eventually it led to the rebirth of the Hebrew language and to the rebuilding of our ancient homeland, Israel. In Russia the Haskala Movement centered largely in the Hovevei Zion (Lovers of Zion) Society, which at first appealed mainly to the elite. With the meteoric rise of the political Zionism of Theodore Herzl, the indigenous striving for the rebuilding of Eretz Yisroel (Israel) became a mass movement and nearly everybody in Serei, as in most of Eastern Europe, became a Zionist. In fact the rebirth of Israel is due to the incessant striving of thousands of little Sereis.

While I was spending my first year in heder Mother was busy founding a modern Hebrew day school in Serei for the proper education of her "ben yohid" (only son) Moshe Simcho, and the children of like-minded parents. She lined up about twenty children and furnished a classroom in the vacant apartment of our duplex house across the hall from our home. She then went to the capital city of Grodno and returned with a young teacher who could teach modern Hebrew by the progressive method of "ivrith b'ivrith"—to learn spoken Hebrew without the aid of another language. I recall the two years I spent under the tutelage of this dedicated teacher with a great deal of nostalgia.

Mr. Draznin, my new teacher, was a tall, handsome, broad-shouldered man with thick black hair, a prominent nose and a heavy mustache. He was immaculately dressed in modern Western clothes with a winged celluloid collar and a gray tie of patterned English cloth. He brought with him to Serei a library of children's books by modern Hebrew writers as well as translations into Hebrew from world literature. This teacher instilled in us a love of books and a love of learning and he taught us to speak fluent Hebrew. Young as I was, I devoured books by the dozen and I became the class librarian. My sense of curiosity about the outside worlds, which these books opened for me, was insatiable and I have remained an avid reader all my life.

The books that had the greatest influence on my Zionist education were the historical novels by the modern Lithuanian Hebrew writer Avraham Mapu—especially his *Ahavath Ziyon* (*The Love of Zion*), *Ashmath Shomron* (*The Guilt of Samaria*) and *Ayyit Zavuah* (*The Hypocrite*). I was also deeply impressed by the historical novel *Daniel Deronda* by George Eliot, the English novelist. It brought renewed hope and a fresh breath of air in the sea of hatred that enveloped us; it is also served as a shining example of a righteous Gentile "hasid umot haolam." In addition to these books I also read books on the legends of the Jews as well as translations from Russian, German, French, and English literature and books by other Hebrew writers. Mr. Draznin also taught us to read and sing poems by Chaim Nachman Bialik, the national Jewish poet, and poems by the celebrated poet Judah Leib Gordon, who, in one of his famous poems, bemoaned his fate as "the last of the Hebrew poets." It is well to recall that in 1906 the Hebrew language had not yet emerged as a living tongue and that Eliezer Ben Yehuda and his family were still in the early stages of their historic struggle in Jerusalem to revive Hebrew as a spoken tongue after two thousand years of disuse.

The study of literature, grammar, and Bible was frowned upon by many pious Jews of Serei as conducive to apicursus (atheism) and at best as a sinful waste of time and a diversion from the all-important study of the Talmud. Mr. Draznin instilled in me a love of the Hebrew language and the Bible as well as a deep respect for writers and classical literature. These loves acquired at the ripe age of seven never left me.

Because of his great influence on his times and beyond, a few words about Avraham Mapu are in order. Mapu was born in 1808 in Slabodka, the poverty-stricken suburb of Kovno. He is recognized as the creator of the modern Hebrew novel and as one of the foremost exponents of the Haskala (Enlightenment) Movement. Avraham Mapu's two major novels, *Ahavath Ziyon* and *Ashmath Shomron*, had Biblical settings and depicted life in Ancient Israel, especially in the times of Isaiah. These books fostered pride in our national past and the love of Zion. They also opened for us the prospect of a free life in an independent Israel in the face of the intolerable political, social, and economic restrictions under which we lived in Russia. Mapu's books were published in many editions and were translated in all of the European and many other languages. His novels made the Bible come alive for me and their profound influence has never left me. Later on when I reached the age of eight and "the time had come to advance to more serious studies"—which meant the study of Tanach (Bible)—I plunged into the new subject with great eagerness and anticipation as a result of the groundwork laid out by this inspiring teacher.

School hours in the modern heder were still from 9 A.M. to 9 P.M. In addition to Hebrew language and literature, Mr. Draznin taught us Jewish history, Humash (Pentateuch), writing, and composition. Mr. Draznin had a free hand in shaping the curriculum and he did a grand job. He was apparently an idealist who, in accordance with the precepts of the Haskala Movement, came to Serei to help spread "enlightenment." It may be well to compare my curriculum at the age of six and seven to the drivel that is being spoonfed to our children today.

A short time after teacher Draznin came to Serei, Mother decided to play

Cupid and enticed him to meet the hazan's (cantor) daughter. The effort was successful and one day the teacher's parents and family arrived for the wedding which was to take place in the schoolroom across the hall from our home. Suddenly a hitch developed. The parents of the groom learned that their son was marrying a poor girl without a dowry—an unheard-of and humiliating situation. After a brief delay and some hurried consultations, Mother came up with a brilliant idea—she took two hundred rubles from the secret hiding place in our home and gave it to the teacher, who quickly showed his parents that he did receive a dowry. The parents were delighted and allowed the wedding to proceed. What they did not know, and apparently never learned, was that after showing the money to his parents Mr. Draznin promptly returned it to Mother, who just as promptly returned it to our secret hiding place.

At the age of seven my education had advanced to the study of Tanach (Bible) and I was matriculated in a special Tanach heder. My rebbe for Tanach was a man with a fine reputation as an excellent teacher by the name of Bialystotzky. My first day in this school, which was located in a two-story brick building near the lower end of Lange Gass, was so exciting and stimulating that I have never forgotten it. I do not recall the teacher's appearance but his voice still rings in my ears. In majestic stentorian tones, while pacing across the small room, he began to recite by heart Chapter One of Isaiah. Every word

Moshe Simcho Schulzinger (Shulsinger) at age seven, 1908.

landed like a sledgehammer and both the words and the sound etched themselves into my memory forever.

> *"Shim'u shomayim*
> *V'hazini eretz—*
> *Ki adonoi diber:*
> *Bonim gidalti v'romamti*
> *V'hem posheu bi.*
> *Yodah shor koneiu*
> *V'chamor eivus beolov;*
> *Yisroel lo yoda*
> *Ami lo hisbonon."*

> "Hear, O Heaven,
> And listen, O Earth—
> It is the Eternal speaking:
> I reared sons and brought them up
> But they have rebelled against me.
> The ox knows its owner
> And the ass its master's stall;
> But Israel knows nothing,
> My people understands nothing."

Frequently I find myself reciting these words of the greatest of all Prophets and the sense of exhaltation which they evoked in me as a child has never diminished. I was very happy with my new teacher and the broad vistas that the words of Isaiah opened for me, the incomparable imagery and poetic beauty of the prophet, the eloquence of his religious message, and his clarion call of hope in a glorious future for Israel and for all mankind, have made me proud of my heritage and an eager champion of our people's legacy.

Unfortunately, this wonderful experience was cut short after only a few brief weeks when I fell sick with scarletina (scarlet fever), from which I nearly died. Without a physician, antibiotics, or any other medicines to speak of, scarlet fever was a deadly disease in Serei. The moment the feldsher (paramedic) made the diagnosis, wailing and crying broke out from the four women of the household and continued until the crisis was well over. In the meanwhile I was mostly in a coma with my temperature reaching daily to 105° F. A whole galaxy of folk remedies were proposed and most of them were tried. The standard remedies were—ice packs, aspirin, chicken soup, and seltzer (soda water). Then came the more exotic prescriptions such as changing my name so that if the Angel of Death came to look for Moshe Simcho and there was no one to answer by that name, he would leave without his prey. Another sage remedy was for the family to go to the cemetery and prostrate themselves at the graves of saintly forebears. During a brief interlude of consciousness I heard Mother dickering with a peasant for mare's milk, but by the time the milk arrived I was again unconscious so I never learned what mare's milk tastes like. When nothing seemed to help, Mother resorted to an act of sheer desperation—she rushed into the men's section of the synagogue during the Sabbath morning services and, with a piercing shriek, tore open the Ark of the Torah and began to cry. The women in the gallery opened the windows to the men's section and joined in the wailing and the men, with their regular services interrupted, began to recite Tehilim (Psalms). It is said that there was not a dry eye in the sanctuary. No one tried to get Mother off the bimah (pulpit), and only when she felt that the Lord could not possibly remain indifferent to the petitions of an entire congregation did she quietly leave the synagogue in the firm belief that her fervent prayers had been heard.

I do not know for certain which of the remedies were the most effective. They certainly bolstered the spirits of the household and the nursing care was superb. The crisis came, the fever broke, and the lucid intervals began to lengthen. During one of my lucid moments I asked a question which again threw my mother, my two sisters, and my Tante Toibe into a fit of unrestrained crying and wailing. I had taken sick just before Rosh Hashanah, the high fever had broken a few days before Yom Kippur, and it occurred to me at the time that the keeper of the heavenly ledgers of life and death had a problem. Since the fate of every being is determined on Rosh Hashanah but the verdict can still be reversed through prayers and atonement on Yom Kippur, in which ledger—I asked—is a verdict of death entered; in the ledger for the old year or the new year? I was only seven years old at the time, so how was I to know that such a simple question would evoke so much consternation? But the grownups knew something else. They knew that preoccupation with death in such circumstances was a bad omen and they reacted accordingly. Soon after posing my question I again lapsed into a coma and I never learned the answer to my question.

Convalescence from this illness was long and troublesome. Greatly weakened, I fell prey to complications including a skin infection, probably impetigo, which covered most of my body, and later on an ear infection which kept draining for months. I thus spent the winter of 1908 indoors recovering from illness and I missed out on my beloved studies of Tanach (Bible). Having become an avid reader under the tutelage of Mr. Draznin, I spent my time devouring one fascinating book after another. During this illness and later during the four years of World War I (1914-18) I discovered what a powerful force serious reading can be in widening one's horizons and advancing one's education.

As soon as I had fully recovered from my illness I was matriculated with the new teacher for Talmud, Mr. Davidowich, who had just been brought to Serei for this very purpose from the famous Talmudic academy of Radin. Mr. Davidowich was a relatively young man of medium height and stocky frame with a round, benign face and a flowing, reddish beard. He was an excellent teacher and was adept at making difficult subjects easy and interesting. As he entered the classroom he would tell us to proceed on our own from where we had left off the day before while he would wrap himself in his full-length talit (prayer shawl). After making the prescribed brocho (benediction) while putting on the talit, he would open the Gemora (Talmud) and spend about half an hour in serious study. His preference of study over prayer was a shocking experience for children who were drilled in the supremacy of prayer. I later learned that the teacher knew what he was doing after all. My introduction to Gemora was through the tract of "Bobo Kama" and I spent three years (1908-10) studying the Talmud in my home town and later another three years in three different Yeshivoth (Talmudic academies)—in the capital of our state, Suvalk (1911-12); in a small shtetl, Skidel, near the capital city of Grodno (1912-13); and in a neighboring shtetl, Lazdei (1913-14).

While studying Talmud in Serei I became a masmid (a diligent persevering student) to the delight of my teacher Davidowich and my parents and to my own satisfaction. During one of the question and answer periods I posed a question on a subject I no longer can remember which brought my teacher to a state of excitement. Stroking my cheek he said to me: "Meishele, du bist an oker horim (Meishele, you are an uprooter of mountains)." At the age of eight or nine this was quite an accolade and it gave me great stature in the eyes of my fellow students.

The accolade Oker Horim was bestowed on the great teacher Rabba (Ben Nachman), the head of the famous Talmudic Academy of Pumpeditha, Babylonia. Rabba distinguished himself for his subtle and trenchant style of teaching, for his keen intellect, and for his skill as a sharp debater, innovator and solver of difficult legal problems. In his teaching methods he preferred to rely on logical argument and rational inference rather than on established precedent or authoritative case records. Rabba thus became the founder of a school of Talmudic study and teaching that has persisted to this very day. Rabba's contemporary and friendly rival at the Academy of Pumpeditha was Rav Yosef, who stressed proficiency and erudition of the oral and written texts. He became a veritable encyclopedia of sayings, maxims, and decisions of great Rabbis and he considered these as binding as if they were revealed to Moses on Mt. Sinai. Rav Yosef and his method of teaching thus became known as "Sinai." Most of the Rabbis were in favor of the "Sinai" method of teaching and chose Rav Yosef to head the Academy of Pumpeditha. Rav Yosef, however, refused to accept the exalted honor and deferred to Rabba or Oker Horim, who became the authoritative head of the Academy. Both methods of teaching were accepted as valid and the opinions of both of these two great teachers are often cited in the Talmud side by side.

Classes in the Gemora school were still daily from 9 A.M. to 9 P.M., and I cannot truthfully say that I ever tired of the subject since it was challenging, informative, and sharpened the mind. Our teacher would habitually skip passages that dealt with sexual relations, adultery, promiscuity, rape, etc. I recall that, along with the other boys, I would regularly return to the skipped passages whenever the teacher was out of the room and dwell at length on the tantalizing subjects. The teacher may have saved himself the trouble of answering embarassing questions on delicate subjects, but as far as I was concerned the skipped passages gave us wholesome sex education and some pleasant diversions.

In 1911, at the age of ten, I left home to study at the yeshiva of Suvalk under the leadership of Rabbi Magentze, a well-known scholar and personality in our part of Lithuania. I considered it a privilege and a great adventure to be entrusted to the outside world at this tender age. The question immediately arose whether I should be placed in a private boarding house, which we could well afford, or whether I should be supported by the school—the customary way. The latter involved public lodging and free meals three times daily in different homes—known as essen teg. Because of my age and being a ben yohid (only son) and the first time away from home, Mother decided in favor of boarding me out. I remained an entire year in Suvalk, boarding at the home of the Garbarsky family, who were friends of ours and related to the Garbarskys of Serei. I was surprisingly very happy in Suvalk and do not recall being homesick. I do not remember too much about my studies in Suvalk but I do recall that I was greatly impressed with the size of the city, its wide and clean streets, and the tree-lined boulevards and sidewalks. Since Suvalk was near the German border, many of the people spoke German and wore modern Western clothes. I vaguely remember Mother's frequent visits and the goodies she would bring me.

The following year my parents enrolled me in a more advanced yeshiva located in a shtetl called Skidel, near the capital city of Grodno. The choice of this yeshiva was determined by the fact that the Rosh Yeshiva (head of the academy) was a former chaver (fellow student) and boyhood friend of my father. At this stage in my education there was no longer any question but that if I was to succeed as a yeshiva bocher (Talmudic student) I must conform to the universal custom of living humbly at public expense. This practice was based on a saying of the Prophets that Torah is advanced by the children of the poor (ki mib'nei aniyim teitzei Torah). And so I was assigned a place of lodging together with several other yeshiva bochorim (Talmudic students) in a volunteer private home. I was assigned seven homes where I was to eat my three daily meals, except that on the Sabbath we ate the Friday night and Saturday meals at the same home. Due to the influence of the Rosh Yeshiva, I received the best lodging place and the best homes to eat that the shtetl had to offer. Our hosts treated us with a great deal of respect and they provided us with an abundance of wholesome and nourishing food, considering it a great mitzvah (commandment or good deed) to encourage the study of the Law.

Skidel was a town of fabricators of raw hides and finished leather products and was malodorous from the numerous open tanning vats, but the balebatim (householders) I met were all lovely people. Three households I remember well. The people where I ate my Sabbath meals were a closely knit, large, happy family and they made me feel like one of them. The house where I was assigned my two Friday meals emitted such a stench from their tanning vats that I would become nauseated before reaching the house. I tried for several weeks to get used to the smells but I finally decided to forego these people's generosity with due apologies to the patron and to the Rosh Yeshiva. A humorous event occurred at the home of my Wednesday meals. This was the wealthiest home in Skidel and there were four of us at the table. The baleboste (lady of the house) was a tall, heavy, good-natured, no-nonsense lady who strongly believed in the adage "Im ein kemah ein Torah (Without good eating one cannot excel in Torah)"—so she served us prodigious meals. One morning the lady surpassed herself by serving us more food than we could possibly consume. The breakfast consisted of large individual portions of bread, herring, fish, and meatballs. After we had already exceeded our capacity and before she ordered us to recite the Birhat Hamazon (Grace after Meals), she showed up with large plates of a thick gruel soup and potatoes and she hurriedly left the room with a strong admonition: "Est, bochorim, est (Eat, young men, eat)." We were in absolute panic. It was impossible for us to eat any more and we dared not offend our benefactress. Suddenly I came up with a brilliant idea: "Lomir essen die shitere un leigen di gedichte in keshene (Let's consume the liquid and put the thick parts in our pockets.)" We rapidly emptied the potatoes and the thick gruel into our pockets and hurriedly drank the soup. During the Birhat Hamazon we felt as happy as "the cat that swallowed the canary."

My advancement in Talmud was rapid. By this time I was able to study

Talmud with commentaries on my own with the Rosh Yeshiva limiting himself to a daily shiur (lecture) of an hour or two. The accepted method of study was for all students to pair off for the purpose of study and discussion, and an effective method of study it was. The academy was situated in the main sanctuary of the synagogue and there were no limits to the hours of study. When we did not eat or sleep or attend to physical necessities, we studied. I became known as a real masmid (diligent student) and as such I spent one night weekly studying until the early hours of the morning. When the balebatim began to arrive for their morning prayers I, along with the others who studied through the night, would join them in prayer. I do not recall that I ever felt tired after a night of study. I was proud of being considered a masmid and felt the same exhilaration as when I used to join my father for Selihos (Penitential Prayers) in the wee hours of the morning as a much younger child. At times we would engage in activities that were frowned upon, such as hiding among the tracts of the Gemora such forbidden books as a Hebrew novel, a musar sefer (book of ethics), or even a Tanach (Bible). Anything distracting from our chief studies was taboo and unthinkable. We studied the Talmud in a kind of sing-song which ranged from the sweetly melancholy to the ecstatic. The words and the tune of the following passage was very popular at the yeshiva: "Omar Rabbi Eliezer, 'Talmidei hahamim marbim shalom ba'olam.'" ("Rabbi Eliezer said: 'Students of the law, or sages, strengthen the peace in the world.'")
The following song was also quite popular:

> *Mai ko mashma lon der regen*
> *Vos zshe lozt er unz tzu heren?—*
> *Dribne tropens oif di shoiben,*
> *Lern! lern! on oifheren.*

> *Mai ko mashma lon der regen*
> *Vos zshe lozt er unz tzu heren?—*
> *Essen teg, un shlingen treren,*
> *Far der zeit farheltert veren.*

> What do we learn from the rain,
> What does it teach us?—
> The raindrops on the windowpanes?—
> Study! Study! Without end.

What do we learn from life,
What does it teach us?—
To eat "days" and swallow tears,
And age prematurely.

Although this song expressed the rebellious sentiments of the Haskala movement of earlier times, its continued popularity suggested an ongoing reevaluation of standards.

During my sojourn in Skidel an episode occurred which troubled me greatly. One night I awoke to discover someone in my bed. I curled up in a fetal position and held my breath as the intruder scampered out. When the same thing was repeated a few weeks later I screamed and was never troubled again. I thought the intruder was one of the older sons of the housekeeper but was not sure about it. Although I was unaware of the man's intention, I knew instinctively that it was evil; I was also afraid of possible physical harm. From my studies in the Bible and Talmud I was familiar with the long lists of abnormal or perverted sexual practices which were mentioned, only to be condemned as immoral, sinful, and harmful. In the environment in which I grew up, "sex" and sexual practices were never discussed and homosexuality was unheard of. My understanding of these subjects from the holy books was that these were evil practices of a pagan society in the dim past. My shock was great indeed to encounter homosexuality at close range in such a highly religious and moral setting. Reflecting on this incident in later years, I have come to realize that there were likely other disquieting stirrings beneath the surface which the existing social milieu did not allow to emerge.

I left Skidel by the middle of December 1913 to be home for my Bar Mitzvah, and I never returned. A Bar Mitzvah (religious maturity ritual) in Serei was an inconspicuous matter-of-course affair and my Bar Mitzvah was no exception. It consisted of being called up to the Torah on one of the three days in the week on which the Torah is read in the synagogue and beginning to wear t'filin (phylacteries) during the morning services. If there were no hosen (groom) or an important yarzeit (a mourner's anniversary) the Bar Mitzvah boy would be honored by being called up to the Torah on the Sabbath for the Maftir (the closing reading of the Torah from the prophets). In my case, there happened to be a hosen in the way so I was called up to the Torah on the preceding Thursday. There were no parties or celebrations as is the practice nowadays. It was not customary for young men to wear a talit (prayer shawl) until they were married, but Mother made a green velvet bag for my t'filin and embroidered it with a Magen David (Star of David) with the word "Zion" in the center and one of the four Hebrew letters denoting the year 5674 in each of the four corners of the Star of David. It was the most beautiful gift I had ever received and I cherish it highly to this day.

A few days after my Bar Mitzvah I was matriculated in the new yeshiva that had just opened in the neighboring shtetl Lazdei. It was housed in the synagogue and was under the leadership of Rabbi Yoffa, the local Rabbi. There was little change in the method of study or teaching and I remained there until the outbreak of World War I on August 14, 1914. In Lazdei I boarded at the home of a prosperous local butcher by the name of Prussak who lived just off the marketplace on the road to Kalvari. The lady of the house was a beautiful God-fearing woman who took care of me in royal fashion. The house and furnishings were spotless and the food was tasty and overabundant. Mrs. Prussak respected my dedication to the study of Torah and she awaited my pleasure as if I were the only thing in her life. The Prussaks had a beautiful daughter by the name of Malke who was about a year or so my junior, but I had no interest in girls at that time. She later emigrated to the United States and established a home in Boston. During my sojourn in Lazdei a teenager declared himself to be the Prophet Elijah and brought a great deal of grief to his family. Aside from topographical differences, Lazdei did not differ much from Serei except perhaps for the large number of sharp horse-traders for which Lazdei was known. Piety and the love of learning was shared by both villages with the rest of Eastern Jewry.

What have the six years I spent in the exclusive study of Talmud done for me? There can be no doubt that they have rounded out my Jewish education and given me a keen insight into the position of the Jew in a non-Jewish world. The study of Talmud is furthermore an excellent vehicle to stimulate the mind and to sharpen deductive reasoning. As a repository of the law, life, and folklore of seven centuries of Jewish history, they also taught me much about the problems that troubled the Jewish people and the world during an important and critical period in Jewish and world history, from 200 B.C.E. to 500 C.E.

The Mishna is written in a pure classical Hebrew and consists of six Sedarim (Orders, or Tracts). It was produced by a group of Rabbis known as Tanaim and was edited at the end of the third century by the last of the Tanaim, Reb Yehudah Hanasi (Yehudah the Prince), also known simply as "Rabi." The Mishna is a compilation of Halachot or legal rulings based mainly on expositions of Biblical verses relating to the "oral law."

The Talmud is essentially an interpretation and elaboration of the Mishna, which in turn is an interpretation of the Torah. The Talmud consists of Mishna and Gemora and was created in the great academies of Babylonia and Jerusalem by many generations of teachers. The authors of Mishna were known as "Tanaim" and the authors of Gemora were known as "Amoraim." The Amoraic period extended from the first half of the third century B.C.E. to the beginning of the sixth century C.E. or, as the Rabbis phrased it—from Rav (the first Amora) to Ravina (the last Amora). Rabbi Yehudah Hanasi, the editor of Mishna, was a contemoprary of Rav.

The Talmud is an immensely rich storehouse of Jewish and universal cultural values. It is an important repository of Jewish religious and civil law, known as halacha, as well as reflections on the cosmos and the creator; the character and lives of the Rabbis; illuminating tales on the religious and social experiences of the Jewish people and their relations with non-Jews; as well as lessons in botany, animal life, astronomy, mathematics, architecture, hygiene, and medicine. All of the latter are encompassed by that part of the Talmud which is known as "Hagadah." Many of the episodes depicted in the Hagadah were idealized and romanticized in later centuries and they served to stimulate the hearts and minds of countless generations, including my own. The Hagadah is, moreover, a rich storehouse of the folklore, customs, superstitions, and legends which were current in Babylonia and in Palestine. The Hagadah is also a rich reservoir of biographical sketches, historical fragments, short stories, tall tales, proverbs, parables, sermons, ethics, conversations, maxims, and reflections. The Hagadah may be described as the imaginitive, artistic, and scientific part of the Talmud and comprises nearly one-third of that vast literary creation. Although the authors of the Talmud addressed themselves primarily to the problems of their own times, they have exerted a decisive influence on the Judaism of succeeding generations and millions of men have found its teachings intellectually stimulating and spiritually refreshing.

My European education consisted primarily of traditional values acquired in the home and the community or learned in heder and the yeshiva. This was interlaced with a two-year stint in a modern Hebrew school which opened a small window for me to the outside world. My education was supplemented by four years of war experiences and was rounded out by two years in a modern Hebrew gymnasium (high school or junior college).

Mariyampole Hebrew Gymnasium, Class V Science Section, 1920.
Honoring Hechalutz (pioneer) group departing for training on farm near Serei. Left to right:
Bottom row: brother & sister Galanti, Frank, Schulzinger
2nd row: faculty: Airov, Anoch, Levin, Lurie; Meyer (director); Levinhertz (2nd director), Yablonsky; Goldshtein (student)
3rd row: Yoel (faculty), x, x, Rubelsky, Kushner, Ruthenberg, Burak, Feivush, and x
4th row: Shulgaser, Charni, x, x, x, x, x, x, Yitzhak Lurie and Goldshtein
top row: x, Avraham Lurie, x, x, x, x, x, x,

CHAPTER FOUR

A Year of Holidays

"The Sabbath is the link between
the Paradise which has gone away
and the Paradise which is yet to come."
(Wylie)

Our faith completely pervaded our lives. We entrusted our neshama (soul) to God in prayer on retiring for the night and thanked Him for returning it to us pure and unblemished in the morning. The three daily prayer services in the synagogue were universally attended and the prayers were recited with kavanah (devotion), taking care not to garble a word or omit a syllable. Although we knew our prayers by heart we were careful to follow the text in the Sidur (Prayer Book). The same prayers assumed a variety of meanings depending on the mood and the needs of the worshipper. In harmony with the meaning of a prayer, and attuned to its spirit, an individual worshipper would occasionally lend special emphasis to a single word or a phrase by raising his voice above the others in prolonged ecstasy. The Rabbi would usually set the

45

pace for the services by ending each prayer aloud and this served as a signal for the cantor and the rest of the congregation to proceed to the next prayer.

Since the dawn of our history the Sabbath had set our people apart from all other peoples and has played a major role in our survival. The Rabbis have said that even as the Jews have observed the Sabbath so has the Sabbath preserved the Jews. Every week, as if by a wave of a magic wand, the pauper's home became a palace, the pauper became a prince, and our sorely tried and oppressed people cast off their worries and remained joyous and gay until the end of the Sabbath. From the lighting of the Sabbath candles by the mistress of the house to the lighting of the twisted multi-colored Havdalah candle (separating the Sabbath from the workday) by the master of the house, we remained happy and carefree. Thinking of mundane matters on the Sabbath was sinful and was effectively banished. A few would even observe a twenty-four-hour vow of silence so as not to desecrate the holy Sabbath by a chance sinful utterance.

In a sense, all of our activities revolved around the Sabbath. People worked hard and pinched pennies all week long to ensure the wherewithall to buy fish, chicken, wine, and white bread for the three festive Sabbath meals. The lack of money to provide adequately for the Sabbath meals would result in a farsh-terten Shabbes (spoiled Sabbath). Such a calamity could not be tolerated in Serei for no one could enjoy his own Sabbath unless everyone else did. Preparations for the Sabbath began by mid-week and we lived in the after-glow of the Sabbath during the remainder of the week. All work would cease by Friday noon and those who were out of town would hasten to return home in time to usher in the Sabbath. The bathing, cleaning, and grooming preparations for the Sabbath were only slightly less rigorous than for major holidays. At least two hours before licht benchen (lighting the Sabbath candles) Father had all his chores completed and he would sit down at the head of the table to recite the Torah portion of the week (Sedra) from the Humash (Pentateuch) with cantillations. This would be repeated three times, twice in the original Hebrew and once in the Targum Unkelus—the Aramaic translation of the Torah by this Greek convert to Judaism. This labor of love done, Father would rush off to the synagogue with me in hand to give me special instruction in the laws pertaining to the Sabbath and the Sabbath Eve services. For me, the highlight of the Sabbath Eve service was always the singing of the beautiful liturgical poem "L'ho Dodi"—"Go forth, my friend, to meet the bride, the Sabbath queen."

Meanwhile at home the womenfolk worked all day preparing tzimmes, cholnt, gefilte fish, several meat dishes, chopped liver, chaleh (twisted egg bread), and other special dishes in honor of the Sabbath. They would clean the house from top to bottom, cover the Sabbath table with the finest white tablecloth, and bring out the silver candlesticks and the holiday tableware. This done, they would dress in their most attractive garments and Mother, bedecked with a wig and a Sabbath kerchief, would approach the table to bench licht (light and bless the Sabbath candles). Exactly at the moment of sunset Mother would light the candles, close her eyes, cover her face with the palms of her hands, and recite the benediction over the lighted candles. At this moment a glow of beauty and serenity would appear on Mother's face and one could readily see the Neshama Y'seira (Heightened Spirit) accompanied by a flock of joyous angels entering her being to dwell therein for the duration of the Sabbath. Every member of the household shared her experience.

The Friday night Sabbath meal was truly a memorable event. As soon as Father would enter the house from the synagogue he would begin to sing "Malahei Hashalom (Angels of Peace)," the song of greeting to the Sabbath angels. He would then recite the Kiddush (sacramental blessing on the wine), wash his hands, make a broche (benediction) over the chaleh, and distribute slices of chaleh around the table to each member of the family. Not a word was spoken by anyone during these proceedings. Mother would then serve the delicious gefilte fish, which Father preceded and followed with a modest slug of vodka. Most unforgettable of the sacred Sabbath day was the singing of z'miroth (Sabbath songs) in which the entire family participated. We were a musical family and loved to sing, and the joyful melodious Sabbath hymns were a perfect means of expressing our cheerful mood. We sang between each of the numerous courses and finished our Sabbath meal at a late hour with the singing and recitation of the long version of the Birhat Hamazon (Grace after meal) when we were literally exhausted.

The most beloved z'miroth, which we continued to sing for decades in our home in Cincinnati were: "Yo Ribon Olam," a hymn of praise to the Creator of the universe; "Tzur Mishelo O'halnu," a hymn of praise to the 'Rock' (God) from whose storehouse we have partaken; "Yom Ze M'hubod Mikol Yomim (The Most Distinguished of All Days)"; and many others. These beautiful hymns with their jingling meter and haunting melodies expressed in a wonderful medley the adoration of God, the love of the Sabbath, and the great longing of Israel for spiritual and physical redemption in the Land of our Ancestors. The Sabbath evening meal always ended with the drinking of hot tea and was occasionally followed with a visit to a friend by the womenfolk, while the younger children would often fall asleep before the end of the sumptuous banquet.

A bonus Sabbath event was an orah oif shabbes (a wayfarer at the Sabbath table). Not infrequently an itinerant Rabbi, a magid (preacher), a meshulah (a solicitor for outside institutions), or a casual traveler would remain in our village for the duration of the Sabbath. Everyone, including the poor, considered it a great mitzvah (meritorious deed) to have a guest at their Sabbath table and they would compete for the privilege. The shammes (sexton) would usually arrange for the distribution of the orhim (wayfarers) on some kind of rotation basis. Occasionally, however, a misunderstanding would arise and a good-natured quarrel would result over whose privilege it was to take the orah home. The orah was occasionally a learned man or a man with a pleasant voice who would enliven the Sabbath table with words of wisdom, a new Sabbath song, or absorbing tales from the outside world.

The Sabbath morning services started early and ended before the noon hour. The distinguishing features were the beautiful chanting of the musaf (supplementary prayers) by the hazan (cantor), who had a pleasant voice and adhered to traditional melodies and intonation. The cantillation of the Sedra (Torah portion of the week) and the even more melodious cantillations of the Haftorah (readings from the prophets) were most pleasing to the ear. In connection with the abandonment of hazanut (cantorial music) and cantillations in some American houses of worship, it is well to recall a teaching of the Kabbalists (mystics)—"There are halls in heaven that are open only to the voice of song." The reading of the Torah was preceded by an auction in which members of the congregation competed for the privilege of being called up to the pulpit for the reading. It was a good-natured, mildly riotous affair in which the bidders were encouraged to raise the ante. Those who were observing yarzeit (memorial anniversaries), bridegrooms, and Bar Mitzvah boys did not have to compete. They made voluntary offerings during the mishebeirah's (blessings in honor of someone) that followed the reading of each of the seven portions of the Sedra and the Maftir. Sermons by the Rabbi were on topical religious subjects and were delivered only on major holidays and on Shabbat Shuvah—the Sabbath before Yom Kippur.

The Sabbath noon meal was a repeat performance of the night before with the addition of cholnt. The cholnt in Serei was a unique culinary delight which had every imaginable delicious taste and aroma. It consisted of chunks of meat, potatoes, beans, chicken fat and spices, as well as kishke (stuffed derma), and other ingredients—and all the pots of cholnt of the entire village were left stewing for eighteen hours in the sealed baker's oven on Shulgass (Synagogue Street). We had two pots of cholnt and they were carried home wrapped in cloth, by myself and one of my sisters. We competed for the privilege and were delighted to bring Mother's creation back to our Sabbath table—except in wintertime and on rainy days when we had to step gingerly to avoid the unthinkable.

After the Sabbath noon meal, which lasted until mid-afternoon, the entire family usually retired to take a nap. Upon arising, Father would seat me near him at the head of the table to find out what I had accomplished during the week in heder. He would then begin to study with me the "Pirkei Avoth (Ethics of the Fathers)" during the summer months, and "Borhi Nafshi" (Psalm 104—A Hymn to Providence) and other Psalms during the winter months. Across the street from us was an inn owned by the Borowsky family, which later emigrated to Pittsburgh, Pennsylvania. From the window I could see the children of the neighborhood playing games in the Borowsky court-yard. I was eager to join them but my feeble entreaties were usually cut short by Father with:—"Dos is gut far prostakes (This is good for the ignorant)" or, "Es past nit far a yingel vos vet a mol zein a rov (It is unbecoming for a boy who will some day be a Rabbi)." We often wonder about the small things that mold our lives; besides indicating my Father's aspirations for me, his admoni-tions played no small part in stimulating my hunger for knowledge and my lack of interest in sports during the rest of my life.

The third prescribed Sabbath meal—Shaleshudes—was a lesser version of the other two meals and was served late in the afternoon. The menu consisted primarily of cold leftovers. The singing of z'miroth (Sabbath songs) was less elaborate, while the customary benedictions and grace preceding and follow-ing the meal were the same as with the other Sabbath meals. Immediately after Shaleshudes Father and I returned to the synagogue for additional studies. This was followed by minha (afternoon prayers), which in turn was followed by responsive recitation of Psalms led by the member of the Hevra Tehilim (Psalm Society) in which the entire congregation participated. The recitation of Psalms lasted until sunset, when the Sabbath ended with the maariv (evening) service followed by the lighting of the twisted multi-colored candle and the Havdalah ritual.

The last hours of the Sabbath at home were marked by a sobering and saddening of the mood with Mother actually crying over the passing of the enchanted holy Sabbath. As soon as Father returned from the synagogue Mother lit the Havdalah candle and Father chanted the Havdalah benediction for the benefit of the household, stressing the importance of "light" by raising his fingernails to the candle and highlighting "fragrance" by smelling from the special spice box (b'somim). The Havdalah benediction to the "Creator of light and fragrance" pointed up the difference between the holy and the profane, the enchanted from the mundane, the blissful Sabbath rest from the hurly-burly of the weekday, light from darkness, and Israel from the heathens. The most touching leavetaking of the Sabbath came from the lips of the pious Jewish women. The soul-stirring chanting of my mother in the twilight hours before the Havdalah service still rings in my ears:

> *"Got fun Avrohom, fun Yitzhok un fun Yaakov!*
> *Der Heiliger Shabbes kodesh geht avek...."*

> "God of Abraham, Isaac, and Jacob,
> The Holy Sabbath is coming to an end.
> May the new week bring us health, life,
> And all that is good:
> May it bring us sustenance, good tidings,
> Deliverance and consolation. Amen."

A considerable part of our time was devoted to prayers in the synagogue. On the Sabbath day we spent about six hours in prayer, somewhat longer on major holidays, twice as long on Rosh Hashanah, and eighteen hours on Yom Kippur. On Shavuoth, the day on which according to tradition the Torah was given, some worshippers would spend all night in the synagogue reading from the Torah. On Yom Kippur some worshippers would remain in the synagogue wrapped in the white kittel (religious robe) and talit (prayer shawl) absorbed in devotional prayers from sunset on Erev (the Eve of) Yom Kippur until after sunset on the Day of Yom Kippur.

The most solemn days on our calendar were the Yomim Noroim (the Days of Awe), which began a month before Rosh Hashanah (New Year) and ended with Yom Kippur (the Day of Atonement). On Rosh Hashanah, also known as Yom Hadin (the Day of Judgment), we believe that the entire human race passed in judgment before God and the fate of each was "recorded"—while on Yom Kippur the verdict was "sealed." During the ten days between Rosh Hashanah and Yom Kippur, also known as Asereth Y'Mei T'Shuva (the Ten Days of Penitence) an adverse decree could still be averted through penitence, contrition and prayer. The climax of the Rosh Hashanah service is the blowing of the shofar (ram's horn) during the morning service as a reminder that the Patriarchs were ready to sacrifice their lives for their faith, and to call upon God for help "while he is near." The Days of Awe were days of soul-searching, pondering, and trying to improve our ways through prayer, charity and good deeds. They began a month before Rosh Hashanah on the second day of the month of Elul and they were marked by the daily blowing of the shofar after the morning services and the addition of special prayers. During the Days of Awe we were told, "Even infants in their cribs tremble before God." But we were also reminded that God was merciful, that He was ever ready to forgive the true penitent, and that the closer we get to Him the nearer He comes to us. During the month of Elul we took account of our spiritual life and began to make amends for past errors as a fitting approach to Rosh Hashanah, the Ten Days of Penitence, and to Yom Kippur. In the process we experienced a great spiritual uplift.

The Yomim Noroim brought with them a sad and somber mood. The prayer services became longer and the prayers were recited with greater kavanah (devotion). People became more charitable, more introspective, and more compassionate. Quarrels were mended, and slights, or possible slights, and offenses were atoned for by begging forgiveness. The women made their plans for the holiday meals weeks in advance. New garments or new shoes were bought in honor of the holidays (l'koved yom tov), or at least something symbolic was acquired to help usher in a new and hopefully better year.

During the entire month of Elul (the Days of Awe) special services of atonement (s'lihot) were held in the synagogue at two o'clock in the morning when the gates of Heaven were open to prayers of contrition and supplication. For a seven-year-old child to be awakened in the middle of the night to go to the synagogue to atone for his sins was a fairly traumatic experience. Yet once in the street in the dark stillness of the night with crackling frost under foot and millions of glittering stars above, I felt a tremendous exhilaration at being witness to such high drama. The gates of Heaven were open, God and His angels were looking down, and little me was being asked to help weigh down the scales of heavenly mercy for the sake of the young.

At the turn of the century in Serei, we took our religion seriously and we followed its precepts willingly and joyfully. I cannot recall ever participating in these activities out of fear or superstition, although such feelings undoubtedly existed. It was rather an expression of joy and thanksgiving for having been born a Jew and for the privilege of serving the God of our Fathers who has given us the Torah. To this day I find myself humming the words and the enchanting tune of the shammes (sexton) of Serei as he would awaken us at midnight with a gentle knock on the door during the s'lihot season with the sing-song "Shteit oif! Shteit oif! Laavodas haborei!" ("Arise! Arise! To serve the Creator!")

The two days of Rosh Hashanah (New Year) marked the beginning of the Ten Days of Atonement. After a whole month of preparation with special supplications and thoughts of penitence, we were now full of reverence and trepidation. We spent most of these days in the synagogue absorbed in prayers pleading for our very lives and for the lives of our loved ones, our people, and the world. The thick holiday prayer book, the Mahzor, admirably served these needs. This marvelous compilation of hymns, poetic and philosophic thoughts, and appropriate passages from the Bible, Talmud and Kabbalah, reflected the history and the spirit of the Jewish people throughout the ages. It was truly pure balm for our souls.

The Rosh Hashanah festive meals were in the usual holiday spirit and we were treated to the finest courses in Mother's cook book. There were several unusual features to these meals—the twisted chaleh (egg bread) was round to symbolize continuity and honey was spread on it to symbolize a sweet year. We also sampled several varieties of sweet new fruit to enable us to recite the benediction of Shehehiyanu—a prayer of thanksgiving for having survived to witness this day.

On the third day of Tishrei (the day after Rosh Hashanah) we observed Tzom Gedaliah (the Fast of Gedaliah). This is a commemorative fast mourning the massacre of the prominent Jewish leader Gedaliah (and his followers), who was Governor of Judea for two months after the destruction of Jerusalem by Nebuchadnezzar in the days of Jeremiah in 586 B.C.E. Although it did not carry the impact of the fast of the 9th day of Av, the fast marking this event commemorated the end of organized Jewish life in Judea since those who remained in Jerusalem panicked out of fear and escaped into Egypt.

The Sabbath between Rosh Hashanah and Yom Kippur, known as Shabbat Shuvah (the Sabbath of Repentance), was observed as part of the Ten Days of Penitence with special prayers expressing regret for past wrongdoing and a determination to correct our ways in the future. The name "Shabbat Shuvah" is taken from the first words of the Haftorah for this Sabbath by the Prophet Hosea:

> "Return, O Israel, unto the Lord thy God
> For thou hast stumbled in thine iniquity.
> Take with you words
> And return unto the Lord.
> Say unto him, 'Forgive all iniquity,
> And accept that which is good.' "

The day before Yom Kippur was a beehive of activity. After the morning prayers we performed the expiatory ritual of Shlogen Kapores during which a special prayer was recited while a chicken or a rooster about to be sacrificed was being rotated over our heads. After taking the kapore to the shohet (kosher slaughterer), the men folk went to the bod (bath house) and then rushed home to put the finishing touches to our holiday attire. Last minute efforts were then made to mutually forgive and beg forgiveness from each member of the family, neighbors, and friends, while the women had the extra chore of preparing the sumptuous meal before the fast.

Some of the men would enter the synagogue on the way from the bod and the mikvah (ritual bath) to receive malkos (flagellations) at the hands of the shammes (sexton) as an atonement for possible sins committed against God during the year. The appropriate number of flagellations was forty or forty less one, delivered gently with a strap on the lower back part of the anatomy. As a child with a penchant for getting into places where he did not belong, I overheard a middle-aged man, with his pants down, exhorting the shammes to hit harder—"What kind of malkos are you giving me?" said the penitant. "Shlog besser (hit harder), I don't feel a thing!" While there are many ways of appeasing God, offenses against people can only be atoned through restitution and forgiveness.

The fasting meal (farfasten) was eaten around a festive table with the recitation of special prayers. The head of the household blessed each member of the family and we were then off to the synagogue. We were always careful not to be late for the special minha service which preceded the ushering in of Yom Kippur with the awe-inspiring and beautiful prayer of Kol Nidre.

On Yom Kippur Eve everyone brought with him a large candle to the synagogue which was lit just before the maariv (evening) service. One of he most indelible memories of my childhood is the scene on Yom Kippur Night in the synagogue where a packed congregation of worshippers, wrapped in their white kittels (religious robes) and taleisim (prayer shawls), pleaded with God for their lives and for the life, health, and happiness of their families, all of Israel, and the entire world. On one such occasion, Rabbi Goldin arrived somewhat late and the entire congregation arose in unison in honor of the Torah which he represented. As the Rabbi passed the central bimah (pulpit) he noticed a worshipper lighting his candle. Since it was already past sunset when such an act is forbidden the Rabbi muttered, "Osur! (It is forbidden!)" The flabbergasted transgressor, by way of reflex action, blew out the candle— thus commiting a second sin on top of the first. The paralyzing shock and consternation of the Rabbi and the entire congregation, after they had worked so hard to cleanse themselves of sin, was overpowering.

The solemnity of the Days of Awe, Rosh Hashanah, and the Days of Penitence weighed heavily on our minds, but none of these compared to the gravity of feeling on Yom Kippur, the "Yom Hadin" (Day of Judgment), when our very lives hung in the balance. The prayers were recited with unusual care and devotion, extraneous thoughts were banished, and there was intense concentration on the full meaning of the supplications. In addition to the silent prayers, certain passages were recited aloud in unison with great fervor.

The Yom Kippur evening services began an hour before sunset and lasted until three or four hours after sunset, while the Yom Kippur day services lasted from 7 A.M. until half an hour after sunset. Not a prayer was omitted from the long liturgy and, except for the very young, not a single worshipper left the synagogue. Yom Kippur was an uplifting, stimulating, and purifying experience and was a source of spiritual sustenance for the entire year. Especially attractive and soul-stirring were the Kol Nidre, the Musaf and the Neila (closing) services. Our hazan (cantor) was a true baal t'filah, which means that he had a pleasant voice and rendered a traditionally meaningful interpretation of the prayers without distracting frills. After the closing maariv service on Yom Kippur Day we returned home exhausted and hungry but full of hope that our prayers were heard.

Preparations for the nine-day feast of Succoth (the Feast of Tabernacles) began immediately after breaking the Yom Kippur fast. The entire family entered our permanent succah, Father pulled on the rope which opened the tilting roof, and we began a bit of symbolic decorating. The real decorating of the succah was done by the women of the house during the next four days. Since the feast of Succoth is also known as Hag He'Asif (the feast of the Harvest) the succah was decorated with a variety of seasonal flowers, gourds, plants, and fruits. We ate all of our meals in the succah and each morning we recited the broche (benediction) over the lulov (palm branch) and essrog (citron) in the succah. The lulov, which was decorated with myrtle and willow branches, and the essrog symbolically combined the four different varieties of plants (arbah minim) into a meaningful whole. The essrog represents beauty and utility, the lulov stands for beauty without utility, the hadass (myrtle branch) denotes utility and the aravah (willow branch) represents neither beauty nor utility. Anyone who could afford it bought a lulov and essrog and they were handled with great care and reverence. Besides their use in the home they were also used in the synagogue during the recitation of Hallel (Praise the Lord, Psalms 113-118) prayers, during the recitation of Hodu (Thank the Lord) and Ono Hashem (O Lord, I beseech Thee) and during the Hakafoth (the procession around the bimah).

The five days between the first two days of Succoth and the eighth and ninth days (Hol Hamoed) were a semi-holiday when we were permitted to do some essential work. On the intervening Sabbath, known as Shabbes Hol Hamoed, we enjoyed the reading of the Book of Koheleth (Ecclesiastes). I was always impressed by the beauty of the cantillation and the exhalted wisdom of this remarkable scroll attributed to King Solomon. After achieving everything he desired—wisdom, wealth, power, pleasure, and general acclaim—in Koheleth he concludes that all is vanity and vexation of the spirit, that there is nothing new under the sun, and that true happiness can be achieved only through fearing God and observing His Commandments.

On the seventh day of Succoth, known as Hoshana Rabah, during the morning services we circled seven times around the bimah (pulpit) in a procession with the lulov and essrog in hand while reciting the Hoshana ("Hosana—help us, O God"). We concluded the morning service by beating the aravah against the pews, thus marking the end of the essrog and lulov services for the year.

The eighth day of Succoth, known as Sh'mini Atzereth (the Eighth Day of Assembly) was celebrated as a solemn festival in its own right, it being the day in which the heavenly verdicts of Rosh Hashanah and Yom Kippur were ratified. Eating in the succah was no longer mandatory on this day.

The high point of the Succoth festival, also known as Z'man Simhatenu, (our Season of Rejoicing) was reached on Simhat Torah (Torah Jubilee), the last day of Succoth. On this day the weekly reading of the Pentateuch was completed and was begun all over again. On Simhat Torah every male past Bar Mitzvah was called up to the reading of the Torah. The small children were gathered on the bimah under the cover of a large talit (prayer shawl) worn by an adult, and they repeated in unison the brahot (benedictions) before the reading of the Torah. The synagogue was crowded on Simhat Torah, even as on Yom Kippur, and everyone was in a festive mood, eager to celebrate and anxious to take part in the joyous Hakafoth (the seven processions with the Torah around the bimah). The Holy Ark was emptied of its contents and both young and old joined in singing and dancing before the holy scrolls that were carried in rotation by everyone present. The proceedings represented true democracy in action and denoted that the Torah belonged to everyone—the poor and the rich, the ignorant and the learned, the simple and the wise. On Simhat Torah, even as on Purim, worshippers were encouraged to drink to excess—and some did. Unaccustomed as these people were to hard drinks, some of the sights and antics were hilarious. Rejoicing with the Torah was a great mitzvah and the merriment was truly intoxicating.

The long winter season between the fall festival of Succoth and the spring festival of Pesach (Passover) was broken by two important semi-holidays— Chanukah, at the beginning of winter, and Purim near the end of winter. Chanukah commemorates the rededication of the Beth Hamikdash (the Temple) on the 25th day of Kislev 165 B.C. by Judah Maccabee after it had been defiled by the Greek ruler Antiochus the Fourth. This madman who ruled over Judea and considered himself a god, tried to hellenize the Jewish people by introducing idol worship in the Temple. On Chanukah we celebrate a triple victory—an important military victory over the Syrian Greeks, the regaining of national independence, and the triumph of religious freedom over the suppression of conscience. Chanukah also commemorates a series of miracles—the few defeated the many, the holy defeated the profane, the righteous defeated the wicked, and a one day's supply of ritually pure oil that was found in the Temple lasted eight days.

In commemoration of the latter miracle, Chanukah is celebrated for eight days with a nightly candle-lighting ritual beginning with one candle on the first night and increasing to eight candles by the eighth night. The fire of devotion and self-sacrifice which these lights symbolize inspired future generations to emulate the great heroes of the past. As children we looked forward to Chanukah since we played a central part in the lighting of the candles, the singing of the brahot (benedictions), and the singing of "Maoz Zur" (Rock of Ages) and other inspirational songs. We also enjoyed playing the Chanukah game of dreidlach (tops), receiving presents and Chanukah gelt (money), and eating potato latkes (pancakes), which were served nightly throughout the festival.

Six weeks after Chanukah, on Hamisha Asar B'Shvat (the Fifteenth day of Shevat), we celebrated another minor holiday. This holiday is known as Rosh Hashanah L'Ilanoth (the New Year of Trees). On this holiday we ate fruits which grew in Eretz Yisroel (Land of Israel)—namely dates, figs, and bokser (carob). Although there were no special ceremonies, the holiday served to focus our attention on the Land of Israel and its flora and to keep alive our traditional appreciation of God's gift to man—the fruit tree. The planting of trees by school children in modern Israel has added new meaning to this festival.

Four weeks later, on the evening of the fourteenth day of Adar, is the beginning of Purim—the gayest festival in our calendar. The day preceding Purim was observed as a fast to commemorate the two days of fasting which Mordechai and the Jews of Shushan (the capital of ancient Persia) observed at the urgent request of Queen Esther.

All of our holidays were happy occasions, each having a meaning and flavor all its own, yet Purim was somehow different. It was a delightful semi-holiday distinguished by eating homentashen (three-cornered pockets of dough filled with poppyseed or jelly) and the exchange of gifts. There were also playlets by local talent called Purim Spiels which dramatized the story depicted in the Book of Esther. The reading of the "Megilath Esther" on the eve and on the morning of Purim was especially exciting. We came to the synagogue prepared with all kinds of handmade noisemakers called graggers and at each mention of "Haman Haagagi Zoreir Hayehudim (Haman the Hagagite, the persecutor of the Jews)" all Hades broke loose with a great deal of noise and derision for Haman by stomping our feet and noisily swinging our graggers. The older people would merely stomp their feet or stealthily pound on the inside of their lacterns. They would then help quiet us down so that the reading could proceed. Although the story of Esther and Mordechai was well known to us, we looked forward to hearing it again and again because the story and the melody were so enchanting. We knew from experience that the would-be persecutors of our people were always around. The triumphant ending of the story expressed our age-old determination to survive, and the symbolic vengeance on our tormentors was ever so sweet. The story of Purim reminds us of the Biblical admonition that "there is an ongoing conflict between God and the 'Amalekites' throughout the generations, and that because of the eternal hatred for the eternal people" it behooves us to be well fortified in our faith if we are to survive.

Preparations for Purim began several weeks in advance of the holiday. The poppyseed, which was the primary filling of the homentashen and which grew in our garden, had to be finely crushed to make it edible. This was accomplished by pounding the seeds with a heavy wooden masher in a large stupe (pestle) which was carved out from the trunk of a tree. Since there were only two stupes in all of Serei, they were passed around in a pre-arranged system of rotation until they were finally returned to their owners. Other holiday items which were in short supply and were passed around in a similar manner were: the Pesach stupe which was used to grind matzo into pesachdike mehl (flour) or farfel; pesachdike mednize (a brass cooking vessel used to brew mead—a Passover drink of hops and honey); extra large pots and pans to make preserves; and the essrog and lulov on Succoth.

The exchange of gifts on Purim consisted in the main of large or small homentashen and other specially prepared goodies which were distributed by the children on kerchief-covered platters. The mutual visitations, the mystery as to what was under the covers, and the element of surprise created a carnival spirit which was greatly cherished. The Purim Spiel was a highly stylized dramatization of the story of Esther performed in the Yiddish language in song. Weather permitting, it was presented on the Shulhoif (Synagogue Place) near the Alte Shul (Old Synagogue). Abbreviated versions were also presented from house to house. Since we had never seen a real show, we considered it great entertainment. The grotesque performances by the untutored children and adolescents were accentuated by their comic appearance in the ill-fitting antiquated garments of their parents or grandparents, their imaginative paper crowns, and their crude disguises behind flowing beards of black wool.

The preparation for Pesach (Passover) began immediately after Purim and lasted four weeks. With spring in the air and with the need to eliminate any possible doubt that the house was kosher for Pesach, every room and every piece of furniture was scoured. The walls were whitewashed, linen, bedding and tablecloths were taken outside for airing, and everybody got something new to wear l'koved yom tov (in honor of the holiday). The special Passover drink, mead, required several weeks to distill and filter. The turkey, which was carefully raised for the occasion, had to be fattened by stuffing without causing a sudden demise of the delicate bird. Pesach dishes, glassware, pots and pans, and tableware all had to be scoured and koshered by burial in the ground or immersion in scalding water. Pesachdike chicken fat or goose fat for cooking and baking had to be prepared, as well as pesachdike eingemachts (preserves) and a variety of jams.

Baking the matzo was the big event. It began with a sifter coming to the house to sift the pesachdike mehl under carefully supervised conditions. Arrangements at the matzo bakery had to be made long in advance. The most desirable time for baking the matzo was during the third week before Pesach, preferably during the first daily session in the wee hours of the morning when the oven was real hot and the staff was refreshed. One's turn for baking the matzo was in a way a measure of one's standing in the community. The turn of the poor people was during the least desirable first and last weeks of the four-week matzo baking period. Our turn was usually in the first daily session during the middle of the most desirable (third) week. The baking of the matzo was a cooperative affair of the baker, the family, four or five professional helpers, and a mashgiach (religious supervisor). Every member of the family participated in the event in auxiliary or in supervisory capacities.

In the bakery there was a long wide table at the head of which stood a woman who mixed flour and water to make and knead the dough into a proper consistency. A broche on the baking of the matzo was made by Mother. The dough was then cut into appropriate sections which were passed on down the table to be rolled into thin flat wafers. Straight lines of perforated holes were then made through the matzo wafers with a sharp-toothed wheel guided by a moving roller and the raw matzo was then placed on a long flat ladle and placed in the oven. The baker used two or three ladles and, while one row of matzo was baking, another ladle was prepared. My sisters and I helped with rolling and perforating the matzo. The baking was fast and was in the nature of a sacrament reminiscent of the hasty historic exodus of our ancestors from slavery into freedom and from a strange land to the land which was promised by God to our forebears and their seed. All who were engaged in baking the matzo wore clean white robes and headgear and no food was allowed on the premises. After paying the baker and tipping the helpers, we wished each other a happy and kosher Pesach and departed behind a porter who carried the matzo to our home on his shoulders in a large woven basket. The matzo we baked served our needs during the eight days of Pesach and for two or three months thereafter.

On the eve of the day before Pesach we performed the rite of Biur Hometz—

or the removal of all bread products from the house. Since there was no hometz to be found anywhere as a result of the extensive cleansings, small pieces of bread were distributed on the window sills of each room so that the benedictions and rites of Biur Hometz could be performed. On returning home from the maariv services, Father would light a candle and hand it to me and with the entire family in tow we would proceed from room to room to gather in the hometz. With the candlelight focused on the hometz, Father would carefully sweep it into a large wooden spoon with the aid of a goose feather and just as carefully deposit it into a paper bag. It was my task the next morning to take the bag with the hometz to the public bath house and throw it into the huge oven. On the same trip we would also take the tableware that needed to be koshered and have the bedder (keeper of the bath house) dunk it into the kettle of boiling water.

Another task on the morning of Erev Pesach (Passover Eve) was to sell the hometz (farkoifen hometz). That meant to sell the hometz we possessed on the premises to the Rabbi, who in turn sold it, along with the hometz of the rest of the village, to a Goy (non-Jew) for a small fee. The Goy knew that the sale was a religious rite and a legal fiction and never claimed possession of his purchase. During this visit to the Rabbi, or on a previous visit, we also made our contribution to Moos Hitim—the special fund to provide matzo for the poor. At noon all hometz dishes and leftover hometz foods were removed from the house but we were forbidden to eat matzo until after the proper benedictions during the Seder Service in the evening. After the customary bathing at the public bath house, we were ready for Pesach and the Seder—the most joyful religious family ceremonial event of the year.

New garments for Pesach were mandatory for everyone who could afford them so as to be absolutely certain that no crumbs, or hometz, were left in the pockets. Those who could not afford new clothes were broken-hearted and had to be satisfied with carefully cleansing and washing their old holiday clothes. Tailoring a new garment was a weighty matter. The texture, the color, and the quality of the cloth had to be agreed upon and was seriously discussed by the entire family until a consensus was reached. The garment of a growing boy was not tailored to fit but to be "grown into" and so was always oversized and had to be adjusted with various temporary devices. There were at least two or three fittings at which there were some more consultations. When the cloth of a garment faded after several years of wear, it was frequently retailored by turning the garment inside out. We had three kinds of tailors in Serei—a master craftsmen; a tandetnik—a tailor of cheap, ill-fitting clothes usually worn by the peasants; and a latutnik—an expert at applying patches.

The traditional Seder was observed in all homes. We did not omit a single passage from the Hagadah (a compilation of the story of the exodus from Egypt) and most of it was done to the tunes of enchanting music and numerous symbolic rituals. Father was seated at the head of the table in a comfortable armshair, wearing a white kittel (robe) with pillows to lean on under his left arm to symbolize his status as a free man and a prince. To emphasize his high rank and position, a pitcher of water and a basin were brought to the table so that he could wash his hands before the Seder service. In regal fashion, his cup was filled with wine by members of the household and there were other reverential gestures. The injunction of Rabbi Eliezer that "he who prolongs in relating the story of the exodus from Egypt is most praiseworthy" was observed at our home to the fullest and the Seder celebration seldom ended before midnight. The young children greatly enjoyed their exalted status as the center of attention. Bravely they asked the Arba Kushyot (Four Questions), including "How does this night differ from all other nights?" And they received the answer immediately and throughout the Seder ritual. Equally enjoyable were opening the door for the Prophet Elijah, finding the affikomen (carefully hidden pieces of matzo) for which there was an award, the jingling songs, the banquet table, and the gay mood.

With the official ceremonies of the Seder over, most of us promptly retired for a well-deserved rest, but Father proceeded with the reading of the entire "Shir Hashirim (Song of Songs)" with its traditional melodious chant. The "Song of Songs"—that beautiful Biblical poem full of expressions of tenderness and love—was believed to describe the reciprocal relationship between God and His people Israel. Father's heart too was ever full of love and gratitude toward the God of Israel. During Hol Hamoed (the four days of semi-holiday between the first two days and the last two days of Pesach) light, essential work was permitted. Otherwise, it was a holiday for all intents and purposes. The distinguishing Pesach foods were matzo balls and chremslah (matzo meal pancakes). The absense of bread, bread products, and any unleavened dishes was of course the most notable feature.

Seven weeks from the second day of Pesach we celebrated the festival of Shavuoth (the Feast of Weeks). The Sefira (counting of the intervening days) was begun by reciting daily the benediction of the Omer (wheat offering) after the maariv service. The Sefira was at first considered an expression of the eager anticipation of the festival of Shavuoth that commemorates receiving the Torah—it being the main reason for our departure from Egypt and the main driving force behind our continued existence as a people. In later centuries, as persecutions filled the pages of our history, the Omer season became a period of semi-mourning during which we abstained from weddings, grooming, and all celebrations—except on Lag B'Omer, the thirty-third day of the counting of the Omer, when all delayed festivities took place. History relates that dreadful calamities befell our people during this season, including a pestilence which wiped out tens of thousands of Rabbi Akiba's followers during the second century and appalling massacres at the hands of the Crusaders at the end of the 11th century. The religious services on Shavuoth were noted by the reading of the Scroll of Ruth which deals with the conversion of the "righteous" Moabite to Judaism and the descent of the dynasty of King David from her marriage.

The menus of Shavuoth were marked by the emphasis on dairy products and the absence of meat dishes, possibly as an expression of mourning. Among the delicious dishes served were kugel (pudding), made of broad noodles and cheese, and cheese blintzes (crepes) topped with sour cream. A legend traces the custom of eating dairy products on Shavuoth to the day of receiving the Torah at the foot of Mount Sinai. By the time our teacher Moses finished expounding the laws of the Torah, it was too late to obtain kosher meat that would conform to the new dietary laws. But milk, cheese, and other dairy products were on hand.

The seventeenth day of Tamuz was a fast day commemorating the onset of the siege of Jerusalem by the Romans which led to the destruction of the Second Temple and eventually to the loss of sovereignty and dispersion of the Jewish people. In fact, it marked the beginning of a period of mourning over many other tragedies which had befallen the Jewish people through its long history. This period of mourning and soul-searching lasted for nearly eight weeks until after Yom Kippur, the Day of Atonement.

The saddest day of the year was without doubt the ninth day of the month of Av, or Tisha B'Av—the day on which, according to tradition, the First and Second Temples were destroyed. On this day we wore mourning garb— namely old tattered clothes and sandals over white stockings. We abstained from all food and drink from sundown till sundown, we sat on low stools or crates both at home and at the synagogue, and we avoided music or any kind of pleasurable activity. We spent the greater part of the twenty-four hour period in the synagogue praying, reciting kinot (dirges and laments), reading the lamentations of Jeremiah "Eiha yashva badad ha'ir—behold how desolate has become this metropolis," and recalling the various national tragedies—especially the loss of both Temples, the loss of sovereignty, and the exile of the Shehinah or the Divine Providence from the Temple. The crying, the wailing, and the audible sighing were heartrending and were accompanied by deep prostration as at the loss of a dear one. Even small children were carried along by the mood of deep mourning and they wept along with the adults. It is related that during his Eastern campaign Napoleon chanced upon such a scene in the synagogue of a shtetl. In response to his puzzled query, Napoleon's adjutant explained that the Jews were mourning the loss of their ancient Temple and sovereignty two thousand years before, upon which Napoleon remarked: "A people that remembers the loss of their sovereignty that long ago will live to see it restored."

Despite the spirit of gloom and despondency of this festival of Tisha B'Av, I felt an inner glow and a spiritual uplift when the congregation, led by the cantor, recited the dolorous outcry of Jeremiah and the beautiful poem on the same theme by the celebrated poet of the Middle Ages, Rabbi Yehudah Halevi. The words and haunting melodies of these powerful statements are deeply etched in the storehouse of my memories. Halevi begins his lamentations with "Eli Zion v'orea k'mo isha b'zarea v'hivsula haguras sak al baal neurea—Wail, O Zion, and your cities, like a young woman in her (labor) pains and like a maiden in her mourning garb, over the loss of the husband of her youth." Elsewhere Halevi cries: "Zion alo sish'ali lishlom asiroyih—O Zion! How I yearn for the welfare of your captives."

The Sabbath that followed the fast of Tisha B'Av was known as Shabbath Nahamu (Be-Comforted Sabbath). In the Haftorah reading for this Sabbath the Prophet Isaiah uttered his "Be comforted, my people" message in which he prophesied that Israel will yet be rebuilt. We faithfully believed in Isaiah's prophecy and we felt comforted, but Fall was already in the air and the beginning of the Days of Awe was only three weeks away. The spirit of despondency of Tisha B'Av thus seemed like a fitting prelude and a natural transition to the feelings of trepidation at the Approaching Days of Judgment. Our year of fasts, feasts, and holidays was now at an end and a new cycle was about to begin.

CHAPTER FIVE

Institutions and Practices

> "The truth of religion is in its rituals."
> (Powys)

In addition to the activities which revolved around the Sabbath, the festivals and the synagogue, there were numerous social and philanthropic needs that Serei was deeply aware of. In a sense, our social and charitable activities were an extension of our religious activities, for in addition to the problems to be solved there were mitzvoth (rewarding commandments) to be earned. Among the organized social activities were: Malbish Arumim (clothing for the needy), Gemilas Hasodim (free loans), Hahnosas Kalah (dowry for needy brides), Moos Hitim (matzo for the poor), Bikur Holim (visiting the sick), Hevrah Kadisha (burial or holy rites society), Hahnosas Orhim (shelter for needy travelers), Talmud Torah (schooling for the poor), Maoz Ladoh (help for the oppressed), Pidyon Sh'vuyim (ransom for prisoners), and the Hekdesh (home for the destitute). Quite a formidable range of activities for a village of one hundred Jewish families.

63

Besides the local charitable societies there were outside institutions to which we contributed. Every home had a number of charity boxes (z'doke pushkes) in which the woman of the house would drop a few coins on the eve of every Sabbath and yom tov (holiday), just prior to licht benchen (lighting the candles), as well as on other happy or sad occasions. The most prominent of these charity boxes were those of Yeshivath Rabbi Meir Baal Hanes (the yeshiva of Rabbi Meir the miracle worker of Tiberias), the Diskin orphanage of Jerusalem and other orphanages, homes for the aged, and yeshivoth (Talmudic Academies). The white and blue box of the Jewish National Fund was added during the first years of the current century and it became very popular.

Not infrequently, a variety of visitors would come to Serei. The most welcome among these were the itinerant Rabbis or maggidim (preachers). They would usually spend the Sabbath in the village and preach in the synagogue between the minha and maariv services. They were in the main inspiring speakers who would tell us wonderful stories about our glorious past and exhort the eager listeners to love God and obey His commandments. The preachers would invariably close their sermon with the phrase: "U'vo l'Zion goel bimheiro v'yomeinu v'nomar omen—May the Redeemer come to Zion soon in our own days and let us say amen." Among the other visitors were meshulahim (solicitors) for yeshivoth and charitable institutions and the poor from other communities who needed help to support their families. There were also victims of a fire or some other calamity and those who needed money for a daughter's dowry or some other worthy cause. The solicitors would go from house to house and tell of their needs in a matter-of-fact manner. No one ever questioned their stories or refused to help. Even those who were themselves recipients of charity seldom turned anyone away empty-handed. Every effort was made to receive the solicitors with understanding and friendliness, which helped ease their burden and make their task less onerous.

Since coins were in short supply we used a community script known as pruta to give to the meshulahim. Before leaving town the solicitors would then exchange the script for ordinary coins with aid from the Rabbi. The value of a pruta can be gauged from the facts that a Russian ruble was worth fifty cents, there were one hundred kopeks in each ruble, each kopek was worth two groshen, and each groshen was worth one hundred prutas. At this rate of exchange, even the poorest could affort to give charity. Fortunately, many items could be bought for a groshen or a kopek in those days.

Marriages in Serei were arranged by the marriage broker or shadhan. A handshake between the parents of the bride and the groom was considered binding once the terms of the marriage were agreed upon. The terms usually involved such items as the amount and nature of the bride's dowry; the date, size, and other incidental details of the wedding ceremony; the duration of room and board for the married couple, to be provided by the parents of the bride; the shadhan's fee and other sundry considerations. Once the terms were agreed upon, a festive engagement ceremony (T'noim) took place, at which time the formal engagement contract was signed. There was a customary waiting period of one year between the T'noim and the wedding. During this period the hosen-kaleh (groom and bride) were permitted some modest freedoms that were otherwise frowned upon.

A wedding was a memorable community event and lasted a week. The wedding ceremony began with the capelie (music band) of four musicians walking up the street to fetch the groom and his family and neighbors. The entire group, dressed in their finest holiday garments, then marched to the Shulhoif (Synagogue Place) to the sound of music and the hosen and his parents were placed under the hupah (wedding canopy). The capelie then proceeded to the bride's home and accompanied her together with her family and the remainder of the community to the waiting hosen. The capelie consisted of a violin, a base, a flute, and a drum. None of the musicians could read notes and they were all self-taught. Their attempt to play traditional Jewish wedding music was a gallant effort which was only partly successful, for not infrequently each took off in a different direction. Although the audience was largely unsophisticated, the merriment created by the cacophony added to the happiness of the occasion.

During the traditional ceremony under the hupah, the bride and her parents circled seven times around the groom in deference to his status as the master of the new household. The wedding party, led by the capelie, then proceded to the bride's home for the festive meal to the sound of "hosen-kaleh mazel tov (good luck to the bride and groom)." There was invariably dancing in the street by the grandmothers of the newlyweds. While facing the couple they would dance backwards in the traditional mock dance called the Kosher Tantz. The entire village was invited to the Seudat Mitzvah (the prescribed festive meal) immediately following the ceremony, and everyone came. Special pains were taken to invite the poor and they were often given seats of honor. All of the assembled participated in the singing of the traditional Shevah Brahot (Seven Blessings), but it was the ever-present badhan (bard) who made the occasion most memorable. The badhan usually improvised easy or forced rhymes to suit the occasion. He manipulated his lines to evoke alternately tears or laughter to the tune of a stylized traditional melody accompanied by the capelie. There was a great deal of circle- and square-dancing and other efforts to entertain the newlyweds. The bride and groom fasted on their wedding day and they were not allowed to see each other on their wedding day until they were under the hupah. Shaving the bride's hair on her wedding day to diminish her attractiveness to others was already a matter of memory except among the Hassidim, but going to the mikvah (ritual pool) and wearing a sheitel (wig) were mandatory.

The groom was called up to the Torah on the Saturday preceding the wedding and he had first priority to read the Maftir (the last and most honored portion of the Torah reading). The seven days that followed the wedding were celebrated at a more leisurely pace but the singing and dancing continued and everyone considered it his duty to add to the happiness of the hosen-kaleh and thus earn an important mitzvah (good deed). The mahatonim (family of the married couple) and the out-of-town guests usually remained over the entire Sheva Y'mei Mishte (Seven Days of Feasting).

The first child was usually born exactly on time and the father would name the girl child in the synagogue on the nearest Sabbath, Monday, or Thursday as he was called up to the Torah. In the case of a male child, the naming took place at the brith (circumcision rite). The brith was performed at the home of the parents in the presence of family, friends, and neighbors. The traditional ritual of the Brith Milah (circumcision covenant) has changed little over the years except that the moel (circumcizer) no longer uses his mouth to stop the bleeding. This practice was abandoned some time ago as unsanitary, unnecessary, and aesthetically unacceptable. Paradoxically, recent studies have shown that human saliva contains a clotting factor, a healing factor, and an antibiotic factor—explaining, perhaps, the reason for the earlier practice in a less sophisticated age. The circumcision rite, which was initiated by Abraham, is considered a religious covenant between the Children of Abraham and the God of Abraham.

If the first child was a male born to parents who were neither Cohens or Levites we had a Pidyon Haben (redemption of the first born) ceremony on the thirty-first day after his birth. In the presence of family and friends, the father redeemed his son from the ancient duty to dedicate his life to the service of God. Around a festive table in the synagogue, the father handed the child to a Cohen. Following an exchange of prescribed declaratory statements and prayers and the payment of five silver-rubles to the Cohen, the redeemed child received the priestly blessings and was returned to the father. The feasting then proceded in accordance with one's means. We also had special religious invocations on reaching Bar Mitzvah at the age of thirteen, on dedicating a new house, on recovery from illness and on embarking on or returning from a journey.

Death and dying, even as birth and marriage, were surrounded with elaborate religious rites of sanctification. The first consideration in illness was to implore divine help for recovery through special personal and public petitions of atonement which included a brief confessional. Seeking competent medical help was a practical as well as a religious duty. It was strictly forbidden to depend on faith healing or to rely on miracles. During terminal illness or when death became imminent, one of the most important concerns was not to die without Vidui (confession). The Vidui was a full Yom Kippur confessional and was recited, unaided if possible, or with outside help if necessary. The last words of the dying were "Sh'ma Yisroel—Hear, O Israel, the Lord our God, the Lord is one." The final confessions of faith were preceded by the well-known declaratory exhortations: "The Lord is, was, and shall be for ever and ever; blessed be His name whose kingdom is forever and ever; and the Lord is God." If the dying person lingered a while longer, these declarations of faith were repeated over and over again.

Visiting the sick was considered a great mitzvah and was scrupulously observed; the poorer and lonelier the sick person, the greater was considered the mitzvah. Visiting the sick, it was felt, might contribute to recovery, while not visiting might contribute to death. The Bikur Holim (Visiting the Sick) Society played an important role in seeing to it that this mitzvah was carried out in an orderly fashion. Reciting special misheberahs (invocations) in the synagogue on behalf of the sick during the reading of the Torah was considered especially beneficial for recovery and no one failed to invoke these misheberachs. After recovery from an illness, the recovered person was called up to the reading of the Torah and he recited the benediction of Hagomel (thanksgiving).

Immediately upon expiration, members of the Hevra Kadisha (Holy Rites) Society came to the house and took charge of all the necessary arrangements. They began with the cleansing and ritual purification (taharut) of the deceased, performed by a special male or female squad. The deceased was then dressed in the ever-ready tahrihim (burial garb) and the men were also wrapped in their talit (prayer shawl). The body was then placed on the floor and covered with a special black blanket, candlesticks with lit candles were placed around the body and a minyan (ten members) of the Hevrah Kadisha began reciting Psalms, which continued uninterrupted day and night until the funeral. Through all these proceedings the members of the family remained discreetly in an adjoining room. They bore their grief in silence except for occasional outbursts of wailing by the women and crying by the children. The bereaved were spared the painful commercial problems surrounding funerals elsewhere. Visitors would pronounce the traditional "Boruh Dayan Emes

(Blessed Be the Righteous Judge)" and would depart in silence after shedding some tears. There were no attempts to console the bereaved and there were no handshakes.

In accordance with tradition, the funeral took place within twenty-four hours before sunset. Funeral services were conducted at the home of the deceased and at the gravesite. There were no hespeidim (eulogies) except on very rare occasions as at the funeral of tzadikim (unusually pious persons). On extremely rare occasions the deceased would be carried past the synagogue, the doors of the synagogue would be opened, and a hesped (eulogy) would be delivered. The funeral service began with Kriha (the rending of garments) followed by the reading of prescribed Psalms and prayers and the recitation of the traditional "El Moleh Rahamim (Lord Full of Compassion)." The body of the deceased was then placed in a temporary coffin on a horse-drawn hearse and the procession to the cemetary began.

Nearly everyone in the village accompanied the family to the cemetery. The procession was preceded by the children of the Talmud Torah who chanted Psalms in unison all the way to the cemetery. Immediately behind the hearse walked the shammes (sexton), who jingled coins in a charity box and recited "Tzedoko tatzil mimoves (charity saves from extinction)." No one shirked his duty and everyone deposited a coin. The final rites at the gravesite consisted of placing a small sack of Eretz Yisroel erd (Israel soil) under the head of the deceased with shards over the eyes and twigs between the fingers of both hands, all of these symbolizing faith that "in the end of the days" the dead will arise and reassemble in Jerusalem. Burial was on the bare ground with improvised rough boards on all sides and on top. Before leaving the gravesite everyone present threw a lump of dirt into the grave while reciting, "Odom m'ofor v'sofo l'ofor (from dust thou came and to dust thou returneth)." The burial ceremony was known as Tziduk Hadin (Resignation to God's Judgement). No attempt was made to soften the harshness of the proceedings. The prescribed Psalms were recited, the male mourners chanted the Kaddish (memorial prayer), and the mourners departed between two rows of friends who recited: "Hashem y'nahem eshem b'toh aveilei Zion v' Yerusholayim (May the Lord comfort you amongst the mourners of Zion and Jerusalem)."

Upon leaving the cemetery and again on entering and leaving the mourner's home, all would wash their hands and recite: "Bilah hamoves la netzah (He maketh death to vanish in life eternal)." The washing of the hands, a purification rite, was repeated before the mourners re-entered their home. The mourners fasted on the day of the funeral and ate sparingly upon returning from the cemetery. Festive meals following a funeral and during Shiva (seven days of mourning) period were alien to us and were frowned upon as a Goyish (non-Jewish) custom. During the Shiva we dressed in our oldest garments, we sat on low stools or boxes, we wore no shoes, and we ate sparingly. All mirrors, pictures, and ornaments were either removed or covered with white linen. Between and after the three daily services we recited Psalms and read from the Book of Job. The mourning period lasted thirty days (Shloshim), while mourning for parents extended twelve months. Listening to music or indulging in any kind of merriment was forbidden except on the Sabbath and on holidays when it was forbidden to mourn. The Jewish cemetery in Serei was situated on a dirt country road to the south of the shosei (paved road) to Alyta. A stone fence, an open wrought-iron gate, and old stone grave markers are all I remember of the Beth Hakvaroth (cemetery) of Serei, which is also known as the Beth Hahayim (House of the Living in Eternity).

CHAPTER SIX

A Shtetl Called Serei

> "A man full of piety and knowledge is always rich; it is a bank that never fails; it yields a perpetual dividend of happiness."
> (G.H. Lewes)

My birthplace, Serei (Serijai), was built atop a low hill and its gentle slopes and was tucked away at the southern tip of the small triangular Baltic state of Lithuania (Lietuva). It was an old village surrounded by rolling hills, fertile farms, lush meadows, small orchards, lakes, and forests. In the dim past primordial forests dominated the landscape and the local inhabitants, who spoke a strange ancient tongue, supported themselves by hunting, fishing, and cultivating small parcels of land. In the course of time, additional stretches of forest were cleared by the hardy Lithuanians to provide tillable soil for their expanding families.

In a series of conquests during the thirteenth century two great Lithuanian leaders, Gdiminis and Vitautas, converted their small primitive land into a major kingdom. They subdued Latvia, White Russia, and large parts of the

Ukraine and Poland, and they extended the borders of Lithuania from the Baltic Sea to the Caucasus and the Black Sea. During this period the pagan Lithuanians were also converted to Christianity as a result of a series of "misunderstandings."

Gdiminis and Vitautas invited Western European Jews to settle in Lithuania to help with the management of fiscal affairs and the development of commerce and industry. Gdiminis also brought large numbers of Rabbinic and Karaite Jews as captives during the wars of conquest. These enlightened rulers granted the Lithuanian Jews a charter of rights to protect them from minor tyrants, the anti-Jewish guilds, the jealous and fearful native city-dweller, and the anti-Semitic clergy. This charter of rights was a model for the protection of minorities and served to attract many more Jews into Lithuania, especially from Western Europe, where violent persecution of Jews was rampant at the time. For a period of four centuries Lithuanian Jews enjoyed complete freedom to engage in the economic activity of their choice and to develop their own religious, cultural, and social institutions. This era came to an end when Lithuania was conquered by the Russians in the seventeenth century and both peoples were subjected to severe discrimination and oppression.

In 1920 Lithuania regained its independence and lost it again in 1939 to Communist Russia, in 1940 to Nazi Germany, and in 1944 again to Communist Russia. As a result of the revolutionary and cataclysmic events of the two world wars, the shtetl (village) Serei no longer exists. The Serei I am describing is the one I knew at the turn of the century.

Serei had one long street in a north-to-south direction that was appropriately called the Lange Gass (Long Street). Running west from the middle of Lange Gass was the short Shulgass (Synagogue Street) which led to the Shulhoif (Synagogue Place). A little further down Lange Gass to the left was the marketplace and across the street stood the church. At each end, Lange Gass split into V-shaped bifurcations which gradually eased into the countryside. The village was framed at each end by military highways (shosei) running in an east-west direction. The highways were built of compressed crushed rock and were quite serviceable. They were primarily intended to facilitate the defense of the region in case of war with Germany and we were the indirect beneficiaries.

There were about one hundred and fifty families in Serei—one hundred Jewish and fifty non-Jewish. In the countryside the vast majority of the peasants were hard-working, self-sufficent Lithuanians. They raised a great variety of products which they sold to the Jewish merchants or householders. On the outskirts of Serei were two medium-sized landed estates which were owned by local Jews, one by Yosef Garbarsky and the other by the partners Nun and Zeman.

Serei was surrounded on all sides by shtetlach that were in most respects indistinguishable from our own. In the vicinity were Lazdei, Simne, Alyta, Vishei, Meretz, Leipun, and Druzgenik (a resort town on the River Nieman). All of these shtetlach were about thirty kilometers or a three- to four-hour drive by wagon from Serei. Further southwest was Seni, Suvalk (our state capital), Yagustov, and the German border. Further northeast were Butrimanz, Stoklishok, Troki, and Vilna. Vilna (Vilnius) was the ancient capital of Lithuania and the most revered seat of Jewish learning in the Diaspora; it was also known as the Jerusalem of Lithuania. Northwest of Serei were Kalvari, Mariyampole, and the German border; north were Balbirishok, Pren, and Kovna (Kaunas), the capital of Lithuania; and south were Kopcheve, Sopotkin, Halinke, and Grodno. Grodno was a capital city and an important place of Jewish learning—it also served as our center of supply for manufactured goods. At one time or another I had visited or lived in each of these places before I emigrated to America in 1921.

Life in our shtetlach was, in the main, primitive and hard. The winters were long and cold with frequent blizzards and huge snow drifts, but sleigh-rides and ice-skating provided some fun for the small fry. Our summers, though relatively short, were most enjoyable because of the mild climate, the abundance of delicious fruits, the fragrance and heavenly scents of the country air, and the joy of bathing in the lake; but the short spring and fall brought us a fare of rain, mud and slush. We could have readily skipped these dreary seasons were it not for the Jewish holidays that came just in time to bring us joy and laughter and happiness.

Most of the houses were single-family homes of ancient vintage with vegetable gardens of variable sizes and a barn or stable in the back of each. The houses were mainly of unhewn logs with plastered and whitewashed walls on the inside and floors of wood or compressed clay. There were a few brick houses, several two-story buildings, and a few houses that sported colored tile roofs. Most of the roofs were of wooden shingles and quite a few were of thatched straw. With only a primitive bucket brigade to fight fires and the lack of a ready water supply, shtetlach like Serei lived in constant fear of destruction by fire. Details of huge conflagrations were frequently mentioned and fires were dreaded as much as the plague or a pogrom.

There were no sidewalks, electricity, or refrigeration in Serei. Most of the houses were heated with wood in huge brick ovens which also had sections for cooking and baking. The top of the oven served as a warm place to sleep in the sub-arctic cold of our long winter nights, while the bottom of the oven, which usually opened on to a rear foyer, provided warm shelter for the egg-laying chickens. All houses had double windows and shutters to keep out the cold and to provide a measure of privacy. The lighting was by kerosene lamps in the more affluent homes and by wooden slats in the homes of the poor and the peasants. The smoke of the burning slats would meander across the ceiling and leave by way of a hole in the wall, a window, or an open door.

Our house was a comfortable one-story duplex of unhewn logs with a roof of wooden slats. There were shutters on all the windows and these were closed nightly from within. The front entrance to the house was by way of a small covered wooden terrace. A three-step stairway connected the terrace to the street and there were wooden benches on each side of the terrace. A double door led to a small foyer with doors on each side and a window straight ahead. The door to the right led to an apartment which we rented out and which served at one time as my schoolhouse. The door to the left led to the place which I called home. It opened on an oblong room whch served as our den and dining room. This room had a window on the left facing the street, a door straight ahead led to the living room, a door to the right led to the kitchen, and a door slightly removed from the entrance led to a small bedroom which also housed the sleeping section of the large oven. The other furnishings of this bedroom were a bed, a wardrobe, a night table, and a chair. The only furniture in the dining room was a long wooden table along the window with benches on each of the long sides and chairs on each of the short ends. There was enough room around the table to accommodate our family of six and several guests. It was the most used room in the house and was the nerve center of most of our activities, especially on the Sabbath and holidays. The plastered walls were whitewashed annually and the bare wooden floors were sprinkled with yellow sand on the eve of every Sabbath in accordance with an ancient custom.

The living room was the formal room of the house and was used primarily to entertain guests, while at night it doubled as a bedroom for my sisters. It had a window on the left which looked out on the street; another window, facing the entrance, looked out on the double driveway which led to the rear of the house; and a door to the right led to the master bedroom. The wall adjoining the entrance was lined with three-inch glazed white tiles and it formed the outer covering of the ceiling-high second brick oven that kept us warm through the winter. The furniture of the living room was decorative and included a table, chairs, a day bed, and a wardrobe with a mirror. The white lace curtains were decorous and spotless and added a touch of elegance.

The master bedroom was small and included two beds, an end table, a wardrobe, and a chest. The bedroom had two windows, one facing the driveway and one facing the courtyard. The kitchen contained a table, some cabinets, and the working ends of the two wood-burning brick ovens. The smaller oven had a small compartment which was used to keep food warm, while the larger oven was used for cooking and baking. A door next to the oven led to the rear foyer, where another door led to the second apartment. One of the fond memories of my childhood is crawling into the large, dark chicken coop under the oven to bring out the warm, freshly laid eggs for the breakfast table by the light of a candle.

In the rear of our house, behind three-quarters of its width, were two buildings unique for Serei. One was a large, low-ceiling one-room shop which housed the primitive machinery and equipment of our soft drink facility, and next to it was a large ice house. The ice house extended some twenty feet underground and provided excellent year-round cooling for the lemonade, kwas, and soda water which we sold in Serei and in the neighboring communities of Lazdei, Leipun, and Kopcheve. Replenishing the ice was a major annual undertaking in which the entire household participated and provided lots of fun for me and my sisters. The project began with a crew of sturdy men who cut large squares of ice from the village lake. The ice was then transported to the ice house by several sleighs making repeated trips to the lake. A crew of skilled workmen unloaded the ice by means of a chute and another crew distributed and packed the ice for maximum efficiency. The ten days that it took to fill the facility were a semi-holiday for the household. Besides serving our own domestic and business needs our ice house was greatly appreciated in the summer by some of our friends and neighbors. Towards the end of the summer when most of the ice had melted, it was quite a chore to climb down the ladder and up again to reach the cool food or drinks.

Between the house and the shop was a large connecting room that served as a warehouse for the temporary storage of full and empty bottles. To the right of this room was a permanent succah with a latticed ceiling and a tilting roof on pulleys. A door on the wall opposite from the entrance to the succah led to the ice house. Behind the shop and the ice house was a fertile fenced-in garden, some three hundred feet deep, on which we raised all kinds of vegetables and flowers for our own use. Among the edibles were cucumbers, tomatoes, cabbage, corn, potatoes, spinach, shchav, celery, radishes, watermelons, sunflower seeds, etc. We hired a peasant to till and fertilize the soil while the planting and harvesting were done by the family. At the end of the garden were a stable to house our horse and two cows and a large barn to store the wagons, the garden equipment, and the fodder and grain for the cattle. To the right of the barn was the outhouse, of which the less said the better—except perhaps that it was an unforgettable experience, especially when the weather was foul, the call urgent, and the time to traverse the distance too short.

Our house was located near the southern end of Lange Gass on the west side of the street near the beginning of the downslope and the Government building. Our street was paved with cobblestones and a row of large flagstones of irregular size and shape in the center. This row of stones helped the children play a hop-skip-jump game up and down the street and helped everybody to negotiate through the slush and mud that engulfed us in the spring and fall. The short side streets on both sides of Lange Gass were unpaved and they were seas of mud for about four months of the year.

The right fork of the southern end of Lange Gass led to a fair-sized lake where we went bathing and swimming in the summer. Since we bathed in the nude, there were designated areas for male and female bathers and they were separated by distance and by clumps of trees and shrubs. The lake was about a one-hour walk from the village and was approached through lanes of sweet-smelling orchards and ripening fields. It was a pleasant, exhilarating walk and the activities on the lake, which included an occasional ride in a fishing boat, were eagerly anticipated by the children and adolescents. This nostalgic memory is marred by the fact that this lake was the site of the brutal extermination by machine gun of the entire Jewish population of Serei at the hands of the Nazis and their local Lithuanian collaborators on the eve of Rosh Hashanah, 1941.

The left fork of the southern end of Lange Gass led, after an hour's walk through heavy sand, to the farm of the only yeshuvnik (farmer) near Serei who supplied some of the townspeople with kosher dairy products. Another half-hour's walk down the road led to the landed estate of Nun and Zeman. Parts of this estate were turned over, in 1919-20, to a group of young Zionist student pioneers from the gymnasium of Mariyampole for the purpose of Hachshara (preparation for kibbutz life in Israel). A son of Mr. Zeman became a prominent local Communist, and after World War II he became secretary general of the Lithuanian Communist Party and editor of the newspaper *The Lithuanian Pravada*—thus the virtual ruler of Communist Lithuania.

The northern end of Lange Gass ended abruptly facing a saloon. The head of the family inhabiting this landmark had the dubious distinction of being the only Jew from our area to be exiled for life to Siberia for allegedly setting a fire which resulted in a fatality. The "Sibirnik," as he was subsequently called, was a swarthy man with a deep, dark complexion and was hare-lipped. The man's family seemed to be nice people, indistinguishable from the rest of the community, and they seemed to carry their burden and shame with admirable stoicism.

The fork of Lange Gass to the right of the saloon led to the post office and to the homes of the town's more prosperous citizens, who were nearly all Poles or

Germans. The left fork led to the military road and beyond that to the landed estate of Yosef Garbarsky. Yosef Garbarsky was a tall stoop-shouldered man, very positive and assertive in his manner and highly respected for his wealth and his wisdom. He wore the same outer garment as long as anyone could remember and was considered somewhat eccentric. Yosef Garbarsky had a hazoka (claim) to chant, on the feast of Shavuoth in the synagogue, the Aramaic poem "Akdomoth Milin V'shoryoshuso." I have never forgotten this imposing man standing on the central bimah (pulpit) wrapped in the talit (prayer shawl) and chanting the "Akdomoth" with its beautiful traditional melody—his vibrant and resonant voice filled the synagogue and the passion and clarity of his diction testified to a deep attachment and understanding. To this day I often find myself chanting the words and the melody of this beautiful poem as I learned it from this remarkable man. His wife was a charming, genteel lady and was related to my future wife Pupi and my niece Chana. A beautiful daughter, Sonya, and a son, Herschel, who later became the town's physician, were my contemporaries. As a tribute to the alleged wisdom of Yosef Garbarsky and my mother Basheva, they used to say in Serei that if Yosef Garbarsky had married Basheva the pair could have ruled the land. The Garbarsky family were the first to succumb at the hands of their Lithuanian farmhands when the Nazis came to Serei.

One of the important landmarks of Serei was the Kanzelarie (Government Building) which housed a two-cell jail, vital statistics, property records, the three-man Russian police force, and three Russian civil officials. It was a spacious two-story building of limestone situated near the beginning of Lange Gass on the east side of the street and the level part of the hill. Three houses southward, on the corner of Lange Gass and the intersecting shosei (military road), lived my future brother-in-law, Yitzhak Hirsh Slavaticki, who married my beloved sister Rivka. My sister Rivka, who was two and one-half years my senior suffered a martyr's death in 1941 together with her husband, their son Avram, her aged mother-in-law, and the entire Jewish community of Serei. Their older child, Chana, escaped their bitter fate when she came to live with us in Cincinnati in 1936 as a young child.

Other landmarks in Serei were the two synagogues, the marketplace, the church, the sod (orchard), the heder (Hebrew school), the Beth Hakvaroth (cemetery), the city lake, Finkel's Hachsania (holstery), the shlosserei (metal workshop), and the apteik (pharmacy). Features of the one-of-a-kind variety were—one Jewish drunkard, one psychotic, and one blind-deaf mute man. There were also a feldsher (paramedic), an akushorin (midwife), a melamed (beginner's teacher), a teacher of Tanach (Bible), a teacher for Gemora (Talmud), a Rabbi, a hazan (cantor), a shohet (kosher meat slaughterer), a

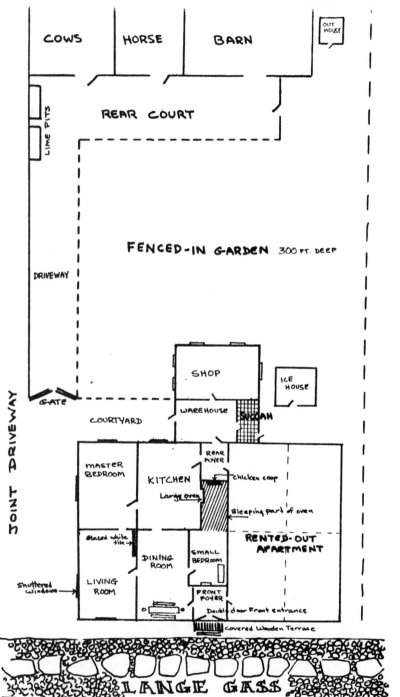

COWS HORSE BARN OUT HOUSE

LIME PITS

REAR COURT

DRIVEWAY

FENCED-IN GARDEN 300 FT. DEEP

JOINT DRIVEWAY

GATE

COURTYARD

SHOP

ICE HOUSE

WAREHOUSE SUCCAH

MASTER BEDROOM

KITCHEN

REAR FOYER

chicken coop

Large Oven

Sleeping part of oven

Glazed white tile

RENTED-OUT APARTMENT

DINING ROOM

SMALL BEDROOM

Shuttered Windows

LIVING ROOM

FRONT FOYER

Double door Front entrance

Covered Wooden Terrace

LANGE GASS

SCHULZINGER HOME

shammes (sexton), a bedder (bath house keeper), two butchers, and two balegoles (wagoners). The others were peddlers, shopkeepers, saloon keepers, wholesale and retail merchants, and a number of exporters. The exports went primarily to Germany and consisted of grain, potatoes, fodder, poultry, turkeys, geese, sheep, cattle, horses, hemp, hog bristles, horsehair, hides, leather and timber.

Four houses north downhill from our house was the Shulgass (Synagogue Street). It was a narrow, unpaved lane with a dozen or so crumbling houses on either side of the street, and it was the most traversed and poorest part of the village. Down the gently sloping hill Shulgass opened up on a wide square, the Shulhoif, with the kloise (small synagogue) on a hillock on the left, the town's only well (brunim) in the center, the Alte Shul (old synagogue) on the right, and the bod (bath house) and the lake straight ahead. There were houses on all sides of the square and their inhabitants carried the same stigma of poverty and low social status as those who lived on Shulgass. In this area lived the shammes, the bedder, the dard'ki melamed (beginner's teacher), the baker, as well as the two butchers, the two cobblers, a tailor, a capmaker, and one balegole. We were a rigidly stratified society and the inhabitants of these streets were on the lowest rung of the social ladder. Yiches (family standing) was of great importance and upward mobility was next to impossible. The only exceptions to the rigid rule were the Talmudic scholars, who were highly prized and respected regardless of humbleness of origin. The lowly occupations and the poverty of the neighborhoods otherwise stigmatized the inhabitants. The acquisition of wealth or a respected occupation were of some help in overcoming the stigma of "lowly" origin or lack of yiches, but not altogether. These attitudes were somewhat relaxed as a result of World War I and the revolutionary changes that followed, but they were never really abandoned.

The Alte Shul was a large ancient structure of clapboard and was the main synagogue of the village after the new synagogue on the lower part of Lange Gass was destroyed in the great fire before the turn of the century. Architecturally, the Alte Shul had four tiers which narrowed at each level toward the top. There were large, stained-glass windows in the main sanctuary and small, plain windows in the women's section (weibershe shtiebel) on the second floor. The entrance to the main sanctuary was on the ground floor along the western wall and the entrance to the women's section was around the corner along the northern wall.

The Alte Shul was partly sunk into the ground and we had to stoop to enter. There was a large foyer at the entrance and there were two large rooms on either side of the foyer which were used for study by prushim (ascetic Talmudic students) and occasionally for special services by late worshippers.

There was an Aron Hakodesh (Holy Ark) in each of these side rooms along with tables, benches, and shelves full of books. The weibershe shtiebel was immediately above this section of the shul.

At the entrance to the main sanctuary, immediately on the left, was a large copper water container with an attached copper basin to catch the overflow and a large copper cup on a chain. The water was used to wash the hands before reciting "Asher Yotzar" (the benediction after visiting the bathroom) and for ablution of the hands of the Cohanim (Jews of priestly descent) by the Levites before the "Birhat Cohanim" (the blessing of the congregation by the Cohanim). Next to the water vessel was a huge wood-burning brick oven faced with glazed white tile. While the men warmed themselves around the oven many a yarn was spun, political and other important events were discussed, and daily news or gossip was disseminated. Besides heating the sanctuary, the oven also served to thaw out the half-frozen, early-rising worshippers who would rush into the synagogue nearly undone by the sub-arctic cold.

The floor of the main sanctuary was reached by way of a broad three-step flagstone staircase about fifteen feet wide. In the center of the sanctuary was the large bimah (pulpit). On the eastern wall facing the large bimah was the Aron Hakodesh (Holy Ark) with a small bimah in front of it and a lectern for the hazan (cantor) in front of the small bimah. In the rear of the shul, in back of the central bimah, was a long table with benches. There were also long tables with benches along the northern and southern walls of the rear part of the synagogue. In the front part of the synagogue were about a dozen pews facing the Aron Hakodesh with identical pews along the northern, southern and eastern walls. Ownership of a pew along the eastern wall was a highly prized possession and a badge of honor. These pews were originally assigned to people of great piety and learning and were subsequently inherited. Each seat had a chest for the storage of the talit, t'filin, prayer books, and study books, and each pew had a portable lectern to support the heavy prayer books or books of study. The walls were painted white and were decorated with appropriate Biblical quotations. The Aron Hakodesh was of mahogany wood and was a work of art of ancient vintage. The carvings on the Ark were an intricate design of lions, deer, rams, grapes, shofars, essrogim, lulovim, and cherubs. There were two eternal lights in the shul, one in front of the Aron Hakodesh and the other in front of the central bimah. The eternal lights were small kerosene lamps with red glass covers.

The seating order along the eastern wall was in accordance with one's rank in the hierarchy of learning. The Rabbi sat on the left side of the Aron Hakodesh and the hazan on the right side. Our seat was next to Mr. Kabaker (a respected merchant of yard goods), one seat removed from the Rabbi. Since my father was away in Cincinnati during most of my years in Serei, I was the proud possessor of this badge of honor (or yiches) by virtue of hereditary right, and I basked in its glory. Many years later, as an established resident of Cincinnati, I mused over this situation when I heard a member of the prestigious Losantiville Country Club declare, "If I leave nothing else for my children but a membership in the Losantiville Country Club, I will die a happy man."

The seating in the other pews was along the lines of diminishing standing in learning or wealth. The poorest and least learned were seated along the tables in the rear of the synagogue. These same tables were cleared immediately after services for the customary daily hours of study. The table along the northern wall belonged to the Hevra Shas (Talmudic Society), which was led by the Rabbi. In this study group there were frequently heated discussions, loud expostulation, and many questions and answers. It was the largest and most respected study group in the synagogue. The two tables along the southern wall were assigned to the Hevra Mishna (Mishna Society) and Hevra Ein Yaakov (Ein Yaakov Society) respectively. These groups contained the lesser learned members of the synagogue and they were led by the most knowledgeable members of their groups or by a member of the Hevra Shas. The dedication of these two groups to learning and study was not less than that of the Hevra Shas, but there were fewer discussions or debates because of the highly narrative nature of Mishna and Ein Yaakov and the lesser depth of study.

The love of learning was great and the learned were admired and respected. The fondest hope of every parent was that his or her offspring would grow up to be a dedicated student of the Talmud, and no sacrifice was considered too great to achieve it. Many worshippers would frequently shorten or rush through their prayers in order to have more time for study. The synagogue was thus more commonly called "Beth Midrash (House of Study)" than "Beth T'filah (House of Prayer)."

Studying was done individually and in groups. It took seven years of study, one page every day, to complete the study of the Talmud by the Hevra Shas Society. At the conclusion of the last line of the last tractate of the sixty-three tractates of the Talmud, there was a celebration with the joyous and jubilant exclamation in unison by all the members of the study group of "Hazak! Hazak! V'nithazek!—Be strong! Be strong! And let us be strengthened!" The entire congregation joined in the celebration, known as Siyum. At the Siyum brandy and kichel (cake) were served, the Rabbi delivered a learned address, and the group began the study of the daily portion of the Talmud all over again. Similar celebrations were held at the conclusion of their studies by the

Mishna and the Ein Yaakov societies and at the conclusion of individual tractates of Talmud, but they were on a lesser scale.

The totally unlearned belonged to the Hevra Tehilim Society. The members of this group engaged in the responsive reading of Tehilim (Psalms), following their leader in a traditional sing-song. The reader stood on the central bimah and the followers gathered all around. They followed a daily repetitive order and, from frequent repetition most of the group knew the Tehilim by heart— even though few knew their meaning. The reading of Tehilim usually took place between the evening services of minha and maariv. Most memorable was the Tehilim Zogen (Recitation of Tehilim) on the Sabbath. The lengthening shadows near the end of the enchanted day gave a special flavor to the sweet, sad sing-song of their plaintive voices. When some of these Tehilim zogers came to America they were often considered learned men because of their ability to quote Biblical passages in the Hebrew.

The weibershe shtiebel (women's section) was forbidden territory to men and was governed by one of the women—usually by one who was able to follow the services in the main sanctuary and thus was able to keep the women worshippers in step with the men. Another consideration was the ability to read the "Tzena Ur'ena"—a Yiddish anthology of Biblical and pious tales—to the other women, most of whom were unable to read. In the absence of a regular leader, my mother would often fulfill this function. On such occasions I could see the small curtained window in front of Mother's pew open ever so slightly in order to learn where the men were in the service ritual. The "Tzena Ur'ena (Go Forth and See)" was an extremely popular and remarkable book. It consisted of a miscellany of tales, homilies, midrashim, and exegetical comments woven around a Yiddish rendition with paraphrasings from the Pentateuch, the haftarot (Prophets), and the megilot (scrolls). The work was written in a lively, simple, and flowing style and was first published in 1590 by a Lithuanian Jew, Rabbi Yaakov Ashkenazi, from Yanow. It was reprinted in more than two hundred editions with many revisions. Most women read this fascinating volume at home over and over again until they knew it by heart.

The smaller synagogue, known as the kloise, was a small wooden structure and was the house of prayer for most of the balmelohes (artisans) and the unlearned poor. I visited this synagogue only once out of curiosity and it did not appear inviting. The town's water well occupied the center of the Shulhoif and water was fetched by lowering a wooden bucket attached to a rope on a pulley. The water was distributed to the more distant areas of the village by a wasser treger (water carrier) who carried his load in two buckets on a wooden yoke.

The bod (bath house) and mikvah (ritual pool) provided for the sanitary and ritual needs of the community. The first thing one saw on entering the bod was a huge, wood-burning oven with a copper kettle encased in it. The bathroom proper housed an open wood-burning hearth filled with large stones, and steam was obtained by pouring cold water on the glowing stones. The bathers poured buckets of cold water on their hot flesh and whipped themselves with little brooms of birch or willow branches. The cleansing and the stimulating effects were superb. No soap was used or needed. Occasionally the bedder (bath house keeper) would surprise his unwary clients with a few lashes of his broom or with a bucketful of cold water on their overheated bodies. The squirming of the victims and the inevitable yelling of "hu-ha" never failed to amuse the others. The top wooden benches of the steam room were meant for the hardy souls who would yell and squirm with delight. In the absence of bathing facilities in the home, attendance at the bath house was a true hygienic necessity and was utilized by young and old every Friday afternoon in preparation for the Sabbath. The bath house also served as a social and educational center of sorts. The bedder, on the other hand, was at the very bottom of the social totem pole.

In the bath house I received my first lessons in human anatomy and I learned that it was not quite true that all men were created equal. There were those who were almost ape-like with their dense coats of body hair and there were others who were totally hair free. I also learned that differences in size and shape were magnified by the naked state, that some men had unusually large breasts, and that certain peculiarities of gait were actually due to a kile (hernia) which sometimes rivaled the bucket for size. There were also a few bath tubs and two mikvahs (ritual pools) in a side room of the bath house which were used by adult men and women for ritual purposes. The soiled water from the bath house flowed through an open ditch directly into the lake.

The village lake was surrounded by marshes and was unsuited for swimming. It also lacked the necessary privacy for bathing in the nude. Bathing suits had not been heard of in Serei at that time. There was some fishing and boating on the lake and in the winter time we cut ice from it and went skating on the frozen waters using shoe leather instead of skates—which, again, were unheard of. The most important role of the lake, however, was its use for the Tashlich service on Rosh Hashanah. On that day, before the afternoon (minha) services, our entire community went to the lake to cast away our sins and to gain spiritual cleansing by emptying our pockets and symbolically throwing accumulated crumbs or lint into the flowing water. It was a joyful ritual and was repeated on both days of Rosh Hashanah with recitation of the prescribed prayers.

Near the shore of the lake grew water lilies and other water plants in great abundance. There were also wide stretches of green algae. In the evenings we were amused by the solo and choral singing of the crickets and the frogs, while in the distance across the lake there beckoned the strange, mysterious, and forbidden world of the Goyim.

The Jewish world we knew was all we had and all we cared to have. Our relation to God was trusting, loving, and intimate. We could plead to him directly in an hour of need and we knew that he would not let us down. The rich and the poor lived in a beautiful symbiotic relationship. The rich, "by heavenly grace," enjoyed olam haze (material well-being) but they yearned for olam haba (heavenly bliss), which they could only obtain through compassion for the poor, while our poor were willing to relinquish part of their heavenly reward in return for relief from their suffering on earth. Our relations with our non-Jewish neighbors were also amicable and mutually beneficial—we traded worldly goods to our mutual advantage and we were perfectly content to be left otherwise alone if the others would only consent.

We were steeped in the faith of our fathers to the point of martyrdom. Our chief concerns, young and old, rich and poor, was the study of Torah, the fulfillment of the Taryag Mitzvoth (613 meritorious deeds), and the accumulation of as many g'milut hasadim (compassionate deeds) as possible. Concern with material things was considered a necessary evil—something to be tolerated but not indulged in. Some of our well-to-do were known to complain that by being rewarded on earth they were being denied their due share in heaven and it troubled them. The suffering of the poor, on the other hand, was mitigated by an abiding faith that they would be rewarded in the hereafter. In our milieu the synagogue was the true nerve-center of the community and the hub of all our activities from cradle to grave. No one would ever dream of missing any of the three daily services in the synagogue. When such an omission was occasioned by illness or incapacity, we felt a need to atone for the transgression. The attachment to the synagogue was shared by the women even though attendance at daily prayers in the synagogue was optional for them.

Relations with our non-Jewish neighbors was, although satisfactory, never too close. We bought everything they produced and sold them everything they needed. The exchanges, for money or barter, took place on Sundays after church services, on Tuesday market days, and in special monthly fairs in our village and in neighboring communities. Some of our people made a living traveling from farm to farm selling, buying, or bartering on the spot. These traders were known as karabelniks and they would return home early every Friday in good time for the Sabbath. Occasionally, the Goyim would bring their produce to town on odd or non-market days, usually in connection with the Jewish holidays. They would bring turkeys for Pesach, chickens and roosters for Kapores (Atonement) on the eve of Yom Kippur, or s'chach (evergreen branches) for the succah on the eve of Succoth. Occasionally, because of the closeness of the holidays, a peasant would get mixed up and would bring roosters for Succoth or s'chach for Yom Kippur. This caused a great deal of merriment, but we bought the unwanted products anyway out of rachmones (compassion). Firewood and kindling wood were other products that were brought to town at odd times.

Although we spoke Yiddish and the Goyim spoke Lithuanian, it was not a barrier to trade. We learned a few words of Lithuanian and the Goyim learned a few words of Yiddish, and in a pinch we used sign language. No one felt a need for more extensive means of communication since there were no social or cultural exchanges between us whatsoever. The two communities actually lived side by side as friendly strangers. We were united only by our trading and by the common bond of oppression at the hands of the Russian overlords. Occasionally, when a disagreement or a misunderstanding arose as a result of the language barrier or for some other reason, we would compromise in favor of the Goyim in order to promote good will. In case of a serious disagreement, the Goyim would often insist that the Rabbi adjudicate the conflict, knowing from experience that they would not be wronged.

After the Sunday and holiday church services the Goyim would disperse to their favorite stores or saloons. Frequently there was heavy drinking which led to fights or other disturbances. These altercations would be settled with the help of the saloonkeepers, their own fellow villagers, or the police. After a few hours some of the men would be lying dead-drunk in the back of their wagons and their women would drive them home. When there was no one to drive the poor drunkard home, the saloonkeeper would stretch him out in the back of his wagon and the horse would take his master back home—once he was headed in the right direction and given the signal to proceed.

There were a few Goyim in Serei who spoke a passable Yiddish. These were usually the Shabbes Goyim—the gentile who would turn off the lights, stoke the fires, and perform other chores forbidden to us on the Sabbath, without being asked. For these services they would receive a piece of gefilte fish or a slice of chaleh—which was considered a fair exchange. The karabelniks (Jewish peddlers), on the other hand, learned to speak a passable Lithuanian as a result of their daily contacts with the Goyim. Despite the good relationship between our peoples, there were two days in the year on which we were in fear for our very lives—these were the days of Christmas and Easter Sunday. By the time the Goyim left the church on these holidays, we had become "Christ-killers" to them. To avoid provocation or incidents until the wrath subsided, we would barricade ourselves in our homes behind shuttered windows and barred doors. With deep anxiety we would watch our erstwhile friendly neighbors pass our homes with fire in their eyes and murder in their hearts.

At all times, and especially on these holidays, we were at the mercy of the three Catholic priests who ministered to the religious needs of the illiterate Goyim of Serei and its environs. The pagan Lithuanians were among the last of the European peoples to be converted to Christianity. Among the concessions that the Church made to keep their loyalty was acquiescence to an arrangement where the priests' "housekeepers" were also their wives. These "housekeepers" of the priests were often our only contacts with the non-Jewish religious hierarchy. The children of these households, commonly known as the priests' children, were usually sent to regional schools and many of them wound up in the priesthood, as government officials, or in the professions. Because of the intensive pressure from the Russian Government and the more subtle social pressure from the more cultural Poles and Germans, most Lithuanians who went to school became assimilated and they frequently shunned their origins. The same was true of most of the clergy. The peasants, on the other hand, remained fiercely loyal to their roots, but they were a leaderless mass. The estrangement of the peasantry from their assimilated anti-Semitic leaders and their community of interest with their Jewish brothers in oppression and in trade were important factors in the satisfactory mutual relationship between us.

Occasionally a bishop or a high ranking Russian official would come to Serei. He would be greeted by a Jewish delegation consisting of the Rabbi and a few of our dignitaries dressed in black frock coats and silk top hats. They would offer their respects and their wishes for the visitor's well-being, holding up the traditional offerings of a twisted chaleh and salt or a Sefer Torah (Scroll of the Pentateuch) depending on the rank of the visitor or the requirement of the occasion.

An important contact between ourselves and the non-Jews of Serei was the pharmacist, who was a liberal Pole. He also accepted Jewish pharmacists-in-training for the required internship experience. This pharmacist, together with the chief of police and the senior priest, would annually come to the synagogue on Yom Kippur night to listen to Kol Nidre. They would be escorted by ushers to seats of honor and they would depart immediately after the Kol Nidre, visibly impressed.

The church, situated atop a hill on the east side of the middle of **Lange Gass** and across from the marketplace, was a large sandstone structure built in classical Greek style with a Gothic spire. Several flights of broad flagstone stairs led up to the entrance of the church. An extensive green lawn and many trees surrounded the church and the entire compound was encircled by a low stone fence. At the rear of the church were the dwellings of the priests as well as the Christian cemetery. We never really got a good look at the church since it was forbidden for us to look at it or at the graven images which were carried during religious processions, but since it was surrounded by Jewish homes it was impossible not to absorb some details. During religious services on Sundays and holidays the entire congregation, led by the priests, would parade on the lawn around the church, carrying aloft gilded crosses, statues and banners with images of Christ, the Madonna, the Apostles, and other saints. On some holidays these processions would pour out into the street and they would pass our house on the way to the outskirts to bless the crops in the fields. In the case of funerals, the procession would proceed to and from the Kanzelarie (Government Building).

Der Mark (the marketplace) was a large square off the middle of the west side of Lange Gass, five houses north of Shulgass. There was a long row of stores down the middle of the marketplace in an east-west direction, with a dozen stores on each of the long sides and five stores on each of the short sides of the compound. The stores were attached to each other and were built of brick with red tile roofs, probably as a result of the last conflagration. There were also many stores around the periphery of the marketplace. These differed from the center stores in that the proprietors lived in the rear of their stores. Two short dead-end streets branched off the far end of the marketplace and a narrow, unpaved lane connected to the Shulhoif. The marketplace itself was paved with cobble stones.

On market days the marketplace was jammed with peasants, their products, and their wagons and horses, as well as with the wagons and horses of traveling merchants. The peasants brought to market all the products that went for export as well as honey, fruit, firewood, kindling, homespun yarn, linen, rope, and handicrafts. They bought manufactured cloth, ready-made caps, suits, shoes and boots, hardware, herring, kerosene, axle grease, harnesses, combs, lace, mirrors, and cheap costume jewelry. The Lithuanian peasants usually went barefoot at home or they wore wooden shoes called klumpes which were similar to those worn by the Dutch. However, they wore shoes or boots when they came to market or to church. The great variety of encounters, scenes, and images and the many sounds and smells of the marketplace have left indelible memories.

In the middle of the far end of the marketplace stood the apothecary—our major health facility. It was an imposing brick structure on the outside and a clean, roomy, high-ceilinged place on the inside. On entering the apothecary, one was struck by the variety of strange medicinal odors coming primarily from disinfectants like iodine and creosote, smelling drops and perfumes. One was also impressed by the abundance of strange, multicolored vials, containers, and symbols. There being no physician in Serei the pharmacist, along with the feldsher (paramedic) and the midwife, ministered to all of our medical needs. The main pharmaceutical products dispensed at the pharmacy were aspirin, iodine, castor oil, alcohol, leeches, suction cups, cotton, bandages, disinfecting solutions, carbolic acid, valerian drops, turpentine, etc.

On the marketplace were located the two main hardware stores and the two main textile stores. One of the hardware stores was owned by the Zif family, which later moved to Vilna, and one of the main fabric stores was owned by the Kabaker family with which we shared pews in the synagogue in Serei. Later we shared a deep friendship with their descendants in Cincinnati. The other fabric store was owned by the Nun family, some of whose members emigrated to Pittsburgh.

The downhill extension of Lange Gass below the marketplace had many vacant lots, a reminder of the many houses which were not rebuilt after the big fire which consumed nearly half of Serei near the end of the 19th century. At the beginning of this section of Lange Gass, on the right side, was the shlosserei (locksmith and wrought iron works), which was a family enterprise of the four Zwilling brothers and their children. Across the street lived Alter Araner, who owned a hardware store and whose son, a chemical engineer, lives in New Jersey. At the far end of the street lived Alter Sandler, a brother of the wholesale merchant Max Sanders of Cincinnati. Another resident of Serei who emigrated to Cincinnati is Mr. Louis Neman (Nemchinsky), whose son Albert is a Cincinnati attorney. This family lived next to my brother-in-law and sister, Yitzhak and Rivka Slavaticki. The family of the late Isadore Fleischman, whose drugstore was next to my offices in Cincinnati for nearly half a century, lived on the Goyishke Gass on the shosei to Seni. Our Rabbi, Yisroel Goldin, and his family, who were related to my cousins in New Milford, Connecticut, lived at the end of a narrow lane off Lange Gass across from the entrance to Shulgass. The entire family emigrated in the Twenties to the United States. One son, Yaakov Goldin, emigrated to Eretz Yisroel and owned a hostelry in Tiberias. One daughter, Rachel, married a dentist in Detroit and two sons, Yosef and Chaim, served as Orthodox Rabbis in the East.

Justice in Serei was practically nonexistent except for what was imposed by the Russian police. It happened that once a tenant of ours maliciously refused to pay his rent, which was one hundred rubles a year, and he also refused to vacate the uninhabited apartment. After every possible remedy was exhausted,

Mother consulted an attorney in Lazdei by the name of Kubelsky—who was none other than an uncle of the famous American comedian Jack Benny. Mr. Kubelsky advised Mother that under the existing system of justice the situation was nearly hopeless unless some ghosts appeared in the dark of night and stealthily emptied the apartment while the village was asleep. One morning the village awoke to a most unusual event—it seems that ghosts visited our house and emptied the locked apartment. Mother promptly reported the event to the chief of police who, with a wink in his eye, uttered one word, "Mudretz (well done)."

Major crime was rare in Serei but we did occasionally hear of a murder or a highway robbery. Thievery, on the other hand, was common and the peasants considered it almost a sport. As a result, the shopkeepers watched their merchandise with a thousand eyes, especially on market days when the stores were full of people. The watchfulness was frequently of no avail and the losses had to be absorbed by higher prices. The general moral tone of the Goyim was relatively low. Illegitimacy was common and was reluctantly accepted as an unavoidable evil. Extramarital sex and illegitimacy did not exist among the Jews of the shtetlach, and if they did exist it was not known. Even marital sex was limited and circumscribed by religious stricture and was sanctified by a variety of injunctions. After the war I heard that there were harlots in the larger cities. I knew nothing about the subject except what I had learned in the Bible and Talmud, but since there was smoke there must have been fire. The country environment of the shtetlach was fiercely intolerant of any such license.

Some of our biases towards the Goyim may be illustrated by the words of a merry Yiddish folk song:

> *Geht a Goy in sheinkel arein*
> *In sheinkel arein, in sheinkel arein*
> *Trinkt er ois a glezele vein*
> *A glezele vein, a glezele vein—*
> *Oi! Oi! Oi!—shiker is a Goy*
> *Shiker is er, trinken muz er*
> *Veil er is a Goy...*(repeat last two
> lines)

> *Leift a Yid in shulchel arein*
> *In shulchel arein, in shulchel arein*
> *Chapt er dort a k'dusha arein*
> *A k'dusha arein, a k'dusha arein—*

Oi! Oi! Oi!—nichter is a Yid
Nichter is er, davnen muz er
Veil er is a Yid...(repeat last two lines)

A *Goy* goes to the saloon,
To the saloon, to the saloon.
He drinks a glass of wine,
A glass of wine, a glass of wine—
Oi! Oi! Oi!—drunk is a *Goy*,
Drunk he is, drink he must
Because he is a *Goy*...(repeat last two
lines)

A Jew runs to the *Shul*,
To the Shul, to the *Shul*,
To recite a *k'dusha* (sanctification),
To recite a *k'dusha*, to recite a *k'dusha*.
Oi! Oi! Oi!—sober is a Jew,
Sober he is, pray he must
Because he is a Jew...(repeat last two
lines)

Eighty years later in the United States, non-Jews, by and large, still drink to excess and Jews in the main still practice moderation but they no longer hurry to the synagogue to pray or seek "sanctification."

For many centuries Jews had lived in Serei and in other shtetlach of Eastern Europe in accordance with a strict interpretation of Jewish religious laws and traditions. The ambition of every boy of ability was to become a Rabbi or at least a God-fearing man, learned in the law and full of good deeds—and to raise children and grandchildren who were also learned in the law.

During the four centuries that ended with the Holocaust, the Lithuanian Jews experienced a Talmudic and cultural revival comparable to the golden periods in France, Spain and Babylon. Talmudic academies sprung up all over the land; new insights, new ethical concepts, and new methods of study and interpretation were developed; great learning became widespread and the views and rulings of famous Lithuanian Rabbis were solicited and respected by Jews all over the world. The great Talmudic academies of Lithuania—such as Wolozhin, Mir, Telzsh, Slabodka, etc.—attracted the best young minds and their products were eagerly sought by Jews everywhere as spiritual leaders or as teachers in their Talmudic academies.

There was also another side to Serei—the Serei of Hayyim Zak, one of the pioneers of the Haskala (Enlightenment) Movement in Russia. He was a self-taught Rabbinic scholar, a linguist fluent in ten languages, a philosopher, an educator, a writer, and a beloved leader who was highly respected by young and old, by the traditionally pious as well as by the "Enlightened." Zak was an advocate of national revival through the introduction of secular education in the heder and the uplifting of the Jewish people through learning professional and technical skills. In his scholarly efforts he collaborated in translating the Bible into Russian and Maimonedes into German. He was also a foreign correspondent of the first Hebrew Haskala periodical, *Hameasef*, in Koenigsberg, Prussia. The ultimate goal of Zak's activities was to advance the emancipation of the Russian Jews. Zak was a man of impeccable ethical and moral virtues, a lover of people, and a superb story-teller who represented in his person a synthesis of the tradition of Jewish learning and piety and a liberal secular outlook. With all of his prodigious activities and achievements, he continued a life-long practice of reviewing the Talmud every three years.

Zak lived in the early part of the nineteenth century. Sometime during his adulthood he moved from Serei to Zagar, a small town in northern Lithuania and a major center of Haskala, where he soon became known as "the Father of Haskala in Lithuania." Zak was influenced in his zeal for Haskala by Moses Mendelssohn of Germany and by the Gaon of Vilna, the greatest Rabbinic luminary since Maimonedes. The Gaon advocated the study of the sciences, languages, mathematics, philosophy, and other secular subjects as an aid to a clearer understanding of contemporary life and the teachings of the Talmud. The Gaon of Vilna happened to have spent some time in Serei studying in the Alte Shul together with his chaver (friend) Reb Meir, who was a native of Serei.

As a result of the Haskala Movement, some Talmudic students from Serei and from other villages like ours spread out in increasing numbers into the world's centers of learning. Some enrolled in Russian, German, and other European universities while others became famous scholars or writers without the benefits of a formal education. The Haskala Movement had its successes and its failures, but in Russia it never succeeded in attracting the masses. In the course of time the leaders and practitioners of Haskala became disillusioned with their efforts when they discovered that acculturation did not ameliorate anti-Semitism, advance emancipation, or help solve any of the major Jewish problems. At the same time, the rest of the people concluded that the light was not worth the candle—especially when they learned that Haskala in Germany led to an epidemic of mass conversions and that many of the Maskilim (advocates of Haskala) in Russia became lax in their religious practices—and that some even converted to gain acceptance. They reacted to these developments with a ban of Haskala and they retreated to the proven safety of Torah, piety, and good deeds.

The Haskala Movement eventually faded away in two opposite directions. The nationalists gave up on the Galut (Diaspora) and became Zionists, while the assimilationists drifted into the revolutionary movements or left the fold. Many Talmudic students became the fathers of the modern Jewish literature in Hebrew and in Yiddish while others won enviable reputations in the sciences, the professions, and in other fields of endeavor.

When I left Serei in 1920 there was not the slightest hint of the cataclysmic events which were soon to destroy one-third of European Jewry and devastate the world I knew. The destruction came from without and from within. In addition to the grievous losses caused by the Nazi Holocaust, irreparable damage also resulted from the destructive and corrosive influences of the Bolshevik Revolution, the two world wars, and the total urbanization of our people. These critical events led to a loss of religious and cultural strictures and to the onset of revolutionary changes the outcome of which cannot be predicted.

CHAPTER SEVEN

War and Revolution

> "He who hits with the sword
> shall be beaten with the scabbard."
> (Job)

The world I have described was as seen through the eyes of a young, deeply religious Jewish country boy, a world unadulterated as yet by the materialism and urban decay which was already degrading moral values in the world at large. Major Jewish centers like Vilna and Warsaw were being drawn into the same whirlwind, but the vast majority of Jews resided in the shtetlach of the Eastern European Diaspora and these Jews remained true to the beliefs, practices, and traditions of their forebears. Despite persecution and adversity, we were proud of our heritage and gloried in the great happiness and spiritual riches to be culled from the study of Torah. We were fired by the vision of a Zion rebuilt whence the word of God will once again arouse a confused humanity to "do justice and walk humbly with God," and we were firm in our beliefs that in the end of the days the Messianic dream of Isaiah will be fulfilled and there will come to be a world of uninterrupted peace, compassion, and happiness for all mankind.

World War I, which suddenly erupted around us like a volcano, shattered many worlds including the one which our people knew, nurtured, and loved for hundreds of years. The war was fifty years in the making but was triggered by a relatively minor event, the killing of an Austrian archduke by a Serbian patriot in distant Sarajevo. A series of events then followed which, like the foredoomed events in a Greek tragedy, plunged the world into one of the greatest blood baths in human history. It was the old Biblical story repeating itself—Abel had something that Cain wanted "so Cain arose and slew Abel." The Germans wanted "a place in the sun" which, as they conceived it, they could attain only through conquest. So Germany methodically conceived and built a gigantic war machine which by 1914 was straining at the leash to get into action and achieve its mission. They therefore prevented the settlement of the Sarajevo incident by way of apology and compensation, which could have easily been achieved. France, on the other hand, was eager to take "revenge" for its humiliating defeat by Germany in 1870 and to regain the provinces of Alsace and Lorraine which they had lost to Germany. England was anxious to eliminate a troublesome upstart competitor in world markets and a potential threat to its position as the world's dominant power. Austria-Hungary, the most concerned power in the tragic Sarajevo affair, hoped to prevent its imminent collapse by whipping up patriotic sentiment. It was a dying empire being torn apart by cross currents of hatred, by the multiplicity of divergent cultures and peoples of which it was made up, and by the shortsightedness of its administrative and ethnic policies. The Turkish Empire was a morass of internal decay and corruption and had been known for decades as the "sick man of Europe." It likewise hoped to postpone the day of reckoning, through a victorious war, by aligning itself on the German side. Russia, as usual, was fishing in muddy waters and hoped to inherit parts of the collapsing Ottoman and Austria-Hungarian empires. The United States ultimately became involved in the war on the side of the Allied Powers to help "save the world for democracy."

World War I started on August 1, 1914 when the German and Austrian Armies marched across the frontiers of Belgium, France, and Russia. This was preceded by the delivery of an unacceptable twelve-hour ultimatum by the Germans and partial mobilization by Austria and Russia.

Serei was about seventy-five kilometers from the German border so the war was immediately upon us. The moment the war broke out Mother hurriedly left for Halinke to bring Grandfather to Serei. The road to Suchovolia, where his other two daughters lived, was already cut off. Mother returned with

Grandfather safely to Serei and he shared our fate throughout the war. The first thing we noticed when the war began was endless columns of Russian infantry, cavalry, and artillery passing through our city along the shosei (military highways) that framed our town on each end. The foot soldiers were well dressed and well armed and seemed to be in high spirits. The cavalrymen were in dress uniform wearing blue pants with broad red stripes on the sides or red pants with blue stripes.

The Germans had planned for a holding operation on the Russian Front while the Austrian Army engaged the Russians in combat in the South and the bulk of the German Army delivered a lightning knockout blow to the French in the West. As frequently happens, however, something went wrong when the Russians failed to cooperate and crossed the German border into East Prussia which bordered on our region. The Germans were thus forced to withdraw several divisions from the French Front in order to stem the Russian advance into Germany. They were also forced to divert several divisions from France to support the Austrian Army, which proved no match for the Russians. The meticulous plan of the German High Command for a fast conquest was thus thrown into a cocked hat when the Western Front developed into the bloody, lengthy, and exhausting trench warfare for which the Germans were ill prepared.

The early involvement of the British was not anticipated by the Germans and the arrival of the Yankees was the final blow. What concerned us in Serei was that after a few early victories by the Russians, the Germans counter-attacked and drove the Russians across their own borders. During the first few months of the war, Serei changed hands several times. Once or twice the Germans simply bypassed Serei, which had no garrison and had no military value. Our only battle experience was when some stray artillery shells fell in the city and a neighbor of ours was killed by one of these shells near our barn. There was no property damage as a result of the shelling.

Soon after the outbreak of the war, the Russians began to mobilize owners of wagons and horses to help them with their transportation problems near the front. Even though I was only thirteen years old (approaching fourteen) I could pass for seventeen, and Mother knew that something had to be done to save me from a dangerous plight. With her usual resourcefulness, she devised an ingenious solution. Our horse was removed from the barn and was placed in our permanent succah, which was then cleverly camouflaged. Unwilling to rely totally on this stratagem, she also arranged for me to go into hiding. Before this was accomplished, however, I was picked up to join a work batallion to dig trenches. It cost Mother a fifth of vodka and I was released. In the middle of the night I was then spirited out of town together with another boy my age by the name of Elie Sandler. We both found a safe haven for about six weeks in a haystack on the farm of Elie's grandfather which was off the beaten path, between Leipun and Druzgenik. Mr. Sandler was the father of the prominent Cincinnati wholesaler Max (M.R.) Sanders and the great grandfather of Jack Heines of Cincinnati. Within two months after the onset of the war two Russian armies, the First and the Second, were trapped and totally annihilated, one at the Masure Lakes and the other at Yagustov Forest where some six years earlier Tante Toibe and I had spent a whole night when the driver lost his way.

Some three hundred thousand Russian soldiers were taken prisoner by the Germans in a brilliant pincers movement. There were also untold numbers of killed and wounded and the loss of most of the Russians' military equipment. It was a pathetic sight to behold when the hungry, weary, bedraggled, and dispirited Russian troops who escaped from the battle marched through Serei on their way back from the front lines of war. Very few had any weapons left and many of these retreating soldiers wore ill-fitting civilian dress including frock coats, fedora hats, and even women's dresses. Many of the soldiers marched barefooted in the near-freezing weather. After the retreat ended a new Russian army began to march through Serei towards the German front. The remarkable thing about this new army was that it did not carry any weapons. The reason for this curious phenomenon, we were told, was that the new army would get its weapons from the soldiers it was to replace when it arrived at the front. We knew then that the Russians had lost the war, for they had no industrial base to replenish their weapons and their allies on the Western Front had none to spare.

After their great defeat on the battlefield, the Russians sought and found a scapegoat in the Jews. Suddenly an edict arrived that all Jews must leave their homes within forty-eight hours and move south away from the front. We were lucky at that, since some villages were given only a few hours to pack and leave. I had secretly returned home from my hiding place a few weeks earlier—just in time to witness the humiliating retreat of the remnants of the Russian Army. Soon after the initial shock of the cruel eviction edict, Mother oriented herself and decided to sacrifice some of our valuable belongings and to take along with us into exile the machinery and other essential equipment of our bottling works. Mother hired two large freight wagons and the dismantling of the shop and the loading began. Our own horse had become useless from standing several months in the cramped quarters of the succah and it had to be destroyed. Our immediate destination was a shtetl called Stoklishok, which was about sixty kilometers southeast of Serei or seven to eight hours travel by horse and wagon. Mother made one trip back to complete the evacuation and the locked house and keys were turned over for safe-keeping to a good friend of the family, a local Gentile carpenter by the name of Yanukas.

Almost overnight Jewish refugee committees sprang up in every community to which the refugees flocked. These communities went out of their way to share with us their homes and anything else that was needed. Our household presented a special problem since Mother insisted that we neither needed nor wanted relief. All she asked for was a place to set up shop so that we could earn our own living. Within a few days the machinery was reassembled and we were again in business making and selling soft drinks. Grandfather, who was by now ninety-four years old, was a great comfort to us in our new status as refugees. With his sweet smile and his kind and loving demeanor, he immediately captured the affectionate attention of the townspeople and the whole family basked in his glory. Unfortunately for us, there were two breweries in Stoklishok and pretty soon we were perceived as competitors and we were reported to the authorities for violating one regulation or another. Mother, never lacking in resourcefulness, found the right approach to postpone any drastic action by the police. However, within six weeks of our arrival in Stoklishok, a new edict arrived declaring that the refugees were too close to the front and we were again given forty-eight hours to move on.

By this time we were expert in dismantling and loading our equipment and in the designated time we were again on our way walking behind the loaded wagons. Grandfather was comfortably seated atop one wagon while the rest of the family took turns to rest our feet atop one or another of the wagons. Our next stop was a railroad junction near Vilna called Troki. It took about two days to reach our new destination and we were pretty tired and worn out when we got there. As in Stoklishok, we were received with open arms by the local refugee committee. Temporary food and shelter were provided and, as before, Mother insisted and we received a suitable place to reassemble our equipment and to start earning our own way. Our new home and shop was a spacious place atop a hill across from the railroad station somewhat removed from the street. We were not molested while in Troki and we remained there for about nine months, producing and selling our product until war conditions forced us to move on to Vilna in September of 1915.

We had not seen any warfare since we left Serei. In Troki we saw the daily movement of trainloads of soldiers and war material from our vantage point across the railroad tracks, but these soon became a matter of routine. Occasionally we would see Red Cross trains passing by and we could gauge the intensity of the fighting from the length of the trains. One day in September, we heard a strange zooming sound which grew steadily louder. We rushed outside and noticed several planes overhead and we witnessed the first bombardment by air of the railway station. We had never seen a plane before and the bombardment so near us was a terrifying experience, so we rushed indoors and huddled in a remote corner of the house. When the noise subsided and we considered it safe to venture outside, we were horrified by the sight of a dead man sprawled on the ground near the entrance to our house and the poor man's brains plastered all over the nearby wall. We correctly concluded that the Germans meant to occupy Vilna and began to pack. Within two days we were out of Troki—this time without a Russian edict—and we settled in the safety of Vilna where we remained for two and one-half years, or until near the end of the war.

Troki was an interesting experience for me since it was a major center of Karaite Jews—an ancient sect which was also known as Karaim or B'nai Mikra (Sons of the Scriptures). The Karaites emerged at the beginning of the eighth century in Babylonia and Persia soon after the birth of Islam, and they were perhaps influenced by the persecution of the Jews by the new militant regime. The Karaites recognized the Scriptures as the sole and direct source of religious law—to the exclusion of the "oral law" as embodied in the Talmud. The irony of this movement is that they came to liberalize Judaism from the "excessive" body of law which the Rabbis had developed and they wound up more rigid and doctrinaire than the "Rabbanite" Jews whom they tried to supplant. Over the centuries the Karaites produced many theologians, writers, scholars, and poets, and they lived amicably side-by-side with the main body of Jewry, each considering the other as Jews and as members of the same family. Following a literal interpretation of each word of the Torah, the Karaites became excessively strict in such matters as marriage, ritual purity, circumcision, kashrut, and the observance of the Sabbath. In Troki we found the Karaites closeted in their homes on the Sabbath, sitting in the dark and cold, eating cold food and even abstaining from cutting bread on the Sabbath for fear of violating the literal interpretation of the law. They also applied rigid restrictions in eating meat and in marriage outside their own sect.

The main body of Jewry, on the other hand, as a result of systematic reinterpretations of the written law (the Torah), evolved an elaborate and complex body of law that made it possible for the Rabbis to adjust to changing conditions. The compulsion to find approval within the law for difficult problems often reached such extremes that it was said of some of the Rabbis that they could find a "hundred and fifty reasons for approving as kosher that which was not." Another distinction between the two groups was that the Karaites were admonished to interpret the words of the Torah in accordance with their own conscience—which, in practice, led to a great deal of confusion and to unnecessary restrictions as well as license. The interpretation of the law among the Rabbanite Jews, on the other hand, was left to the most learned and authoritative Rabbis who acted as a sort of Supreme Court with the proviso that in case of disagreement the most lenient opinion prevailed. Despite their differences, the Karaites often availed themselves of the religious facilities of the Rabbanites when the need arose. Attempts to convert Rabbanite Jews and people of other beliefs to their own faith was an important part of the Karaite creed.

A dramatic sudden change in the friendly relations between the Rabbanite Jews and the Karaites took place when Czar Nicholas I decided to destroy the friendly relations between the two Jewish sects. He accomplished his aims by giving the Karaites special privileges such as owning land, the right to engage freely in commerce, and freedom from military service. All other Jews, on the other hand, were subjected to the unspeakable horror of the kidnapping of small Jewish boys for the purpose of conversion and twenty-five years of service in the army in remote regions, pogroms, special restrictive taxes, and innumerable other economic restrictions. As a result, the Karaites began to consider themselves as non-Jews and a deep hatred developed toward the Rabbanites. Sometime around the middle of the 19th century, they successfully petitioned for the expulsion of the Rabbanite Jews from Troki. Anyone interested in affecting changes in established religious practices by radical or doctrinaire means should ponder over the history of the Karaites.

An interesting epilogue to the Karaite story occurred in more recent times. During the Holocaust the Karaites declared themselves as non-Jews and were thus spared from persecution. Some Karaites were even said to have collaborated with the Nazis in exterminating Jews. In 1942 when the Nazis were reconsidering their attitude towards the Karaites, they called on three Rabbis to testify on the subject. In order to save the lives of the Karaites, the Rabbis testified without hesitation that the Karaites were not Jews, knowing full well that the contrary was true. Soon after the birth of the State of Israel some seven thousand Karaites came to Israel to escape persecution in Arab lands. They were received with open arms and were accorded the same privileges as are enjoyed by other Jews under the "Right to Return" laws. The State of Israel also helped the Karaites to establish their own religious courts, to build synagogues, to print prayer books, and in many other ways.

Although I was almost fifteen by now, it was not until we came to Troki that I became interested in girls. One afternoon I noticed two lovely girls strolling up and down the street in front of the railroad station. They were my own age, apparently well-to-do, and they were dressed in the customary brown dresses and black aprons of girl students in the gymnasium. Both girls were of medium height and they had round faces, healthy complexions, and Semitic features and were slightly buxom. They were rather vivacious and conversed in a fluent Russian which I did not understand. They might have been twins, but we lacked a common language to ascertain such details. One of the reasons I was attracted by these girls was that they were Karaites and I knew that we belonged to hostile camps. We saw each other almost daily at about the same time and place—except on the Sabbath, when they remained secluded. During these enchanted brief encounters there were no physical or verbal contacts, we were quite content to exchange friendly furtive glances in passing. It is nothing more than a pleasant memory, but for some unexplained reason I did not notice any other girls in Troki nor for that matter during the next two and one-half years of our sojourn in Vilna.

Vilna was a new and exciting experience for me and it became the safe haven of our family for the remainder of the war. As soon as we arrived in Vilna we were met by a refugee committee and were housed in a comfortable apartment in one of the housing compounds on Troker Gass. Within a few days after our arrival the German Army entered the city in triumph, on the heels of the meek retreat of the Russian forces, and they remained as an army of occupation until December 30, 1918. The Germans were received wth flowers and dancing in the streets by Jews and non-Jews alike. Although they were a foreign army, they were viewed by the population as liberators—an eloquent commentary on the cruel, stupid, and corrupt Czarist regime. Within a few weeks the Germans had installed a smoothly functioning civil administration complete with identity cards, food rationing cards, and a normal functional economy. Later on, however, came searches for copper and precious metals, forced labor battalions, and food lines.

Although we had never lived in a large city, we did not meet with any insurmountable problems and the adjustment to city life came easy. We felt at home almost immediately since we found ourselves amongst our own people who cared about our welfare and who differed little in their outlook and practices from the people of Serei. Vilna, we found, was a larger version of places like Serei. We already knew that fabled Vilna was something unique and special. On close observation we learned that its fame was well deserved.

Under the German administration it was no longer possible to operate our soft drink works without a permit or to obtain one at the cost of a fifth of vodka. After giving the matter some thought, Mother went to the committee on refugees of the Jewish Federation of Vilna and asked for a recommendation to the German authorities. When told that it was an impossible request, Mother asked to see the head of the Federation—the highly esteemed physician and community leader Dr. Jacob Vigodski. The kind doctor listened attentively to Mother's impassioned plea that by helping her with a recommendation to the authorities he would help us retain our dignity and that by helping us earn our own living he could use our share of the meager resources for those refugees who could not help themselves. Dr. Vigodski praised Mother for her forceful and eloquent pleading and he gave her a strong recommendation to the German authorities, despite his misgivings about its effect. The next day Mother was received at the Governor's office, first by an adjutant and then by the Governor himself. In simple words, half in Yiddish and half in German, Mother explained how she managed to support herself and her family as war refugees by our own efforts and that a benevolent German administration could not possibly deny her such a simple request as a permit to produce a good and desirable beverage that would make us self-supporting. The Governor was impressed by Mother's passion for self-help through work and by her diplomatic skill. She returned home triumphantly with an operating permit in hand. Our product did not become an outstanding success in Vilna, but with the entire family at work producing and selling our soft drinks, we managed to remain independent during our two and one-half years in Vilna without having to resort to public help.

In the course of its five-hundred-year-old history, Vilna gained a place of honor among Lithuanian Jewry and it became the unchallenged spiritual center of Eastern European Jewry. The Jews of Vilna produced world-famous Rabbis, scholars, writers, and artists and its leaders played a prominent role in all of the spiritual trends and movements in Jewry. The Gaon (Genius) of Vilna is recognized as the greatest Rabbi since the eleventh century, yet Vilna produced many other great and distinguished Rabbis. Vilna was also a major center of yeshivoth, Jewish scholarship, the Haskala Movement, the Hebat Zion (Lovers of Zion) Movement, and later it became a center for such modern movements as Jewish revolutionary organizations, labor trade unionism, the Jewish Socialist Bund, Labor Zionism, and General Zionism.

The Mizrahi (religious Zionist organization) was founded in Vilna as well as the first Hebrew secondary school in the Diaspora. Vilna was also a center for the secular educational and Yiddish cultural movement and the largest Jewish center in the world for the publication of books. Vilna was also noted for the variety and scope of its philanthropic institutions and for the excellence of its communal organization and leadership.

The Jewish leaders about whom we had heard a great deal during our stay in Vilna were Rabbi Yitzhak Rubenstein, Dr. Jacob Vigodski, and Dr. Tzemah Shabbad. All three were dedicated, selfless public servants who gave of themselves without stint at great personal sacrifice in order to alleviate the suffering of their fellow Jews and to improve their lot. They were all highly respected and they were looked up to because of their fine personal and leadership qualities. They all served in turn as heads of the Jewish Community Council of Vilna, and Dr. Vigodski was the chairman of the Community Council's commission on aid for refugees. They were also leaders in the Zionist organizations and in Jewish education, and they were the esteemed and effective representatives of Vilna Jewry in the councils of city and state governments. I was especially impressed by the fact that of the fourteen members of the Vilna Jewish Community Council, seven were busy practicing physicians.

The Gaon of Vilna, Rabbi Elijah, who lived from 1720 to 1797, was the pride and symbol of Jewish Vilna. He was a saintly recluse, devoted to piety and scholarship, and at the same time he stressed the power for good of individual human will and effort, and the benefits of reforms by men of wisdom. Through his writings and those of his disciples, he revolutionized the study of the Talmud, emphasizing the value of practical interpretations through a solid knowledge of the text and a reliance on early sources. He stressed the importance of grammar, the correct and distinct pronunciation of the Hebrew in prayers and in the reading of the Torah, as well as an adequate grounding in Bible and in Mishna. He helped establish scholarly contact between Jerusalem and the Diaspora. He stimulated research into early post-Biblical history and he encouraged the study of mathematics, astronomy, and the other sciences. He was well versed in world literature, he wrote a book on geometry, and he stimulated the translation into Hebrew of Euclid and Josephus. The Gaon was favorably disposed towards the Karaites and yet he fought fiercely against the founder of Hassidism, the Ba'al Shem Tov, out of fear that it might result in a new schism in Judaism. I visited the Gaon's shtibel (prayer house) on several occasions and I reflected in awe and reverence before the roped-off seat where the Gaon of Vilna "labored in the vineyard of the Lord."

Vilna was one of Russia's main gateways to Western Europe and the Jews of Vilna had no competitors in trade and commerce. They had also developed many light industries—fabricating suits, hats, gloves, socks, tobacco, etc. Every phase of the industrial process, from the acquisition of the raw materials through production and salesmanship, was done by local Jews. The Jews of Vilna were in the main simple and hard-working people and were willing to engage in any type of work from the highly skilled to common labor. The 75,000 Jews of Vilna in 1915 worshipped in some two hundred synagogues; each trade or craft had its own house of worship which was named after the trade. To mention just a few, there were the tailors' shul, the shoemakers' shul, as well as shuls for masons, roofers, carpenters, bakers, furriers, cap makers, glaziers, undertakers, porters, water carriers, brick layers, drivers, chimney-sweeps, printers, bookbinders, merchants, harness makers, etc. The same diversity existed in their social service organizations, their study groups, and their self-help societies. There were some one hundred sixty study and social service societies in Vilna and these often carried the name of some Biblical verse.

The prayer houses in Vilna were highly frequented and they served a variety of purposes. Even small synagogues had several morning and evening daily prayer services, while between services they were utilized as study halls, social clubs, and union meeting places. The membership of some trades was so crowded that one synagogue could not serve all its members. Thus, there were separate synagogues for bakers of white bread and bakers of roseve bread (pumpernickel), for tailors of stylish garments and tailors of plain garments, and for retail clerks and wholesale clerks. An innovation that I had never heard of before was a manzbilshe shul (men's synagogue) and a weibershe kloise (women's synagogue) from which the opposite sexes were excluded.

Vilna was a city of tradition, above all the tradition of Torah, but Torah study in Vilna was more comprehensive than elsewhere and it included secular wisdom, science, philosophy, and critical judgment. After work hours Jews would gather in their innumerable small synagogues to study the Sedra (Bible reading) of the week, Mishna, Gemora, Ein Yaakov, Hayei Odom—exactly as in Serei. Among these hard-working Jews, even as among the Tanaim and Amoraim of old, there were great scholars who would lead their fellows in the interpretation and discussion of the lesson of the day. In the evenings large audiences would fill synagogues or lecture halls where they would listen attentively and courteously to the sermons of itinerant preachers, lecturers on secular subjects or exhortations of all kinds. Often lengthy and heated discussions would arise, but it was all done in a spirit of fair play, or serious concern for the subject at hand, and with a remarkable degree of tolerance for opposing views. There were Rabbis in Vilna who could recite Goethe and Schiller by heart, and there were religious teachers who were members of secret revolutionary groups.

On Sabbath eve, boys and girls and young working people would flock to the small corner lending libraries and they would carry off stacks of books to satisfy their thirst for knowledge and new horizons. On Sabbath morning, thousands of Jews would fill the Great Synagogue, the Shulhoif, and the neighboring streets to listen to the great cantors for which Vilna was famous. They would then discuss the merits of a new cantorial composition or rendition and some would repeat cantorial snatches all day long. No artist could ever hope to have a more attentive or appreciative audience. On Yom Kippur

Eve the top German authorities would come to the Great Synagogue to hear the rendition of Kol Nidre, even as the Russian Governor before them. Cantor Hirshman, who became world famous in Warsaw and later in New York, began his career in the Great Synagogue of Vilna. It was the first time I ever heard a great cantor and the combination of a beautiful voice and beautiful music added new dimensions and new meaning to the ancient beautiful prayers I knew so well. I was greatly impressed by the formal dress, the decorum in the synagogue, and the grandeur of the structure.

The Great Synagogue was built at the end of the 16th century on land donated by a nobleman. It was the only way the Jews of Vilna could obtain permission to build a synagogue. In time, many small synagogues were built around it so that the Great Synagogue could only be reached through a courtyard. On the inside the synagogue had magnificent high-vaulted ceilings supported by huge brown marble columns. The bimah was in the center and was built in the shape of an oversized hupah (canopy) supported by slender brown marble columns. In front of the bimah was a huge, beautiful crystal chandelier and on the eastern wall was an artistically carved Aron Hakodesh (Holy Ark) with two curved wrought-iron stairs leading up to the Ark while embracing the lectern for the hazan (cantor). The Jewish dignitaries of Vilna would come to the Great Synagogue on Sabbath and on holidays dressed in tails and silk top hats to grace their seats of honor. I was so overwhelmed by the atmosphere in the Great Synagogue that I made it my business to come to the synagogue early enough to assure myself a desirable seat.

The other large synagogue of Vilna was a palatial structure in classical style on Zavalna Street and it was surrounded by a tall iron fence and many trees. It was called the Chor Shul (Choral Synagogue) and was known for its strict decorum, its beautiful choir, and as the place of worship for the somewhat assimilated wealthy people. The interior was decorated in bright colors, the bimah was moved from the center to surround the Aron Hakodesh as in most of our synagogues in the United States, and the dignitaries were seated on the bimah, again dressed in tails and silk top hats as in the Great Synagogue. The services were strictly Orthodox, but this synagogue lacked the majesty of the Great Synagogue. The atmosphere in the Choral Synagogue was alien to my spirit and background and I did not visit it too often. My attitude softened when I visited the Choral Synagogue on Simhat Torah and observed that these lukewarm Jews observed this joyful holiday with no less enthusiasm than the rest of us. I was especially impressed by the enthusiasm of the gymnasium students, who were dressed in elegant uniforms with shiny buttons resembling those of army officers. I was filled with pride and envy to the brim.

Next to the Great Synagogue was the world-famous Strashun Library. It was built by the great-grandparents of the Cincinnati Strashuns and it was operated and maintained by the Strashun family until it was destroyed by the Nazis. There were some 35,000 Jewish books and rare manuscripts assembled in this library and it was the richest collection of Jewish books in possession of Eastern Jewry. The Strashun Library was a gathering place for serious students young and old, Orthodox and modern. They came to study Rabbinical responsa or modern novels in a spirit of harmony and great tolerance. The Strashuns came from a long lineage of great Rabbis, merchants, and bankers and two synagogues in Vilna bore their name. Their Cincinnati descendants seemed to know very little about their illustrious background.

In the courtyard approach to the Great Synagogue there were also the famous Ramales Yeshiva and Synagogue whence sounds of the Talmudic students could be heard day and night. There were also several small stores in this courtyard and in front of these were vendors of hot chick peas, fresh pastries, pretzels, and other edibles. The sounds of the vendors praising their wares in earthy terms would often rise to a crescendo and would merge with the sounds of the yeshiva and the loud prayers from the surrounding synagogues in an harmonious symphony of sound which proclaimed faith and sorrow and pleaded for justice and dignity. This was the heart of Jewish Vilna—poverty-stricken yet vibrant and radiating beauty of soul and touching simplicity. Even the poorest toilers were the bearers of refinement and spiritual exaltation. There was, of course, a seedy side to Jewish Vilna, such as pickpockets, swindlers, beggars, oppressors of the poor, and even prostitutes. There was also a great deal of disease, especially tuberculosis due to malnutrition and living in damp and old basements and sub-basements, but these blemishes were so insignificant that they were lost in the splendor of the whole. Jewish Vilna had fully earned its accolade as the "Jerusalem of Lithuania" for its gigantic intellectuals, its reverence of God and man, its spirit of self-sacrifice (kiddush hashem), its thirst for knowledge, and its genius for extending a helping hand to brothers in need, in dignity and in love.

The several hundred charitable and social societies of Vilna were operated at the grassroots level by committees or boards with a minimum of help or supervision from the overall central organizations—the Federation of Charities (Tz'doko G'dolo) and the Jewish Community Council. The collection and distribution of charity was developed in Vilna to a fine art with special emphasis on anonymity in the giving as well as in the distribution of alms and in the preservation of the dignity of the recipients. Several ordinary people, both men and women, were so successful in their methods of collecting and distributing charity that they became one-person institutions and their methods were adopted by others. I once visited a free soup kitchen where a hot, filling gruel was served to anyone for the asking. I was greatly impressed by the quality of the food, the cleanliness, and especially by the humane and friendly approach.

The center of the city, the Jewish Ghetto, was medieval in appearance with narrow, short, crooked streets randomly paved with cobblestones. The houses opened into an enclosed courtyard with a solid gate at the entrance that was closed and guarded at night. The houses were mostly three stories high with narrow balconies running around all four sides of the courtyard, and they were built of stone or brick covered with white plaster. There was frequently a water pump in the courtyard and there were sanitary facilities of a primitive nature. The Central Ghetto was surrounded by wide streets and boulevards on which there were palatial government and private buildings as well as private homes. Vilna was a city of many ethnic groups in which the Jews were about forty percent of the population, and the White Russians were the next largest group; both groups were equally mistreated by the authorities. There were also Poles, Lithuanians, Karaites, Tartars, Germans, Russians, and French. On the outskirts, the city was surrounded by sandy mountains and woods, and the narrow River Vileika meandered through the city.

The Jews of Vilna frequently spoke with pride of the Ger Tzedek (the Righteous Convert). He was a young Polish count, Valentine Potocky, who converted to Judaism and became an avid student of the Talmud and observed all the commandments. He was ultimately burned at the stake for his beliefs and was buried in the old Jewish cemetery. A large, strange tree grew up at his gravesite. It was bent at a right angle near its root and, after extending for some distance horizontally, it sprouted out luxuriously in all directions. It was pointed out as a symbol of strong will and faith that overcomes all difficulties.

Among the many lectures I attended in Vilna, one in particular stands out. The lecturer was a tall, thin, slightly stooped, graying man with long hair extending to his shoulders, a Vandyke beard, dreamy eyes, and an oblong sad face. He was S. Anski (Rappaport), the author of the famous mystic drama *The Dybbuk* (The Possessed). The lecturer told the audience about his travels through the Russian Pale of Settlement as a folklorist, and of his efforts to collect and preserve Jewish folk tales and folk music. According to Anski, there was an untold wealth of material hidden among the Jews of the shtetlach and it would take decades of specialized effort by professionals like himself to save this precious material for future generations. Some of this material was preserved through the literary efforts of Sholem Aleichem, I.L. Peretz, Peretz Hirshbein, the Nobel Prize winners Agnon in Hebrew and Isaac Bashevis

Singer in Yiddish, Professor Z. Idelsohn in his Thesaurus of Jewish music, I.L. Cohen, and others. The bulk of the material, however, together with its possessors, has been lost forever in the Holocaust. In Vilna, we experienced for the first time the thrill of seeing theater performances by a professional Jewish theater troupe. I remember particularly the production of *The Dybbuk* by the predecessors of the Vilner Trupe. This group of first-rate actors later became world famous and they played to packed audiences in the United States (including Cincinnati) and in other countries around the world. They had a large repertoire of Jewish plays but their most famous production remained *The Dybbuk*.[1]

With the German occupation of Vilna we settled down to a fairly routine existence, safely removed from any theater of operation. As the war dragged on, more and more shortages appeared in food and other necessities. We had to spend many hours in lines, usually for one product at a time as it became available. This chore usually fell to my sisters. Mother and Tante Toibe were busy around the house or producing our wares. Zeide Avremel spent most of his time in shul and enjoyed the attention and respect he was accorded wherever he went. As for myself, I tried to keep out of sight to avoid mobilization into the civilian work battalions which the Germans had introduced. Legally I was still too young to rate the honor, but because of my physical maturity it was the better part of wisdom not to be seen. The mood of the Germans varied with their fortunes on the Western Front, but most knew that they had lost the war when the United States joined the Allied Powers against them. The overthrow of the Czarist regime in March 1917 boosted the German morale considerably, and there was great jubilation when the Communists gained the upper hand in St. Petersburg and they sued for peace. The Treaty of Brest-Litovsk, which took the Russian Army out of the war and awarded to Germany most of the large area of Russia which they had occupied, produced a significant boost in their spirits. But this did not last long and with the staggering losses at the hands of the newly arriving American troops on the Western Front, we began to hear loud voices of revolt amongst the soldiers of the army of occupation.

One day in the Fall of 1917, I saw people streaming from all directions toward the Governor's Palace on Georgevsky Prospect (later known as Adam Mickievicz Boulevard). I joined the crowd and found myself in the midst of a large number of German soldiers in their fatigue dress in an obviously angry

---

[1] For more details about Vilna see *Jerusalem of Lithuania*, Volumes One and Two by Leyzer Ran, printed by the Laureate Press, from which some of the material about Vilna was taken.

mood attacking their superior officers and tearing off their insignias of rank. After a while, the Commanding General of the Vilna garrison appeared on the balcony of the palace to address the soldiers in the crowded square. His words were few but telling. "Comrades," he said, "I know how you feel and how disappointed you are at the unfortunate turn of events, but please remember that we are all Germans and that we must maintain discipline as long as we are on foreign soil. When we return home then will be the time to discuss and effect changes we may wish to consider." The square emptied promptly and peacefully.

Only much later did I learn that the attempted revolt in Vilna was in sympathy with the mutiny of the German garrison of Kiel which demanded the abdication of the Kaiser. By this time the Austro-Hungarian and Turkish empires were near collapse from starvation, exhaustion and internal dissent, and revolutionary ferment was rife in Germany itself. The Bolsheviks, who were now in control in St. Petersburg also, had their hands full trying to consolidate a shaky hold on the government of Russia while bloody civil war was spreading all over the country. Under these circumstances, when Russia sued for peace on November 20, 1917, it was promptly accepted by the Central Powers and fighting on the Eastern Front ceased December 1, 1917. Haggling over peace terms went on for about three months mainly in an effort to get the Allied Powers to join in the peace process. When this effort failed, Germany imposed onerous peace terms on Russia and a peace treaty between Russia and the Central Powers was signed on March 3, 1918. The Bolsheviks did not shed any tears over the humiliating defeat of their country as it served to strengthen the revolutionary fervor of the population by pointing up the ineptness of the Czarist regime. Besides, the Bolsheviks were convinced at that time that world revolution was near and when it came they would regain all of their losses.

With the end of the war and revolutionary upheaval all around, we began to think about returning home to Serei. After due inquiry we learned that our village was intact and that it was safe to return. There was no disagreement on our next steps. As soon as weather permitted, which meant May or June, we would embark on our journey home. Means of transportation in our region were poor at best, and as a result of the war they were non-existent. We therefore decided to buy a horse and wagon and travel on our own. At the appropriate time, Mother and I went to the market and, using our combined wisdom, we settled on a frisky white horse. A sturdy wagon and harness came with the horse and we paid 130 rubles for everything. Since our old horse was brown and a plodder, we secretly hoped that a change of color and pace would save our new horse from the sad fate of that former one.

As we had left home with two large wagons and four horses, it was evident that a good many things would have to be abandoned. It is never easy to part with essentials that were laboriously acquired with the sweat of one's brow, and so a great deal of soul-searching went into the discarding process. At the bottom of the wagon went the machinery, next came the barest essentials of our household goods, and each of us carried a light bundle of soft wares on our shoulders. As on our way into exile, all of us walked along the wagon except for Zeide Avremel, who was made comfortable atop the overloaded wagon amidst pillows and perenes (down covers). We were all in good spirits, eagerly anticipating our return home and the regaining of our property and our former status and dignity as balebatim (houseowners) in our familiar surroundings.

We left Vilna on a Sunday by way of Troki, intending to retrace our trek from Serei. About ten or eleven kilometers outside of Vilna we passed through the village of Ponar, a winter resort where some of the Jewish youth of Vilna would go skating and sleigh-riding. Two decades later, during World War II, most of the saintly Jews of Vilna and its environs were forcibly led to the outskirts of Ponar, where they were machinegunned by the Nazis and were buried in a huge ravine. The victorious Soviets finished the destruction of anything Jewish that remained in Vilna after the Holocaust, with the exception of the Choral Synagogue which they converted into a museum. The well-known Russian poet Yevtushenko wrote a chastising commemorative poem "And There Is No Monument in Ponar" which alluded to the refusal of the Russians to permit a suitable monument for the Jewish martyrs at Ponar.

Our trip home was more than we had bargained for. Our spirited horse balked repeatedly when the heavily laden wagon got bogged down in fine sand down to the axles. Mother, Tante Toibe, my sisters, and I would then put our shoulders to the wagon and help the horse along. He would also be rewarded with some oats and a brief rest. The road to Serei was a long sandy treck through virtually trackless dense forests for the greater part of the journey. Six days later, after repeatedly losing our way, we arrived in Alyta totally exhausted and barely in time for the Sabbath. We had traveled day and night, stopping from time to time on the road to rest and to obtain some nourishment. We remained in Alyta over the Sabbath and stayed with our old friends the Guries. Early Sunday morning we left Alyta and arrived in Serei just before noon. We were pleasantly surprised to find our home and all of our belongings intact exactly as we had left them three years earlier. We were among the first families to return home, but gradually nearly all of the exiles returned and nearly everyone found their homes intact. We were astonished that the Goyim did not plunder or destroy our homes. Two decades later the same Lithuanians and their offspring brutally killed the entire Jewish population of Serei—men, women and children—in cold blood on a signal from the Nazis. What happened in the intervening decades to account for this regression to barbarism? The Holocaust is so incomprehensible as to border on the insane. Some of the unfolding events will shed some light on the evolution of the madness in this small corner of the world.

Although our homes were intact, we found Serei a ghost of its former self with stores and houses boarded up, streets deserted, and none of the essentials of life such as bread, kerosene, candles, or other necessities to be found. Whatever we did find was obtained at high prices from the peasants and through barter with each other or with members of the German administration. Shortages of all kinds continued for a long time and store shelves filled out very slowly. We reassembled our bottling works without difficulty and gradually re-acquired a cow, chickens, and all of the essentials that we had lost during the war. But life in the shtetl—social, economic, and spiritual—never returned to where we had left off before the exile.

Within a few weeks after we returned home we suffered a grievous loss. Zeide Avremel became ill and he was put to bed almost as soon as we arrived in Serei. The seven days and nights of travel under primitive conditions and the prolonged exposure to the elements caused a respiratory infection which developed into pneumonia. There was no physician in Serei and there was not even a paramedic to advise us. In our ignorance and helplessness we suffered with Zeide, not knowing what to do, and after several weeks of illness he went into a coma.

On the Friday night on which he died, while still unconscious, he recited by heart the entire Sabbath Eve service in a strong and melodious voice. He then regained consciousness and asked for me to approach his bedside in order to receive his blessing. He began by saying that he knew his end was near and that he wished to tell me a few things about his life that might be useful to me. In a weak and halting voice he related how hard he had worked all his life to support his family and to raise five God-fearing daughters; how happy he was to see his daughters married to honest and learned Jewish men; how he dealt fairly with everybody, whether Jew or Gentile; how he had suffered in his long life robbery, mugging, cheating, and arson, without hatred and with forgiveness in his heart to everyone who had wronged him; and he ended with the admonition that I should remain a good Jew ("zei a guter Yid"). All the while that Grandfather was talking my heart was breaking and I did not stop crying inwardly. As soon as he finished transmitting his ethical legacy, Zeide Avremel lapsed back into a coma and the death rattle began. He died within a few hours, valiantly struggling for breath to the very end, a giant of a man and the sweetest person I had ever known.

It was the most tragic Sabbath our family had ever experienced. We realized and lamented our great loss, but we were denied the usual outlet to express our grief since mourning is forbidden on the Sabbath. Our pent-up grief was released at the end of the Sabbath and it was like the sudden rush of water through a broken dam. Zeide Avremel was ninety-seven years old when he died and he was interred Sunday morning in the Jewish cemetery of Serei in the traditional manner. His legacy lives on through his good deeds, his example, and his progeny. It was a modest funeral because of the scant number of returnees, but everyone had something special to remember about this good and saintly man.

Soon after Grandfather died we began to prepare for the harsh winter by accumulating firewood and filling our shelves and cellar with the customary staples. There was also a need to replenish our wardrobes, which we had lost or outgrown during the war years. My own pride and joy was the acquisition of a fur coat called a "bekeshe." Grandfather had willed me some beautiful snow-white Persian lamb furs and Mother decided to make me a fur coat. Since the fur was customarily used on the inside for greater warmth and since yard goods for the outside of the coat were unavailable, Mother bought a German officer's overgarment and our local tailor used the underside of this coat for my new garment. My new fur coat was a beautiful dark green and it was tailored in the exotic style of a shlachtzitz (Polish rancher). I enjoyed the warmth and the dignified appearance of this garment for several years and I discarded it reluctantly, along with my full-length boots, when I reached Cincinnati in 1921.

Early in January 1918, we learned that the Germans had left Vilna and that the city was governed by a local soviet of workers and peasants. The rhetoric and oratory of the Communists at that time sounded like an updated version of Hosea and Amos. Even nationalistic and religious youths like myself felt that the Bolsheviks were about to fulfill the prophetic vision of Isaiah that "nations will change their swords into plowshares" and that "the lamb and the lion will dwell together in peace." In the prevailing mood it was not too difficult for me to get Mother's permission to return to Vilna to enter a gymnasium. In my innermost thoughts I was also anxious to explore the Communist paradise in action. In the ensuing anarchy there were no longer any borders nor any armies to contend with, so there were no hindrances on this score. Two practical problems presented themselves—there was no certain means of transportation and there were doubts about the value and acceptability of our currency, which was still the German Occupation scrip. To solve the exchange problem, I decided to take along two one-pound bags of saccharin. This product was used in our shop and was thus readily available; I also surmised that it was in short supply in Vilna and should thus be readily convertable into cash.

It was mid-January when I left home for Vilna by way of the neighboring shtetl Alyta. To withstand the rigors of our sub-arctic winter, I dressed warmly in multiple layers of special clothing. I remained several days in Alyta and, after extensive inquiry, I found a peasant who was returning to the vicinity of Vilna and he agreed to take me along for a fee. He assured me that travel was safe and that there were no difficulties in entering the city. After two days of travel in an open sleigh, we arrived on the outskirts of Vilna at about midnight. It was a moonlit night and the temperature was somewhere below zero when we suddenly heard a shout—"Stoy! (Stop!)". Before us stood a soldier in a Russian military uniform and he ordered us to dismount. While securing his bayonetted gun with one hand, he frisked me with the other and easily discovered one of the two bags of saccharin which lay unconcealed in the top pocket of my burke (felt overcoat). He immediately placed me under arrest and began to denounce me as a smuggler, a filthy capitalist, and an enemy of the people—using, all the while, the most vulgar and brutal language, for which Russian soldiers are famous. He also repeatedly threatened to shoot me on the spot, or said that I would be shot by the authorities. In the meanwhile, the peasant was released with a gentle reprimand. After arranging for a replacement at the guard post, the soldier then ordered me to follow him to headquarters in the city.

During the long walk to the city the soldier seemed to have tired of his threats and I used the invective-free interval to tell him my side of the story. In my halting and broken Russian I tried to tell him about my faith in the Bolshevik Revolution, that I came to Vilna to acquire an education, and that I brought the saccharin with me to exhange it for currency because I did not know what kind of money was being used in Vilna or whether it was legal to carry any kind of currency, especially German scrip. I concluded by saying: "Comrade, what purpose would it serve for you to trudge the several miles into the city and back again on such a cold night? If I violated the law why don't you just confiscate the saccharin and let me go?" It seemed that my words made an impression on the soldier for he slowed down and then he told me to proceed to the city on my own. For a few moments I felt in fear of my life, thinking that he might carry out his threats and shoot me in the back as I walked away. I finally heaved a sigh of relief when I perceived that the distance between us was increasing and that the soldier was heading towards his post.

I proceeded immediately to the home of the Zifs, who had not returned to Serei at the end of the war and who were by now the owners of a small electric station in Vilna. I had hoped to receive from them some sage advice on such matters as schooling opportunities, lodging, and converting my saccharin into cash. They seemed happy to see me even though we were not related, and they were visibly incensed at my experience the night before. After advising me on the various matters that had brought me to them, they suggested that I meet a friend of theirs, a well-placed Jewish commissar who they felt would arrange for a return of the confiscated saccharin. I had great respect for the worldly wisdom of my successful townspeople and agreed to meet their friend the Communist commissar at a nearby cafeteria. It was toward evening when I met the commissar. He was a thin young man, dark complected and in his twenties. He was dressed in civilian clothes without insignia and he was altogether unassuming. We sat down in a quiet corner and I began to tell him about my mission to Vilna and the frightening happenings of the previous night. As soon as I finished my story he pulled out a hand gun and placed me under arrest. He commandeered a horse-drawn cab and without uttering a word he accompanied me to an improvised house of detention where he turned me over to a guard. I was truly frightened and was at my wits' end trying to understand how my friends could have so grossly misjudged the situation to put me in such a mess. I also weighed the possibility that I was the victim of a deliberate plot with evil intent.

The place of detention turned out to be the ornate ballroom of the Governor's Palace on Geogevski Prospect which I had passed many times during our sojourn in Vilna as wartime refugees. The ballroom was already jammed with men and women of all ages when the doors closed behind me. The detainees were mostly well-dressed men and women of the elite. Some of the women wore evening gowns or were wrapped in expensive fur coats while some of the men wore the golden-braided uniforms of Russian officials. As the night dragged on more and more people were brought in. Some of them were half-dressed, having been dragged out of bed in the middle of the night. Almost all of the detainees were pale, worried, frightened, and shocked by the sudden turn of events, and all were exhausted from lack of sleep and hours on end of being on their feet. From snatches of hushed conversation I learned that a wave of terror had just begun, aiming to eliminate or intimidate the former ruling classes and the wealthy and to secure authority with a mere handful of cohorts. Some in the huge hall were former Czarist officers, some were caught trying to escape to a foreign country, while others were arrested for possessing gold, jewelry, securities, or foreign currency. The punishment for these "crimes," I learned, was summary execution by firing squad—from which few escaped.

Soon after daybreak, heavily armed guards began to remove some of the assembled in groups or individually to face trial before "The People's Revolutionary Tribunal." My turn came at about 10 A.M. when I was fetched by a fully-armed soldier and was placed in a waiting taxi for transportation to the Palace of Justice. I suffered the shock of my life when, upon entering the taxi, I found that my guard was none other than the soldier who had arrested me thirty-six hours earlier on the outskirts of Vilna. On the way to the People's Court the soldier reminded me repeatedly of my pending execution by the firing squad. By this time I had no reason to doubt his words. I was truly frightened and expected that he himself would probably perform my execution. When he led me into the waiting room of the Tribunal and ordered me to wait in a corner, I felt somewhat relieved. The medium-sized room was jammed with people awaiting their turn to be called before the Tribunal. There was standing room only and the trials were brief. My place in the corner was near a door which led to the chamber of the People's Tribunal and I could hear the verdicts as the door opened and the hapless victims were being led out one after another or in groups. Like the ominous refrain in a Greek tragedy, I could hear only one verdict—"Streliat (Firing Squad)."

My guard stood at a distance watching me without uttering a word. For some reason, unknown to me, he disappeared at three o'clock. Although I did not see anyone replacing the guard, I was so petrified by the proceedings that I remained glued to my corner, passively awaiting my turn. The hours dragged on and the waiting room began to empty when I finally found myself the last to be called. It was 11 P.M. when I was ushered into another medium-sized room with five ordinary people dressed in civilian clothes with Russian loose shirts over their trousers seated at the head of a long table. "What brings you here, citizen, at this late hour?" said the Chairman of the Revolutionary Tribunal. Despite the fatigue and the complete physical exhaustion and fear, I quickly oriented myself and realized that, if I was not called by name and if they were inquiring about my business, there was no protocol. So without flinching an eye I replied: "Comrades, I came to complain about the unsanitary conditions of my housing compound." I gave a fictitious name and address and was assured that my complaint would be investigated and corrected.

I walked out of the torture chamber in a state of disbelief and instinctively held my breath as I passed the guards. I looked straight ahead, avoiding the gaze of an occasional passerby, and I kept on walking in a measured gait until I was safely out of town. I was careful to take a different route than the one which brought me into town and I carefully avoided the main roads, bridges, farms, dogs, and people. The peasants were already beginning to tend to their morning chores when I ventured to put up with one of them for rest and food. By this time I was beyond the reach of the Communists, who were barely in control of the city at this time. I never returned to my lodging to pick up my belongings. After a reasonable rest I walked some more, then I hitched until I finally obtained paid transportation back to my home in Serei.

Although the family had no inkling of my narrow escape, I found them worried and restive since stories about the terror had begun to trickle through. I remained subdued and chastened for a considerable length of time after my shocking experience in Vilna. I thanked God in my heart and formally in the synagogue by reciting the benediction of Hagomel—for having spared my life and for having saved me from the Communist "paradise." I was reminded how God had saved Daniel from the lion's den in days of old. Amidst the warmth and love of my family I quickly recovered from my ghastly ordeal, but I never forgot how much cruelty can be perpetrated by man in the name of humanity and lofty goals. I have often wondered who was to be credited for saving my life. Was it the soldier who may have had reasons of his own to avoid the Tribunal? Was it the Zifs who intervened on my behalf with their "well-placed commissar"? Or was it due to a fortunate series of circumstances?

CHAPTER EIGHT

A Memorable Visit

> "What we learn with pleasure
> we never forget."
> (Alfred Mercier)

With the capitulation of Germany came a relaxation of the travel restrictions which the occupational forces had imposed. Throughout the war we were greatly concerned about the fate of our relatives in Suchovolia and as soon as we learned that the roads were open, Mother decided to go to Suchovolia to visit her sisters. It was near the end of December 1918 when Mother and I embarked on this journey. The roads were covered with a deep snow and the temperature was hovering around zero. Since we were to travel in an open sleigh and blizzards with biting, whistling winds could come unannounced, we prepared for the worst and dressed in our warmest special clothing. These consisted of several layers of warm underwear, one or two sweaters, boots over several pairs of woolen socks, voliakes (pressed felt boots) over the leather boots, a fur coat, a burke (felt overcoat) over the fur coat, earmuffs, a fur hat, and a felt hood over that. We entered the sleigh with some difficulty, but not a bit of our clothing was superfluous. To complete our protection against the elements, our feet and legs were tucked in under a large fur leg-spread.

We began our journey early in the morning and our frisky white horse which we had bought in Vilna proved equal to the task. The sleigh-ride was smooth and pleasurable and we arrived in Sopotkin before nightfall. Our cousins, the Dulsky (Doll) family, had already returned from their wartime exile near Bialystok and so we stayed with them overnight, exchanging all the while our wartime experiences. We learned from them that Halinke had been destroyed by fire during the first weeks of the war and that our family in Suchovolia were all well. The next day we verified the total destruction of Halinke for ourselves and then proceeded through the dense forest to Sucho-volia. I had never met my aunts, uncles, and cousins except as a very young child and I looked forward to this reunion with joyful anticipation. Reality exceeded my expectations and this visit remained a memorable event in my life.

From the moment of our arrival we were overwhelmed by much love and care, which bespoke of the personal warmth of my newly-found relatives and of the closely-knit family ties. Suchovolia was about five times the size of Serei and, being near the German border and near the capital city of Bialystok, was somewhat more advanced than Serei. But, in the main, the Jews of both towns differed little in their ideas, ideals, attitudes, and way of life.

Mother's two older sisters, Henie Rochel and Malke, married two brothers, Hatzkel and Mordechai Yosel Krutzel. Tante Henie Rochel had six children—Yudit Pribulsky, Yudel, Harry, Chaye Gitel (Golden), Chavke (Allen-Cherow), and Chana (Druyan). Tante Malke had five children—Rochel Leah (died in childhood), Yudel Rabinowitz, Frieda (Leemon), Chaya (Gladstone), and Velvel Rabinowitz.

Both families lived in a large, two-story brick building painted white and situated on the marketplace of Suchovolia. It was the largest and most impressive building in the shtetl and was known as Henie Rochel's Moyer (brick building). In addition to these two families it also housed the family of my widowed cousin Yudit Pribulsky and her children—Sander, Chanele (Steinberg), Valia (Yanovsky), and Shleimke. The building also housed the businesses of the two families. Tante Henie Rochel had a soda-water-and-kwas soft drink shop as well as a glass and china store, while Tante Malke operated a dry goods store. Both uncles, Hatzkel and Mordechai Yosel had been in America and—like my father—had returned home "for want of a proper Jewish religious environment in the United States."

In both households, as in many other Jewish households at that time, the women were in charge of the businesses. There were several cogent reasons for this apparent anomaly—where the men were "learned" the wives and the religious mores demanded that the men not waste their time on such mundane matters as working for a living; all preferred that the men continue to work "in the vineyard of the Lord"—studying Torah. When the men did try to help out on market days, they proved themselves most inept and were scoffed at by their wives as if they were small children underfoot. Both of my aunts were pious, compassionate, hard-working women, and were devoted to their families and to the poor and the needy. They were also dedicated to their people, their community, and above all to Eretz Yisroel (Israel). Like the other sisters, they had a ready wit and a remarkable native intelligence, and they walked on the run. At sunrise they would rush to the synagogue with the heavy Korban Minha Siddur (Prayer Book) in hand in order to start the day off in communal prayer, even though a thousand chores awaited their attention at home and even though, for women, this practice was beyond the call of religious duty, precept, or custom.

Tante Henie Rochel was a tall and slender woman with a majestic bearing, a beautiful long face, sparkling blue eyes, and a dark Mediterranean complexion. She was quite talkative and possessed a great deal of practical wisdom. She was fiercely proud of her husband Hatzkel's yiches (lineage) and she would often boast to her Christian friends: "Moi muzsh iz tshtire dzeshtche Rabinov (My husband is a descendant of thirty-four generations of Rabbis)." My uncle Hatzkel Krutzel was a broad-shouldered man of short stature with a ready smile, a flowing gray beard, and a beautiful voice. He was a kind, simple, and compassionate person and he loved to conduct Sabbath and Holiday services in the synagogue. Tante Henie Rochel kept a jar full of ready cash in her house and she would dip into it whenever a person in need would appeal for help, such as after the loss of a cow, the burning down of a house, or some other calamity or urgent need. To alleviate the recipient's embarrassment she would invariably say: "This is only a loan. You will repay me when you have the money." But she knew full well that the advance would rarely be returned.

Tante Malke Krutzel (Rabinowitz) possessed all of the wonderful virtues of her older sister, Henie Rochel, but she seemed somewhat withdrawn as if in deference to a wiser and older sister. She was extremely kind, charitable, and pious, with a slightly stooped bearing. Like her older sister, she was dedicated to her children and her community. A distinguished trait of Tante Malke was to finish every meal with a morsel of bread. This was done exactly before the Birhat Hamazon (Grace after Meals) as if to add emphasis to the relevance of the benediction or to stress the importance of the humble but life-sustaining bread. Her husband, Mordechai Yosel, was a good-natured, outgoing man with a ready wit and a beautiful voice and, like his brother Hatzkel, he was very much appreciated as a cantor.

When Mother and I came to Suchovolia some members of both families were already in the United States. Two of Henie Rochel's children, Chaye Gitel (Golden) and Chavke (Allen-Cherow), were in New York, while at home were cousins Yudit (Pribulsky), Yudel, and Chana (Druyan). Tante Malke also had two children in the United States, Yudel Rabinowitz and Frieda (Leemon), who were both in Detroit, while at home were Chaya (Gladstone) and Velvel (Walter Rabinowitz). We arrived in Suchovolia towards evening and found that cousins Chana, Chaya, and Velvel had just left for a Zionist youth meeting. My second cousins, Chanele and Valia, who were a few years younger than myself, offered to take me to the meeting—which I readily accepted. I found a large number of young boys and girls debating the merits of various approaches to the rebuilding of Zion, some advocating the socialist approach of the Poale Zion while most were non-socialist Zionists like myself. After listening for awhile, I asked for the floor and, with the characteristic brashness of youth, I made a number of rhetorical statements which seemed to have pleased the audience and gave me special stature among my cousins.

Tante Henie Rochel and Uncle Hatzkel and their oldest daughter Yudit were all martyred by the Nazis. Their other children and grandchildren had settled in Israel or the United States soon after the war. Tante Malke and Uncle Mordechai Yosel and their children emigrated to the U.S. and lived for many years in Detroit. The change of the family name from Krutzel to Rabinowitz occured at Ellis Island. When Uncle Mordechai Yosel came to the U.S. at the turn of the century the immigration official had difficulty pronouncing the name Mordechai Yosel Krutzel, so he said to Uncle: "I will give you a nice Jewish name—Rabinowitz." This was a common experience in those days. Many years later, on a visit to Detroit, I asked Uncle Mordechai Yosel what business he was in. "Mine is the best business," he answered with a grin, "I get paid and I keep my merchandise." "It sounds like a riddle," said I. "It is very simple," said Uncle, "I am a Rebbe and the Jewish boys are not interested in what I teach them, so I get paid and my Torah remains with me."

While reminiscing about Suchovolia my mother said: "Some of my best years, the years of my childhood, I spent in Suchovolia. Down by the lake, in the rear of Haim Yankel's brewery, we went to wash our laundry; from the yellow hill I would drag yellow sand in a burlap bag to spread on the floor in honor of the Sabbath; from Motke the wine merchant I bought a bottle of wine for Kiddush and on the Sabbath we would play with nuts together with the children of Enye the Widow. After my marriage I once came with my husband on a visit to Suchovolia. We were both dressed in our best garments and wore hats in the latest style. It was such a rarity for people to be well dressed on a weekday that we were mistaken for nobility and Jonathan

Rabinowitz removed his cap, bent low, and greeted us formally in Polish: 'Dzien dobri, panovie' (A good day, your eminences)."

Suchovolia boasted of many fine people and there were sagas and legends to be spun about each family. Two personalities deserve special mention—Rabbi Avremel Einhorn, who served the community for fifty years, and Peretz Hirshbein, the foremost Yiddish playwright who, in his youth, spent some time in Suchovolia as a guest of the Pribulsky family. Reb Avremel, as the Rabbi was affectionately known, was a kind and saintly man, a great Rabbinic scholar, and a scion of a long line of Rabbis. He stressed the study of Torah, ethical conduct, and a love for Eretz Yisroel. He lived in great poverty and his wife helped support their five children, yet he turned down a proposed raise in his salary knowing how poor most of his congregation was.

In his religious rulings, Reb Avremel always leaned towards leniency. Once he was confronted with the kashrut of a freshly slaughtered cow. Knowing that an adverse ruling meant the ruination of the poor butcher, he spent an entire night in search of a plausible lenient ruling. Unable to find one, he called a minyan (ten Jews) to his home and, by virtue of the authority of a minyan—which constituted a kehila (congregation)—he declared the meat "kosher," a drastic but religious effective solution to a difficult problem. Reb Avremel once asked Moshe the Balegole, "What would you do if your wagon broke down on your way to town on the eve of the Sabbath?" "What would I do?" replied Moshe, "I would cry out, 'Sh'ma Yisroel (Hear, O Israel).' " "That's right," said Reb Avremel, "That's what I hoped you would say." At another time he asked Peretz Hirshbein to tell him what he was writing about. "I write," said the playwright, "about good and evil, justice and injustice, morality and immorality." "In that case, you are writing about the Ten Commandments," said the Rabbi. "Something like that," replied Hirshbein. "Very good, very good," said the Rabbi. "Yet I am worried that your writings may lead young people astray from the path of Torah."

Reb Avremel had good reason to be concerned. Every one of his five children abandoned their traditional upbringing and chose the path of "Enlightenment." One of his sons left home barefoot at the age of fourteen; eight years later he was practicing medicine in New York having graduated from the University of Berlin. Dr. Max Einhorn soon became famous as a gastroenterologist, as a professor of gastroenterology for several decades at the New York Post-Graduate School of Medicine, and as the inventor of the Einhorn stomach tube and of many diagnostic tests and treatments. Upon retirement in 1922, Dr. Einhorn contributed $500,000 to build a new wing at the Lenox Hill Hospital in New York.

Of Rabbi Einhorn's two daughters, one received a Ph.D. in Philosophy and the other an M.D. from the University of Berlin. His two other sons became wealthy merchants in Warsaw. Yet the good Rabbi mourned the rest of his life over the loss of his children. "What good are their achievements," he said to Hirshbein, "if they cease to be observant Jews? Material gain only means another kugel, another tzimmes (favorite Sabbath dishes), but nothing truly worthwhile." In 1910 Rabbi Einhorn set an example for the Jews of Suchovolia when he left at the age of seventy-five to settle in Eretz Yisroel, where he died a year later.

Peretz Hirshbein and his boyhood friend, Yitzhak Pribulsky, were brilliant and dedicated Talmudic students. Both eventually developed literary ambitions and, under the influence of the dynamic Pribulsky, they left the Yeshiva for tolerant Vilna—the mecca of aspiring literary talents. Yitzhak Pribulsky, being physically frail, got sick from exposure to cold, dampness, and starvation in the cellars of Vilna and returned to Suchovolia, where he married my cousin Yudit Krutzel and became a teacher and wrote freelance. After Yitzhak's death, their oldest son Sander, who was my own age, came to Serei to live with us—the intention being to help lighten the burden of a young widow with four small children and to help solve some disciplinary problems. My mother and Yudit were contemporaries and they grew up together as playmates in spite of their aunt-niece relationship.

Peretz Hirshbein came to Suchovolia twice at Yitzhak's invitation and he spent a great deal of time discussing his literary ambitions as well as topics for future plays with his friend. Hirshbein traveled often to fairs with cousin Yudit, who was a charming lady and an unusually able businesswoman. In their travels, Hirshbein helped Yudit sell her china and kitchenware from the back of her wagon while observing life in the marketplace. These experiences served as material for some of Hirshbein's later writings. One of his plays, *Die Neveila* (The Carcass), is based on finding the dead body of a stranger who had drowned accidentally in a Suchovolia well on the eve of the Sabbath. The body had apparently been in the well for some time before it was discovered. In addition to the great shock and consternation over the ghastly event, the question arose as to whether the cholnt (Sabbath meal), which had been cooked with the tainted water, should be eaten or not. Reb Avremel ruled that since it is a sin to desecrate the Sabbath and to waste food, and since the well was of ample size and depth, it was permissible to eat the cholnt. The dayan (religious judge), on the other hand, ruled that eating the food might result in death from food poisoning and since the saving of lives takes precedence over all other considerations, the tainted Sabbath food should not be eaten. Those who did eat the cholnt suffered nausea and vomiting and those who did not eat had a farshterten Shabbes (ruined Sabbath), but the debate as to which ruling was more correct went on for a long time.

Many decades later, during the 1940's and 1950's, Peretz Hirshbein was our house guest in Cincinnati on several occasions in connection with his lecture tours. He was a tall, slender, graying, handsome, and aesthetic-looking person, with dreamy eyes and an oblong, expressive face. He was an excellent public speaker and was considered one of the Fathers of modern Yiddish literature. Hirshbein lived in Los Angeles together with his wife Esther and their only son Amos. In addition to being a brilliant playwright, he was also a gifted artist. During one of his visits to our home he excused himself after dinner to telephone his wife in Los Angeles. In measured stentorian tones he began to declaim, as if on center stage, "Esther, dos redt Peretz Hirshbein (Esther, this is Peretz Hirshbein speaking)."

A story of a different nature has to do with a young Jewish girl in Suchovolia known as the nafke (harlot). I was not privy to the details which earned her this accolade, but I do know that in that religious moral climate even minor infractions of the rules of modesty would have sufficed. She could have earned the condemnation of the community by too-careful grooming; excessive exposure of arms, legs, or neck; looking straightforwardly at a man who was not her husband instead of keeping her eyes glued to the ground; or by misplaced trust or even malicious gossip. The penalty was harsh indeed. Besides being ostracized by the entire community, the victim could never hope to get married or find decent employment. Her only recourse, usually, was to leave the community or to emigrate—difficult choices in an economy with meager opportunities. In this particular case, there appeared a white knight who married the girl out of a strange combination of pity, compassion, and love. However, this was not the end of this girl's tragic life. A daughter born of this marriage died in her early teens and the mother succumbed a few years later. The husband, who was a strong, tall, handsome man when he braved the displeasure of his family and community and married her, became fanatically religious, emigrated to Canada, and never remarried.

CHAPTER NINE

In the Aftermath

> "The wind ceased
> and there was a great calm."
> (Bible)

On the day on which Bolshevik Russia capitulated to Germany and a year before the Germans in turn capitulated to the Allies, an event of historic importance occurred in London. On November 2, 1917 the British issued the Balfour Declaration, in which they declared their support for the establishment of a homeland for the Jewish people in Palestine. Although the exciting news was a year late in reaching us, the joy it brought and the hopes it raised were overwhelming. Overnight living legends sprung up about Lord Rothchild, Chaim Weitzman, Rabbi Stephen S. Wise, and Justice Brandeis—all of whom had played a part in the negotiations which preceded the formulation and the issuance of the Balfour Declaration. Every one of us considered it a personal triumph, an act of redemption, and a fulfillment of our ancestral two-thousand-year-old dream. Indeed, we all thought of ourselves as the lucky generation of Jews who were fortunate to live in such Messianic times. With little to go on except the bare outline of the blessed declaration, the young people began to organize in hechalutz (pioneer) groups, and in Serei we promptly formed a chapter of the Zeirei Zion (Young Zion) organization. Since Serei was small and backward, its response was subdued compared to the enthusiasm and the multitude of activities which the Balfour Declaration had evoked in larger Jewish communities.

None of us were aware of the major role which President Wilson and his principal advisers, Colonel House and Secretary of State Lansing, had played in the issuance of the Balfour Declaration. Despite the British indebtedness to Dr. Chaim Weitzman, the celebrated scientist and president of the World Zionist Organization, for his scientific achievements during World War I, the British had misgivings about issuing this declaration. They were reluctant to offend the Turkish Government, which ruled over Palestine and with which they were still at peace, and they did not wish to displease the Arabs, who they were wooing. The British, therefore, insisted on prior approval of the declaration by the United States government. Another point of contention was the insistence of Justice Brandeis that the stated aim of the declaration should be the establishment of a homeland for *the Jewish people* instead of the original version which declared in favor of a homeland for *the Jews*. With the active and enthusiastic support of President Wilson, the declaration was issued as amended by Justice Brandeis.

1918 was a miserable year for us in Serei. In addition to the many physical deprivations and the great personal loss we sustained in the passing of Grandfather, we became keenly aware of the cultural poverty of our tiny community and we suffered from boredom. We especially missed the lectures, the theater, the libraries, and the rich communal and religious life to which we had become accustomed in Vilna. My sisters and I fell back on studying languages through self-tutoring and testing each other. We studied Russian and German grammar and literature, we memorized poetry in both languages, and we recited these to each other. Our favorite authors were the Germans Schiller, Goethe, and Heine, and the Russians Pushkin, Lermontov, Tolstoy, Turgenev and Dostoyevsky. Despite these efforts we found life in Serei dull and we felt trapped and unfulfilled.

By late summer 1918, most of the refugees had returned home and life in Serei began to normalize. But at the age of seventeen, with few activities to stimulate my interest, I began to feel the boredom weigh heavily on my mind and I fell back on socializing. There were not too many young people of my own age and social standing in the village, but a group of four girls used to gather at the home of the Sandlers and I, together with several other boys, joined them to sing, dance, cajole, and do some of the other things that young shy adolescents engage in. Despite the ravages of the war years, the weakening of religious strictures, and the corrosive effects of exile, our traditional upbringing and the strict small-town climate precluded anything beyond a furtive kiss or some cuddling. I used to pair off with the older of the two Sandler sisters or with a newcomer to Serei, Hadassah Rubinchic, who used to come to our house to socialize with my sisters. The Sandler girl was a pretty, well-proportioned, unsophisticated girl who later married in Serei and was killed in the Holocaust together with her entire family. Hadassah Rubinchic was a petite, well-bred, and well-educated girl with a sweet disposition and fair complexion whose father was a Hebrew teacher and freelance writer in Yagustov. She emigrated to Israel and married an attorney in Tel Aviv. In later years, during my visits to Israel, she was always very happy to see me and was considered a friend of the family by my mother and my sister Sheine. Her husband, a fine, quiet man, became my mother's legal adviser.

On November 11, 1918 Germany signed the Armistice with the Allied Powers and World War I came to an end. Almost immediately the German army of occupation began to evacuate our region. The Lithuanians declared their independence and began to organize a provisional government with the help of two well-known Jewish leaders from Vilna—a legal expert on government, Shimshon Rosenbaum, and Dr. Tzemah Shabbad. Because of a shortage of educated Lithuanians, many Jews were mobilized to help the new state in its shaky beginnings. In the meanwhile, American Jewish leaders, working through President Wilson and the American peace delegation at Versailles, were helping to obtain international recognition of Lithuanian independence. In return for recognition, the Lithuanian Government undertook to grant full and equal rights as well as cultural and religious autonomy to Lithuanian Jews. Concretely this expressed itself in the establishment of Jewish primary and secondary schools, Jewish libraries, a chain of Jewish people's banks, a ministry for Jewish affairs headed by Shimshon Rosenbaum, subventions for Jewish religious needs, and abolition of all existing discriminatory laws and practices. Other minorities were granted similar rights.

Because of three hundred years of enforced cultural assimilation, Lithuanian was spoken mainly by the illiterate peasantry and the clergy. There was hardly any literature to speak of, the Lithuanian language suffered from the atrophy of disuse, and it had to be rebuilt from scratch. Unbelievable as it may seem, there were learned Jews in Vilna who were experts in Lithuanian and they were extremely helpful in the process of rejuvenating and reconstructing the language.

At first the Lithuanian Government and people were grateful to their Jewish fellow citizens for their help in securing and nourishing their independence, and we hoped that we were witnessing the beginnings of a new era in interfaith relations—perhaps akin to the golden period of the Jews in Spain. To many of us the equality and the friendship we were experienceing seemed like a mirage that was destined to vanish with a sudden and rude awakening, but there were others, especially among the liberals and socialists, who truly believed that a new day had arrived. The realists felt that it was too much to expect a backward, monolithic society, in which hatred of minorities was a way of life, to change in a meaningful way. It was an especially unrealistic expectation as far as the Jews were concerned. When people are indoctrinated from birth to hate Jews because "they are guilty of deicide" or because "Jews are responsible for every social, economic, or political evil"—it must be expected that Jews will become the scapegoats when the going gets tough.

The provisional Lithuanian Government, although headed by the liberal Professor Valdemaras, consisted largely of Jew-hating reactionary priests. As the Lithuanian schools began to graduate youths, they were recruited to replace Jews in their positions in the Government and the Army. Pretty soon the sons of the peasants were being encouraged to move to the cities to compete with Jewish businessmen in commerce and industry. A system of subventions and other concessions to Christian businessmen was then introduced which made it difficult for Jews to compete on equal terms. In no time at all a clerical dictatorship took over the Government. Liberal elements were eliminated from Government positions, and gradually most of the rights promised to Jews and other minorities were eliminated too. These violations of the Lithuanian Constitution and the League of Nations Charter were vigorously but uselessly contested. Eventually, under a variety of pressures and pretexts—such as the continued state of war with Poland, the persistent Communist ferment from within and without, the venomous anti-Semitic teachings by the reactionary clergy, and the vicious agitation by the Nazis against Jews—the Government of Lithuania became a full-fledged dictatorship. A pogrom environment against Jews became a national policy—long before the Nazis plunged a naive and credulous world into the blood bath of World War II and the Holocaust.

In nearly every country which had gained independence in the aftermath of World War I, restrictions against Jews were imposed almost immediately by those who had been oppressed. In Poland, attacking and killing Jews, pogroms, and economic oppression became a national preoccupation. It was clear to me that the poison of hatred against the "unlike" had penetrated so deeply in "Balkanized" Europe that a new war was inevitable and that the Jews would be the first to suffer. Even while the successful end of the war was being celebrated, the Jews were already being blamed for the successes of the Bolsheviks by the Poles, the Ukranians, the White Russians, and the various hordes of Cossacks. The Russian counterrevolutionaries who fought against the Communists for about four years took revenge against numerous Jewish communities—in victory and in defeat—with plunder, killings, and rape. The first refugees from Poland who tried to save themselves from the wrath of their tormentors filled every shtetl of Lithuania. Among the refugees who came to Serei and lived at our home for several months were the Doll family from Sopotkin and my cousin Yudel Krutzel from Suchovolia.

In the spring of 1920 the word spread that a Cincinnati Jew had arrived in neighboring Lazdei to visit his family and that he brought with him letters and money for people in various parts of Lithuania. We learned that der Americaner (the American) had a letter and money for us from Father and we promptly got in touch with him and invited him to be our guest for dinner. Mr. Philip Tennenbaum was the first American to visit our area since 1914 and we had not heard from Father in the intervening six years. Mr. Tennenbaum had left Lazdei some thirty years earlier to become, together with his brother, the successful proprietor of the Tennenbaum Brothers Furniture Company on the corner of 12th and Main Streets in the Over-the-Rhine area of Cincinnati. He was a pleasant and friendly man who, in spite of three decades with his "nose to the grindstone" in America, had not lost his native down-to-earth manner and compassion and he brought happiness wherever he went.

During his visit to our home and at a subsequent meeting when we traveled together for several hours from Mariyampole to Serei, I questioned Mr. Tennenbaum at length about life in America and in particular how Jews felt about their new country. He spoke of life in America in glowing terms as the goldene medine (precious country) and grew ecstatic about how proud he was to be an American—a sentiment, he assured me, that was shared by all other Jews. I loved every word he uttered about America and it confirmed my conviction that I must build my future in the United States. When I asked Mr. Tennenbaum how he enjoyed his visit to Lithuania after such a long absence, he replied: "Everything is wonderful except the fried liver. Wherever I go they serve me fried liver. Es kricht mir shoin fun haldz (I cannot stand it any more)." Apparently, in their eagerness to please the "American Angel of Mercy" (as he was called), people learned through the grapevine that "der Americaner gleicht leber (the American likes fried liver)," and this is how the poor man was unwittingly punished. Philip Tennenbaum died young, and so did his daughter Reva (Mrs. Abe Munich), who for several decades was a social friend of ours in Cincinnati.

In the letter which Mr. Tennenbaum delivered, Father described his loneliness and how he had missed his family these long years, and he urged us to join him in America as soon as possible. Mother was not too eager to emigrate to

America for several reasons—economically we were fairly comfortable in Serei and Mother, who enjoyed being a businesswoman, was frankly concerned about losing her independence. Except for our eagerness to be reunited, we had no compelling reason to uproot and to undergo the painful process of acclimating in a new and strange land. But the strongest argument against emigrating was that my two sisters were of marriageable age and both had local suitors. We also knew that Jewish immigrant brides were not in great demand in America. From my own point of view things looked altogether different. I was anxious to see and to get to know my father, whom I had hardly known except as a small child. I knew I had a better chance to receive a higher education in the United States, and as the year 1920 progressed I became convinced that the improvement of the Jewish position in Eastern Europe since the end of the war was a temporary respite from the long history of persecutions and that the endemic anti-Semitism was too deeply rooted to yield to any easy solutions. My decision to emigrate to the United States with or without the rest of the family soon became firm and unshakeable.

Once my mind was made up to emigrate to the United States, I attempted to get the approval of my family. My mother and my oldest sister Sheine were adamantly opposed to my going, while my younger sister Rivka and Tante Toibe gave me their blessing. When the day of departure arrived, Mother and Sheine stubbornly refused to see me off or even to say goodbye. My guardian angel Tante Toibe again came to the rescue. As in my childhood, she hugged me and kissed me and wished me happiness in my new undertaking and a safe journey. My sister Rivka was the only one to accompany me to the Sandlers, from whence I left by cart on my fateful journey. Mother had hoped that withholding her consent would deter me from leaving. I understood her feelings, especially since the close call I had had in Vilna, but I was convinced that I made the right decision and that I had to establish my priorities for my own sake as well as for the sake of the entire family, hoping that time would prove me right. The pain and sadness of my leaving without Mother's blessing lingered on for a long time.

Before leaving Serei for the last time, I participated in a party given by the Sandlers for the boys who were going away. There were some twenty of us in all—many of these were refugees from Poland who had escaped with their lives when the newly liberated Poles celebrated their independence with a campaign of terror against young Jews. Most of the boys were headed for Canada, Mexico, or South Africa, and a few were going to the United States. The determining factors as to where one was going were the ease of admission and the presence of family in those countries. Among those who were not leaving were the host of the party, Alter Sandler, and my future brother-in-law, Yitzhak Hirsh Slavaticki. Sandler was a friendly and kindly young man with a strong, athletic physique, about five years my senior, and he was courting my sister Sheine. The Sandler family was well-to-do and they were decent, charitable, hardworking people, but they lacked the desirable status of the learned and their occupation as wagoners (fuhrmans) put them on a lower level of the social scale. Thus an otherwise desirable match for Sheine became nearly impossible because of prevailing standards. Yitzhak Hirsh was an intelligent, friendly young businessman about three years my senior who married my sister Rivka several years later. Yitzhak Hirsh was of short stature with a robust physique, a round face with receding hairline and pink cheeks, white skin, and a frequent twinkle in his eyes. His mother, Bashe, was a sister of Pupi's grandmother Iti from Lidvinove. Another participant at the party was a refugee who was the son of Rabbi Magentze of Suvalk, my first yeshiva teacher, who was headed for Palestine.

The author at seventeen dressed in his bekeshe (Squire's fur coat). He left Europe dressed in this coat and was taken for a potentate.

The party lasted well into the night. All restraints were cast aside and we ate and drank and talked and sang until past midnight. Very few of the participants had ever tasted hard drinks, but this time we consumed vodka as if it were water and we violated a number of other sensible rules. We were not trying to prove anything. It was, perhaps, an expression of bravado on the eve of facing an unknown future in distant lands. When the party broke up we were all feeling quite "happy" and Yitzhak Hirsh and I staggered home, arm in arm but facing in opposite directions. We were singing aloud with gusto and abandon and we woke up the town on this beautiful moonlit night. I tried to sneak into the house silently by removing my shoes, but then I toppled something over and woke everyone up. I became sick almost immediately and was sick all night long. I nursed a headache for several days and could not stand the smell of liquor for many years after the big blowout.

CHAPTER TEN

The Gymnasium

"Mikol m'lamdai hiskalti
(I have gathered wisdom
from all who taught me)."
(Talmud)

Before I continue my story with my trip to America, I must go back and describe an important episode of my last years in Lithuania. In the spring of 1919 I learned that a Hebrew gymnasium (high school or junior college) had been opened in the nearby capital city of Mariyampole. I contacted the school and learned that I would be eligible for admission to the fifth grade if I passed examinations in arithmetic, algebra, geometry, European history, and Hebrew. I obtained whatever textbooks and stenciled notes I could find and returned home determined to accomplish the formidable task in the six months that remained before the opening of the fall term. I was chagrined at my total ignorance of secular subjects and was especially dismayed that at the age of eighteen I was unskilled in simple arithmetic. I applied myself to the task at hand with a diligence and singleness of purpose that I had not known since my days in the yeshiva. I do not recall that I was handicapped by the lack of teachers and at the appointed time I passed the examinations in all of the required subjects and was admitted to the fifth grade of the "real" (Science) section of the Hebrew gymnasium of Mariyampole.

Mariyampole was one of the larger cities in our area with a population of about five thousand, half of it Jewish. It had an old Russian gymnasium called called Bullat, to which Jews were being admitted. Mariyampole was an enlightened community with many active Zionists, Maskilim (enlightened persons), and a fair number of prosperous industrialists, businessmen, and professionals. With the rise of expectations engendered by such major events as the collapse of the Russian Empire, the rebirth of Lithuanian independence, the promise of Jewish cultural and religious autonomy for European Jewry, the Balfour Declaration, and the hope for a Jewish homeland in Palestine—a group of community leaders headed by Shmuel Gan decided to found a Hebrew gymnasium modeled after the Hebrew gymnasium in Herzliya in Tel Aviv. Given their meager resources, it was a daring move based purely on faith and determination. The gymnasium opened for instruction early in 1919 and it was the first Hebrew gymnasium in the new Lithuania. Even more remarkable was their decision to divide the school into two sections—a humanistic section with emphasis on languages and the liberal arts and a "real" section with emphasis on mathematics and the sciences.

The director and three of the teachers were German Zionists who were drafted for these positions after they were demobilized from the German Army. The other teachers were all local talent. It is remarkable that such a fine group of teachers could have been assembled in such a short time. Without exception they were dedicated and competent teachers who were thrilled by their pioneering mission. The students were also, in the main, well behaved and well-mannered adolescents who were eager to learn and were proud to be enrolled in this trail-blazing effort in secular Jewish education in Lithuania. The director, Dr. Max Meyer, was a Greek and Latin scholar and a former editor of the German Zionist weekly *Das Yiddishe Rundshau*. He was born in an assimilated home but became a staunch Zionist as a university student under the influence of Sh'maryahu Levin, the revered Zionist orator and wit, and Zalman Shazar (Rubashov) who later became the third President of Israel. Dr. Meyer was a handsome, quiet-spoken man and projected nobility of character, manners, and appearance. After three years as director he retired in favor of his protege, Dr. Abraham Levinhertz. Dr. Meyer emigrated to Israel in the mid-Twenties and lived for many years in retirement in Haifa, where his home became a mecca to his former students. He died in 1967.

Our teacher for mathematics, physics, and German was Dr. Levinhertz, who was a tall, lean young man with a drawn face and the bearing of a Prussian Junker (army officer). He was a strict disciplinarian, a dedicated

Zionist, and a very able teacher. He had some difficulty with his Hebrew, especially with the suffixes for masculine and feminine genders, and he also had to be helped by his students when he was unable to find the suitable Hebrew word for the German equivalent. When a student complained about getting a low grade for a minor error in arithmetic he retorted: "A second is a small unit of time, but if you are a second late for your train, you can hear the whistle but the train has left." Dr. Levinhertz was always neatly dressed, wearing an open winged collar and tie. He married a Mariyampole society girl by the name of Mecklenberg. In the late Twenties the couple emigrated to Israel, where Dr. Levinhertz served for many years with distinction as the director of a high school in Kfar Motzkin. He was a native of Koenigsberg, Prussia and had become a Zionist under the influence of the Hebrew philosopher and proponent of cultural Zionism, Ahad Ha'am. Dr. Levinhertz had served four years as an officer in the German Army at Verdun during World War I and had previously taught mathematics and physics in Jerusalem and at the Technion in Haifa.

Our two other German teachers were A. Yoel, a quiet, well-mannered man who taught geography and botany, and A. Enoch, a slim, short, mild-mannered man with thick eyeglasses who taught gymnastics and sports. Both of these teachers were natives of Hamburg, Germany and were recruited by Dr. Levinhertz. They, too, emigrated to Israel in the late Twenties, where they were employed by the municipality of Tel Aviv. The early exodus of the German teachers was motivated by their Zionist convictions and by their disillusionment with the unfavorable political trends in Lithuania.

Our teacher for Lithuanian language was a heavy-set Lithuanian, Mr. Inzulitis, who was constantly in hot water because of the frequent changes in the grammar of his newly resuscitated language. To his great embarrassment, rules of grammar which he laboriously explained to us one day had to be unlearned several days later. To make things worse, many of the students had little interest in the difficult language since it played no practical role in our future plans. Our teacher for Russian and history, Mr. Zvi Airov, was a kind, mild-mannered, and well-liked man but he was slovenly and distraught. He perished in the Holocaust. Dr. Max Meyer, our director, taught Greek and Latin to small classes.

Mr. Haim Lurie, a graying, heavy-set man with a trim goatee and pince-nez, was our teacher for Bible, Hebrew literature, and Talmud. It was a new experience for me to find that Mr. Lurie covered only one or two lines during each session since I was accustomed in the Yeshiva to study several pages of Talmud daily. It was, of course, a totally different approach to the subject as Mr. Lurie would dwell at length on the historic or philosophic significance of the text or on the place of an Aramaic expression in the Hebrew literature, and was concerned only in passing with the Halahic (Religious Law) intent of the passage. I thus discovered new meaning in an old and well-known subject. Two of Mr. Lurie's sons, Avram and Yitzhak, were classmates of mine, and the entire family emigrated to Johannesburg, South Africa early in the Twenties. Our teacher for art, Mr. Max Bond, emigrated to the United States, where he gained some fame as a painter. It may be of interest to note that nearly all of the first teachers of the gymnasium emigrated from Lithuania within a decade of its independence. The rising wave of anti-Semitism and Fascism was a harbinger of worse things to come and those who could help themselves left.

Admission to the gymnasium was for me a dream come true and one of the highlights of my young life. I soon became known as a top-ranking student and I had no peers in Hebrew literature and composition. Some of my compositions were passed around among the teachers who, I was told, admired the richness of my Hebrew idiom and the maturity of analysis and expression. Under the influence of the Bullat Gymnasium, we organized a highly vocal student council which played an active role in curricular and administrative matters as well as in arranging for student plays, operettas, choirs, and dances. I was an active member of the student council and took a prominent part in the Biblical operetta *Shimon V'levi Ahim* (The Brothers Shimon and Levi). In the revolutionary spirit of the times, we even had a student strike about some contrived nonsensical problems. As I recall it, it was mainly a covert desire to express our rebellious spirit and to test our sense of power. At a meeting of the student body I was designated as the chief spokesman and, after two meetings with the director and a committee of the teachers' council, the strike was settled to everyone's satisfaction. I believe that the students were trying to have a voice in matters of curriculum and discipline and the subject was referred to a joint committee of the councils of the teachers and the parents with power to act.

My first visit home after I entered the gymnasium was a day of triumph long to be remembered. I was the first native son of Serei to return as a gymnasist (a high school student) from the first Hebrew gymnasium in Lithuania and was dressed in the elegant and enviable uniform of a student. The uniform consisted of a white Russian blouse with shiny buttons from the neck down, over dark pants; a wide leather belt with a shiny buckle, and a blue-and-white cap with a Mogen David (Star of David) above a shiny visor. Carrying a riding stick in one hand, I strutted up and down our long street proud as a peacock in its colorful plumage and felt the gaze of mothers and daughters from behind hastily parted curtains. My greatest triumph came when passing Finkel's

Hostelry with Mother one day. Moishe Finkel, one of the foremost citizens of Serei, said to Mother: "Do you remember, Basheva? I told you ten years ago that your son will grow up to be an important man." I appreciated this expression of confidence in me since it came from a world-wise, successful businessman whose brother had just returned from Berlin to become Serei's first physician.

There were two girls in my class named Frank and Galanti. One was very pretty and both were extremely intelligent and bright. They both perished in the Holocaust. All of the girls in the gymnasium were under the tutelage of the wives of Doctors Meyer and Levinhertz for their extracurricular activities, while the boys were on their own. Soon after I entered the gymnasium I fell in love with a junior schoolmate called Pupi, who later became my life's companion. I thus never experienced the girl-chasing game, except what I learned by hearsay. Among the boys the conversations usually revolved around schoolwork, the teachers, Zionist aspirations, world events, the emerging new Lithuania, and occasionally girls. On one occasion one of the boys described an experience on the outskirts of town where a peasant girl was available for a fee. She was pretty and vivacious but crude, and when she sprawled herself out in the straw exhibiting her charms, he could not resist the temptation. A moment later, he continued, he was in tears crying over the human degradation and the loss of his innocence. We were all flabbergasted and there were no comments. On another occasion, one of the boys brought up the subject of ham and what a delicacy it was. Although most of us were no longer observant, we were shocked by the idea of such a gross violation of the Jewish dietary laws and the boy's daring to admit it in public. The subject was promptly dropped and the classmate felt chastised.

I was well provided for during my sojourn at the gymnasium. I had roomy, comfortable quarters and nourishing, tasty meals. In addition, Mother would frequently send me packages of sweets and other delicacies for snacks. One of these that I well remember was the delicious smoked goose that I hung on the pantry wall. Whenever my fancy took to it, a slice of smoked goose would satisfy all of my culinary cravings. During my stay in Mariyampole I made my one and only effort to learn to play the violin. This was a "must" for every self-respecting Jewish boy in Russia with any kind of claim to musical talent. It was a flop, freely admitted, on all sides. My only other recreation was the game of chess, which I had learned as a child but never previously pursued.

An event of great moment took place before the 1920 school year came to an end. Near the beginning of the summer vacation the great Zionist leader and highly revered folk hero Vladimir Zhabotinski came to Mariyampole to address our student body. Although of short stature and pock-marked, he was greatly admired as a fiery orator, a linguist, a poet, a gifted journalist and editor, as the founder of the Jewish Legion which helped expel the Turks from Palestine at the end of World War I, and as a recognized Zionist leader who considered himself the true heir of Theodore Herzl. His message was: "We must not rely on the British and the Balfour Declaration to give us a homeland. If we want to have a Jewish homeland in Palestine we will have to learn to till the soil, to establish settlements and to mobilize an armed force to fight for our rights if necessary. At this juncture," he continued, "cultural pursuits are a luxury which we can ill afford. You must leave the school and enlist in the service of your people as pioneers."

There was so much logic and conviction in his words that a group of about thirty students, including me, decided to leave school and enroll in a pioneer group to prepare for emigration to Palestine as halutzim (pioneers). We named our kibbutz (group) P'duth (Redemption) and we obtained from a Jewish landowner permission to work on his land during the summer alongside his peasant farmers to gain experience in cultivating the land. As soon as school closed for the summer the entire group—mostly boys and girls from the fourth, fifth, and sixth grades—left for Mr. Nun's farm, which was only a few miles from Serei. The land was poor, the work hard, and I soon began to discover some flaws in Mr. Zhabotinski's rhetoric—at least as far as I was concerned. I could not quite agree that cultural pursuits were a luxury and I discovered that not everyone is fit to be a pioneer. The burning sun, the sore hands, and the aching muscles soon quenched my romantic notion of becoming a hard-working pioneering settler in Palestine. I was too proud to admit my mistake and to give up, so I continued to work through the summer and learned every phase of farming in the fields and in the barn, under the most primitive and difficult conditions. My spirits were low and I became moody and if it were not for the frequent visits of Pupi and an occasional visit home I surely would not have made it.

There were two girlfriends of Pupi in Kibbutz P'duth who tried to bolster my spirits. One was Chaya Hendelman, a classmate from the humanistic section of the fifth grade. She was a lovely, vivacious girl and somewhat of a flirt. She remained a member of Kibbutz P'duth after many of its members returned to school at the end of the summer. She eventually emigrated together with the entire group to Palestine where she married and raised a family in Raanana. She remained a pioneer all her life. Another classmate was a pretty girl named Rasia (Ruth) Yacobson. She was a serious intellectual girl who was also compassionate and deeply concerned with alleviating the ills of poverty and injustice. She came from a fine family which lived on a landed rural estate. A distinguishing feature was her rolling of her *R*'s like the

Scottish. She too returned to school at the end of the summer and she graduated gymnasium with distinction. She later emigrated to New York, where she married and raised a family. Both she and her husband (Misha Schneider) were teachers in the Sholom Aleichem Yiddish folk schools and were close to the leftist intellectual Yiddish movements of the big city. Rasia was an interesting and lovely person despite some of her doctrinaire views. Together with other students who had joined Kibbutz P'duth, I returned to the gymnasium in the fall of 1920 and enrolled in the sixth grade. But my heart was no longer in my studies and by the end of the year I was on my way to Cincinnati to join my father and to enroll at the University of Cincinnati.

CHAPTER ELEVEN

Pupi

"How beautiful you are, my love,
how beautiful you are!"
(Song of Songs)

The monthly school dances at the gymnasium became major events in our lives and they were eagerly anticipated and long remembered. With the exuberance of youth and the eagerness of neophytes, we would dance all night. Then, in the wee hours of the morning, we would leave as a group or in pairs for a stroll in the beautiful nearby city park, and return home at the break of dawn. With the approval of the faculty there were no classes on the day following the dance, giving us plenty of time to recuperate, to savor, to dream, and to prepare for the next school day. For me personally these dances were of special significance as they played a fateful part in my life. At the very first dance I spotted the most beautiful girl I had ever seen or hoped to see. Her name was Rachel (Pupi) Gurvitz. I was mesmerized by the sight of this fourteen-year-old beauty wearing a bordeau-red dress. An arresting and distinguishing feature of this beautiful creature was her unusually large bluish-green eyes. With them came a round face, pink cheeks on a clear white skin, rustic sculptured features, raven black hair in long braids, and a stately

Rachel Gurvitz (Pupi) at sixteen.

bearing. It was the proverbial "love at first sight." I asked her to dance, she
accepted, and we both knew it was a momentous time in our young lives. I was
not much of a dancer and she patiently tried to teach me the intricate steps of
the waltz, the polka, and the mazurka. She had the patience of Job and never
complained when I stepped on her toes and caused her pain or when I turned
out to be a disappointment as a dancer. After our first meeting we never really
parted. We saw a great deal of each other whenever we were free from school
work, taking advantage of every spare moment so our romance could bloom.

Rachel or Pupi (doll), as she was affectionately called by family and
friends, boarded together with her younger sister Leah and her two younger
brothers, Gedalke and Sroli, around the corner from my own boarding home,
which faced the marketplace of Mariyampole. I became a big, loving brother
to these lovely children and I tried to help them with their studies, especially
Hebrew. Leah Gurvitz was a pretty, sweet, chubby little girl of twelve and was
seldom seen without a smile on her face or a tune on her lips—traits which she
retained the rest of her life. Gedalke was a handsome, tall, lean, dark-
complected boy with a ready wit, a lovely manner, and a fine, active mind.
Sroli was a chubby, ruddy-faced, dark-complected boy who came to the
gymnasium shortly before I left and I didn't know him too well. Once, Leah
asked me to help her with a literary composition with which she was having

some difficulty. I helped her, as I had done many times before, and she almost flunked the course. The teacher thought her composition was too good and he apparently suspected the source. Pupi was enrolled in the third grade and the others in lower grades. The Gurvitz children boarded with a friend of the family from Lidvinove, Moshe Mendel, and his unmarried daughter. They were friendly, loving people and I remember them especially for their good sense to leave us alone when Pupi and I were tenderly embracing in the foyer, trying to grow up on each other's shoulders.

The school year 1919-20 in Mariyampole was a year of uninterrupted happiness for both of us and we savored it to the fullest. Before the school year was over we exchanged rings, became secretly engaged, and vowed eternal love and marriage. During the holiday and summer vacations I visited my beloved Pupi at her parents' home at their landed estate in Katkishok, where I was eagerly received with love and affection. The rural environment of Katkishok was a perfect setting for our romance to develop. We spent many hours in their lovely orchard, on the lake, or in walks along the brook through their luxurious meadows. Pupi was always eager to see me come, her mother Beile enjoyed my rich repertoire of Yiddish and Hebrew songs, and her father Yosef loved to engage me in discussions on Zionism, the rebuilding of Palestine and world events.

Pupi's parents, Beile Rutshtein Gurvitz and Yosef Gurvitz, at their wedding in 1903.

Pupi's parents were both lovely, modern people who seemed out of place in the primitive rural setting of their country home. Pupi's mother, Beile Rutshtein Gurvitz, was born in a large family to a prosperous supplier of foodstuff to the Russian Army, and they lived in the neighboring shtetl of Lidvinove. She, and each of her ten siblings, received a good secular education in a gymnasium, and when all the boys and girls would return home for summer vacation the house exploded with song, laughter, and merriment—especially on Sabbath Eve. With an abundance of musical talent, their songs would fill every corner of the house and would spill over through their small village even as at the home of Hatzkel Sereisky in Halinke. Their favorite song on Friday nights was the popular song by composer-poet-attorney Warshawsky:

Freitig oif der nacht
Is yeder yid a meilach
In yeder vinkele leicht
Un dos ganze oiz iz freilach.

On Friday nights
Every Jew is a king
Every corner shimmers
And the entire abode rejoices.

Mother Beile was a good-looking, dark-complected, slim young woman of medium height with small, correct features and dark brown hair. She was somewhat quiet and subdued, but she was well read and she loved to play the piano when she was not busy raising her six children or attending to household chores. Pupi's paternal grandfather Shepsel, a frugal no-nonsense kind of man, was a successful businessman who kept his nose to the grindstone. He had five brothers, all of whom were important businessmen. Once Pupi's younger sister Leah came running to her grandfather shouting, "Zeide! Zeide! Lazdei brent!" ("Grandpa! Grandpa! Lazdei is on fire!") After verifying for himself from atop a hill that there was indeed a big conflagration in Lazdei, he turned to his excited granddaughter and said, "Don't worry, my child, it is not Lazdei that is on fire; America is on fire." "How so?" asked Leah. "America will send money and the people will build newer and nicer homes," answered Grandfather.

Pupi's paternal uncle Archie, who was a partner in their business, died in Katkishok in his forties during a typhoid epidemic. His son Hershel, together with his entire family, were exiled by the Soviets in 1940 to Bisk, Siberia near

Pupi's Grandfather Moshe Rutshtein, a prosperous supplier of the Czar's armies, at the age of ninety.

the Chinese border. His only crime was that he was the owner of the local electric station and a wealthy man. This act of Russian Communist cruelty saved them from the Nazi Holocaust a year later, but Hershel had to struggle the rest of his life to make ends meet as a janitor under primitive conditions in a harsh environment. Another uncle, Yaezi, emigrated to France and lived in Paris for many years. During World War I he had business connections with the General Motors Company and after the war he emigrated to the United States, where he continued his business career. During his terminal illness, Yaezi came to Cincinnati to live with us. His early traditional upbringing revealed itself in his dying delirium when he recited whole chapters from the Prophets in the original Hebrew.

Both of Pupi's maternal grandparents were of short stature and they were meticulously neat and tidy and properly well-dressed at all times. Grandmother Iti was a mild-mannered woman of the old school. She had a round face with pink cheeks on alabaster white skin. She wore a traditional wig with a few strands of her own hair on top and she was very pious. Pupi's grandfather, Moshe Rutshtein, had a small, neatly trimmed, grey beard and dressed in Western style, usually topped by a black bowler. Like many other important businessmen who dealt with high government officials and traveled abroad, he was somewhat lax in his religious practices. Both of her grandparents died at a ripe old age.

Pupi's father Yosef was an exceptionally handsome and tall young man with bluish-grey eyes, a luxurious growth of black wavy hair, a thick mustache, and a trim Vandyke. He was well educated and well read, a Maskil with

a modern worldly outlook, and he was a dedicated Zionist. Like myself, Yosef
Gurvitz was the only subscriber in his village to the Hebrew Zionist weekly
Hazfira, and the magazine would then circulate from hand to hand. He was a
friendly, compassionate man with a great deal of common sense and excellent
business acumen. He was born in the nearby shtetl of Balbirishok, to a family
of prominent businessmen who dealt largely in exports to Germany of forest
products, grain, and leather. Yosef, together with his father Shepsel and older
brother Archie, bought the estate of Katkishok in 1912. It consisted of a large
six-story flour mill, a well-stocked lake which also served as an alternate
source of power for the mill, a large forest, two good-sized orchards, several
hundred acres of tillable land, and vast meadows. Six families of Russian
peasants lived on the estate and they were in charge of cultivating the land and
attending to the livestock. During my last year in the yeshiva in Lazdei in 1914
I would occasionally take a walk along the brook that ran through the
meadows of Katkishok. I was totally unaware that at the end of the brook in a
small house by the mill and the lake there was a little girl at play who five years
hence would become my bride.

Pupi's birthplace, Balbirishok, was located on the River Nieman and did
not differ much from any other shtetl; along this river flowed most of the trade
that the Gurvitz family conducted with Germany. A story which Pupi loved to
relate is of two neighbors one of whom, Malke, was a shrew and the other
Sheine, as sweet as can be. One day, as the women were hanging their laundry
to dry on a party fence, Malke began to harp on her perennial complaint that
the fence really belonged to her and that Sheine had no right to use it—a
frequent cause of quarrels in the shtetlach. In her charismatic fashion Sheine
kept smiling in amusement and did not utter a word in reply. Finally Malke
became exasperated and broke down in tears "Sheinele feigele (dearest Shei
nele), why don't you at least answer me?"

Pupi's numerous aunts, uncles, and cousins on both sides of her family were
eventually scattered in many cities and countries. Among these were—Kovno
Vilna, Gomel, Moscow, New York, Miami, Chicago, Pittsburgh, Los
Angeles, Louisville, and Mexico City. The men were nearly all important
manufacturers or businessmen. In post-Revolutionary Russia they became
prominent physicians and engineers. One even made it to the Soviet diplo
matic corps. One uncle, Grisha, was among the seven prominent Jewish
physicians that Stalin had singled out prior to his death for prosecution at a
show trial preliminary to exiling all Russian Jews to Siberia. On the then
existing scale of values, Pupi's family belonged to the wealthy upper class
while my family belonged to the Torah-oriented middle class. In 1920 these
differences in yiches (lineage) no longer mattered.

One day, late in December 1920, while I was on my way to Kovno to arrange for my travel papers, the coach stopped in Balbirishok at midnight for a rest. It was a cold, moonlit night and I again thought of Pupi and her birthplace. What I saw were old, small log cabin homes, partly sunk in the ground, with roofs of thatched straw covered with moss. But I knew that inside these poor exteriors there was a wealth of culture, learning, warmth, goodness, and compassion. In Kovno I had to get my passport and obtain an American visa. I received the passport within a few days but I was disappointed to learn that in order to obtain the American visa I had to travel by train to the Latvian capital city of Riga where the American Consul for the Baltic region resided. This was my first train ride and Riga was the first large Western-style city I had ever seen. Although I was greatly impressed with both, I took both experiences in stride as if I were a seasoned traveller. Of Riga I remember mostly the beautiful, wide boulevards and the stylish dress of the people. I was especially impressed by the multi-colored marble exteriors of so many of the public buildings—mostly in beautiful shades of brown and pastel colors. As the son of an American citizen, I was issued an entrance visa to the United States with courtesy and dispatch and I returned promptly to Kovno, ready to embark on my great adventure.

During my stay in Kovno, which lasted about a week, I was well received by Pupi's youngest aunt, Rachelle (Gefen). She was a beautiful, friendly young woman of medium height with a freckled, round face and reddish hair. She was also a gracious hostess and was elegantly dressed. Like all of her ten siblings, Rachelle was well educated and was proficient in piano and ballet. She loved and admired Pupi and she seemed to approve of our relationship. Rachelle was later happily married to a wealthy industrialist and she perished in the Holocaust together with her husband and her two small children, Sorale and Abba. I also spent some time in the company of Pupi's cousin, Nechama Gurvitz. She was chubby, with a beautiful face and a very pleasant and friendly demeanor. She was good company and her weight and her thick eyeglasses distracted little from the warmth of her personality. In the years that followed she became a practicing dentist, and both she and her family perished in the Holocaust.

Before I decided to emigrate to America I discussed my plans with Pupi and asked her approval. It was a difficult decision to make since it entailed a possible wait of many years and parting from her entire family. Fortunately, I had no problem with my beloved for she knew and approved of my dreams, and she promptly agreed to join me in the United States at the proper time. The parting was more difficult than we had anticipated. We were deeply in love and were attached to one another and, without voicing our forebodings,

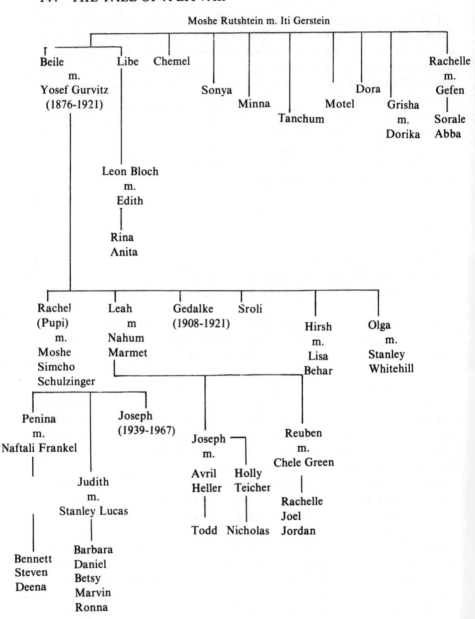

were worried lest something happen to rend us asunder. After crying and kissing and many good-byes, we finally parted with heavy hearts.

On leaving Pupi on Cheshvan 30, 5684, I gave her a picture album which I had bought in Riga. It bore the following inscription in Hebrew which I had adapted from a Russian poem by Lermontov:

To Rachel from Moshe—

Even as flowers
That bloom in summer
Excel in beauty
The blossoms of spring,
So does
The tender sorrow
Of our parting
Excel
The glow of feeling
At the time we met.

CHAPTER TWELVE

Between Two Worlds

> "In this world of change
> naught which comes stays
> and naught which goes is lost."
> (Swetchine)

With my exit papers and train ticket in hand, I boarded the train to Berlin at the Kovno railroad station and I was on my way to America in a state of excitement and exaltation. To my pleasant surprise, a fellow traveler in my compartment was the brother of Nechama Gurvitz, a cousin of Pupi. He was a well-educated, wealthy businessman who was on his way to Berlin on business. We struck up a conversation and almost immediately plunged into a discussion of the most discussed topic at the time—Communism. Despite my sad experience with the Communists in Vilna, I was still a "parlor" Communist at heart and was reluctant to give up the basically Messianic Communist ideal—"From everyone according to his ability, to everyone according to his needs." It seemed so reasonable, so logical, and so promising for a better humankind and a better world that I was willing to overlook the existing terror, brutality, dictatorship, and injustice as unavoidable evils that would vanish when the ongoing civil war came to an end and the Communist regime became firmly established. I embellished my arguments with all of the familiar cliches and spoke with the passion and dogmatic certainty and brashness of youth.

To my great surprise I found Mr. Gurvitz an eloquent, forceful, and unabashed advocate of outright capitalism. In the naive, wishful, revolutionary environment of the times, an avowed capitalist was as extinct as the dodo bird. His arguments seemed absurd and archaic, but even though I would not yield, they fell on fertile soil and I admired his courage to swim against the tide. Mr. Gurvitz spoke of such strange things as incentive, private initiative, individual freedom, competition, the efficient accumulation of capital, the enlightened employment of wealth to increase employment and improve the standard of living of ever-larger numbers. Finally, he continued, in the vein of the Prophets, life is a struggle, abuses are likely to appear in the best of societies, and we must ever be on the alert for the bad and the antiquated and try to correct these in time. We parted as warm friends and in time his views became my convictions. Mr. Gurvitz did not survive the Holocaust. In the decades that followed I often thought of my chance encounter with this wise man. I can almost hear him summarize our discussion on revolutionary change with the words of Shaw: "Revolutions have never lightened the burden of tyranny, they have only shifted it to another shoulder."

I spent several days in Berlin trying to arrange for my transatlantic passage and when I failed I left for Antwerp, Belgium, which was a busy transatlantic port at that time. I arrived in Antwerp on a minor holiday and my spirits were lifted when I saw all those happy faces. Students were dancing in the streets, all gaiety and laughter, and I recalled the Liturgical passage "Ma tov u'ma naim shevet ahim gam yahad (how wonderful it is when brethren dwell together in harmony and peace)." Why could not all peoples be like that? Surely the United States must be like that, and my spirits were high indeed. The regular shipping lanes which were interrupted by the war had not been re-established as yet, and so I bought passage on a tramp steamer, a converted troop carrier named *The Cedric*, which was due to sail to New York out of Liverpool by way of London. I had time to spend a few hours in that port city before boarding ship. While Berlin and Antwerp were clean, bright, and cheerful, what I saw of Liverpool appeared gloomy, cold, and uninviting.

I spent the entire month of January 1921 in transit between Kovno and New York. All this time I wore my school uniform and my distinguished-looking fur coat. On boarding *The Cedric* on January 16th, I was led to a row of five-tier bunks that filled a huge room several floors below deck and was pointed to the bunk I was to occupy. I was overcome by the stench of the foul air and the ugliness of the place and, without uttering a word, I grabbed my suitcase and ran out of the room. I climbed the stairs up and up until I ran into a steward with golden braids on his blue uniform. Without hesitation I handed him a five-dollar bill and said, "I want a cabin." I was willing to pay the difference between the cost of the bunk in steerage and a cabin, but the steward took me to a beautiful, empty cabin on one of the upper decks and without further ado told me I could have it. I thanked him profusely, and the double-tiered private cabin remained my home for fifteen days of what, it was said, was one of the most severe winter crossings on record.

The Cedric was a small ship and before long we were engulfed by a gale. The ship was buffeted by thirty foot waves and was helplessly tossed from side to side and from bow to stern. For a few days I stoically resisted the seasickness to which nearly everyone had succumbed. The miserable feeling finally caught up with me and I kept to my bunk most of the time after that.

During the first few days of reasonably fair weather, I ventured occasionally on deck and made a few friends among the passengers, most of whom were young Romanian Jews. They were a gay carefree group of young people, not too well educated or indoctrinated in Judaism, a distinctly different breed from those I had known in Lithuania. Before the storm overtook us, two of the boys had managed to attract girls to their cabins, not realizing that they were risking permanent denial of admission to the United States on grounds of moral turpitude. It reminded me of the moth and the flame.

The grandeur and vastness of the ocean and the power and fury of the waves were overwhelming to this fair-weather mariner from Serei. I was overcome by a sense of humility and I gained a new understanding of the reverence with which the pious looked upon God's creation. I also thought of Jonah and his stormy ocean crossing on the way to Nineveh, where God had sent him to save the city from destruction. But most of the time I was too sick to think of anything.

Some hours before landing in New York all of the passengers flocked to the deck to watch the maneuvering tugboats and to look at the skyline. It was an enchanting and awe-inspiring sight. Although I had seen several large European cities by now, this was different. This was mine—the most beautiful city of my adopted country. As to the skyline—I had never seen skyscrapers and they appeared to me like one of the world's Seven Wonders.

We landed in New York Harbor and were taken in groups by towboat to Ellis Island, where all new immigrants were being processed. The disembarking was slow but orderly. Overladen with suitcases and bundles, we were led to a huge processing hall where each of us claimed a spot on the floor while awaiting a call or announcement. The cavernous size of the room with its tremendously high ceilings and gigantic windows made us all shrink to insignificance. Most of the passengers looked pale and haggard from the long and harrowing ocean crossing. They seemed confused by the sudden onrush of events and they appeared worried by the numerous tasks, chores, and immigration procedures that lay ahead. I was called up promptly and passed the immigration formalities rapidly. Within a few hours after landing I was a free man and alone on the streets of New York.

PART TWO

AMERICA 1921-

CHAPTER ONE

Cincinnati

From Ellis Island I went directly to Grand Central Station. I was overwhelmed by the vastness of the concourse and the huge masses of people who were pushing and shoving and rushing about, oblivious of everyone and everything. Everyone seemed like a world unto himself. The absence of greetings or any other expressions of friendliness or concern was a shocking experience. People were friendly when I stopped to ask directions or pose a question, but a sense of impatience pervaded. I bought a train ticket to Cincinnati and sent a telegram to my father giving the name of the station and the time of my arrival. After a short wait in New York, I was on my way to Cincinnati, the Queen City of the West, the Gateway to the South.

The sixteen-hour train ride to Cincinnati was exciting and revealing. Wherever I looked I saw something new and grand. The people on the train were relaxed and friendly and some were curious about my gymnasium uniform and my unusual fur coat. I, in turn, was absorbing impressions fast and furious. I remained awake most of the night and was on the platform every time the train made even the briefest of stops. I was struck by the wide-open spaces, by the size of the country, and by the architectural differences of the stations. During the few daylight hours of the trip I noticed the richness of the countryside, the good condition of the soil, the buildings, and the livestock on the farms, and was ecstatic about my new country.

I left Europe wearing my bekeshe (squire's fur coat) and my blue-and-white

153

student's cap with its prominent Star of David, so that Father could see me "in my glory" before I was reduced to a "greenhorn." I did not realize what a good turn I had done myself in clinging to my old garb. It seems that people everywhere mistook me for some kind of potentate or foreign diplomatic representative, and I was treated with unusual respect and deference throughout my journey. Even the reception committee that greeted me upon my arrival in Cincinnati looked puzzled and did not know what to make of the "greenhorn" who somehow did not fit the stereotype.

I arrived in Cincinnati at 8 A.M. on February 1, 1921 and was met at the Grand Central Station at Third and Elm Streets by my father, my first cousin Moshe Meir Dunsky—the oldest son of Tante Toibe, and by my second cousin Ben Doll—the son of Leibe and Alte Dulsky (Doll). As could be expected, it was an emotional meeting between Father and myself for, having parted in 1912, we hardly knew each other. I felt flattered that my cousins came to meet me since it involved considerable inconvenience. My cousin Ben Doll, who was an ardent Zionist, was visibly impressed by the Zionist insignia on my cap, while Cousin Moshe Meir made me feel at home with his unusual warmth and kindness which reminded me of his mother, the gentle Tante Toibe. My father, who was obviously elated to see me, was dressed in his Sabbath clothing and was grinning from ear to ear. He bombarded me with questions about the health and well-being of Mother, my sisters, and Tante Toibe, as well as about conditions in Lithuania and the well-being of a number of people in Serei that he remembered. My cousins also asked numerous questions, principally about conditions in the land of their birth—and I expounded freely.

Despite my great happiness at finding Father in good health and at having arrived safely in the country of my dreams, I could scarcely conceal disappointment over some first impressions. The train station and the surrounding buildings were gloomy and dirty, while soot and the smell of incomplete combustion of coal filled the air. The streets behind the station were also unclean and most of the buildings were old and ordinary. I was also annoyed by the corruption of the spoken Yiddish. It was an admixture of incorrect Yiddish and ungrammatical English.

After meeting at the station, the four of us walked to Father's boarding house at Eighth and Mound across the street from the main Orthodox synagogue known as Shachnes Shul. Mrs. Pastor, with whom Father was boarding, was a fine, tall, and friendly lady in her sixties and we were her only boarders. Without too much fuss, Mrs. Pastor immediately made me feel at home and henceforth treated me like a son. She was the grandmother of Dr. Herman Pastor and Roy Pastor, both of whom became my lifelong friends in later years. As soon as I had rested from my overnight train ride, and on the very day of my arrival, Father took me to the Rosenberg Brothers store to buy me American clothes.

Sam and Isadore Rosenberg were the prosperous owners of a department store on Central Avenue and George Street. They had come to Cincinnati from Mariyampole some thirty years earlier and they still had a sister there. They were very happy to see the newcomer who studied in their home town and they plied me with innumerable questions about people, places, and conditions. I was interested to observe the transformation that three decades in the goldene medina (golden country) had wrought on these former Lithuanian immigrant Jews. The comparison was quite favorable in many respects. Both brothers were soft spoken and polite and they spoke a surprisingly good English. They were both gray, past middle age, and overweight—the mark of prosperous Americans. Isadore Rosenberg was the long-time president of the Adath Israel Congregation, Cincinnati's foremost Conservative synagogue, while Sam Rosenberg was president of the Talmud Torah (religious Hebrew school). Isadore's daughter, Pearl Silverberg, became our lifelong friend in later years. The Rosenbergs fitted me out with a new suit, a hat, shoes, and shirts, and charged them to Father's account. They also offered me a teaching position either in the Talmud Torah or at the Adath Israel religious school. I accepted their offers with thanks but deferred the start of teaching to a later date—after I had acquired a better command of the English language.

During my first week in Cincinnati numerous visitors came to inquire about family in Lithuania. Among the visitors was Max Sanders, a prosperous wholesaler and a fine gentleman, who came to inquire about his parents and his brother, Alter Sandler of Serei. Another immigrant from Serei, Mr. Louis Neman (Nemchinsky), came to inquire about his parents and family. Mr. Philip Tennenbaum, whom I had met a year earlier in Serei, also came to see me. The other callers were mostly friends of my father who had come from Lazdei and Mariyampole and other Lithuanian shtetlach, and they were all eager to learn about conditions in the "Old Country." Despite the great distance between Serei and Cincinnati, these visitors made me feel as if I were back in Serei. This sense of kinship with Serei was strengthened in the synagogue where I went twice daily for services together with Father. There I met the same kind of Jews I had known in Serei and I was surprised to note how little most had really changed despite two or three decades in the United States. Many of these landsleit (fellow countrymen) I got to know quite well. Among these was the hazan (cantor), Mr. Zeff, who came from Lazdei and who conducted the services in a strong and resonant voice in the traditional style.

The Rabbi, Reb Yaakov Yitzhak Gershon Lesser, was a venerable, friendly old gentleman who came to Cincinnati in 1880 (by way of Chicago) from my mother's home village of Halinke where he had served as Rabbi. He remembered my grandfather and was overjoyed to greet "Avremel dem garber's an einikel (the grandson of Avremel the tanner)." After the prayer services, as I sat down with Father at the long table in the rear of the synagogue for the daily study hour of the Talmud, I recognized some fine Talmudic scholars among these worshippers. Their method of study in Yiddish was identical with what I had known in the Yeshiva and, except for their American dress and the frequent admixture of English words, these new Americans could not be distinguished from their counterparts in any of the shtetlach of Eastern Europe. Among the people of this elite group that I remember best are the brothers Reb Ephraim and Mordechai Schiff, Reb Mosche Elchonon Miller, Reb Eli Danziger (Dunsker), Reb Elias Shur, Reb Moshe Levin, Reb Baruch Samuels, and Reb Ber Manischewitz.

An embarrassment that I long remembered occurred on my second day in America when several visitors came to see me. As soon as they were seated, Mrs. Pastor as hostess brought in a large bowl of fruit, mostly oranges and bananas. Seeing that no one was partaking, I neatly peeled a large orange, divided it carefully into its segments, and offered a segment to each of the guests. In Serei, where the cost of oranges was prohibitive, this was the customary way of serving. Seeing the amused faces, I promptly perceived that I had committed a social error, but the deed was done.

On the eve of my first Sabbath in Cincinnati, I was invited by Mr. Frank Posner to come to his home in the fashionable suburb of Avondale to meet his family and to be their guest for the Sabbath meal. Mr. Posner, who was an insurance agent with the Union Central Life Insurance Company, was a friendly, short, and stocky man who had come to Cincinnati as a child. His wife, a tall, hospitable, intelligent woman, was born in Cincinnati and was the sister of attorney David Rosenbaum. They had two unmarried daughters, Helen (Greenberg) and Dorothy (Schwartz). The girls were well bred and friendly but they seemed somewhat puzzled by the strange guest. Up to that time I had never traveled on the Sabbath, so I walked from downtown Cincinnati to Avondale—a distance of five miles, mostly uphill. Unable to gauge the walking time in advance, I arrived at my destination one and one-half hours late, somewhat exhausted and embarrassed. I enjoyed the pleasant atmosphere of the Posner home and the well-served Sabbath meal. I was hampered in conversation, however, by my limited English vocabulary, by my atrocious accent, and by the reluctance to expose myself to ridicule. Yet somehow I managed and I returned home late in the day, pleased and grateful.

I received a similar Sabbath invitation from the Sanders but I do not recall that I walked that time.

Following a few days of rest, my father broached the subject of tachles (goals)—what I intended to do. I told him that I meant to enroll at the University of Cincinnati and seek a professional career. My father did not think much of the idea. "America is a business country and it appreciates only businessmen," said my father. "With your education and ability you will become a successful businessman in no time at all." "How do I start?" I asked. "I will introduce you to my wholesale house," he said, "and they will give you a line of credit. I will also introduce you to some of my customers and in time, after gaining experience as a customer peddler, you will open your own business with a good chance of becoming as successful as the Rosenbergs." I was somewhat shocked by my father's suggestion and I let him know in no uncertain terms that I knew what I wanted, that I knew how to achieve it, and that becoming a businessman was not part of my plans.

I then proceeded to seek some sage advice from my cousin Ben Doll. I told him that I would like to enroll at the University in the fall and inquired about facilities where I could acquire a passable command of the English language during the intervening seven months. Ben suggested that I enroll at the public night school classes for immigrants where his brother and sisters were studying. One session at that school was enough to convince me that this was not for me—too many of the students in that class lacked the basic education to proceed faster than at a snail's pace. The next day I suggested to Ben that I would like to enroll in one of the regular high schools as a special student in English and, if possible, to attend all four grade levels simultaneously. I was interested primarily in acquiring the correct sound and "feel" of the language rather than following a prescribed schedule. The rest, I was certain, I could do for myself—even as I had done on entering the gymnasium at Mariyampole. Ben looked at me quizzically and expressed some doubt, but I suggested that he take me to the high school where he was attending night classes and that he help me explain my plan to the principal. My cousin Ben Doll, who was three years my senior, had come to Cincinnati from Sopotkin in 1913 as a young boy. By now he was the proprietor of a jewelry store and he had a good command of English and was a wise and able spokesman. The following day Ben took me to Woodward High School on the corner of Thirteenth and Sycamore Streets, and introduced me to Mr. Roberts, the principal. Mr. Roberts listened attentively as I was explaining my plan in my bookish English and, to my great surprise, agreed that I could take English I, II, and III for credit and that I attend Grade IV as a "free" listener in American History. I was elated at the favorable turn of events and gladly agreed to his suggestion. I was forthwith enrolled as a day student and Mr. Roberts took me around to show me the classrooms and introduced me to the teachers with appropriate recommendations.

The reading in English I was *Hiawatha* by Longfellow and in English II *A Tale of Two Cities* by Charles Dickens. When I started to read the first ten pages of assigned reading in *Hiawatha*, I found it an impossible task. I had to look up nearly every other word in the English-Yiddish dictionary and it took me several hours of continuous effort to finish one page. A greater shock awaited me when I discovered on re-reading that I had gained very little understanding of the subject and had acquired too few words to make the method worthwhile. In desperation I proceeded to read the assigned number of pages whether I understood the text or not, and to look up only key words. During the remainder of the school year I spent sixteen hours daily on my reading assignments with time out only for meals and personal needs. Before long I was considered a star pupil and was frequently called up to the front of the class as an example during spelling bees. At the end of the school year I received A's from each of my teachers and I fulfilled the entrance requirements for English at the University.

At Woodward High School I attained much more than a working knowledge in English. I learned for the first time that not all Gentiles were confirmed anti-Semites bent on persecuting Jews just for the hell of it. On the contrary, I encountered so much friendliness, decency, and outright desire to be of help that I began to re-think my hitherto biased attitude towards Gentiles. I had never really met any non-Jews on a personal level or, for that matter, on any level at all. All I knew from my earliest childhood was that most of our problems came at the hands of Gentiles who hated and persecuted Jews. We knew that there were exceptions but these were rare. God's chosen few, whom we called Hasidei Umot Haolam (The Just Gentiles), were destined to share God's grace in Paradise along with the righteous of our own. The friendly attitudes of Mr. Roberts, the principal, Miss Shiel, my teacher of English II, and the others, taught me that these Gentiles were practicing the Biblical injunction "Veohavto et hager...." ("Thou shalt love the stranger for you were yourselves once strangers in the land of Egypt.") I found the same friendliness and eagerness to be of help all through my next eight years at the University and at the College of Medicine. It bolstered my good feelings towards my adopted country and the realization grew that the United States was indeed a unique and shining example among the nations of the world. As the years passed this feeling became deeply rooted and it has never left me.

In mid-June of 1921, as soon as I completed my high school studies, I made my way to the University of Cincinnati to seek admission to the fall term. The

Dean of Admissions, Dr. E.L. Talbert, was friendly and outgoing and I was admitted as a regular student with advanced standing in German and Mathematics. With the attainment of a working knowledge of English and admission to the University behind me, I called on Sam Rosenberg to redeem his promise of a teaching position at the Talmud Torah. He arranged an interview for me with the new director of the Talmud Torah, Dr. Abraham Simon, and I was promptly hired to teach modern Hebrew. For the first time in my life I was now self-supporting.

Within six months after I arrived in Cincinnati I received a letter from Tante Toibe expressing a strong desire to come to Cincinnati. Her two sons, Moshe Meir and Yitzhak Dunsky, although annoyed by their mother's long-delayed decision to come to the United States, promptly made all the necessary arrangements for her coming. As had happened during most of her life, trouble again stalked behind this major event in her life—her reunion with her sons, whom she had not seen since they left as young boys for America some fifteen years earlier and her reunion with me, to whom she was greatly attached as a surrogate son. When we learned the date of her arrival, Yitzhak volunteered to meet his mother at the boat and to help her with the immigration procedures at Ellis Island. When he arrived at Ellis Island Yitzhak was informed that his mother's boat had arrived earlier than expected and that she was placed on a train to Cincinnati. He wired that we should meet her in the morning at the Cincinnati Grand Central Station and that he would follow. Our hopes were dashed and we were thrown into deep gloom when the train arrived and Tante Toibe was not on it. While waiting for Yitzhak's return from New York, we began frantically to trace her whereabouts with the help of the Hebrew Immigration Aid Society (HIAS) in New York. We learned that since no one had come to meet her, Tante Toibe was being detained by the immigration authorities. In the meanwhile, Yitzhak returned to Cincinnati and, upon learning about the turn of events, took the evening train back to New York. This time Yitzhak found his mother and he returned with her to Cincinnati the following morning.

Tante Toibe looked tired and exhausted when we met her at the station and she was more dead than alive by the time she arrived at the home of her older son, Moshe Meir. As a result of the physical exhaustion of the lengthy journey from Serei, the severe emotional strain surrounding her coming to America, and the shocking experience at Ellis Island, Tante Toibe fell into a coma almost as soon as she arrived at her son's home and she did not emerge from it for over a week. The attending physician, Dr. Eli Fogel, one of the few Eastern European Jewish physicians in Cincinnati and himself a descendant from Serei, did not know what to make of the strange malady. It took almost two

The wedding picture of the author's sisters Rivka and Sheine in 1924.
From left to right: Rivka, Yitzhak Hirsh Slavaticki, Mother, Avram Ber Ravad and
Sheine. Rivka and her husband were martyred by the Nazis together with the entire
Jewish community of Serei on the eve of Rosh Hashanah, 1941. Sheine and her
husband emigrated to Eretz Yisroel soon after the wedding and Mother emigrated to
the U.S.

months for Tante Toibe to recover from her ordeal, and we were all very
happy to see her regain her health and had the chance to enjoy her presence
and to get reacquainted. Almost immediately Tante Toibe became strongly
attached to her grandson Yitzhak (Irvin) Dunsky, who was only a toddler at
that time. She also made many acquaintances among the women in the
neighborhood and at the Washington Avenue Synagogue around the corner,
and she seemed quite content to enjoy a measure of happiness. Since we lived
in the same house we saw each other quite often, although my studies did not
leave me as much time as I would have liked. To gain more privacy in the
crowded apartment, I used to retreat to a third-floor attic room to study and
Tante Toibe would come up frequently to bring me some snacks and to chat.

Tante Toibe's son Moshe Meir was one of the finest men I ever knew and he favored in sweetness our grandfather Avremel and his mother Toibe. He was kind, friendly, and outgoing, and he shunned controversy. His face would light up on the slightest pretext and when confronted by a wrong he would resort to Grandfather's saying: "Zol meine ibergein (let me be the loser)." Moshe Meir was a charitable man and he was loved and admired by all who knew him. He was an ardent baseball fan and a dedicated member of the Poale Zion (Labor Zionists). His wife Goldie was the daughter of my father's oldest brother, Yitzhak of Semyatich. She was a very kind person but she suffered from chronic illness. Tante Toibe was much aggrieved by this situation and did her best to alleviate the suffering of her beloved son Moshe Meir and his four young children. Tante Toibe's own chronic illness and her angelic nature made it possible for her to feel the suffering of others. The Dunsky children are Chana (deceased), Yitzhak (Dr. Irvin), Bessie (Rothman), and Abe, who succeeded his father in the restaurant supply business. In 1928 Tante Toibe contracted pneumonia, to which she succumbed after a valiant struggle of several weeks. Dr. Fogel was the attending physician, and as a senior medical student I was able to bring her a measure of comfort, but with her chronic lung disease and the absence of antibiotics in those days, the tragic outcome was foredoomed. Her seven years in Cincinnati were probably the best years of her life. I mourned her, missed her, and remember her as much as my own mother.

In the spring of 1924, Father returned to Lithuania, where he visited several yeshivoth to find a suitable match for my older sister Sheine. He found what he was looking for in the yeshiva of Ponievezh. With his mission accomplished he promptly returned to Cincinnati. In the fall of 1924 my two sisters were married in Kovno on successive days. Sheine married a young Rabbi from Shavel, Avram Ber Ravad, and they soon left Lithuania to settle in Eretz Yisroel, while Rivka married her long-time suitor, Yitzhak Hirsh Slavaticki, and they remained in Serei. With her daughters married, Mother finally felt free to come to Cincinnati and she joined us within a few months after the weddings. Father bought a house on Prospect Place next to Moshe Meir Dunsky and my parents became reunited for the first time in many years.

Mother was delighted to join Father and me in the goldene medina (precious country) and to be near her sister Toibe, her cousins and life-long friends Alte and Leibe Doll, and her sisters in Detroit and Toronto. Within a few weeks after her arrival, Mother enrolled in evening classes for immigrants at the Avondale Public School and in an amazingly short time she was reading the Cincinnati English Newspapers—the *Post*, the *Enquirer* and the *Times Star*. She made many friends amongst her contemporaries in the Orthodox Jewish community, she basked in the glory of my achievements, and she seemed to be well satisfied—except that she missed her daughters and she worried frequently about their well-being. In the course of time, Mother became more and more absorbed with religious matters and she became unhappy about the flagrant violations of Jewish religious customs and practices by so many. One lovely summer Sabbath day when I asked her why she stayed indoors she said, "My son, when I sit on the porch and I see my fellow Jews lighting cigarettes or riding in their automobiles, thus desecrating the Sabbath, I sin with my eyes—so I would rather not see it." Mother joined a number of charitable organizations and the ladies auxiliary of the synagogue and she adapted readily to her new environment in Cincinnati, but the death of Tante Toibe was a great shock to her. A year later, with the beginning of the Great Depression, Father decided that he had worked long enough to satisfy his physical needs and that the time had come to dedicate himself more fully to his spiritual needs by settling in Eretz Yisroel. Mother concurred in this decision and they left Cincinnati in 1931 to settle permanently in Israel.

The next three decades were the happiest years in my parents' lives. They considered themselves extremely fortunate that they succeeded in fulfilling the important injunction to live in the Eretz Avot (Land of the Patriarchs), as Israel is often called. Father spent all of his time in study and prayer while Mother dedicated a great deal of her time to welfare work and social institutions, and both became highly respected members of their community. After a brief stay in Tel Aviv, my parents settled permanently in their own home in Herzliya, part of which they dedicated as a house of prayer for themselves and their neighborhood. On their way from Cincinnati to Israel, my parents spent several months in Serei visiting with my sister Rivka and her family as well as renewing old friendships. They long remembered that last visit to their place of origin and with their daughter whom they never saw again. In Tel Aviv and Herzliya my parents lived near Sheine and her family and they enjoyed the growth and development of their grandchildren and great-grandchildren. Mother died in 1959 at the age of ninety and Father died in 1963 at the age of ninety-four. They were both interred in Herzliya. While my parents were alive we conducted an extensive correspondence and I visited them frequently.

Despite the initial unsatisfactory impression which the city had made on me, Cincinnati soon revealed itself as a city of great charm and as a most pleasant place to live in. Built on a high plateau on the northern bank of the Ohio River, Cincinnati is surrounded by seven hills—the narrow plateau along the river and the lower foothills are the city proper, and the more distant hills are the park-like suburbs. The beautiful panoramic views from the hills of Kentucky and the Ohio countryside are breathtaking in many places. Cincinnati originated as a military fort during the Indian wars near the end of the eighteenth century when it was known as Fort Washington. In 1802 it was incorporated as a town and was at first called Losantiville, but was soon renamed Cincinnati in honor of the then-governor of the Northwest Territory, of which Cincinnati was the first major settlement.

During the century since it had become a city in 1819, Cincinnati rapidly increased in size from three square miles to seventy, and from a population of 9,000 to 400,000. The population, although mostly white Anglo-Saxon, had thirty percent people of foreign stock and ten percent Blacks. Of the foreign element nearly forty percent came from Germany between 1845-60 and about 20,000 were Jews, most of whom had arrived after the Russian pogroms of 1881. By 1921 Cincinnati extended some thirty miles along the Ohio River and some seven miles north and it contained within its borders many beautiful parks, numerous cultural institutions of high quality, and a varied and flourishing industry. Over the decades that followed, Cincinnati expanded greatly in area but the size of the population has remained virtually unchanged.

When I came to Cincinnati it was already a major center of commerce and industry with seven railroads and nineteen truck lines entering the city and numerous barges and boats plying the Ohio River on the way to the Mississippi. Among the numerous industrial concerns were the manufacturers of garments, shoes, leather, machinery, machine tools, chemicals, soaps, distillation products, meat packing, printing, publishing, autos, etc. Among the unusual features of Cincinnati were: the ownership of a major railroad line, the first municipal university in the United States, the first cooperative system in engineering education where students alternate between periods of academic studies and periods of practical experience in the field, the first city manager form of government, a full season of summer opera, bi-annual music festivals, an outstanding symphony orchestra, numerous choral and literary societies, and excellent schools of music and the performing arts.

After World War II, Cincinnati changed considerably in many respects due to the influx of large numbers of Appalachians from Kentucky and Blacks from the south, the movement of industry from the city to the suburbs, the extension of the suburbs many miles into the countryside, the depopulation of the downtown city basin and its eventual conversion into a commercial and civic center, and as a result of economic, cultural, and scientific innovations.

In the early Twenties people in Cincinnati were still talking about the defunct, corrupt political gangs of Heineke and Cox and about the beginning of a new day in clean government. Under the New Charter Movement, which was led by the prominent attorneys Murray Seasongood and Charles P. Taft, son of the former President William Howard Taft, clean city government became firmly entrenched in Cincinnati. Another dream of half a century—to build a magnificent central railroad station for the seven railroads servicing Cincinnati—was realized, but soon the airplane made railroad transportation obsolete. The horse-drawn trolley that was still operational when I arrived was soon replaced by the electric trolley, then in turn by the electric bus, the motor bus, and finally by the individual automobile that virtually supplanted mass transportation. Among the regrettable losses are the cable incline cars to Mount Adams, Clifton, and Price Hill.

In the service areas, the laundry industry was replaced by home washing machines, and the milkman, bread man, fruit and grocery venders and the mama-and-papa stores were replaced by supermarkets and shopping centers. In entertainment, the numerous theaters and vaudeville houses were replaced by home television and small movie houses. A fine system of public education has mushroomed numerically but deteriorated in quality. In economics the Great Depression has led to the Great Recession by way of several cycles of boom and bust. Over the decades morals have deteriorated and religious affiliations have shrunk significantly. On the positive side, the lifespan has increased by several decades, personal comforts have multiplied, and individual human rights have become more secure.

Cincinnati also occupies a special position in American Jewish life largely as a result of its leadership and institutions. The Cincinnati Jewish community is the oldest west of the Allegheny Mountains. The first Jewish inhabitant, Mr. Joseph Jonas, arrived in Cincinnati in 1817 from England by way of Philadelphia. By 1824 there were twenty Jews in Cincinnati and they founded the B'nai Israel Congregation, also known as Rockdale Temple. In 1840 Polish Jews founded a synagogue which later became known as Adath Israel Congregation, and in 1841 German Jews founded the B'nai Yeshurun Congregation, also known as Wise Temple. Until 1854, all Jewish congregations in Cincinnati were Orthodox. This changed with the arrival of Isaac Mayer Wise as Rabbi of B'nai Israel Congregation and the arrival a year later of Max Lillienthal as Rabbi of B'nai Israel Congregation. Both of these Rabbis were products of the Post-Napoleonic German Liberal Movement of Mendelssohn and they were both confirmed internationalists. They believed that God had designated the United States to lead the world to universal brotherhood and that a reformed ethical Judaism should be in the vanguard.

Both Rabbis began their careers as educators and they were both controversial figures before they came to Cincinnati. Lillienthal tried to reform Jewish education in Russia along lines akin to his native Munich. After five years of intensive effort in the late 1830s, he earned the enmity of every segment of Russian Jewry as well as the ultimate mistrust of the Russian Government. He left Russia secretly and he came to the United States in the early 1840s. Isaac

Mayer Wise, who was a native of Bohemia, came to the United States at about the same time as Lillenthal. He became the Rabbi of a congregation in Albany, New York, but a Rosh Hashanah sermon of his aroused such a furor that the services broke up in physical violence and Wise was booted out of the synagogue. In Cincinnati, amidst their German Jewish immigrant landsmen, Lillienthal and Wise found fertile soil for their ideas and are counted among the important founders of Reform Judaism in America.

The mass emigration of German Jews to Cincinnati during the four decades beginning in the Thirties of the past century and the activities of Wise and Lillienthal have left a permanent imprint on Cincinnati and American Jewry. The more dynamic Rabbi Wise was the founder of the Hebrew Union College Seminary for Reform Rabbis and he served as its first president for a quarter of a century. He was also responsible for founding the Union of American Hebrew Congregations, the Union of American Rabbis, and the first Jewish Anglo-American weekly, *The American Israelite*, which is still being published in Cincinnati. All of these institutions subsequently served as prototypes for the Conservative and Orthodox segments of American Jewry. Rabbi Lillienthal served for many years as a member of the Cincinnati Board of Education and the University of Cincinnati Board of Trustees, and he made important contributions to both.

The Reform or Liberal Movement, as it is now known, has had its ups and downs and has undergone a series of metamorphoses. The problem with universal brotherhood as a primary goal is that it is wonderful as an ideal but elusive in practice. The Rabbis of old have been preaching the ideal of human brotherhood over the milennia, but they tempered it with caution, patience, and historical perspective. Some of the early reformers, epecially David Einhorn, David Philipson, Kaufmann Kohler, and others, were even more radical than Wise and Lillienthal. They were all too eager to abandon the accumulated heritage of centuries of martyrs for the sake of tenous temporal benefits. In recent decades the Reform Movement has made heroic efforts to recapture lost ground by restoring many ancient prayers, customs, and rituals and by returning to the principle of peoplehood, as well as by its enthusiastic support of the State of Israel.

In addition to becoming a center of Jewish scholarship and a storehouse of invaluable Jewish treasures at Hebrew Union College, Cincinnati also gained national recognition for pioneering in Jewish social services and in Jewish education. Cincinnati is also known for two national distributors of kosher products, the Manischewitz Matzo Company and the Osherwitz Salami Company, both of which originated in Cincinnati.

CHAPTER TWO

Marriage and Family

> "When a man meets his fitting mate
> society begins."
>
> (Emerson)

From the time I left Lithuania I continued a regular correspondence with my Pupi, who remained a student in Mariyampole. We kept each other informed about events of interest in our lives and kept the fires of love burning. One day in the fall of 1921 I was shocked to learn that Pupi's father had died suddenly after a brief illness. It was a catastrophic blow to the entire family and I grieved over his passing along with the more immediate members of the family. I had learned to admire Pupi's father and I deeply regretted the passing of this fine man who was only in his early forties. Despite their relative security, I also knew about some of the bleak circumstances in which his untimely death had placed his widow Beile and her six young children. My heart went out for Pupi and I wished I could have been with her to help her bear the grief and to share the burden that now fell upon her as the oldest child in the family. All I could do was to write more often and with more feeling, knowing full well that only time could soften the blow.

With the death of Yosef Gurvitz, the management of the family business fell on the shoulders of Pupi's cousin Hershky Gurvitz, who began to push the family aside in every possible way. Yet all the children remained away in school and when the family eventually moved to Kovno, Beile's sisters and their families gave them all the moral support and the occasional financial help they needed.

Pupi's father had had a great love for Eretz Yisroel which he instilled in his children. Early in 1921 he had written to his friend Moshe Yankowsky in Haifa, inquiring about the business opportunities for settling in Eretz Yisroel. He was especially interested to learn if he could buy or open a flour mill in Eretz Yisroel. In two letters in a literary Hebrew, dated March and April 1921, Mr. Yankowsky had informed Mr. Gurvitz that the mood in Eretz Yisroel was very depressed as a result of the recent Arab riots, which had caused many casualties and substantial destruction of Jewish property. He also had informed Pupi's father that the economic opportunities in the flour-mill business were limited because of the planned construction of a modern flour mill in Haifa by the Rothschilds at a cost of half a million dollars, and the existence of many long-established mills. Mr. Yankowsky had closed the letter by saying that although the economic opportunities in Eretz Yisroel were limited and the difficulties of supporting a family of eight should not be underestimated, Mr. Gurvitz's wealth of $20,000 and his long experience as a successful businessman should help him find his niche in the community, but the ultimate decision must be his own.

In the fall of 1921, accompanying a shipment of logs down the Nieman River to Germany, Yosef Gurvitz contracted an infection from the bitter cold and the inclement weather of the season. He went to Badneuheim for expert medical treatment but they were unable to save his life. A year later, Pupi and her family sustained another blow when Pupi's brother Gedalke contracted tuberculosis. Pupi left school and took her brother for a lengthy course of treatment in a tubercular sanatorium in the Black Forests (Schwarzwald) of Germany. She remained with Gedalke during his stay in the sanatorium and she helped nurse him and did everything possible to save his life, but he died six months later despite all efforts.

I knew Gedalke as a very bright, cheerful, and handsome youngster, and I loved him as I did the rest of the family. This calamity, coming so close on the heels of her father's untimely death, was a numbing experience. Since she was at such a great distance, I was worried about Pupi's own health and well-being. I was, frankly, concerned about the possibility that she might contract the dread disease and about how she would stand up under the strain of the double blow. As I recall it, our relations grew even closer and I tried in my letters to do all I could to comfort her. The tragedy of it is that with modern antibiotics both of these beautiful lives could have been spared.

In the spring of 1925, as soon as I was admitted to medical school, I shared the good news with my Pupi and suggested that the time had come for her to join me in Cincinnati and get married. In 1925 marriage was still a lifetime commitment and, as a rule, was not undertaken until one could support a family. My financial resources were as yet meager and tenuous and I still had four years of medical school and two or three years of incomeless internship and residency ahead of me. Although these were the "boom years" that preceded the Great Depression, even an established physician was not assured of earning a livelihood. What complicated my decision still further was the awareness that Pupi had been only sixteen when I last saw her and that the lapse of four and one-half years under such diverse environments surely had wrought changes in both of us that would need to be reconciled. Fortunately, our mothers strongly approved of the match and both of us had abiding faith in each other and in the future.

I was elated when Pupi's acceptance of my formal marriage proposal arrived by return mail, and I proceeded immediately to make all the necessary arrangements for her arrival. To avoid undue delays under the stringent immigration laws of 1924, I arranged for Pupi to come as a student by getting her admitted to the University of Cincinnati. Pupi arrived in New York a few months later, on the day before Yom Kippur in 1925, and she was promptly detained on Ellis Island for deportation as an unauthorized bride. An unguarded statement aroused the suspicion of the immigration authorities that the beautiful girl before them was more than a student. Fortunately my New York relative Mr. Silverman, who came to meet her on my behalf, obtained legal counsel and she was promptly released to continue her journey to Cincinnati. I did not go to New York to meet Pupi at the boat because of the need for discretion and also because I was tied down in medical school with examinations at a critical time in my freshman year.

I waited for Pupi's arrival at the Grand Central Station in Cincinnati full of excitement and anticipation. As soon as I spotted her getting off the train I ran towards her and we kissed and embraced and shed tears of joy that our dreams had finally come true. She looked as stunning and as beautiful as ever and she displayed a practical, no-nonsense manner which I found especially appealing. During the five years that we were separated, Pupi had grown from an attractive teenager to a beautiful young woman in her full bloom. Yet there was a momentary sense of disappointment, perhaps due to the sudden realization that a long-cherished memory of tender youth had vanished. Although I was considered a good-looking young man, time had not passed me without blemish, especially since I had become substantially bald. I hoped, though that Pupi would not find the changes in me too unpleasant. Actually, the process of adjustment proceeded fairly rapidly as far as our mutual relations were concerned, although it was much more difficult for Pupi than for me. Like all immigrants, she had to acquire a new language and she had to adjust to new customs, new friends, a new country, and an entirely new cultural environment. She also missed her mother and her family and she had to adjust to living together with my parents—a proverbial source of irritation and bad tempers. I did everything possible to smooth over all the inevitable early difficulties and I believe that I succeeded in making Pupi happy.

Pupi matriculated at U.C. as a special student to fulfill the requirements of the law and she registered for classes in German literature, while in the evenings she attended classes in English for immigrants at Avondale Public School. There she met the two daughters of Hebrew Union College professor and musicologist Zvi Idelsohn, and they became close friends. She also met Nechama Hochstein, the daughter of Rabbi Hochstein, Rachel Wolf (Wigser), and the two Muskat girls—the sisters of Dr. Muskat. These girls and the Poale Zion (Labor Zionist) group and the Ivriah (Hebrew Culture) group made up our social setting during the remainder of the Twenties while I was completing my medical education and Pupi was getting acclimated in her new environment. Our wedding was scheduled for June 15, 1926 so that I could finish my first year in medical school and obtain my citizenship before getting married.

The wedding took place in the living room of my parents' home as planned. The decorations and all the other arrangements were a mixture of the old and the new with a distinct European Jewish flavor. Pupi and I decorated the large living room with colorful bunting and other decorations, and we strung overhead a huge blue-and-white Mogen David which extended from wall to wall. The entire family was invited to the wedding and they all came. Our wedding, in effect, served as a welcomed family reunion. Tante Malke and her husband, Mordechai Yosel Rabinowitz, came from Detroit; Tante Mirke and her husband, Rabbi Meir Levy, came from Toronto, and Tante Toibe came from next door. We also had as our wedding guests all of our cousins and their small children from Detroit, New Milford, Connecticut, and Cincinnati. Among the other guests were our friends of the Poale Zion, some of my parents' friends, a few landsleit, and Rachel Wolf with her fiance, Dr. Abe Wigser. It was a rather large assemblage for a private home.

The wedding ceremony took place under the hupah in the living room and was performed by Rabbi Louis Feinberg and my uncle, Rabbi Meir Levy. Between courses, around the festive tables, there were greetings and toasts and a great deal of communal singing of Zionist and Jewish popular songs in Yiddish and in Hebrew; there was also some dancing of popular Jewish dances like the Sherele. At a fairly late hour the Sheva Brahot (Seven Benedictions) were sung and the Birhat Hamazon (Grace after the Meal) was recited in

The family grouping at the author's wedding on June 15, 1926. Seated left to right: Tante Toibe Dunsky, Uncle Rabbi Meir Levy, Tante Mirke Levy, Pupi and author, Mother, Father, and Tante Malke Rabinowitz. Children seated in front: Shirley Rabinowitz (Klein) and Adele Allen (Bayer). Standing in the rear: Cousins Goldie and Moshe Meir Dunsky, Jenny and Yitzhak Dunson, Julius Rabinowitz holding Doris (Kashtan), Mary Rabinowitz, Eva (Chavke) Allen-Cherow, and Ida (Chaye Gitel) Golden.

unison. All the guests lingered until past midnight and, in accordance with Old-Country custom, the out-of-town guests remained for several days and there was no honeymoon. Through all of these goings-on, my bride remained as calm and as beautiful as ever and the groom was dazed. On the day following the wedding I took my aunts and uncles for a tour of the city in my old Chevrolet and they appreciated it very much. My uncle, Rabbi Levy, was a good-looking man and with his long black beard he looked like Theodore Herzl. He was dressed formally in a frock coat and silk hat and he soon began to feel uncomfortable in the June heat. Tante Mirke then turned to Uncle and said: "Meir, a car is just like a living room. Take off your hat and make yourself comfortable." He seemed to cherish the advice and he took off his silk hat and put on a yarmulke (skullcap).

A few months after our wedding, Pupi and I decided to take a trip to New York for our honeymoon. My Chevrolet had a long and honorable history but it was falling apart. I had bought it in 1922 for $150 and it had served me well to go to school, to attend to my rental property in Mount Adams, and to take Pupi, my parents, and Tante Toibe for rides on Sundays. But at this juncture the seats were torn, the roof leaked, the tires were worn, and some serious trouble developed in the transmission and the motor. Buying a new car was out of the question, so I decided to rebuild the car with used parts and the mechanical know-how which I was to acquire as I went along. I started to take the car apart in sections in my backyard and I bought all the replacements I needed from used-parts dealers, but I soon discovered that I needed special equipment to lift the motor and to replace the piston rings, the flywheel, and the transmission. I arranged to have the car towed to a repair shop on Knott Street and, with the proprietor's permission, I proceeded to rebuild my old jalopy. With some help from the mechanic in the garage, I completed the job in about a week's time and I was promptly offered a job for the summer, which I declined with thanks. Pupi then helped take a hand in the project and we replaced the roof and the tires and Pupi made beautiful new seat covers. We were now ready to embark on our delayed honeymoon, which began with a three-day trip to New York through the Allegheny Mountains and the narrow winding roads of West Virginia and Pennsylvania.

We had made it without any trouble to the outskirts of Wheeling, West Virginia when the car began to lose power and we could proceed only at a snail's pace. A farmer-mechanic along the road advised us he would attempt to correct the strange malady but that it might take forty-eight hours. My instincts told me to decline the offer and to take a chance on reaching the city somehow. With a great deal of trepidation we did make it to the city, where a young boy in his teens looked under the hood, turned a screw with his penknife, and declared that the problem was fixed. When I asked the boy how much I owed him he refused to accept payment for "doing practically nothing," but he thanked me profusely when I pressed two quarters into the palm of his hand. We had no further mechanical trouble on the way to New York and back, but negotiating the numerous steep mountains of the Alleghenies was something else. Our car had an inefficient four-cylinder engine and in order to make it to the top of each steep mountain we had to gain sufficient momentum on the downhill of the preceding mountain to carry the car at least halfway up. Failing in this maneuver meant that the motor would get overheated from driving in low gear and the water in the radiator would evaporate in steam. When this happened it meant a long delay in the middle of nowhere to allow the motor to cool, to fetch a replacement of water for the radiator, and to continue the struggle uphill in low gear at a very slow pace. This was such a common occurrence that there were entrepreneurs on each mountain selling water to the unlucky motorists. Pupi was so impressed with the performance of our rebuilt car that she dubbed it "The Spirit of Cincinnati."

My cousins Yitzhak and Jenny Dunson and their friends the Mayerhoffs, who started out with us in their brand-new car, succumbed to the rigor of the mountains and they arrived in New York a day after we did. In New York we saw a vaudeville show at the recently completed Rockefeller Center, took in some of the sights, and spent considerable time visiting with Pupi's family— the Gurwitzes and the Rochelsons—and a few classmates from the gymnasium. From New York we proceeded to New Milford, Connecticut, where we spent a week with my cousin Ida (Chaye Gitel) Golden, her husband Harry, and their family.

On the way back home to Cincinnati, Pupi and I talked a great deal about the members of the family we had just met for the first time, about the reunion with our classmates, and what we had learned about each other's family and friends. We were in high spirits and I had a chance to air some of the hundreds of Yiddish, Hebrew, and Russian songs that I still remembered and which Pupi and her mother loved so much. We also reminisced about the past and reviewed some of the things that had happened to us during our long separation. A long trip in the country is conducive to reminiscing, especially with a captive and eager audience at your side.

Pupi told me about some of her courtships and those who sought her hand in marriage. There was a Mr. Levin, a wealthy young man in Kovno with a good business and a chauffeur-driven limousine. Everybody in the family thought he was a good catch but Pupi, her mother, and her Aunt Rachelle preferred that she remain loyal to her first love. There was also a distant cousin in Balbirishok (a brother of Rose Levitt of Pittsburgh) who invited Pupi for a ride in his fancy buggy and then threatened to ditch her and let her walk home through the mud unless she promised to marry him.

On my part, there was nothing as romantic as that. A recent immigrant with a heavy accent was not exactly a "catch" in those days when accent-free English was so highly prized. I had also made it a practice to tell my dates that I was engaged to be married and that I had nothing to offer except an evening's companionship—spelling out the details as I went along. My frankness soothed my conscience but discouraged most of my dates. There was one girl, Sophie, who did not mind acting as a proxy. She was a pretty, vivacious, and friendly girl and I enjoyed her company and was grateful to her. Sophie was a sister of one of my Poale Zion friends and she later married a fine man in a neighboring city and raised a family of her own. Both she and her husband, unfortunately, died at a relatively young age. An adventure of a different kind happened two days before Pupi and I were married when a prominent local developer came to my parents' home in the role of a matchmaker. He proposed a large sum of money as a dowry and a life of ease for me if I would agree to marry the sister of a friend of his, "one of the wealthiest men in Cincinnati." We handled the situation as discreetly as possible but could do little to minimize the embarrassment of the well-meaning gentleman. The young lady in question did marry a physician and we often met socially, but the incident was never mentioned.

During the ensuing four years, while I was completing my medical education and serving a no-income internship at the Cincinnati General Hospital, we continued to live with my parents in their home. With little income of my own to speak of and with spare time at a premium, these were most difficult years for Pupi. I did my best to alleviate the situation and hoped for the best. In 1929 we finally established our own home in a modest second-floor apartment on Reading Road near Rockdale Avenue. A research fellowship in experimental medicine, which I was awarded at the end of my internship, made the move possible.

As soon as we were on our own, Pupi and I agreed that it was time to start raising a family. On June 17, 1930 the great event took place—the birth of our first child. She was a beautiful baby and we named her Penina Toibe. The first name, meaning Pearl, is a Biblical name that Pupi and I just happened to like, and Toibe was the name of that precious jewel, my Tante Toibe, who had died in 1929. Pupi did well under the excellent care of her obstetrician, Dr. Samuel Rothenberg, the father of my classmate Dr. Robert Rothenberg. Excessive sedation and analgesia and two weeks of hospitalization with bed rest were the prevailing practice at that time. Fortunately, little harm was done. Our friends chipped in with presents, a comfortable crib and all the other facilities were prepared in advance, and we settled down to raise our first child. My mother was very happy with the first grandchild she had ever seen and she was eager to help, but only up to a point. To her way of thinking the raising of a child was the sole responsibility of the mother.

Among ourselves Pupi and I usually conversed in Hebrew and we decided to make Hebrew the mother tongue of our children, until we encountered some practical problems. One evening we left Penina in the care of a babysitter and upon returning home we found that Penina had been crying ever since we left. The babysitter was at her wit's end trying to appease her. It seems that as soon as we had left Penina asked for mayim (water), the babysitter did not know what it meant, and nothing else would do. The language problem was solved when Penina returned one day from playing with other children and announced to Pupi, "From now on your name is no longer Ima (Mother), your name is Mommy."

In 1932 Pupi gave birth to our second daughter, whom we named Judith Esther. She was a beautiful baby and a happy child and was a most welcomed addition to the family. After Judy's birth we moved from Mitchell Avenue to a nicer apartment on Beatrice Drive, to raise our two daughters in greater comfort. Two years later we moved from our second-floor apartment on Beatrice Drive to a spacious first-floor apartment on Glenwood Avenue. The private park-like surroundings of our new home provided the children with trees to climb on, flowering shrubs to admire, small gardens to tend, and various small buildings to hide in or to use as play houses. There was also plenty of room for bicycling and outdoor games, and the spacious veranda was greatly utilized by all.

Our Glenwood apartment building was the last word in the Baroque 19th century style of mansion. It was originally the home of Mr. James Gamble of Procter & Gamble Company, and was now owned by the former Governor of Ohio Mr. Myers Y. Cooper. It was a three-story rough-stone structure with bay windows, high ceilings, and a spacious veranda running around the entire front and part of the side of the house. The original mansion had been divided into three spacious apartments, one apartment to a floor. Our apartment on the ground floor had a large double living room which was richly paneled in beautiful cherry wood, with numerous built-in shelves for books and bric-a-brac. There was also a spacious dining room as well as a large kitchen, three bedrooms, and two baths. Other features of the living room were two large crystal chandeliers, a large inlaid color tile fireplace, and two picture windows. It was in this apartment that Pupi had her first real opportunity to display her superb artistry in entertaining, decorating, table decor, cooking, and serving—which everyone admired. From the time we moved into our Glenwood apartment and for the next twenty-five years, our home became a meeting place for many cultural activities and a hospitality haven for nearly all of the emissaries and dignitaries visiting Cincinnati on behalf of cultural, educational, and Labor Zionist causes. That meant frequent guests for dinners to which a few local friends were usually invited; it also meant taking the visiting guests to public gatherings and, not too infrequently, taking the guests back to our home for practical talks, private cultural repartees, or for singing favorite tunes into the wee hours of the morning. We remained in this apartment for six years, until we moved to our own home at 4000 Red Bud Avenue in 1941.

With the exception of the usual colds and childhood diseases, we did not encounter any problems in raising our daughters. Our dedicated pediatrician, Dr. Samuel Okrent, was always on call and he responded cheerfully and effectively. In 1936, Penina was enrolled in University School, a fine nonsectarian elementary and college preparatory school founded by the old German-Jewish families and administered by a non-Jewish staff. My teacher and colleague, Dr. Hiram Weiss, suggested that we enroll our children in this school and, because of its excellent teaching staff and fine reputation, Pupi and I agreed it was a good idea. The school met nearly all of our expectations, but a semi-crisis occurred at Christmas time when the children were taught Christmas carols and engaged in other pre-Christmas activities—despite the fact that the vast majority of the children were Jewish. To account for her lack of interest in the festivities, Penina explained to her first-grade teacher that in her home we celebrated Chanukah instead of Christmas. The teacher was astonished, for her knowledge of Chanukah was even less than Penina's knowledge of Christmas. With the teacher's encouragement, Penina sang several of the Chanukah songs in her repertoire, and these made such a hit that the teacher asked us for descriptive material about the Jewish holidays. We provided her with the descriptive and pictorial material she asked for as well as some additional songs with music. We also invited the children of Penina's class to our home for a Chanukah party of supervised Chanukah games and latkes, or potato pancakes. Both the Jewish and non-Jewish children enjoyed the experience. Some of the Jewish parents greatly appreciated our initiative in introducing Jewish content, while others grumbled. As a result of this experience and the changing times, celebrating Christmas by Jewish children became less and less fashionable at the school and the identification with Jewish customs and the celebration of Jewish holidays became more acceptable. The tragic events of the Nazi period hastened the evolution of this process.

Judy's childhood was also a happy one and she joined Penina at University School when her turn came. She received the same Jewish education as Penina in daily afternoon classes at the Talmud Torah, and their Jewish education extended over the entire twelve-year period of their public education. Both Penina and Judy also spent many summers in the Pocono Mountains in the Hebrew educational camp Massad.

During the early years of her childhood, Judy had an adorable speech defect in which certain letters were only partly vocalized or were transposed. Dr. Azriel Eisenberg, the director of the Bureau of Jewish Education and a close personal friend, repeatedly urged us to make a recording of Judy's priceless speech pattern before she outgrew it. For some reason we did not consider it proper to do so, which is regrettable. During the summers of the 1930s and early 1940s, we did a great deal of traveling with the children to the national parks, caves, and summer resorts of Ohio, Kentucky, Tennessee, and Michigan. These excursions usually took place on extended weekends or on national holidays. We frequently invited another couple to join us on these trips. Among the invited couples were Lillian and Mitchel Miller, Dora and Moshe Kushnir, and Chana Wigser Halfin and her husband. Kushnir and Halfin were teachers at the Talmud Torah and Miller was a pharmacist. We all had in common our European background and social compatibility. During these trips, Pupi and I did a great deal of singing and the children and our guests would invariably join us in what amounted to a continuous and almost endless recital. We all had a grand time. During the early war years, we would often stop our singing while traveling through the hills of Kentucky and Tennessee to hear the familiar voice of Edward R. Murrow on the radio as he announced, "This is London..." He would then proceed to relate the ordeals of the British during the German Blitz on England.

For several years during the Thirties, Pupi and the children would spend their vacations in a South Haven, Michigan resort and I would join them during the weekends. On one such occasion, as we were seated around the table of the main dining room for Sunday brunch, Judy—who was then four years old—stood up on a chair and at the top of her voice called out: "Everybody here meet my pretty daddy!" While blushing, I took a bow to the applause and merriment of the crowd, and kissed my loving little darling for her spontaneous, uninhibited show of affection.

At our Glenwood home, which was next to the park-like Doepke estate, there were many magnificent trees to climb and Penina was especially agile and climbed higher and faster than any of her playmates. Judy tried valiantly to imitate her older sister, but being too young for such "tomboy" activities, she would manage only to fall down and wound up frustrated and crying. Like many young parents, I was an avid photographer and made home movies of our growing family. One reel shows Penina climbing rapidly from branch to branch while Irvin Dunsky lifts Judy up to a low branch, where he holds onto her. Penina then gracefully swings down in triumph, landing on her feet, while Judy begs in tears to be taken down. We have similar joyful records of many firsts—playful scenes with cousin Beatty Golden Perlstein of New Milford, Connecticut and visits to Eden Park, the zoo, and other places of interest to the children.

During the winter of 1937, Cincinnati experienced the greatest flood in half a century when the Ohio River rose thirty-two feet above its normal flood stage and flood waters covered the entire lower plateau of the city basin. Since the central gas and electric station and the city waterworks were also flooded, the entire city was plunged into darkness, drinking water had to be brought in from wells or neighboring communities, and candles and various food supplies were at a premium. The economic and social life of the city came to a halt and small boats plied many streets to rescue those who became stranded in their homes or to salvage valuables. Since one of my two offices was located in the flooded area on the corner of Pearl and Race Streets, I hired a boat to rescue some of my records and I took the children along. What was tragedy for others was excitement and thrills for the children and they have never forgotten this unusual experience. One scene that I remember was the sight of a rich man wading up to his knees in the icy flood waters to bring out a small radio from his flooded store—this may have been the only item in his merchandise-laden store that was not insured. I also recall the tragedy of a large family with small children which had lost everything and was being cared for in a public building by the Red Cross, an old lady being rescued on the shoulders of a city fireman, and small houses floating down the river. The most frightening day was Black Sunday—when the skies remained pitch-black the entire day, heavy new downpour deluged the city, and black smoke billowed in the distance from a huge conflagration in a large industrial establishment that burned out of control for several days.

In the summer of 1936, I received a letter from my sister Rivka in Serei asking my advice about her daughter Chana. In her heart-rending letter, Rivka related that Chana, who was then ten years old, had developed a serious curvature of the spine, probably as a result of a mild case of infantile paralysis. The only place they could take her for treatment was to Koenigsberg, Germany, and they were unable to take the necessary funds out of Lithuania under the existing laws. I agonized over the matter for awhile because of my awareness that it was a costly, long-range problem and that the end results were uncertain. I concluded that it might be best if Chana came to Cincinnati where I could supervise her treatment, realizing full well that it could be a permanent move. With Pupi's consent, I was about to so advise when a complication arose in the person of my cousin Julius Rabinowitz who was visiting with us from Detroit. When I told Julius of our decision, the usually cool and reserved man became greatly agitated and began to tell me in no uncertain terms that I was making a serious mistake. He argued that I was being unfair to my own family by bringing a sick child into their midst and that I would most assuredly regret my ill-conceived decision when it would be too late to change. His best advice was that I should send Rivka the necessary financial help but not remove such a young child from the care of her parents with whom she belonged. His sincerity and his arguments called for a fresh look at the problem. In the end, we concluded that, under the circumstances, our original decision was the correct one and I advised my sister accordingly.

A few months later, in September of 1936, Chana arrived in Cincinnati wearing a tag on her lapel with our name and address in large, bold letters.

Chana was a happy, beautiful, and intelligent child and she seemed to be happy as a full-fledged member of our household. With Penina and Judy as junior playmates, it did not take long for Chana to learn to speak English and to adjust to her new environment. We entrusted the care of her scoliosis to a competent orthopedist, Dr. Joseph Freiberg, who had succeeded his father as head of the Department of Orthopedics at the College of Medicine of the University of Cincinnati. Unfortunately, the state of the art in the treatment of scoliosis was in its infancy and most of the maneuvers were experimental. Chana was placed in a full body cast for an entire year and periodic manipulations were carried out to prevent further damage and to help straighten the curvature. After many years of treatment the payoff was a partial success, but only Chana knows the full range of agony and frustration she had suffered. We had a tutor come to the house to help Chana with her schooling, and as soon as she became mobile she was enrolled at the Avondale Public School and the Talmud Torah Hebrew School. She was a good student and she eventually graduated cum laude from Walnut Hills High School and the University of Cincinnati. Chana offered no special problems to the household and the children treated her like an older sister.

On a Friday night in the fall of 1937, I went to the Isaac M. Wise Temple to hear an address on the world situation by Rabbi James Heller, who had just returned from a lengthy tour of European capitals. He portrayed the chances for world peace and the outlook for European Jews in very bleak terms. "There is a unanimous opinion in the chancelleries of Europe," he related, "that World War II will break out in the fall of 1939." I immediately dispatched letters to my sister in Serei and to Pupi's mother and her married sister in Kovno, advising them to liquidate their affairs on an urgent basis and to leave Europe before it was too late. To further emphasize the seriousness of their plight, in graphic language I urged them to view their situation as if they had been struck by a sudden natural calamity and had to flee for their lives. I immediately forwarded to them all the necessary documents and affidavits of support that would facilitate their entry into the United States. Although rabid anti-Semitism was raging in Lithuania as in the rest of Europe, nobody took my warning seriously. My sister Rivka had an old mother-in-law in her nineties, which made it impossible for her family to leave. Pupi's mother chose not to leave Kovno because her youngest daughter Olga was a dental student, and Pupi's sister Leah and her husband Nahum did not relish the idea of leaving their large family for the uncertainties of a far-off land. Basically, none of them left Europe because they lulled themselves into believing that the danger was exaggerated or was at worst only transitory. In the summer of 1940, during the so-called Phony War in France, Pupi's sister Leah, together with her husband and two small sons Joseph and Reuben, did manage to escape by way of Italy, with the help of the documents I had sent them in 1937. After arriving in Cincinnati they lived with us in our Glenwood apartment for a number of months. After the inevitable period of adjustment, and after acquiring a workable knowledge of English, Nahum got a position as an accountant while Leah became a Hebrew teacher. The family established its own home in Cincinnati, where it remained for thirty-five years. Their sons graduated from the Cincinnati public schools and the University of Cincinnati to become physicians, and the entire family now resides in Los Angeles.

On May 19, 1939 our youngest child and only son was born with the usual joy and excitement that goes with such an important event. He was a handsome, dark-complected boy and Pupi's delivery went extremely well. We named our son Joseph Nahum—Joseph after Pupi's father and Nahum (comfort) from Isaiah's exhortation "Nahamu, nahamu ami—Be comforted, my people." At the time of Joseph's birth, Jews everywhere were shocked by the brutal decision of the Jew-hating British Foreign Secretary Bevin to close the gates of Palestine to further Jewish immigration. It meant the abandonment of the promise to establish a homeland for the Jewish people in Palestine. This edict, embodied in a "white paper" of the British Government, was especially onerous when European Jews were trying so desperately to escape the extermination by the Nazis and when every country in the world had closed its doors to Jewish immigration under Nazi blackmail and pressure from native anti-Semites. Immigration to Palestine was their last hope and slamming the gates of Palestine shut created a mood of grim and utter despair. Isaiah's prophecy of a great future for the Jewish people at the time of Israel's great national tragedy, when the First Temple was destroyed and Israel's sovereignty was lost, came to mind when we were naming our newborn son and we added the first word of Isaiah's prophecy to his name.

The brith a week later was an outstanding event. The two large rooms of the ritual section of the old Jewish hospital were packed with friends and well-wishers, and there was a considerable overflow outside the hospital in the sunshine of the lovely May day. The Poale Zion and our family and friends showed up in force. There were also a number of community leaders with whom I had been working for nearly a decade. Among these were Robert Senior and Morton Heldman from the Bureau of Jewish Education, Carl Pritz from the Jewish Vocational Service, and Adolph Rosenberg and Maurice Sievers representing the Federation. At the conclusion of the brith, I was exhausted from meeting all of the well-wishers and from the stiffling heat, in the absence of air conditioning.

In 1941 the Great Depression was still raging despite the numerous attempts at "pump-priming" by the Roosevelt Administration and despite the feverish activities in the armament industry. The general mood in the country was also depressed because the war was going badly for the Democracies. After sweeping everything in front of them, the Nazis were penetrating ever deeper into Russia and the Soviets were seemingly unable to stop them. Despite the deepening pessimism, Pupi and I decided to buy a home, simply because we needed roomier quarters and we were ready by now for a place we could call our own. Since few people were buying homes and many houses were for sale, we were able to buy one of the nicest houses in North Avondale at a giveaway price. It was a fairly new, twelve-room, three-story brick building, surrounded by beautiful shade trees, numerous flowering shrubs and fruit trees, and a spacious lawn, flower beds, and gardens. The interior of the house was artfully decorated, and expensive drapes and fine Persian carpets came with the house. The house also had many modern conveniences including a twenty-four-cubic-foot built-in refrigerator, built-in vacuum outlets in every room, two furnaces, an incinerator, clothes chutes, and five bathrooms. There was also a spacious screened porch with bamboo furniture and leather cushions. The house was ready for immediate occupancy.

We moved into our new home on December 1, 1941. On December 7th, at about one o'clock in the afternoon as we were arranging our furniture, the radio blared out the shocking news that the Japanese had attacked Pearl Harbor and that the United States was now at war with Japan, Germany, and Italy. A new era began with feverish universal mobilization of manpower and an intensive increase in war production. I volunteered for the war effort along with many other physicians, but as an industrial physician I was declared essential to industry on the homefront. During the four years of the war I volunteered three times, but each time was declared ineligible on the same grounds that I was needed in industry. The fact that I was the father of three small children may also have played a part.

The war years were years of hard work, many personal tragedies, a great deal of uncertainty about the outcome of the war, many shortages, and numerous patriotic and civic activities in support of the war effort. At the same time, there were nagging worries compounded about the fate of our families in Europe and the other Jews there. The victorious end of the war brought a great deal of joy and relief, but also a great deal of anguish and consternation at the horrible cost in human lives and the Holocaust.

During the years that followed the war the girls completed their high school education and graduated from college. Upon graduation from Walnut Hills High School, Penina attended the Tyler School of Fine Art in Philadelphia as a scholarship student through her sophomore year. She then attended the University of Cincinnati before completing and receiving her B.S. degree in

Art Education from New York University. Since graduation Penina has taught art and participated in numerous exhibits of her paintings and batiks. She has sold a considerable number of her works. Judy attended Brandeis University in Massachusetts for one year before she also attended the University of Cincinnati, and graduated cum laude from the College of the Pacific in Stockton, California with a B.A. degree in Art. In 1980 she returned to the University of Cincinnati to receive her Master's degree. Judy has done some painting but her main interest is in her continued study of the history and value of art objects.

As our daughters grew up to become young ladies and later young women, they began to resemble each other to such a remarkable degree that our friends would frequently mistake one for the other. They developed, however, into two distinct personalities. Penina inherited the sweetness of her great-grandfather Avremel Sereisky and became a relaxed, compassionate, well-organized person with a concern for people as her strong point. Judy inherited the sharpness and wit of her grandmother Basheva and her great-grandmother

Family gathering at Penina and Naftali's wedding on January 28, 1951. Left to right: Seated: Leah Marmet, the author, Pupi and Nahum Marmet. Standing: Judy, Joseph Marmet, Joseph Schulzinger, Penina and Naftali Frankel, Olga Horwitz, Herschel Horwitz and Reuben Marmet. Chana was living in Israel at the time.

Chana Dunsky-Sereisky and became a dynamic, creative person with a major interest in Jewish Art and in educational and social activities. Despite these personality differences, our daughters still greatly resemble one another.

Penina and Judy were both married after their sophomore year in college. The wedding ceremony of Penina to Naftali Frankel took place in the living room of our home in front of the fireplace in the presence of some ninety guests. The beautiful bride walked down the regal, winding staircase with its thick Persian carpet, on the arms of Pupi and myself. Rabbi Fishel Goldfeder (Conservative) conducted the wedding service, Rabbi Samuel Wohl (Reform) addressed the young couple in Hebrew, and Cantor Emil Rosen chanted the Sheva Brahot (Seven Benedictions) in his beautiful tenor voice. At one point during the ceremony, it appeared as if the cantor was about to spill some wine on the carpet. Unceremoniously, Pupi reached for a saucer and handed it to the cantor, but he did not want to be disturbed during his artistry. Equally unceremoniously, he grabbed the saucer and clanged it down on the mantle. It was all done very deftly and in good humor and it added to the informality of the home environment.

After the ceremony the guests were seated for dinner in the dining room, living room, and the enclosed porch adjoining the living room. With an abundance of musical talent on both sides of the family, the festivities lasted until 2 A.M. In addition to many beautiful songs by Cantor Rosen, other solos and group singing followed in an uninterrupted succession. Towards the end of the festivities when Cantor Rosen was asked for more renditions, he begged off faintly by chanting, "Four martinis, three manhattans, how much more can I do?" The outdoors had a beauty all its own on that late Sunday afternoon on January 28, 1951. A sudden freeze during a heavy rain had covered the streets with a sheet of ice, and the numerous trees surrounding our home sported hundreds of glistening icicles from their branches. The next day, Penina and Naftali left for New York on their honeymoon and to complete their studies. Penina graduated from N.Y.U. and Naftali graduated from Juilliard and Columbia University, where he received a Ph.D. in Musicology.

Naftali had come to the United States from Israel at the age of nine, just before the outbreak of World War II. He came on one of the last boats out of Eretz Yisroel, together with his parents—Rabbi Joshua and Pearl Frankel, his twin brother—(Rabbi) Reuven Frankel, and sisters Esther (Davis), Dvora (Friend), and Yaffa (Flitterman). He is a fifth-generation descendant of Hungarian Orthodox Jewish settlers in Old Jerusalem and Safed, with a strong family tradition of Jewish learning and cantorial music. The family emigrated to the U.S. after their hostelry was destroyed during the 1937 Arab riots in Jaffa. In 1953 Penina and Naftali returned from New York to make their permanent home in Cincinnati, where Penina gave birth to three children—Bennett Zion (named for my cousin Ben Zion Doll) Steven, and Deena. Although Naftali is engaged in business, music is a continuing avocation and he has conducted choral groups and religious services and has written many original compositions which have been performed over the years. One of his most popular compositions, based on the text from the "Song of Songs" "I am asleep but my heart is awake (ani y'sheina v'libbe eir)," was first rendered at his wedding by Cantor Rosen. His most recent composition is a Friday evening service which was first performed at our granddaughter Deena's Bat Mitzvah in 1979. He also wrote selections for the services for the Bar Mitzvah of their two sons Bennett and Steven. Penina and Naftali met at the Hebrew educational camp Massad, where Naftali was music director and Penina was arts counselor. They now have two grandsons, David and Phillip Frankel.

The wedding of Judy to Stanley Lucas took place on May 4, 1953 in Cincinnati's beautiful Pavilion Caprice at the Netherland Plaza Hotel. There were some three hundred guests and for the first and only time in Cincinnati's history the wedding ceremony was conducted by three distinguished Rabbis representing the Orthodox, Conservative, and Reform branches of American Jewry. Rabbi Eliezer Silver, Rabbi Fishel J. Goldfeder, and Rabbi Samuel Wohl walked down three separate aisles and they joined under the hupah to conduct the marriage ceremony. Cantor Rosen chanted the Sheva Brahot and each of the Rabbis conducted a portion of the Service. Judy walked down the aisle on the arms of Pupi and myself and she attracted everyone's attention with her radiancy and beauty. A reception and a sumptuous dinner followed and there was again some solo and group singing, but the formal atmosphere and the large audience did not lend itself to the abandon and spontaneity of Penina's wedding. It was a very happy and beautiful event and it was the talk of the town for months to come. Following their wedding, Judy and Stanley left for Stockton, California, where Stanley was stationed as a member of the U.S. Air Force and where Judy completed her studies. From California they went to Alaska for a year and Stanley completed his tour of duty there. They then returned to Cincinnati to live and to raise their family of five children— Barbara, Danny, Betsy, Marvin, and Ronna.

Stanley was born in Cincinnati, the youngest of three children of Ruby (Schaen) and Morris Lucas. His brother, Dr. Melvin Lucas, is an anesthesiologist and his sister, Mimi, is married to Julian Moskowitz, a wholesaler in metals. Stanley graduated from the Cincinnati College of Medicine at the age of twenty-one and served a three-year residency in radiology there. Since his graduation, Stanley has established an enviable reputation for himself as a radiologist, as an active member of organized medicine, as president of the Cincinnati Academy of Medicine, and as a man of compassion and sterling character. By coincidence, Stanley's father had come to Cincinnati from Lazdei and Pupi and I knew his family there. They were fine, upright people who succumbed in the Holocaust. A maternal grandfather of Stanley's uncle Eli Harris came to Cincinnati from Serei at the turn of the century and was known as Eliyahu Ben Eliezer Suchovolsky.

Chana's wedding to Morton Rosen took place in mid-summer of 1959 and the ceremony was conducted on the spacious terrace of our home, surrounded by flowering shrubs, fruit trees, and the beautiful gardens cultivated and nurtured by Pupi's magic touch. Rabbi Fishel Goldfeder and Cantor Emil Rosen officiated under the hupah in the presence of some seventy guests, and there was a great deal of solo and group singing following the nuptial dinner. Chana and Mort settled in New York before moving to Hartford, Connecticut and then to Chicago. They were divorced in 1974 and they have one son, Avram, a charming and bright young man of college age named for Chana's only brother, who died in the Holocaust. After many years as a high school teacher in Israel, New York, and Chicago, and after years as a leader and organizer for Habonim youth groups, Chana now holds an important position as the Midwest Regional Director of the United Synagogue of America. She is well regarded in this position and she has many achievements to her credit.

The education and development of our son Joseph proceeded apace and he was a constant source of pride and joy to us. He was an excellent student, a well-mannered and disciplined boy, and he grew to be a good-looking and happy young man. Like his older sisters, Joseph attended Hebrew school daily throughout his undergraduate years at public school, as well as the Massad summer camp. Joseph also spent many hours at the piano under the tutelage of Miss Gertrude Englander, who was also the teacher of James (Jimmy) Levine, the present maestro of the Metropolitan Opera of New York. According to his teacher, "Joseph is musically talented and with hard work he can become a fine pianist." In preparation for his Bar Mitzvah, Cantor Rosen came to the house twice a week and he tutored Joseph in the cantillations for the haftorah (reading from the Prophets) while accompanying himself at the piano. The cantor, who was a superb artist, enjoyed the lessons as much as Joseph and the rest of us. Joseph's Bar Mitzvah was a singularly happy occasion, with many out-of-town guests and a capacity attendance at the sanctuary of the Adath Israel Congregation. Rabbi Goldfeder, Cantor Rosen, and Joseph all performed admirably.

After the Bar Mitzvah, Pupi and I took Joseph on a cruise on the Queen

Judy and Stanley Lucas and their family at Ronna's Bat Mitzvah in 1980. From left to right: Betsy, Danny, Judy, Ronna, Stanley, Barbara and Marvin.

Penina and Naftali Frankel and their family in 1979 on the occasion of Deena's Bat Mitzvah. From left to right: Bennett, Terry, the author, Pupi, Penina, Naftali, Deena and Steve.

The author's niece Chana Rosen and
her son Avram at the time of his Bar
Mitzvah in 1975.

Mary to Europe and then to Israel. Since the trip involved missing several
weeks from school, we obtained permission from the principal on the basis of
recommendations from his teachers and his outstanding scholastic record.
One of the teachers, after praising Joseph's unusual qualities, closed her letter
with "What have you done to deserve such a fine, perceptive boy?" The
five-week overseas holiday was one continuous saga of pleasure and wonder-
ment. We enjoyed the luxuries of the ocean liner, we played shuffleboard and
other games, and we were fascinated by the boundless ocean vista and the
sparkling waves of the summer sea. We also enjoyed meeting some interesting
people, including the former Governor of New York Herbert Lehman, and we
were captivated by the sights and museums of Paris, Switzerland, and Rome
and by three stimulating weeks in Israel. In Israel Joseph was especially
excited about the historical sights, the kibbutzim, Jerusalem, Tel Aviv, and
Haifa, and he enjoyed the fuss that everyone made over him—especially my
parents who had never seen him. While in Jerusalem, Joseph spent a great deal
of time in the company of Zvi Druyan, a brilliant youngster his own age and
the son of my cousin Chana and Dr. Avram Druyan. The two went to sports
events and talked a great deal about the merits of their respective countries
and other subjects of interest. Joseph never forgot this trip and we all
mourned, several years later, the tragic accidental death of Zvi while he was
serving in the Israeli Army.

Joseph graduated from Walnut Hills High School with honors and was
accepted by Harvard, Yale, and Dartmouth. Although he was accepted at
Dartmouth as the most promising freshman of the year, Joseph chose to
enroll as a pre-medical student at Yale. He completed his freshman year at
Yale with a straight A record and enrolled at Harvard for the summer to get

the required course in physics out of the way. He received an A in physics and, after a month of leisure at home, returned to Yale for his sophomore year. Joseph's second year at Yale was a complete disaster. He became depressed and apathetic and his grades plummeted from A's to B's to barely passing. He reluctantly returned to Yale for his junior year, even though the summer's rest seemed to have done him some good. We soon began to receive calls from Joseph intimating that he would like to drop out of school for a year. We considered this option carefully, but after consulting with psychiatrists we could not reach a satisfactory conclusion. From a psychiatric point of view, we were told that if he dropped out of school he might never go back and that it might be better for his mental health if he kept motivated and busy. From a practical standpoint "dropping out" of school was rare in those days and was certain to ruin his academic record.

While we were searching our souls for an answer, we received a call from the master of Joseph's residence hall that made up our minds for us. He advised us to come to New Haven and take Joseph home. Pupi and I found Joseph pacing up and down his small room, greatly agitated and depressed. Our world collapsed with the full realization of the depth of our tragedy. We spoke to all of Joseph's teachers and they had nothing but praise for him and deep sympathy over his illness. We learned that he had been a patient at the psychiatric clinic of the university for several months and that he could return to Yale any time he felt he could carry the load. On our way home we stopped off in New York to attend the wedding of my cousin Dr. Irvin Dunsky to Clare Gerber. Pupi thought that the festivities and the company of well-wishing family might do Joseph some good and Joseph agreed to attend the wedding with us. But the relief was transient and we had to leave early and return home. Besides the overwhelming grief, we were also overcome by a sense of guilt and shame which neither of us was able to alleviate through free and open ventilation. No one at the wedding ventured to talk to us about Joseph's illness, but it was evident that they all knew. The prevailing view at that time was that emotional stress or situational factors were the major underlying causes of aberrant behavior. The accepted mode of treatment was psychotherapy and the use of psychotropic drugs was as yet experimental and was generally frowned upon.

As soon as we returned to Cincinnati, I consulted with Dr. Maurice Levine, the Professor and Director of Psychiatry at the University of Cincinnati and a recognized authority. He recommended one of his top associates as a therapist and Joseph soon began to improve under his care, with long periods of remissions and occasional relapses. During this period Joseph improved sufficiently to get his B.A. degree from the University of Cincinnati. He

Joseph at eighteen.

subsequently held positions at the library of the Hebrew Union College and the main city library, but it was evident that the long-term outlook was not promising.

In 1965 I received an invitation to conduct a seminar on the accident syndrome at the annual meeting of the American Psychiatric Association in Atlantic City. I accepted the invitation in the hope of gaining new insight into the state of the art from a cross section of experts. I learned that, although the field was still dominated by the psychoanalytical school, there were now some grave doubts about its efficacy as a therapeutic tool. I also learned that some psychiatrists were becoming more tolerant of drug therapy in emotional illness. At several specialty seminars I learned that mental illness could be due to certain biochemical deficiencies or imbalances, to disturbances in hormonal transmission of neurologic impulses, or to impairments on a cellular level. There was a strong feeling in these groups that further progress in the treatment of mental illness would evolve from biochemical and biological research and from the increased use of psychotropic drugs.

Dr. Sigmund Freud, the founder of modern psychology, originally conceived of human behavior in purely psychological terms. Later on he concluded that aberrant human behavior would eventually have to be understood in terms of disordered metabolism. Yet the psychoanalytical school virtually pre-empted the field of psychiatry for half a century and drug therapy, which miraculously emptied the mental hospitals several years hence, was then given short shrift. Mental illness is now under vigorous scientific attack by blocking the excessive output of such neuronal mediators as norepinephrin, serotorin, dopamine, and by the correction of deficiencies in some of the trace metals, etc. Thus another human scourge is slowly yielding to the concerted efforts of science.

During spare time at the convention, I discussed Joseph's illness with my classmate Dr. Douglas Goldman, who was board certified in internal medicine, psychiatry, and laboratory medicine. He was experienced in all three fields, had served for two decades as staff physician at the Cincinnati Longview Hospital for Mental Illness, and was committed to the use of psychotropic drugs. Dr. Goldman had written extensively on the subject while most psychiatrists were still vehemently opposed to drug therapy. He offered to treat Joseph with some of the newer drugs and I agreed to try this mode of therapy since by now Joseph had refused to participate in further psychotherapy, which he regarded as worthless. The drug therapy improved Joseph's condition but there were some undesirable side effects and occasional relapses.

In December of 1966, Joseph's condition was evaluated by the Chief Psychiatric Researcher at the Cincinnati College of Medicine and he was pronounced fully recovered. Shortly thereafter Joseph went with Pupi and me to Florida for a rest in the sun. He was subdued most of the time and he often wandered off by himself for long walks, returning with blisters on his heels. We returned home January 1st, but Joseph stayed in bed most of the week, alert but moody. On Sunday, January 8, 1967, I spent several hours at his bedside in an effort to dispel the gloom. We covered a variety of subjects and it seemed that he was getting more placid and at peace with himself. At six o'clock that evening, Pupi and I left for the monthly dinner party of a group of doctors and their wives, at the home of our good friends Dr. Nathan and Mary Kursban. Two hours later we were urgently summoned home to learn that Joseph had ended his life.

Although we had lived with a sense of foreboding for six years, there was nothing in the entire history of Joseph's illness to suggest the possibility of suicide. Being aware of such a danger during periods of depression, I had questioned Joseph's physicians closely about any clues to such an eventuality, but was reassured that no such clues existed. Our world crumbled before our very eyes and the rest of the family felt totally and completely crushed. Within minutes Rabbi and Mrs. Goldfeder and all of our intimate friends came pouring in and they remained with us the greater part of the night doing their best to share our grief and to bring us a measure of comfort. The next morning we received a message which Joseph had mailed just prior to his desperate act. In this beautiful and heart-rending poem, Joseph describes his suffering and anguish over many years, his great love for us and the rest of the family, and he expresses the hope that in time we will understand and forgive and find comfort in his solace.

Take Comfort From My Solace

All life is not beauty, sunshine, and grace.
How can the poets sing of this for all man
Because it is here and now to some—
Others were not given the ingredients to judge it so.
To them it was not the sunshine of a bright new day,
But only the brilliance to show up the other bigger
Blight of their own shortcomings.
So is it not a better world of darkness hiding the
Horror of inner doubt and despair?
Could it not be the soft, gentle lull of stillness and peace
So long sought after and finally known?
This, then, is my solace to you my parents,
Even tho' you cannot understand
And grieve my going from you in body.
Believe me, please believe me,
I have longed for this peace and welcome its quiet oblivion.
As you have always taught me, "Seek your own way and be
Happy therein"—I have done this for myself without wanting
To hurt you my beloved parents and family. I only thought of
My own needs. Take solace in this—I am now at peace.

In time we did find a measure of solace in the memories of the many beautiful experiences we had shared with Joseph prior to his illness, in the love of our daughters and their families, and in the cordial understanding of our friends. An expression of sympathy that was greatly appreciated came from a good friend and highly respected historian, Dr. Jacob Radar Marcus, who had suffered the loss of an only child. After the customary condolences, he took me aside and said: "Morris, you will undoubtedly ponder about what you had done that was wrong and whether you could have prevented this tragedy had you done this or that. Well, don't! Matters like this are beyond our knowledge or understanding." Another friend and former teacher of mine, Dr. Hiram B. Weiss, who had also lost a young child, spoke in a similar vein. Common wisdom says that time heals all wounds and to the extent possible our deep wound has now healed. I often think of Joseph, of the pleasure he brought us, about a stray humorous remark of his, and occasional philosophical detours, about the bane of excessive pride. Occasionally I will re-read some of his lyrical and sensitive poems or I will go back to his textbooks on philosophy, literature, or poetry and try to get some additional clues to his being from his marginal notes or underlined passages. In retrospect, there seems to be a preoccupation with death in some of these—perhaps it began with the onset of his illness—there is no way of knowing for sure. In such moments I like to reflect on the words of Emerson on the loss of a young child: "He has seen but half of the universe who has never been shown the house of pain."

Our daughters Penina and Judy and their husbands Naftali and Stanley and our eight grandchildren were all a great source of strength and comfort to us during the days and months that followed. Happy occasions then came in rapid succession, such as Bar Mitzvahs, Bat Mitzvahs, birthdays, graduations, the marriage of our oldest grandson Bennett Zion Frankel to Terry Arenburg, the birth of our two great grandsons David and Phillip, and the joyous family gatherings on holidays. We also took frequent tours to Israel and to other parts of the world, and we gradually returned to our normal range of activities. Yet our permanent hurt remains.

In the larger scheme of things, the inexorable rhythm of life continues apace with little regard to hurts or detours. Our adolescent grandchildren have passed through the anti-culture revolution of the late Sixties and early Seventies relatively unscathed. Our oldest grandchildren, Bennett and Barbara, are groping for their niche in the business world. Danny has graduated from medical school and is embarking on his training in radiology, and the other grandchildren are at various stages of study on the high school and college levels.

In the summer of 1976, our children decided to celebrate our fiftieth wedding anniversary and they outdid themselves in making it a grand and memorable event. They enlarged to poster size photographs of Pupi and myself at various periods of our married life; they prepared and decorated the tables in good taste and subtle artistry; the cuisine was plentiful and tasty, and they took care of every little detail. There was even a small combo to entertain the several hundred local and out-of-town guests who came to share in our celebration. The beautiful affair was held on a bright Sunday afternoon, on June 13th, in the spacious gardens of our children Judy and Stanley, with a large tent for shade or shelter in the event of rain. Pupi looked stunningly beautiful in her new white floral chiffon dress, and the event culminated on a very happy note.

The festivities actually began at the Adath Israel Synagogue on the preceding Sabbath morning when I conducted the Shaharit service and read the Maftir, after which Pupi, myself, and the children greeted the congregation at a Kiddush. Inspired by the solemnity of the occasion, I wrote a group of poems—some thirty in all—which eventually led to the writing of this volume. The poems began with an ode to Pupi and included poems dedicated to each of our grandchildren, a few poems dedicated to other members of the family, and several poems on general topics. These were read at a family gathering on Saturday evening at a festive dinner held "for family only" at the home of our children Penina and Naftali. Some of the thoughts expressed at this milestone in our lives were then summarized in a set of pithy maxims for the family, even as my father and grandfather had done before me:

Our cultural heritage is our greatest possession; to the faithful the benefits are generous and secure.

America and Israel are humanity's best hope, both are attuned to the wisdom of the ages and the multitude.

Decency, like fresh air, is not exclusive to any region, people, or creed.

A smile, a kind word, a good deed are the least costly things in life, and they should be generously distributed.

Optimism and self-confidence are great qualities, but every good general has a back-up position.

He is happy who is content.

The glory of achievement is transient while the joy of dreaming and striving is forever.

The young should learn from the old and the old retain the trust and resilience of the young.

Let fidelity and truth be your guidelines—unsavory gains are a net loss.

Change is the staff of life, it works best in small portions.

Pupi

There were orchards and meadows
And forests and lakes
And all the things it takes
To learn and know,
To develop and grow.

There was the heder, the rebbe,
The shtetl, the kloise—
The warmth and beauty of a Jewish house
And devotion to all that was ours.

It was a compassionate world,
Devout, honest, and true.
These were the things we knew
When you and I were born and grew.

I was eighteen
And you a mere child
When the two of us met
At a gymnasium event.

Our love blossomed,
Deepened, and welled
Into a bond meant to abide—
Neither distance nor time could divide.

Your exquisite beauty
Cheered many a heart—
Character, talent,
Devotion to duty
Gave inner dimension
To your beauty.

194 THE TALE OF A LITVAK

You built our home on solid foundations—
Hospitality, friendship, resolve, and devotion.
Our lovely children seldom were told,
They simply grew up in the very same mold.

Your holiday tables—artistic creations,
Your colorful gardens show infinite care.
These and other perfections
Are delights beyond compare.

Through the turbulent decades
We shared many joys
And anguish too.
Now it is time to pause
And give thanks—
For all the blessings we knew.

And as we approach our fading hours,
May we add hope
To the serenity that is ours—
For balmy skies
And soft horizons.

June 15, 1976
On our fiftieth wedding anniversary

CHAPTER THREE

The Melting Pot

"Be to her virtues very kind,
Be to her faults a little blind."
(Prior)ˑ

Most American Jews originated in Eastern Europe and came to the U.S. during the thirty-three-year period between 1881 and 1914. It was the greatest mass migration in Jewish history and, with the twenty million other immigrants from Eastern Europe during the same period, was a significant event in the history of the United States. At the beginning of this historic date, there were only three hundred thousand Jews in America, of whom forty thousand had come from Russia. The mass influx of two million Eastern European Jews profoundly changed the shape of American Jewry.

Who went to America and who did not go? The answer lies in the history of Czarist Russia of that period. In 1845, when Czar Alexander II ascended to the throne, he embarked on an heroic effort to pull Russia out of the morass of illiteracy, superstition, and economic backwardness. He freed the serfs and introduced many liberal reforms that began to move the country towards Westernization. Russian Jews played an important part in these efforts and they were rewarded with economic and civic betterment, the encouragement of public enlightenment, and the liberalization of Jewish life. After the assassination of Czar Alexander II by a group of revolutionary terrorists, Czar Alexander III reverted to the brutal, repressive policies of Czar Nicholas I with special vengeance towards the Jews. In the wake of these policies came a wave of savage pogroms, severe economic repressions, political disenfranchisement, and crude anti-Semitic vilifications that left Russian Jewry dazed, dispirited, and hopeless.

Under these extreme circumstances and with the spreading legendary tales about the land of opportunity, freedom, and tolerance beyond the ocean, the hazardous option of emigrating to America took hold and the stampede to get out of Russia began. At first went the young unmarried males, then followed the young girls and the newlyweds, and lastly those with large families. As soon as these immigrants saved a few dollars, they sent for their wives and children and they helped their brothers, sisters, parents, and other relatives to come to America. Especially prominent among those who ventured to come were the poor, the artisans, the economically disadvantaged, the socially deprived, and the disillusioned socialists, anarchists, revolutionaries, liberals, and intellectuals. The latter groups were stunned when their counterparts among the Gentiles joined in the vicious Czarist campaign against the Jews. Belatedly it dawned on them that it mattered not what kind of a Jew one was, the bias and the hatred were the same. Yet most Russian Jews did not leave. Those who remained were, in the main, the wealthy, the economically rooted, the men with large families, and most of the pious and the learned. These groups preferred to weather the storm rather than face a perilous journey to the unknown. The pious were also deterred by the difficulties in observing the Sabbath and kashrut (dietary laws) in what they called the treifene medina (non-kosher country).

New waves of mass exodus from Russia began with the Kishinev Pogrom of 1903 and the pogroms that followed the attempted revolution of 1905 and the loss of the war with Japan. This time large numbers of observant Jews joined in the exodus. By then the religious leaders had perceived that the growing American Jewish community was in need of traditional religious guidance and they cautiously began to encourage trusted young Rabbis and yeshiva students to emigrate to the United States. It may be of interest to note that my father and my uncles Hatzkel Krutzel (Rabinowitz), Mordechai Yosel Krutzel (Rabinowitz), Yacov Leib Schulzinger, and Rabbi Meir Levy did not encounter any job difficulties while adhering to traditional Judaism when they came to the United States. The same experience was shared by many others who were determined to remain observant Jews.

The cost of the ocean crossings and the immediate needs of the immigrants were often covered by the Hebrew Immigration Aid Society (HIAS) or by relatives who had arrived earlier. When they reached New York or Philadelphia, the new immigrants were encouraged by the Jewish leaders to disperse throughout the country, and the local Jewish communities fully cooperated in this effort. When they arrived at their final destination, the immigrants were taken in hand by relatives, landsleit, or the local Jewish agencies, and they were helped to get started. Not all of them were able to make it—some succumbed to illness while others needed public support when they lost their jobs or when economic conditions were bad. The established Jewish agencies acquitted themselves admirably on such occasions, except for a certain ambivalence which somewhat dimmed their efforts. The patronizing attitude of the benefactors often irritated and humiliated the new immigrants and they resented it. The social workers forgot the injunction of Hillel, "Do unto others as you would have them do unto you." Or, as Thoreau phrased it, "If you give money, spend yourself with it; do not merely abandon it to them."

Other irritants were some of the Americanization programs and the wholesale liquidation or absorption of the intimate self-help societies of the new immigrants. In the name of "efficiency" the established philanthropic agencies smothered most of the societies which the new immigrants brought with them from Serei and Vilna, and in the name of "Americanization" they often fostered a repugnant "de-Judaization" in the centers and clubs for immigrants.

The new arrivals were anxious to start working as soon as possible so that they could help the loved ones they had left behind. Many began practicing the trades they had brought with them, others sought work in the factories—usually in the needle trade—or they became peddlers and freelance entrepreneurs. In 1921, many Jewish immigrants were still working in factories, especially in the larger cities. Over the years they knew hunger, illness, loneliness, layoffs, lockouts, and the afflictions of the sweatshop and political laissez-faire attitudes. Many Jewish immigrants plunged into the struggle against the evils of the sweatshops, especially the low pay, child labor, excessively long hours, the six-day work week and the unsafe working conditions. Some of the best labor organizations in the U.S. were founded and led by Jewish immigrants, such as the Amalgamated Clothing Workers Union, the International Ladies Garment Workers Union, and the American Federation of Labor—which were headed by Sidney Hillman, David Dubinsky, and Samuel Gompers respectively. Occasionally the Jewish leadership was called upon to mediate between Jewish employers and their Jewish employees. As the acculturation and economic integration matured, the Americanized children of the immigrants began to expand their parents' businesses and to penetrate other areas of endeavor that were open to Jews. Eventually, relatively few Jews remained in the labor movement—except, perhaps, in some of the larger cities.

Exactly four decades after the Jewish mass immigration from Russia began, I could not help but notice that all was not well with my fellow Jews. At Shachnes Shul I had a chance to observe a fairly large sample of first- and second-generation Jewish Americans who, like myself, hailed from Eastern Europe. I was shocked by what I perceived as an unbridgeable gap between the young and the old. The parents, although Americanized in appearance, actually continued the way of life they practiced in Europe. They were hardworking and frugal, they transplanted to America the institutions they knew back home, and they adhered in the main to their old customs and traditions. Even the more assimilated German Jews, who had arrived some fifty years earlier, still clung to important Jewish traditions and kept their places of business closed on Rosh Hashanah and Yom Kippur—and some even on the Sabbath. The young, on the other hand, seemed to be neither fish nor fowl. Their so-called "Americanization" appeared to me to be gross and superficial and their interest in Jewish religious or cultural matters seemed tenuous at best.

In 1921, the U.S. melting-pot ideal that all immigrants be transformed in the image of WASPs still reigned supreme and most American Jews tried to follow suit. But to the children of the new immigrants "Americanization," as far as I could see, meant chewing gum, the comics, baseball, vulgar language, and deculturalization. Some were even ashamed of their immigrant parents with their funny customs and accents, their "antiquated" religious practices, and their "worthless" cultural baggage. Fortunately, the first-generation Jewish Americans were still in the majority, most of them prospered, and many were able to stand their own ground. In practically no time at all, the erstwhile peddlers and sweatshop workers became storekeepers, landlords, or small manufacturers. They began to acquire or build comfortable homes and they began to build or expand synagogues and other institutions. In Cincinnati, they started to move from the downtown West End to suburban Avondale— and forty years hence to large plots in Amberley Village. Father and I were caught up in the mass migration to Avondale and we moved in with my cousins Moshe Meir and Goldie Dunsky on Prospect Place.

Despite their economic achievements, many of the Jews I met were a dispirited lot. They understood the high price they were paying for their material well-being in terms of estrangement from Judaism and their own children. From the vulgar and cruel attitudes of the young towards their own parents, I knew that my foreign accent and diction would remain an object of ridicule for years to come. So I clammed up and avoided close contact with most of the younger people I encountered. My background had prepared me for a society in which discussions on literary subjects, social problems, Zionism, or religious matters were normal fare. I was shocked to discover that broaching cultural subjects at social gatherings was considered bad manners and that conversations largely revolved around sports, business matters, a variety of trivia, and crude jokes.

The Jewish immigrants did not waste any time entering the mainstream of American life and they did it with relish and enthusiasm. Those who could spare the time went to night school to learn English and they applied for their American citizenship with pride and seldom failed to vote in an election. Election Day was considered a semi-holiday and they would dress up in their finest clothes to exercise their voting rights. It took many decades, however, before they became convinced that they were truly full-fledged members of the "land of the free and the home of the brave" on equal terms with the native Americans. It took even longer for them to appreciate their political strength and importance as a sizeable, important, ethnic minority. The emergence of these feelings of strength coincided with the birth of the State of Israel and matured during the Sixties.

A source of great concern to American Jews was the economic and social discrimination to which they were being subjected and the thinly veiled anti-Semitism that pervaded large segments of American society. Much of the anti-Jewish bias was related to the simultaneous wave of Gentile immigrants from Eastern Europe where anti-Semitism was endemic. It was also fanned by the frequent financial panics for which the Jews were often blamed by one hate-mongering group or another. A great deal of that hate, undoubtedly, had its roots in the religious dogmas of such important church groups as the Catholics, Presbyterians, Lutherans, and some Southern fundamentalists. In the Twenties and Thirties, Jews were still being stereotyped as shylocks, sharpies, and cheats and the "Jew comedians" on the vaudeville stage helped perpetuate the myth. To deal with these problems, several defense and public relations organizations were founded. Among these were the Anti-Defamation League of B'nai B'rith, the American Jewish Committee, the American Jewish Congress, and the Jewish Labor Committee. The Reform movement made public relations with church groups and the clergy an important part of their program.

In 1921 and again in 1924, the U.S. Congress enacted the most restrictive immigration laws in American history. These laws brought to an end the open-door policy on immigration and effectively ended the period of mass immigration of Eastern European Jews to the United States. They also marked the end of an era in many other ways. Henceforth, American Jews had to develop their own cultural resources as they could no longer rely on new waves of immigrants to reinvigorate their religious and cultural needs. The American melting-pot ideal died slowly and it is only in recent decades that it has been replaced by the more acceptable concept of cultural pluralism which calls on every ethnic group to contribute its best towards the common good. How did my family fare as it passed through the crucible of fire that was the melting pot?

Of my mother's immediate family nearly all emigrated to the U.S., while on my father's side, half came to America and the other half went to Eretz Yisroel. My oldest uncle, Hatzkel Krutzel, came to New York in 1899 together with his thirteen-year-old son, Harry. Both worked in the sweatshops of the needle trade and, in 1904, Cousin Chaye Gitel (Ida) joined them in New York. In 1910, after eleven years in the U.S., Uncle Hatzkel returned to his home-town, Suchovolia, Poland, and never came back to America. Major factors in this decision were the refusal of Tante Henie Rochel to join him in the treifene medina and her aversion to part from her widowed daughter, Yudit, and her four young children. Eventually, four of Uncle Hatzkel's six children and two of Yudit's children—Sander and Shleimke Prebell (Pribulsky)—came to the U.S., while his youngest daughter, Chana (Druyan), and Yudit's daughters, Chanele (Steinberg) and Valia (Yanovsky), settled in Israel. Uncle Hatzkel, Tante Henie Rochel, and Cousin Yudit all perished in the Holocaust.

Cousin Harry Rabinowitz (Krutzel), the second son of Hatzkel and Henie Rochel, eventually became a high-priced designer of ladies dresses in New York and he pursued this profession all his life. He was a mild-mannered, good-hearted, charitable man and was unusually handsome. His sunny out-look never changed despite some unfortunate marriages. Upon retirement, he made Aliya (emigrated) to Israel and died at the age of eighty-six in Jerusalem at the home of his youngest sister, Chana Druyan. He left one son.

Cousin Ida (Chaye Gitel) came to the U.S. as a young girl and she worked at low wages in a blouse factory because she did not have to work on the Sabbath. She adjusted readily to her new environment and in 1908 she married Harry Golden, a landsman who was much older than herself. Chaye Gitel was an outgoing, warm, and witty brunette and was greatly admired by all who knew her. Her home was open to relatives at all times and she became the matriarch of the family. Her husband, Harry Golden, was born in Luna, Poland near Suchovolia and came to the U.S. in the 1880s. He landed in Kingston, New York and began earning a living as an itinerant peddler. He later opened a store in Great Barrington, Massachusetts, and when his store burned down he moved to New Milford, Connecticut, where his brothers had settled earlier. He was a quiet, pleasant, pipe-smoking man who, between sales, leisurely exchanged yarns with his farmer customers all day long. Mr. Goldin was related to the Rabbi of Serei, Reb Yisroel Goldin. The Goldins had four children—Anne (Mrs. Norman Dube), Alfred, Beatrice (Beatty Perlstein), and Sybil (Cohen). The Goldins mingled well in the rural community and they were well liked by their non-Jewish neighbors and customers. Their son-in-law, Norman Dube, served with distinction for many years as Judge of the Superior Court of Connecticut.

Cousin Eva (Chavke) Allen-Cherow, whom I had known and loved since I was a child of six, was a compassionate, out-going, caring person. She was especially interested in the aged, the afflicted, and the very young, and, like her mother Henie Rochel, she was always ready to be of help with a kind word and with her limited means. Eva came to New York in 1913 and she worked in a sweatshop for several years. In 1918 she married Isadore Allen (Chalen) of Pontiac, Michigan, a landsman from Halinke. Isadore came to the U.S. in 1912 and joined his father in the scrap metal business. The couple were introduced by Charlie Sayer (Sereisky), whom I knew as a child in Halinke. After less than two years of marriage, Isadore died in 1919 during the Spanish flu epidemic and Eva was left to her own resources—a widow with a one-year-old daughter to raise and in dire financial straits. She struggled valiantly for twenty years trying to raise her daughter Adele in comfort and dignity. During this period she supported herself at first by peddling and later by helping raise orphaned children. In 1940, Eva remarried. Her second husband was Jacob Cherow, a prosperous widower and a childhood sweetheart from Suchovolia with whom she enjoyed a good life for twenty-five years. After the death of her second husband in 1964, Eva made aliya to Israel in 1970 and she died in 1972 in Jerusalem at the home of her youngest sister, Chana Druyan. Adele, Eva's only child, inherited most of her mother's lovely traits. She married Harmon Bayer, a consulting engineer, and they raised a family of four. One of their sons, Eddie, is a scientist at the Weitzman Institute.

Cousin Yudel Krutzel was in his middle thirties when he emigrated to Canada after World War I. I knew Yudel well from my visit to Suchovolia near the end of World War I and when he came to live with us in Serei in 1920 to escape the Polish pogroms. He was a rebellious young man but a shrewd and experienced trader. He entered the fur trade in the Far North of Canada and was reasonably successful. His was a tragic life and he withdrew into himself and became a recluse.

The youngest daughter of Hatzkel and Henie Rochel, Cousin Chana (Druyan), graduated from a Hebrew gymnasium in Bialystok and emigrated to Eretz Yisroel in the middle Twenties. She became a nurse and served with distinction as an aide to the Chief of Radiology at the Hadassah Hospital in

Jerusalem until the age of retirement. Her patients appreciated her radiant smile, her encouragement, and her genuine interest in their problems beyond the call of duty. Chana married Dr. Avram Druyan, a dermatologist, who came from Saratov, Russia and was a co-founder and lifetime secretary of the Israel Medical Association. Dr. Druyan died suddenly in 1956 of a "broken heart" when he learned of the accidental death of their only son Zvi while he was serving in the Israeli Army. The tragedy shook up Jerusalem and the entire family; father and son were interred side by side in the military cemetery of Jerusalem on Mount Zion. Chana, who has been a tower of strength to the entire family with her compassion and her goodness, bore her tragedy stoically and has carried on in her angelic fashion. She is well known in Jerusalem and was honored in 1980 as the Woman of the Year for her volunteer work with Russian immigrants in Jerusalem. She has visited and lived in the U.S. on occasion and her only daughter, Dahlia, now resides in the U.S. together with her husband, Dr. Abraham Lapidot, and their three children, Zvi, Yael, and Dafna.

Cousin Julius Rabinowitz (Yudel Krutzel), Uncle Mordechai Yosel's oldest son, came to the U.S. as a young boy of sixteen, straight from the Slabodka Yeshiva. When he landed in New York, the HIAS organization gave him a ticket to Boston but, while changing trains in Buffalo, he boarded the wrong train and landed in Detroit. He began as a factory hand but after a short while switched to operating a bread route. He later bought a partnership in the bakery and branched out into real estate, insurance, and other successful enterprises. As soon as he saved up some money he sent for his father and sister Frieda (Freidel), and a year later he sent for his sweetheart, Mary (Miriam) Hyman, whom he had known in Slabodka, and one of her brothers. After their marriage in 1908, he brought Mary's parents and her other four siblings to Detroit. Julius was a tall, broad-shouldered, hard-working, practical, no-nonsense man. He was a devoted family man, friendly but overly sensitive and extremely distrustful of public functionaries. After his retirement, Julius resumed his Jewish studies and he came under the influence of an Orthodox Rabbi whom he greatly admired. He developed a pessimistic outlook on life which deepened perceptibly in his later years and he would frequently revert to the refrain of Ecclesiastes: "Evel Avolim"—"All is vanity and vexation of the spirit." He was fond of our Cincinnati cousin, Moshe Meir Dunsky, and he visited Cincinnati frequently—with or without the excuse of a family function. His wife, Mary, was a friendly, petite woman totally dedicated to her home and family, and we were always welcomed guests in their home. Their children—Ruth (Mendelsohn), Milton, Shirley (Klein), and Doris (Kashtan)—followed in the footsteps of their parents received a good secular and Jewish education, and raised lovely families of their own. There are many doctors, lawyers, and businessmen among their progeny.

Uncle Mordechai Yosel Rabinowitz (Krutzel) came to Detroit in 1904 to join his son Julius, who had preceded him to the U.S. in 1902. Uncle did some peddling and worked as a Bar Mitzvah Rebbe. Like his brother Hatzkel, he returned to his native Suchovolia in 1908 for substantially the same reasons. In 1921, Julius made a special trip to Europe to bring his parents and his youngest sister, Ida (Chaya), to America. The pogroms and persecutions in the new Poland and the presence of three of their four children in the U.S., softened Tante Malke's resistance towards emigrating. Like his brother Hatzkel, Uncle Mordechai Yosel had a beautiful voice and excelled as a cantor—an avocation which both brothers loved to pursue whenever the opportunity presented itself. Among Uncle Mordechai Yosel's star pupils is the founder of Revco, Mr. Sidney Dworkin.

Cousin Frieda (Freidel) Rabinowitz came to the U.S. in 1909 as a young girl and worked in an overalls factory for a number of years until she married Joseph Leemon, a young, religious attorney of similar background. I got to know this family rather well when I spent my weekends with them in the summer of 1925 while taking some pre-medical courses at the University of Michigan. Frieda was an attractive young woman with a cheerful, bubbling disposition like the rest of her family. She met her future husband while boarding with Joe's mother, who was a strong personality and the uncontested mistress of the house. With most of the household chores preempted by her mother-in-law, Frieda devoted herself to raising her four children. Her husband, Joseph Leemon, was a frail but unusual man with a very keen mind. He came to the U.S. in 1904 at the age of twelve from Vileyka near Vilna, together with his widowed mother, to join his four brothers who had preceded them to Detroit. He sold newspapers and put himself through school as a self-taught typist and by doing other odd jobs. He became a successful attorney and amassed great wealth in various business enterprises, which included real estate, mortgage banking, and banking. He was a well-read man and at one time was the editor and publisher of a Jewish weekly in Detroit. The Leemons had a large summer home in Grosse Pointe on Lake Huron, where many of Detroit's moguls lived. The entire family were strictly observant Jews and in 1906 the five Leemon brothers founded the first Hassidic synagogue in Detroit, "Nusach Ari." Joseph Leemon was a brittle (juvenile) diabetic who reached a ripe old age through sheer will power and strict dietary discipline. We used to spend many hours on Sundays touring the countryside together with their four small children—Philmore, Norman, Ruth, and Betty.

Phil, a boy of eight with an unusually high I.Q., never stopped asking questions and his father never failed to answer every question patiently and in reasonable detail. It was, I thought, a very wholesome family of great promise. Most of the members of this family are lawyers and businessmen. The sons have continued in law, banking, and finance; Norman has distinguished himself as a pillar of a large Detroit congregation and his wife, Frieda, has served with distinction as National President of the Pioneer Women.

Cousin Walter Rabinowitz (Velvel Krutzel) came to Detroit from Suchovolia in 1920, at the age of nineteen. After a brief apprenticeship with several furniture outlets in Polish neighborhoods, he went into the furniture business on his own. At times he also engaged in housing projects, in which he was moderately successful. Walter was a highly principled, easy-going, good-hearted, and charitable man with a good sense of humor. He married a diminutive girl, Feigel, who came from a fine family in Yagustov near his hometown and was a recent arrival in the U.S. like himself. In 1970 they made Aliya to Israel and spent the last decade of their lives in retirement in Natanya, Israel, where they died within a year of each other in 1980. Walter and Feigel were both dedicated Zionists and they were extremely devoted to each other. They had no children and they bequeathed their estate to the Jewish National Fund.

Cousin Ida Rabinowitz (Chaya Krutzel) came to Detroit in 1921 together with her parents, Tante Malke and Uncle Mordechai Yosel. She was a cheerful, animated girl and she adapted readily to her new environment under the guidance of her older brother and sister. Within a few years, Ida married Yitzhak Gladstone, who was also a recent arrival. Yitzhak quickly went into business for himself—at first as the proprietor of a notions store and later as the owner of several shoe stores. Ida and Yitzhak had three sons, twins Bill and Gilbert, and Norman. All three married Detroit girls and they raised families of their own. This family knew much tragedy. Yitzhak, who was a friendly though high-strung man totally absorbed in his business, died suddenly at a relatively young age from a massive heart attack. The three sons continued in their father's shoe business for a number of years, but the business succumbed to one of the periodic slumps that befell the Detroit economy. Bill, who was one of the pillars in the business and was married to a sister of Senator Carl Levin of Michigan, also died young from a massive heart attack. A few years later Cousin Ida also succumbed at a relatively young age in a tragic accident. The remainder of the family seems to be operating on a reasonable satisfactory level.

I got to know my Detroit relatives quite well because of the closeness of our cities. But more important, undoubtedly, were our mutual affinity as recent arrivals and the many memories and values that were shared. I seldom passed up an opportunity to visit my Detroit relatives.

Tante Toibe's two sons, Cousins Moshe Meir and Yitzhak Dunsky, came to the U.S. in 1904 from Halinke at the age of sixteen and fourteen respectively. They joined their father Hatzkel in Rochester, New York, where all three worked in the garment industry. After two years in Rochester, when their father remarried, the two young brothers came to Cincinnati to be near my father. They worked in Cincinnati's garment industry, which was quite substantial at that time. In about 1917, Cousin Moshe Meir opened a china store in partnership with my father, but the partnership broke up early over the problem of keeping the store open on the Sabbath. The china store eventually developed into a prosperous business in restaurant supplies under the guidance of Moshe Meir's youngest son Abe. Moshe Meir married Goldie Schulzinger, a niece of my father and a recent immigrant from Semyatich (Siemiatycze). The couple had four children—Chana (deceased), Bessie (Rothman), Irvin, and Abe. Moshe Meir inherited all of the fine qualities of his mother Toibe and grandfather Avremel Sereisky. He died peacefully at the age of eighty-six.

Cousin Yitzhak Dunson (Dunsky) remained a tailor most of his life and was a member of the Amalgamated Clothing Workers Union and the Farband (Labor Zionist Order). He was a well-meaning, good-hearted man who was fettered by some inner limitations and misfortune. For several years Yitzhak and his wife, Jenny (Brown), were the proprietors of a country department store. When business went bad, Yitzhak returned to his former occupation and remained comfortably situated. Their only daughter, Ethel, married Dr. Leo Davis of Camden, New Jersey and their three grandsons are physicians. Yitzhak died from a heart attack in his seventies.

Tante Mirke (Miriam Sereisky) and Uncle Rabbi Meyer H. Levy (Meir Zvi Yosefsky) were married in Halinke in 1890. Uncle Meir came to the U.S. in 1892 at the age of twenty-two and Tante Mirke and her infant daughter Ida joined him a year later. Rabbi Levy was born in Yagustov (Augustow), Poland in 1871. Like myself, he was sent away to study at the yeshiva of Suvalk at the age of ten. After Bar Mitzvah he was admitted to the Wolozhin yeshiva, the most prestigious yeshiva in Poland, where he remained for three years. After Wolozhin he served a year as cantor in his hometown and after his marriage he spent a year in the yeshiva of Eisheshok, Lithuania to prepare for his s'micha ordination). He was ordained as a Rabbi by Rabbi Mayofis of Eisheshok, Rabbi Shlomo (Choshen Shlomo) of Vilna, and later by Rabbi Jacob Joseph, the Chief Rabbi of New York. As he was about to embark on a career as a Rabbi in Europe, he was notified to report for service in the Czar's Army.

Rather than suffer the religious hardships and the humiliations of a Jewish private, he decided to emigrate to America.

Rabbi Levy spent the first two months in New York in the home of Rabbi Jacob Joseph, until he received his call to serve as a Rabbi in Syracuse as assistant to Rabbi Herman Hertz, who later became the Chief Rabbi of England. After five years in the Rabbinate, Uncle felt disappointed in his calling and he opted out for the business world. He moved to Rochester, New York and later to Detroit, where he engaged in the coal and insurance business. In 1906, during one of the financial panics that gripped the country, Uncle Meir gave up the struggle and accepted a pulpit in Toronto, Canada.

Uncle's attempt to leave the Rabbinate was motivated by several considerations, the most important of which were the low prevailing salaries in the Orthodox pulpits, the waning respect for the office of the Rabbi, and most important of all, the difficulties encountered by a young, inexperienced Rabbi in his efforts to rein in an unruly religious community that was falling apart. Uncle Meir was not alone in this experience. Many other Orthodox Rabbis gave up the struggle temporarily or for good. Among these was Rabbi Jacob Joseph, a great scholar and famous preacher (magid) who was imported from Vilna in 1888 to serve as Chief Rabbi in New York, only to return to Vilna a broken man. Another was Rabbi Eliezer Silver, who became the leading Orthodox Rabbi in the United States but who left the Rabbinate at one time early in his career to engage in business. In Canada, Rabbi Levy found a more responsive constituency. Since there was greater respect for tradition among the Gentile Canadian population, the Canadian Jews were also more tradition-bound and they adhered to Orthodoxy more readily than the Jews of the United States.

During his long tenure as an Orthodox Rabbi in Toronto, Uncle Meir served several congregations and established an enviable reputation for himself as a pacifier, a wise counselor and a tolerant religious leader. He helped many of the new immigrants get their first jobs and he helped establish many new social institutions in the young Jewish community of Toronto. He also fostered cordial relations with the local press and with the other Rabbis of the community, regardless of their religious affiliations. Throughout his career as a Rabbi, Uncle Meir was also an ardent Zionist and a strong supporter of Israel. He died in 1956 at the age of eighty-five, a fulfilled man who was highly respected and mourned by his community.

The two important Lithuanian institutions, of which Rabbi Levy was a product, contributed greatly to his personality. The well-known Wolozhin yeshiva represented clarity, erudition, logical insight, and the emphasis on the study of Torah for its own sake, oblivious to any practical considerations—

while the little-known but equally respected Eisheshok yeshiva exemplified the love of Torah and respect for its bearers in that a poverty-stricken community of two hundred families undertook to support one hundred serious yeshiva students at their own expense with enthusiasm and great personal sacrifice.

Tante Mirke was born in 1870 and was the first of Zeide Avremel's daughters to reach the American continent. After she came to the U.S. she gave birth to six more children and she greatly relished her dual roles as mother and rebbetzin (Rabbi's wife). At the same time, she was a progressive woman and a smart dresser with a special flare for stylish hats. She was a good-natured and charitable lady and took an active interest in many philanthropic institutions—including an orphanage, a home for the aged, and two hospitals. She wrote to me frequently with great warmth and personal concern. Besides the pleasure of seeing her at my wedding, I also saw her several times during her summer visits at the mineral baths in Mount Clements near Detroit. Tante Mirke died in an accident in 1951 at the age of eighty-one.

Growing up in a large family, especially under the spotlight and restrictions of being a Rabbi's child, has some advantages and many disadvantages. In the Levy situation, it turned out exceedingly well. The five daughters married successful businessmen and the two sons became important businessmen in their own right. All were happily married and all raised fine families of their own. Their fortunes otherwise varied, as will happen in any large family.

Cousin Ida married Louis Goldfine, a drygoods wholesaler of Montreal. Their son Marvin became a Rabbi and died young; their daughter Annabelle married Rabbi Cass of Toronto and both were killed in an automobile accident in 1975 together with their only son and Annabelle's aunt, Lottie Weiss; Ida's other daughter Hadassah is a retired social worker. Cousin Sarah married Hyman Miller of Montreal, who was in the motion picture business. They had one daughter, Annabelle Louis-Mandel, who lives in Pompano Beach, Florida. Cousin Ann (Chana) married Harry Shiller of Montreal, who was in the wholesale button business. Their son Alvin died young and their daughter, Joyce Rosenbeck, is married to an attorney. Cousin Lottie married Morris Weiss of Toronto, who was in the finance business and died young. Their three daughters, who married businessmen, are—Shirley (Mrs. Harry Warner), Barbara (Mrs. Sidney Wilson), and June Bearg, who is divorced. The youngest of the Levy daughters, Belle, married Louis James of Toronto, a clothing merchant who died young. Their only son, Philip, is a disc jockey.

Of the Levy sons, cousin Jules married Mae Wolf, the daughter of a prominent New York physician, and became a motion picture producer. Their daughter Audrey married Lester Cooper, a producer with ABC Television in

New York, and their son, Jimmy Levy, is a motion picture producer in California. Cousin Nathan (Nat) Levy married Alice, who, since his death, now lives in Los Angeles. Nat was in the motion picture distributing business and they made their home in Philadelphia. Their daughters Phyllis Lubliner—whose husband is an interior decorator—and Enid Weitz, who is divorced, live in New York.

I got to know cousin Jules best of all. He was a tall, broad-shouldered, tense and taciturn man, and every inch of him bespoke the executive. A caller who once tried to get Jules interested in a business venture spoke for fifteen minutes without eliciting from him anything more than an occasional "Hmmm" or "Ho!" Finally, the man said, "Jules, whatever your 'take' is in Canada I will double it." This brought forth a three-word reply, "Call me tomorrow." At the same time, Jules could be quite relaxed with those he allowed to know him and he was extremely dedicated to his immediate family. Everything about him had an extra dimension, including the bar in his huge living room, which rivaled for size his father's voluminous library. Jules began working as a young teenager in a factory and at the age of thirteen he became a foreman in a suspender factory. He also did many odd jobs, including a short stint with the Barnum & Bailey Circus. During World War II, Jules served on the staff of General Dwight D. Eisenhower. He later produced President Eisenhower's biography in a movie entitled *Abilene City*. Jules was executive vice-president of RKO Pictures for many years, ultimately becoming an independent motion picture producer. His two floors of offices in the Rockefeller Center of New York City looked like an empire to me and accessibility was highly restricted. Jules and his wife Mae befriended me and I was warmly received and lavishly entertained by them during several visits to their home in New York.

Because of an acculturation gap and the inconvenience of travel between our respective cities, I did not get to know the Levy branch of my family too well. I met the entire family once, at a memorial service for their father. Despite the sad circumstances, the family made an impression of great warmth and personal charm. Cousin Belle James made me feel at home and I have had additional contacts with her through correspondence and telephone conversations. Like most of her sisters, Belle had remained close to traditional Judaism. She has been an ardent worker for Hadassah and Israel and has continued to be interested in her mother's philanthropies. Since Jules' death, Belle has been my best link to the family and I have always appreciated her graciousness.

All of Zeide Avremel's daughters resisted their husbands' wishes to emigrate and settle in America. They were motivated in this primarily by their conviction that Judaism could not survive in the United States. Other factors were the lack of real economic necessity and the absence of pogroms in the region where they lived. The men, on the other hand, though learned and as deeply religious as their wives, yearned for the economic opportunities and the freedom from oppression that America offered. Most of Zeide Avremel's daughters and their families paid dearly for their deep religious convictions, some with many years of separation, others with divorce and martyrdom.

On my father's side, the first to arrive in the U.S. was an uncle of my father, Abraham Stone (Avrom Ben Yaacov Kamenetzky), who came to the U.S. from Stuchin (Szczuczyn), Poland in 1869 as a teenager together with his father, who returned to Poland. He worked as a laborer on the railroads, and when the construction work stopped in Kansas, he found his way to the nearest city where there were Jews—which happened to be St. Joseph, Missouri. He went into the scrap-metal business and eventually founded the Missouri Iron and Metal Works Company (a successful business that is still in existence) together with two other fellow Jews who had worked with him on the railroad, Mr. Epstein and Mr. Adler. Mr. Stone was a very charitable man and an observant Jew. He was among the founders of the first synagogue in St. Joseph and he helped many of his family come to the United States. He married Leah Beile and the couple had one son, William, who was a scholar and a highly respected attorney in St. Joseph. William had one daughter, Helaine, who married Ernest Lane, a German refugee who served as a pilot in the U.S. Air Force during World War II and later became a real estate developer in Milwaukee, Wisconsin. They had two children. Lisa Libman lives in Champaign, Illinois and Dr. Richard Stone is an internist with the Massachusetts General Hospital.

Among those whom Mr. Stone helped come to Cincinnati from Semyatich were my father's uncle, Moses Barlow (Bash), who came to the U.S. in the 1870s, and my father Chaim and his younger brother, Yacov Leib Schulzinger, who came to Cincinnati in 1905. Mr. Stone was an uncle to the Schulzinger brothers and my father studied for awhile in Mr. Stone's hometown of Stuchin as a teenager, together with the local Rabbi's son. The travel expenses reached them indirectly by way of their uncle Moses Barlow, who served as a shochet (kosher slaughterer) in Cincinnati and also did some teaching. He had two daughters, one of whom married a Mr. Friedman. These cousins settled in Paris, Kentucky and became submerged in the area.

In the early 1880s, Mr. Stone helped a cousin of my father, Tevye Sapershtein, come to St. Joseph. After Tevye had saved some money as a peddler, he sent for his wife, Sheine (Bash/Schulzinger), and their son, Chaim Yitzhak, who had married Chana Rivka (Horowitz). The Sapershteins worked for

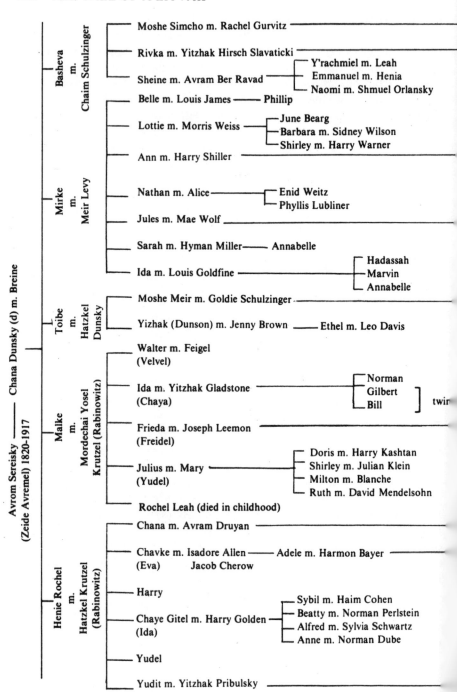

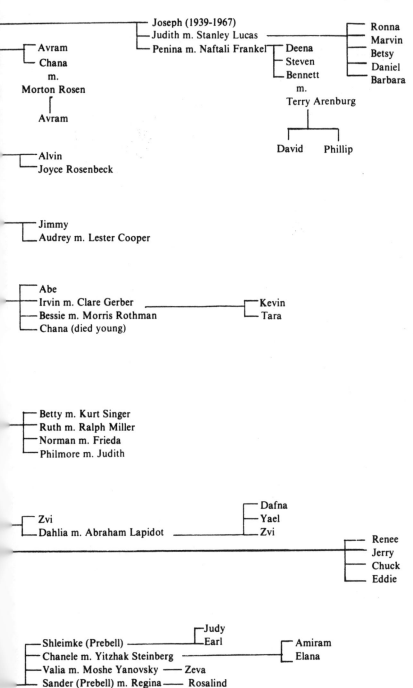

awhile as dairy farmers and then went into the scrap-metal business. The
junior Sapershteins had ten children. Among these were Hazel, Moses Aaron,
William Nelson, Sara Libby (Luke), Rose (Goldman), Miriam (Kranitz), and
Abraham Zelick. Of the St. Joseph relatives, I met only Miriam and her
husband, Lou Kranitz. They visited with us in Cincinnati on several occasions
and Miriam kept me regularly informed about the entire family. Miriam was
an exceptionally fine, out-going, public-spirited person and I was always
amazed at the great interest she took in the smallest events in the family. Lou
was an attorney and a long-time president of the Second District of B'nai
B'rith. His family came from Vilna and there are many lawyers and businessmen in the family. Their son, Ted Kranitz, also an attorney, researched and
published a detailed family tree dating back one hundred years in the United
States. During this period, some ninety families married into the original St.
Joseph group and the clan now counts some five hundred individuals who are
scattered all over the United States. While there is some intermarriage in this
family, it is considerably below the national average. This is remarkable for a
small community like St. Joseph, which had shrunk from three thousand
Jewish inhabitants in 1930 to four hundred at the present time.

In 1929, Chaim Yitzhak and Chana Rivka Sapershtein (Saferstein) left their
children and grandchildren in St. Joseph and emigrated to Eretz Yisroel for
the love of Zion. Their aim was to fulfill an ancient dream of many pious Jews
to live in Jerusalem and to be interred on the Mount of Olives. When Chaim
Yitzhak died in 1933, his wife fulfilled another dream and ordered that a Sefer
Torah (Scroll of the Torah) be written in memory of her dear departed
husband. The Sefer Torah was donated to the village of Herzliya, which was
then building its first synagogue, with the provision that it be used the year
round and not merely on holidays. As the Sefer Torah was being delivered to
the synagogue in a festive ceremony—which included a marching band, a
hupah (canopy), and the entire population of the village in tow—the eighty-
five-year-old Chana Rivka danced in the streets as happy as on her wedding
day.

My parents, who knew the Sapershteins from visits to St. Joseph, invited
them frequently to their home in Herzliya or visited with them in Jerusalem.
After the death of Chaim Yitzhak, these visits became more frequent, and
when Chana Rivka's health began to fail they assumed guardianship over her
and helped place her in a special home for old people without children, of
which my mother was a founder and in which she was an active volunteer
worker. Occasional letters from her children or glimpses at their treasured
photographs helped relieve the loneliness Chana Rivka felt after the death of
her husband. Her last will and testament provided funds for reciting the

Moshe Simcho Schulzinger m. Gitel Bash

Eli Dovid

Yitzhak

Chaim (1869-1963)
m.
Basheva Sereisky

Yacov Leib
m.
Yetta Soffer

Rivka
m.
Weinshenker (Gafni)

Reuven

Goldie
m.
Moshe Meir Dunsky

David Singer

Chana

Bessie
m.
Morris Rothman

Abe

Irvin
m.
Clare Gerber

Tara

Kevin

Sheine
m.
Avram Ber Ravad

Moshe Simcho
m.
Rachel Gurvitz

Rivka
m.
Yitzhak Hirsh Slavaticki

Chana
m.
Morton Rosen

Avram

Avram

Penina
m.
Naftali Frankel

Max
m.
Sara Sobel

Harry
m.
Dorothy Lapirow

Eddie
m.
Carolyn Silverblatt

Maurice
m.
Ann Zussman

Marcia

Joseph
(1939-1967)

Judith
m
Stanley Lucas

Bennett
m.
Terry Arenburg

Deena

Steven

Barbara

Danny

Betsy

Marvin

Ronna

David

Phillip

Y'rachmiel
m.
Leah Katz

Naomi
m.
Shmuel Orlansky

Emmanuel
m
Henia

Yacov

Rachel

Miriam

Rivka

Basheva

Rami

Haggai

Benyamin

Chaim

Malachi

Ayelet

memorial Kaddish and the study of Mishna and Tehilim (Psalms) during the year of mourning and on Yarzeit (annual memorial day), and stipulated that any residual funds be spent for Torah purposes at the discretion of my father. On my visit to Israel in 1947, I received Chana Rivka's personal heirlooms and delivered them to her children in St. Joseph.

The numerous letters of my parents to Chana Rivka's family in St. Joseph have reached me recently due to the kindness of her granddaughter, Mrs. Jonah (Janice Goldman) Cohn of Chicago, who saved them all these years at the request of her mother, Rose Goldman. As a matter of principle, my father corresponded exclusively in Hebrew, which few in their family could understand. When they asked if he would write in Yiddish, he replied that, although he could, it was incumbent on every Jew to use and disseminate the holy tongue. Two of the Sapershtein grandchildren, the children of their daughter Rose Goldman and their families, now live in Israel.

The Saferstein family name underwent many changes in the United States—from Sapershtein to Saferstein, Stone, Safer, Safire, and Sapphire. The family originated in the neighboring communities of Semyatich (Siemiatycze), Chechanow (Czieczanow), and Stuchin (Szczuczyn), Poland and had numerous branches. Large families were common and the father of Chaim Yitzhak Sapershtein, Tevye Hershel, was one of twenty-two children. The journalist Morley Safer and the actress Sylvia Sydney (Sophie Kosow) are allegedly of the Sapershtein clan.

Uncle Yacov Leib Schulzinger came to Cincinnati in 1905 from Semyatich, where he left his wife, Yetta (Yente Soffer), and infant son Max. Yacov Leib struggled for a while as a peddler and as soon as he had saved up some money he sent for his wife and child. In later years he made a modest living as the proprietor of a china store and later on as a butcher. As was customary among many of the new immigrants, their children worked and helped support the family and themselves. Uncle's children sold newspapers on a downtown corner and in streetcars. Three of their five children received a higher education at the University of Cincinnati and all but one got married. Both Uncle Yacov Leib and Aunt Yetta, who hailed from neighboring Brainsk, were friendly, easy-going, hard-working people and so were most of their children. Cousin Max became a painting contractor and married Sara Sobel; Cousin Maurice became an architectural engineer and married Ann Zussman; Cousin Harry was a businessman and an expert in hydraulics and he married Dorothy Lapirow; Marcia was an executive secretary, and Eddie (Edward) became an attorney and married Carolyn Silverblatt. Among Uncle's grandchildren there are two professors, several attorneys, a physician, an accountant, a journalist, a social worker, technologists, and businessmen.

How did our family adjust to their new environment? Despite the hardships which they all endured, most of the first generation did reasonably well, but their offspring exceeded the fondest expectations of their parents. Among the second and third generations there are many physicians, dentists, engineers, lawyers, Rabbis, professors, scientists, actors, producers— as well as many successful businessmen and other professionals. While our family integrated smoothly on the economic level, socially some problems have emerged. Following an identical trend in the general population, marriages have become less firm, the moral fiber is loosening, and the pursuit of the alien cults and practices is spreading. In the religious realm, the first and second generations remained largely within the fold, while in the third and fourth generations intermarriage and alienation are becoming fairly common. So far the gains and the losses are largely in balance, yet there is much to be concerned about. It seems that the intuition of the women in our family was more far-reaching than the wisdom of their learned husbands. Ludwig Lewisohn said it somewhere, "Simple people follow an instinct, an inner monition, an ancestral trend, and supply reasons later."

On our honeymoon visit to New York, Pupi and I had a chance to meet her family when we were entertained for dinner and a social evening at the home of Joseph Gurwitz, a first cousin of Pupi's father. Joseph Gurwitz came from Balbirishok, Lithuania as a young boy during the 1880s and amassed a fortune as a clothing manufacturer, in real estate, and in other business ventures. Both he and his wife were strict observers of the Jewish dietary laws and their apartment had two large kosher kitchens, one for milk products and one for meat products. The home was furnished beautifully and it was our first encounter with what we perceived as great wealth. The Gurwitzes lived in a spacious luxury apartment on one of the upper floors of an apartment building on Riverside Drive at a reported rental of $1,000 per month—an astronomical figure at that time. Both Joseph and his wife were fully acculturated, charming people and they displayed a great deal of warmth and a genuine effort to make us feel at home. We were introduced to their sons, who were law students, and a daughter, who was also in college, and the Gurwitzes invited the other members of Pupi's family to meet us.

Among the invited guests were Joel Gurwitz, a ladies' garment manufacturer and a brother of Joseph Gurwitz; Casper Gurwitz, a manufacturer's agent and a bachelor cousin of Pupi's father; Casper's brother, Philip Gurwitz, a garment manufacturer; and their sister, Rose Levitt, who owned a department store in Pittsburgh. We also met Simon Rochelson—who was married to Pupi's cousin, Michalene, and was employed by Joseph Gurwitz— and Sam Rochelson, his son, a wholesaler in fine linen. The Rochelsons, both father and son, were well versed in Bible, in Talmud, and in modern Hebrew literature, and they were dedicated Zionists and generous in their philanthropies. Both lived to a ripe age and we kept up a close friendship over the years. Sam married late in life to Sadie, a fine musician and pianist and a good-natured, intelligent woman. They had two children, a son Karol, a regional sales executive with I.B.M., and a daughter Zenja, who was until her recent death, a home economist and food consultant for television and movies.

We were afforded a glimpse at another aspect of the workings of the melting pot at a reunion, during our honeymoon trip, with three of our closest classmates from the gymnasium of Mariyampole who came to the U.S. in 1924 and settled in New York. The classmates were Frieda Bergson Mecklenburg, Rasia Yacobson Schneider, and Julius Kushner. We visited with each of them in their homes, to be entertained and to meet other classmates, landsleit, and friends. We also met at a large gathering at the home of Dr. Max and Frieda Mecklenburg, where we reminisced and exchanged experiences.

I had known Frieda Bergson ever since I was a student in the yeshiva of Lazdei in 1914 when I used to accompany my mother to her father's saloon, delivering soft drinks, collecting empty bottles, or settling accounts. Of all the people I met as a child, I remembered her father as a vain, mean, and spiteful man who caused my mother a great deal of aggravation. Frieda's mother, on the other hand, was a fine, genteel, long-suffering, matronly housewife. In the gymnasium Frieda was known as a hard-working, serious student who always worried about staying at the head of her class. She was one of Pupi's best friends, although she was several years her senior. Before leaving for the U.S., Pupi went to Lazdei to take leave of her friends and relatives. When she told Frieda's father that she was going to America to join me in marriage, he became livid with rage and sank his teeth into a doorpost. Had Mr. Bergson known that Frieda would become a life-long friend of mine and that she would spend some of her happiest days visiting at our home, he would have turned over in his grave. Mr. Bergson, his wife, and their only son Moshe perished in the Holocuast.

Frieda was married soon after her graduation from the gymnasium to a young Mariyampole physician, Dr. Max Mecklenburg. For Frieda, who like her father greatly valued yiches (prestigious background), this was the height of achievement since her husband came from a fine family, was a graduate of a renowned German university, and was the brother-in-law of a Dr. A. Levinhertz, the successor of Dr. Max Meyer as director of the Mariyampole gymnasium. Soon after their marriage, the Mecklenburgs emigrated to the U.S., settled in New York and made their home and office on a fashionable section of Park Avenue. Dr. Max Mecklenburg was only modestly successful as an internist and he died at a relatively young age of lung cancer during the

Fifties. Frieda became well known in the Hebrew intellectual circles of New York and she remained active for many years in literary and Bible study circles and by teaching Hebrew. A decade or so after her husband's death, she made Aliya to Israel and settled in Haifa. We visited with Frieda every time we came to New York and she visited with us several times in Cincinnati. We saw Frieda shortly before her death at the age of seventy, when she called on us at the Dan Carmel Hotel in Haifa. Although she was ambulatory, her mind was wandering and the end was obviously near. She left a son in New York who was not in the best of health.

I had not seen Rasia Yacobson Schneider since 1920, when we worked together in the Hehalutz farm training camp near Serei, and later briefly at school. When Pupi and I met her in her home during our honeymoon visit to New York, Rasia had married a fine young man, an engineer, and they made their home in one of the Sholem Aleichem apartment complexes in the Bronx. Both Rasia and her husband were dedicated Yiddishists (devotees of Yiddish) and followers of liberal and socialist causes. When we met, Pupi and Rasia embraced and kissed and both shed tears of joy. Then Rasia suddenly exclaimed in her country brogue, "Oi Rochelle! Ich vil redden un redden un veiss nit vos tsum redden (I want to talk and talk and don't know what to say)." Rasia had not changed much since I had last seen her six years earlier. She looked as attractive and lovable as ever and her rural simplicity and quiet, unassuming intellectual qualities made her even more appealing against the background of the noisy metropolis. This was the girl I might have married had I not met and fallen in love with Pupi. We brought each other up to date on personal happenings and it was truly a joyous reunion. Rasia's brother, who was a classmate of mine in the gymnasium and earned a Ph.D. from a European university, settled in Eretz Yisroel and became an educator in the children's Agricultural School of Bet Shemen. He was an ardent nationalist. We saw Rasia on several other visits to New York but we gradually drifted apart. The Schneiders raised two daughters.

Rasia became a teacher in the Yiddish Proletarian Sholem Aleichem Schools and her engineer husband struggled to get or maintain a job at low pay in the poisoned anti-Semitic environment of the Twenties and Thirties—a state of affairs which was only aggravated by the Great Depression. The Schneiders were caught up in the Jewish Proletarian struggles and in the cultural milieu of their environment. They became non-Zionist, irreligious, socialist Yiddishists—while the Kushners, the Mecklenburgs, and ourselves remained dedicated Zionists, nationalists, Hebraists, and religious tradition-alists. To Rasia, Julius Kushner was a "Babbitt," and we were probably in the same category by association or in our own rights.

Julius Kushner was a friendly, gifted, practical man with a great deal of common sense. He was a native of Mariyampole, where we first met and became close friends. Soon after he came to the U.S. he married Sarah, a charming girl who shared his own values, and he eventually became a successful businessman as a wholesaler of toys and a publisher of children's books. His two sons became prominent Rabbis and his son Harold is the author of the best seller *When Bad Things Happen to Good People*. Julius' older sister, who came to the U.S. at the turn of the century, married Ralph Poyavonsky, who served as Governor of the Virgin Islands for a quarter of a century.

The reunion at Frieda's home was a happy one and was cherished by all. After the usual exchange of pleasantries and personal information, the conversation turned to the future of Judaism in the United States. I expressed my belief that the group's generation that was steeped in traditional and modern Jewish values had an obligation to step into the breach and try to stem the tide of ignorance, emptiness, and crude assimilation that was engulfing our people in the U.S. I was astonished when my words met with derision from Julius. The thrust of his argument was that our first obligation was to get Americanized and that Judaism in the U.S. was doomed to extinction anyway. Despite our disagreement, we remained close friends throughout our lifetime and we visited each other on numerous occasions.

A decade or so later, on one of his business trips to Cincinnati, Julius and I renewed our discussion on the future of Judaism in America while we were taking a long evening walk on Reading Road in Avondale. This time Julius was more receptive to my arguments and he returned home to become an active member of the Brooklyn Jewish Center, the Zionist Organization of America, and various Jewish cultural and philanthropic organizations. Perhaps the deepening Depression or the blasting waves of hatred against Jews had something to do with it. In later years, Julius built a plastics factory in Israel and he helped publish a book called *Lithuania, the Country of my Birth* with an introduction by the late President of Israel, Zalman Shazar. Julius' oldest brother, Alter, who remained in Lithuania and survived the Holocaust in Siberian exile, became submerged among the Lithuanian natives and his family was irretrievably lost to his people. Due to Julius' heroic efforts, one married granddaughter who remained Jewish came to the U.S. and the family now lives in Los Angeles.

During one of our visits to the Kushner home in Brooklyn, we met another classmate of the gymnasium, Harry Goldstein, who was also a native of Mariyampole. Harry was a neat and well-groomed man with reddish curly hair and a lean look. He became an attorney and he married Julius' niece, Miss Poyavonsky of the Virgin Islands. We met Harry once more several decades later during a visit to St. Thomas and were introduced to his fine family. At this time we found Harry comfortably situated in the governor's numerous enterprises and from what we could learn he had never lost his passion for cards. He died at a relatively young age.

Of the pious, learned men I met at Shachnes Shul when I came to Cincinnati, few left followers amony their progeny. Reb Ephraim Schiff, who was a zealot for Torah and Mitzvoth (Commandments), conducted for many years, with the help of his wealthy brother Robert, of shoe industry fame, a one-man campaign to educate Cincinnati youngsters in Torah and the traditional way of life. Many of his wards, including his own children, resented his severe doctrinaire approach and rebelled against it at the first opportunity. Some of his pupils—and most of his children—joined Reform temples, while others gratefully remembered his dedication.

Reb Mordechai Schiff was a quiet and more relaxed person than his brother Ephraim. He was a mashgiach (inspector for kashruth) at the Procter & Gamble company and he kept himself aloof amidst his books. His son, Dr. Leon Schiff, and his grandchildren became physicians and academicians of note. Reb Moshe Elchonon Miller was a pharmacist and was considered the dean of the group. Three of his sons became physicians and one a pharmacist; some of these adhered to Orthodoxy. Reb Eli Danziger (Dunsker) was a quiet, soft-spoken man with a brilliant mind. He was the father of Boris Dunsker, Shiel, twins Sam and Ida (Klein), Dora (Feigelman), and Sonia (Shulman); two of his grandchildren are prominent surgeons. Moshele Levin was the father of Dr. Tom Levin. Reb Elias Shur's son Louis was a garment manufacturer and a grandson is a Reform Rabbi. The progeny of Reb Baruch Samuels, who loved to preach on festive and other occasions, are all successful businessmen and temple followers. Reb Ber Manischewitz, the founder of the Manischewitz Matzo Company, sent his five sons to Eretz Yisroel to study in Yeshivoth. His progeny clung to traditional Judaism.

For many decades, the Cincinnati matzo company was a center of Orthodox Jewish philanthropy and attracted many itinerant Rabbis. The company engaged Rabbi Hochstein to serve as mashgiach and as a one-man reception committee for the numerous distinguished visitors to the plant. Rabbi Hochstein was a friendly, corpulent man of great wit and his home became a popular gathering place for many Rabbinic students from Hebrew Union College, who would come there on the Sabbath to spend a pleasant afternoon. To Rabbi Hochstein is attributed the pun that "Cincinnati's fame rests on two pillars, 'kosher matzos' (Manischewitz) and 'treife Rabonim' (non-kosher Rabbis from the Hebrew Union College)."

Besides the problems of integration and acculturation in the general community, our immigrants were faced with the problem of internal integration—

the Jewish melting pot. For the first time in Jewish history, Jews from every corner of the earth met on a massive scale and they had to reconcile a thousand, often irreconcilable, differences. To mention only a few—they had to bring together the religious and the agnostics, the Orthodox and the Reform, the Zionist and the anti-Zionist, the Hebraists and the Yiddishists, the radicals and the conservatives, the proletarian and the wealthy, the German Jews and the Russian Jews, the Litvaks and the Galitzianer, the Hassidim and the Misnagdim, the greenhorns and the established or assimilated Jews. The struggles were fierce and the process of integration is still incomplete, but what has already been achieved is almost miraculous. A sample of some of these struggles is revealed in my experiences as an active worker in the Jewish community over the decades.

CHAPTER FOUR

The Jewish Community

> "All those who occupy themselves
> faithfully with the needs of the com-
> munity may the Holy One, blessed be
> He, grant them their reward."
> (Talmud)

Four months after I came to Cincinnati, as I was preparing to enroll at the university, I received a call from Dr. David Neumark, who invited me to his home for a chat. Dr. Neumark was a renowned scholar, editor, and Rabbi in Europe before he was invited in 1904 to assume the chair of Professor of Philosophy at the Hebrew Union College (HUC). With my love and reverential regard for Jewish scholarship, I felt flattered by the invitation and became ecstatic when I learned the reason for the unexpected call. Dr. Neumark had learned through the grapevine, he said to me, about my Hebraic, Talmudic, and Zionist background and he thought that I might be the right person to head a Hebrew-speaking cultural society in Cincinnati. In the course of our conversation, Dr. Neumark outlined the following program for the proposed society—the society was to meet monthly for a lecture on some literary or other learned subject in Hebrew; it was to help support needy Hebrew writers; it should help with the publication and distribution of Hebrew books; and it should help advance the use of spoken Hebrew among its members. I gladly accepted the invitation, we named the new society "Ivriah," and I became and remained its president for thirty years. Among the founding members of the society were Dr. Abe Wigser, Sol Richmond, Yosef Gootman, and Professor Samuel A. Cohon (Professor of Theology at HUC). It became a very active group and many prominent Hebrew writers, poets, educators, and scholars found a lively forum at our meetings. The society attracted some thirty members and, at times, students and additional faculty members from HUC. The meetings were held at the homes of members and they became pleasant social and cultural events. It seems like a miracle that the Ivriah Society is still alive and functioning. Professor Neumark lived with his two daughters on East Rockdale near Reading Road. His oldest daughter, Martha, married the journalist Joseph Brainin, who founded the Seven Arts Syndicate. Joseph's father, Reuven Brainin, was a foremost Hebrew writer and journalist with great achievements in the advancement of Zionism and Hebrew in the United States.

Another cause in which I became involved while pursuing my professional education was Zionism. Soon after I came to Cincinnati, I was introduced by my cousin Ben Doll to the members of the Cincinnati branch of the Poale Zion (Labor Zionist Organization) and I was gradually drawn into their activities, despite my aversion for the socialist part of their program. The members of the Cincinnati Poale Zion were a fine group of idealistic young people in their middle or late twenties who had arrived in the U.S. some ten years earlier. They were all older than myself and most of them were struggling to earn a living in business or in small enterprises. Many of them were newlyweds or were about to get married within the fold. Although none of my new friends had ever received a formal secular education, and some had not even received a good Jewish education beyond the level of the traditional heder, they were all imbued with a respect and love for learning and an unquenchable thirst for cultural and intellectual attainment. Fortunately, there were many opportunities to satisfy their needs.

There were seven excellent Jewish daily newspapers in New York alone—six in Yiddish and one in Hebrew—the *Varheit*, the *Morgen Journal*, the *Tageblat*, the *Tog*, the *Forewertz* (Forward), the *Freiheit*, and the *Hadoar*. In addition to news of general and Jewish interest, these papers were full of essays by excellent writers on philosophy, religion, Zionism, history, literature, economics, finance, as well as serialized novels, poetry, reviews, and human-interest stories and letters. Besides the dailies, there were also numerous weeklies, monthlies, and quarterlies, mostly in Yiddish but also in Hebrew and in English. The published material was generally of high quality and provided a rich fare for those who would avail themselves of the opportunity. The members of the Poale Zion read many of these publications from cover to cover and in the process they became a cultural elite and the most informed group among the Jewish immigrants.

There were also frequent lectures in Yiddish and in Hebrew by visiting writers, poets, scholars, educators, and Zionist leaders. Several times a year we were offered dramatic and concert entertainment of high quality by traveling theater groups, concert artists, or cantors. Among the best were the Vilner Trupe, the Habima, the theatrical productions headed by Celia Adler, Maurice Schwartz, Muni Weisenfeld (Paul Muni), and Molly Picon; concerts by cantors Hirshman, Kussevitsky, Rosenblatt, and Roithman; folk songs by Chaim Kotlansky; and recitations by Harris and others. While the cultural environment in which I found myself was eminently satisfactory, it soon became clear to me that our group was a small oasis in an ever-spreading wilderness. All around us were ignorance, senseless assimilation, and the all-devouring philosophy of losing one's identity in the American melting pot. In protest many among the Poale Zion refused to speak English to anyone who understood Yiddish, especially since many Jews were ashamed of the Yiddish they knew so well and preferred to speak an atrocious, illiterate English.

As the Poale Zion viewed the Jewish scene, Orthodox Judaism was a dispirited, dying creed, Conservative Judaism was as yet insignificant, and Reform Judaism was frowned upon as an anti-Zionist, anti-national, assimilationist sect that eventually would lead to the Unitarian Church and beyond. To express their aversion for these tendencies, many of the Poale Zion stayed away from both the synagogue and the temple and organized their own religious services on the High Holidays. Although the Poale Zion were non-observant, they were deeply religious in their own way and fiercely nationalistic. Their outspoken antagonism towards Reform did not stem so much from objections to changes in the liturgy as an abhorrence of the abandonment of such basic tenets of Judaism as belief in Zion, the use of Hebrew, and the observance of the Sabbath. The Poale Zion would point out that Reform Rabbis discarded the talit (prayer shawl) and donned the garb of Protestant ministers; Sabbath services were replaced by Sunday morning services; references to Zion and peoplehood were deleted from their scanty prayer book; the use of Hebrew was reduced to a minimum; Rabbis were being graduated without a proper understanding of Hebrew texts; Rabbinic students were expelled from HUC for expressing Zionist sentiments; and Rabbi David Philipson, Cincinnati's senior Reform Rabbi, demonstratively left any podium at the playing of the "Hatikva"—the Jewish national anthem.

Cincinnati Poale Zion, 1933. Pictured left to right:
Seated bottom row: Rachel Mann, x, William Brown, Lillian Krit, Henach Simkin, Mary Simkin, Dora Kushnir and the author's daughter Penina.
Middle row: Children Bernie Berkowitz and Rena Simkin; Ben Doll kneeling.
Middle row seated: Rochelle Mesh, Mrs. Levin, Abe Tavel, Morris Krit, Sam Skurow, Esther Grad, Sam Schmidt, Ida Schmidt, Yosef Gootman.
Standing rear: Nathan Berkowitz, Mrs. Berkowitz, Mr. Pronin, x, Robert Greenfield, Moshe Meir Dunsky, Abe Block, Fannie Krit, Mr. Mann, Mrs. Skurow, Louis Levin, Sam Grad, Jennie Dunson, Mordechai Goldfarb, Aliza Goldfarb, Sol Richmond, Sophie Richmond, Pupi holding daughter Judy, Bessie Gootman, the author and Morris Kushnir.

Reform Judaism, now known as Liberal Judaism, was saved at the edge of the precipice by the influx of Eastern European Jews, the trauma of the Holocaust, the triumph of Zionism, and—paradoxically—by the resurgence of a militant Orthodoxy. One of the early indications of a trend away from extreme Reform occurred in 1920 in Cincinnati when Isaac M. Wise Temple, named after the founder of Reform Judaism, engaged Rabbi James G. Heller, a dedicated Zionist, as its spiritual leader. A decade later it merged with the "Frum Shul," where Rabbi Samuel Wohl, an ardent Labor Zionist, was the spiritual leader. In recent decades, the Reform movement has restored many of the practices and tenets of traditional Judaism and the gap seems to be narrowing despite remaining basic differences.

The Poale Zion movement emerged in the last decade of the 19th century in the wake of the virulent anti-Semitism and the revolutionary and Zionist ferment that was stirring in the Russian and Austro-Hungarian empires. The leader and ideologue of the movement was Dr. Ber Borochov, a Russian physician. Although they were few in numbers, the Poale Zion soon managed to fragment themselves into several splinter groups. The points of contention were:

1) The degree of socialism to be advocated in the future Jewish state—was it to be pragmatic socialism, revolutionary socialism, or communist socialism?
2) Should the Poale Zion join the Second or the Third Socialist International?
3) Should the Poale Zion join the bourgeoise Zionists in community activities?
4) Should Hebrew or Yiddish be the official language of Eretz Yisroel?
5) Should any other land besides Palestine be considered as the hoped-for Jewish homeland?

The leaders of the Poale Zion in the U.S. were Dr. Nachman Sirkin and Baruch Zukerman among the moderates and Dr. Chaim Zhitlowsky among the leftists. Ben Gurion, the future Prime Minister of Israel, and Ben Zvi, the future second President of Israel, both of whom spent the World War I years in the U.S., also took part in shaping the Poale Zion movement. In 1921 the activities of the Poale Zion began to take on a new life as rhetorical questions gave way to such practical needs as raising funds and building the pioneer institutions of the Jewish homeland. The Histadrut (Israel's labor federation) which played a crucial part in the creation of the Jewish state, was founded by Ben Gurion and his colleagues in 1921 and was charged with the unusual task of developing agriculture, industry, and a suitable labor force virtually from scratch. It fell to the Poale Zion to mobilize volunteers to go to Eretz Yisroel as halutzim (pioneers) and to help raise gift funds in lieu of venture capital— customary investment sources being unavailable since few of the proposed undertakings rated much chance of becoming profitable. During the next thirty years the members of the Poale Zion dedicated themselves to the needs of Eretz Yisroel with an unequaled dedication and singleness of purpose. Numerous representatives came to Cincinnati from Palestine year after year on behalf of new and old labor Zionist causes and institutions, and they were all received in our homes as members of an extended family.

In addition to the numerous fund-raising and cultural activities on behalf of Eretz Yisroel, the Poale Zion were also busy on the American scene and they took an active part in many political, social, educational, and economic problems. In national politics they supported the permanent Socialist candidate for president, Norman Thomas, and they worked for all "progressive" causes. Locally, they supported the charter movement for clean municipal government and in the Jewish community they worked for intensive Jewish education, the strengthening of cultural causes, and the democratization of community institutions. They also participated in the struggle against anti-Semitism and they fiercely combatted all assimilationist tendencies. Although they were a small group numerically, their presence in the country and in the community was very much felt.

Many of the Poale Zion devoted more time to public affairs than to earning a living, and when the dream of a Jewish state became a reality, most of them were spent. Few had prospered, but they were a happy lot and each celebrated the event with subdued pride and rejoiced over the colossal achievement as a personal triumph. Even when the State of Israel meted out honors to "Johnny-come-lately friends" while ignoring the veterans who gave it all, the insensitivity was accepted gracefully as a fact of life. The Poale Zion and Histadrut shlichim (representatives) who came repeatedly to Cincinnati over the years are too numerous to mention, but they included all of the great who eventually became the government of Israel under the leadership of Ben Gurion. Among the active members of the Cincinnati Poale Zion were Yosef and Bessie Gootman, Ben Zion and Becky Doll, Moshe and Dora Kushnir, Lippe and Lillian Krit, Moshe and Fanny Krit, Moshe Meir Dunsky, Abe Block, Henoch and Mary Simkin, Sophie and Sol Richmond, Miriam and Albert Mann, Miriam and Louis Levine, and many others.

Soon after I entered the practice of medicine in the summer of 1930, I also embarked on a career of voluntary Jewish public service. It all began when Dr. Jacob Golub, the Director of the Cincinnati Bureau of Jewish Education

(B.J.E.), called on me and asked me to assume the presidency of the board of the Talmud Torah (T.T.) religious Hebrew school and the chairmanship of the executive committee of the B.J.E. I was surprised and flattered, but begged off on the grounds that I knew very little about their programs and that, as a young doctor struggling to build up a practice and raise a family, I could not possibly spare the time these activities would require. Dr. Golub was a competent and dedicated Jewish educator who had earned a Ph.D. in education from Columbia University and had been a pupil of John Dewey. He had worked hard in Cincinnati for several years to develop an interest in his programs, but became discouraged and depressed over the lack of progress.

On a national level, interest in modern Jewish education had developed rapidly in the wake of the Balfour Declaration and the hopes for a Jewish homeland in Eretz Yisroel. With the end of World War I and the achievement of a measure of affluence, American Jews of Eastern European origin began to vitalize and expand their religious, educational, and philanthropic institutions. A beginning had already been made in 1908 with the organization of a democratic Jewish community council (kehila) in New York City with Rabbi Judah L. Magnes of Temple Emmanuel as the guiding spirit. With a great deal of zeal and dedication, Dr. Magnes began to bring order to the existing chaos in Jewish education and philanthropy and, as a result of his activities, the first Bureau of Jewish Education in the U.S. was established in New York in 1910 with Dr. Samson Benderly at its head. Dr. Benderly, who was a native of Safed and a Johns Hopkins physician-turned-educator, conceived of a comprehensive Jewish educational program to raise the level of Jewish cultural and religious involvement in America. He introduced "ivrit b'ivrit" pedagogy—the use of Hebrew as the language of instruction; he also developed new curricula, experimented with new teaching ideas, initiated pilot schools, organized adult studies, and trained and inspired young students to enter the field of Jewish education. Dr. Golub was one of Dr. Benderly's faithful disciples, but he had become disillusioned with the results of his mentor's concepts and curricula and was soon to opt out of Jewish education. When Dr. Golub called on me to assume leadership it was in the belief that he would be leaving Jewish education in Cincinnati in safe hands.

The decision I was called upon to make was difficult. Since 1918 I had become a "workaholic." I knew that if I accepted the challenge I would give it all the time and energies I could muster and something would have to suffer. Yet, in the end, the tradition of faithful public service which I brought with me from Serei and Vilna—"V'kol haoskim b'zorhei zibur b'emuna"—won over all my misgivings. After discussing the matter with Pupi, I informed Dr. Golub of my favorable decision and I was duly elected president of the

Cincinnati Talmud Torah and chairman of the executive committee of the Cincinnati B.J.E. at specially convened meetings of the respective boards. In accepting the challenge, I also remembered the constructive and honored parts that the physicians Doctors Shabbad and Vigodski had played in Vilna. I was also aware that there were physicians in other communities in the U.S. who were upholding the same tradition.

As I surveyed the task before me, I learned that some fundamental changes had taken place since I last taught at the Adath Israel Congregation school in 1925. The old Talmud Torah on John and Hopkins Streets where I taught in 1921 had folded for the lack of funds and students and most Jewish children were receiving no Jewish education whatsoever, while those who did were getting only a few hours of weekly instruction in congregational Sunday schools or were taught the Bar Mitzvah by private teachers. The Cincinnati B.J.E. had come into being in 1925 to improve Jewish education in the community through a centralized effort. The board of directors of the B.J.E. consisted of representatives from most of the temples and synagogues and others with an interest in Jewish education. The operating budget of the B.J.E. was assumed by the Jewish Welfare Fund, while the Bureau remained an autonomous body. Modern classrooms were built on Rockdale Avenue in front of the old Adath Israel Synagogue, which was located across the street from the Avondale (Samuel Ach) public school. For the first time in the history of the Jewish community of Cincinnati, full-time professional teachers and a professional director were engaged. Yet all of these efforts failed to produce the desired results. The situation in the congregational schools was equally discouraging. They suffered from the lack of competent teachers and the few hours of instruction they offered were insufficient for any kind of impact on the children, beyond learning a few Bible stories and some rudimentary facts about the holidays. Few learned to read Hebrew and the teaching of Jewish history or the Hebrew language was out of the question. At that time any kind of supervision by the B.J.E. was rejected by the Rabbis and the congregations as undesirable, gratuitous advice.

The Talmud Torah operated as an autonomous body under the nominal authority of the B.J.E. and was charged with providing an intensive Jewish education to all of the Jewish children of the community. All of the ingredients seemed to be in place for a successful program—the T.T. had a five-day-a-week, two-hour-a-day program that could deliver an acceptable Jewish education; the location of the T.T. across the street from the public school enabled the children to go directly to Hebrew school without loss of time; and the institution was properly staffed. Yet, after six years of effort, the student body of the T.T. consisted of less than 150 children, half of the classrooms were empty, and the small and irregular attendance was discouraging to the willing children. Some of the difficulties encountered by the T.T. were that the required tuition was an unwelcomed burden for many parents while attendance at the congregational Sunday schools was free; most of the children preferred to play after public school rather than being herded into another classroom; and many of the parents lacked the interest or the control over their children to enforce regular attendance.

A few months after I assumed leadership in Jewish education, Dr. Golub announced his resignation to the startled members of the board of the B.J.E. He suggested a replacement and offered to remain in charge until his successor was installed. After interviewing several candidates, the boards of the B.J.E. and the T.T. chose Dr. Azriel Eisenberg of New York as the new director. Dr. Eisenberg, who had recently earned a Ph.D. in education from Columbia University, came to us highly recommended by Dr. Benderly of New York and by Dr. Emanuel Gamoran, the Director of Education of the Union of Hebrew Congregations, whose offices were in Cincinnati.

Dr. Eisenberg proved to be an able administrator and a dedicated educator and with his friendly and positive approach he soon succeeded in winning many friends for Jewish education in the community. Cincinnati being his first position as director, he was determined to succeed and the result exceeded our fondest expectations. During the first few years of Dr. Eisenberg's eight-year tenure, we were in daily contact on current problems and once or twice a week we spent entire evenings discussing problems, strategy, and methods. The problems were threefold—how to increase attendance, how to increase the interest of the children and thus maximize their tenure, and how to reconcile the divergent views in the community with regard to curriculum. We began with ambitious publicity and registration campaigns to double the number of students from 150 to 300. With a successful outcome behind us, we addressed the problem of tenure. Many of the children were entering the T.T. at the age of ten or eleven and leaving at the age of thirteen, immediately after Bar Mitzvah. This was obviously too short a period to accomplish much of anything. Dr. Eisenberg worked out an intensive program to extend from kindergarden through high school with a curriculum aimed at achieving a good reading and speaking knowledge of Hebrew, a familiarity with Jewish history from ancient to modern times, and a working knowledge of the prayers and holidays.

Within a few years, registration in the T.T. increased to five hundred students and most of our aims had been achieved or were being achieved. The Talmud Torah of Cincinnati became known as one of the best educational systems in the U.S. and we maintained this enviable position for two decades, alongside the Hebrew schools of Minneapolis and Baltimore. Our program succeeded because of the hard work and dedication of the director and his harmonious intimate relationship with the teachers, the board of the T.T., the parents, and influential lay members in the community. The Poale Zion, under the leadership of Yosef Gootman, were of special help in these efforts. To win the interest of the parents, we conducted annual registration drives during the four weeks before Rosh Hashanah. During these campaigns some three hundred volunteers went out into the community to knock on doors and solicit children for the T.T. The obstacles were many but our workers were properly indoctrinated and motivated and they were determined to succeed. They knew that they had a dual task to perform—to register as many children as possible and to educate the parents to the importance of a good Jewish education for their children. The personal contacts of these workers with the parents were followed up with mailings of appropriate literature, telephone calls, and additional contacts by the director or the registration committee when necessary.

Most of the parents were first- or second-generation immigrants. They were imbued with the melting-pot ideal and they yearned for integration into a common humanity. Thus many were not in favor of intensive Jewish education. They argued that learning the mourner's Kaddish and the Bar Mitzvah was enough for them. Others pleaded that their children were too young or too weak and they needed the time to play. Behind some of this reluctance were also the urge for upward social mobility through the Reform school and the practical considerations that the Sunday school was free and met only once a week. We were fully prepared to meet these and many other objections. Although it was required that the parents pay their fair share of tuition, no child was ever denied admission because of the parents' refusal or inability to pay. We arranged supervised play programs for the children before and after school hours and a special committee evaluated the effectiveness of the teachers and the programs on an ongoing basis.

In due time a four-year high school was established, impressive graduation ceremonies were held, and certificates of graduation and prizes were distributed at well-attended festive gatherings. To encourage the high school students to complete the four-year program, we established, in 1933, a paid one-year study program in Eretz Yisroel. The scholarship was awarded annually to the best student upon recommendation of the director, the teachers, and the scholarship committee. Our Israel scholarship was a first for the U.S. and was later adopted by other communities. This prize helped increase student registration and a higher level of achievement. By the time the scholarship program was interrupted by World War II, we had awarded six scholarships and all of our scholars subsequently made important contributions to their communities and to Israel. Our scholarship winners were Nachama Tennenbaum (Mrs. Carl Alpert), Aviva Gootman (Kaufman-Penn), (Rabbi) Simcha Kling, Shoshana Cirkin (Mrs. Martin Grad), Shulamith Gootman (Mrs. Nachum Eden), and (Rabbi) Barry Rosen.

The stalwart members of the board of the T.T. to whom I am indebted were Yosef Gootman, Sol Richmond, A.B. Wise, Sam Burgin, Albert Goldman, and Sol Goodman. Most of these men also served on the board of the B.J.E. Other prominent members of the board of the B.J.E. were Dr. Emanuel Gamoran, Professor Zvi Diesendruk, Morton Heldman, Nathan Ransohoff, Samuel Schmidt, the president Robert Senior, and others. All of the Rabbis of the community were ex-officio members of both boards but their attendance was irregular and their participation was more or less passive. Mr. Senior was an outstanding and most unusual individual. He was of German-Jewish descent and his knowledge of Judaism was not profound, yet he became a tower of strength for Jewish education in Cincinnati and in his own quiet way he helped our cause in every conceivable way over a period of nearly four decades. He was a dedicated horticulturist, a refined and highly cultured man, and a member of one of Cincinnati's foremost and wealthiest families. He was a fine example of an outstanding human being and a proud and dedicated Jew.

The success of the T.T. and the mushrooming of its activities created some envy and discord in the councils of the B.J.E. Although the bureau was, in theory, the parent body of the T.T, it became, in effect, a mere rubber stamp for the activities of its ward. The B.J.E. engaged in some important activities on its own, but these paled into insignificance by comparison with the vitality of the T.T. Among the major activities of the B.J.E. were educational counseling to the congregational schools, adult education, and the promotion of Jewish cultural activities among the young and in the community at large. The cultural activities consisted of Jewish book fairs, theatrical events, concerts, and the encouragement of other forms of Jewish art. An attempt to separate the two boards failed when it was resisted by the T.T. on the grounds that the boards of the B.J.E. and the T.T. supplemented each other and that a successful enterprise should not be tampered with.

In 1939, Dr. Eisenberg resigned to accept an identical position in Cleveland, and he later filled similar positions in Philadelphia and New York. Except for the wider opportunities, higher salaries, and greater prestige that went with the larger cities, Dr. Eisenberg was never able to duplicate the phenomenal success he achieved in Cincinnati. He retired from Jewish education in the late Sixties and has since won fame with the publication of more than sixty books on Jewish religious and cultural subjects.

A special place in Jewish education was occupied by Dr. Emanuel Gamoran, who was a professional educator and made important contributions to Jewish education in Cincinnati and in the United States. Dr. Gamoran came to the U.S. from Russia in 1907 at the age of twelve and received his doctorate degree from Teachers College, New York, after graduating from several Jewish institutions of learning. He was a warm and friendly person, an able and dedicated educator, and a devoted Zionist committed to the upgrading of Jewish education in the Reform movement. Dr. Gamoran was equally interested in the T.T. and in the B.J.E and he could always be counted on for sound advice and counsel. He was a tireless worker for democratic leadership in the community, for adult Jewish education, and every kind of Hebraic cultural activity. His charming wife Mamie, who was an author of children's textbooks and an active member of Hadassah, supported him greatly in his activities. Dr. Eisenberg's beautiful wife Rose and Mamie Gamoran were trusted friends of my wife Pupi and our families enjoyed a close relationship. The Eisenbergs and the Gamorans have remained lifelong friends of ours.

The prestige of our school was so high that we were deluged with applications from educators of the highest competence to fill the position vacated by Dr. Eisenberg. We finally chose as our new director Mr. Mordechai Halevi—a Hebrew and biblical scholar, a competent professional educator, and a charming and witty person. Halevi was much older than Eisenberg and was a first-generation immigrant from the Yeshivoth of Eastern Europe. He was thus completely in tune with the thinking of the members of the board of the Talmud Torah. Mr. Halevi came to us from a similar position in Philadelphia, and after ten years in Cincinnati he retired to live in Israel with his two sons, Amitai and Nadav. Throughout his tenure, the T.T. maintained its high standards of achievement. In 1950 Halevi was succeeded by Dr. Moses Zalesky, when I was no longer active in Jewish education.

After nineteen years as president of the T.T. I resigned, satisfied that I had done my duty for Jewish education in Cincinnati and that it was time for new leadership. Two years later, a committee headed by Yosef Gootman called on me with an urgent appeal to resume the leadership of the T.T. to "save it from falling apart due to internal dissension." Reluctantly, I acceded to their pleas with the understanding that a serious effort would be made to resolve the differences and that my tenure would be limited to this effort. On returning to the T.T., I found the institution in disarray with a rapidly declining registration due in part to incompetent leadership and in part to increasing competition from the congregational schools. In the early Fifties the temples and synagogues became more aggressive in promoting their congregational schools, primarily as a means of attracting and retaining membership. They increased their programs from one day a week to two or three days a week and

Cincinnati Jewish community leaders. Left to right: Philip M. Meyers, Sr., Rabbi Samuel Wohl, Sol Luckman, the author, Maurice Chase and x.

they enriched the content of their curriculum. They made strong appeals to the loyalty of their members and the Rabbis ceased cooperating with the T.T. or even referring to us their serious students for more intensive instruction.

Recognizing the new trend as irreversible, we began to consider new directions. As part of this effort, I appointed a select committee to explore the possibility of introducing Hebrew and Hebraic studies as electives at Walnut Hills High School (a college preparatory school with many Jewish children) and at the University of Cincinnati. After a preliminary inquiry, we learned that both projects were feasible providing they were subsidized. We had no problem in raising the necessary funds, but we ran into strong opposition from some of the Reform members of the board of the B.J.E. and from some of the Reform Rabbis in the community. It was the old "Assimilationist" fear of "setting ourselves apart from the Gentiles" and "flaunting Jewish nationalism."

Another source of opposition came from some people at HUC who contended that there was no need for Hebrew instruction at the University of Cincinnati since such courses were available at HUC. We ultimately succeeded in our efforts simply because the idea was sound; we were thus in the forefront of a trend that a few decades later became widely apparent. Our director, Dr. Zalesky, became the first instructor of Hebrew at the University of Cincinnati, and this gradually evolved into the Department of Judaic Studies at U.C. Another idea that emerged at this time was the establishment of a Hebrew day school. There was, however, a great deal of skepticism about the practicability of the idea and its financial feasibility. Yosef Gootman, who was the originator of many constructive ideas in Jewish education, was the chief proponent of the day-school idea and he nurtured it until it became a reality through his sheer indomitable will. Contributing factors to the founding and development of the Yavneh Day School and the more traditional Chofetz Chaim Day School were the collapse of the Talmud Torah as a viable institution and the coincidental deterioration of the public schools which forced many Jewish parents to the Hebrew day schools as a way out of a serious dilemma.

Dr. Zalesky's tenure as director of the B.J.E. and the T.T. was a complete disaster and I was faced with a serious problem. Zalesky was a pleasant person with a fine sense of humor and he was a personal friend. He was also an excellent Hebraist, a charming host, and a delightful entertainer who, on social occasions, would accompany himself on the balalaika while singing Hebrew, Yiddish, and Russian folk songs. But he had a serious hearing defect and he was a poor administrator, and it became clear to most members of the board that Jewish education would suffer under his administration, especially in view of the adverse trends. I was particularly embarrassed since one of the reasons for my returning to the leadership of the T.T. was to "save" Dr.

Zalesky from a sizable group of board members who demanded his resignation. After considerable soul-searching, I counseled Dr. Zalesky privately to accept a comparable position in Toronto rather than preside over dissent and dissolution in Cincinnati. Many of Zalesky's friends and colleagues were of the same opinion, but instead of taking the honorable way out, Zalesky organized a campaign of vilification centered on personalities and he received a narrow vote of confidence. Shortly thereafter I left office for good and, although we remained friends, I could not forget Dr. Zalesky's unprofessional conduct. For a variety of reasons, the B.J.E. gradually became an anachronism and the T.T. ceased to exist. The spectacle of shrewd professionals manipulating naive laymen is not unique to Jewish education nor to Cincinnati. Unfortunately the reverse is also true. It is the bane of many Jewish community organizations and relief is not in sight.

My successes at the T.T. and the B.J.E. induced other organizations to seek my support, but since I had an aversion for "joiners" I accepted new responsibilities only where I felt I could make a worthwhile contribution. One such organization was Camp Livingston, which was an agency of the Cincinnati Federation of Jewish Charities that offered two weeks of summer camping to underprivileged Jewish children. I was shocked to learn that few of the camp's personnel were Jewish, that the Sabbath and the Jewish holidays were not observed, and that pork and pork products were part of the menu. Most members of the board were women from the finest German-Jewish families, with a token representation from the Eastern European community, who were supposed to be seen and not heard. The charming ladies were absolutely flabbergasted when I began to ask such embarrassing questions as, "Why don't we have Jewish counselors, Jewish nurses, kosher food, a semblance of a religious program on the Sabbath, or the singing of Jewish songs in camp?" I tried to be as tactful as possible, but the ladies were convinced that the poor immigrant children needed to be Americanized by way of total assimilation, and they found my attitude incomprehensible.

When I became convinced that polite repartee would get me nowhere, I began to use some shock treatment, knowing full well that I would have to pay for antagonizing such an influential group of people. Thus, at one of the board meetings I asked, "By what right do you undertake to alienate young children from their parents and their heritage when you know that these children come from Orthodox homes where Kashruth and Jewish customs and holidays are being observed? Such actions," I continued, "could be expected from Christian missionaries but not from a benevolent Jewish organization." As I spoke I could see that I had struck a raw nerve and that I had stirred up considerable antagonism towards me. What I did not know was that I had made them think, for within two years Camp Livingston became an acceptable Jewish summer camp with Jewish programs, Jewish personnel, and Jewish food. With my mission accomplished, I retired from this board at the end of my three-year term. An objective observer could give some credit for these developments to the rise of anti-Semitism and the shock effect of Nazism.

In 1933 I also became a member of the Cincinnati Jewish Community Council, the Jewish Welfare Fund, and the Jewish Public Relations Committee. These were the most active and most prestigious organizations in the community. The other prestigious organizations were the Federation of Jewish Charities and the board of the Jewish Hospital, but the latter two were restricted to the elite of German descent. The sprinkling of Eastern European Jews that did serve on these bodies was mainly from among those who married into German Jewish families or amassed great wealth. The German Jews were also the self-appointed representatives of the Jewish community to the outside world and the "token" Jews in civic affairs.

In the 1930s, the numerically superior Eastern European Jews began to assert their leadership in the community. The German Jewish leaders in Cincinnati at the time were the brothers Walter and Maurice Freiberg, the brothers Max and Robert Senior, Carl Pritz, William Schroeder, Herbert Bloch, Murray Seasongood, and some of their spouses. The only recognized Jewish leader of Eastern European origin was Oscar Berman, a learned and wise man who came from Kovno and amassed a fortune as a manufacturer of a national brand of overalls. The Zionist organizations were small and carried little weight, and so too with most of the synagogues. One of the most active forces in the community was the small but dynamic Poale Zion organization and one of its aims on the American scene was "kibush ha kehilot—to conquer the community councils." This was a carry-over battle cry from Eastern Europe, except that in the U.S. they had to be founded before they could be conquered. The only kehila in the U.S., which was founded in New York City by Rabbi Judah Magnes in 1908, had collapsed with the outbreak of World War I due to the pacifism of its leader.

On the national scene, two organizations were competing for leadership in the defense area at home and abroad—the American Jewish Committee and the American Jewish Congress. The American Jewish Committee was a self-appointed, self-perpetuating organization which represented the established German Jews and was headed by the prominent New York attorney Louis Marshall, and later by Judge Joseph M. Proskauer. This organization was anti-Zionist and anti-nationalist and it operated on the basis of quiet intercession by prominent personalities—an approach we called the "sha-sha (hush-hush)" diplomacy. The American Jewish Congress, on the other hand, represented the Eastern European Jews. It was based on democratic principles and was headed by the great tribune of American Jewry Rabbi Stephen S. Wise. In the Congress, Jewish defense problems were exposed to public scrutiny in the press, in open forums, at mass demonstrations, in the courts, or through use of the boycott weapon.

Philanthropic activities and relief abroad were also conducted by two organizations—the Joint Distribution Committee, which was founded by the German Jews, and the People's Relief Committee, which was founded by the less affluent Eastern European Jews. Here again, the Joint Distribution Committee operated in a quiet, efficient manner, relying on gut diplomacy when dealing with foreign countries and demanding proof of need and a strict accounting when distributing relief, while the People's Relief Committee dispensed its meager resources for the asking with little consideration for efficiency or accounting. People's Relief had a short life and the differences between the defense organizations changed or vanished in the course of time. In retrospect, these organizations often complemented each other, but occasionally they could not get out of each other's way; on the whole, the German Jews built on more lasting foundations.

The Cincinnati Jewish Community Council came into being in 1920 in the wake of the war activities of the local branches of the American Jewish Congress and the People's Relief. It was joined by the Federation of Jewish Charities, probably in order to maintain a measure of control over the activities of the recent immigrants, but also in the interest of communal unity. In the name of efficiency, the Federation had absorbed or dissolved many of the charitable institutions which the Eastern European Jews had founded and there was a great deal of quiet grumbling, but the immigrants lacked the leadership and resources to put up an effective resistance.

When I joined the Cincinnati Jewish Community Council (CJCC) I found it to be a democratic kehila all but in name. It consisted of representatives from every synagogue, temple, cultural and charitable organization in the city and it provided an ideal forum for creating closer relations between the German and the Eastern European Jews. The sessions of the Council were occasionally stormy but we learned in time that neither side had horns. The exchange of ideas led to the awareness of a mutual dependence—the German Jews had the influence of wealth, leadership, tenure, and achievement while the Eastern European Jews represented the power of numbers and a more intimate perspective on Jewish problems.

The representatives of the Poale Zion had a large following in the Community Council. They took a position on every subject and their point of view prevailed most of the time. The chief spokesmen for the Poale Zion were Yosef

Gootman, Ben Zion Doll, and myself. Dr. Emanuel Gamoran, who was a general Zionist, was to all intents a member of our group. Any position one of us took individually or as a group had an automatic majority in the council, so that in controversial matters an effort was made to reach a consensus in committee before or after the Council meetings. Most of the discussions revolved around the raising and distribution of funds which were raised through an annual welfare fund drive and distributed by an allocations committee. Since most of the funds raised in the Twenties, Thirties, and Forties came from members of the two Reform temples, Rockdale and Wise, who were largely of German Jewish origin, these groups also wished to control the allocation of funds. This was unacceptable to the Poale Zion because these groups were primarily interested in philanthropy and had very little interest in Eretz Yisroel or in Jewish cultural and educational causes. We also questioned whether they truly represented the sentiments of their alleged constituency. They did have a point in that most of the funds raised came from about fifteen percent of the community, there being only five hundred to seven hundred contributors in a Jewish community of 25,000. But we questioned the implication of their figures and contended that the reason for the small number of contributors could very well be a lack of effort or a lack of confidence in their leadership; we also challenged them to let us prove our point.

In 1935, I became the chairman of a special committee to broaden the base of contributors to the Jewish Welfare Fund and I threw myself into this task with the same zeal as when I helped increase the enrollment of the Talmud Torah from one hundred fifty to over five hundred. At a special mass meeting of the Poale Zion, I explained the importance of our undertaking and I appealed to them to help me get three hundred volunteer solicitors. I got my three hundred workers, whom I organized into thirty teams, and they spread out into the community knocking on doors to sign up new contributors and get increased amounts from old contributors. Nearly three thousand new contributors were signed up and, although the total amount raised was not large, everybody recognized the magnitude of the achievement and its portents for the future. The astounding results were especially noteworthy considering the scarcity of money in the midst of the Great Depression. After several more years of identical efforts we succeeded in increasing the number of contributors to seven thousand and some of those who started with insignificant donations eventually became contributors in six figures. In 1937 I served as chairman of men's teams in the Welfare Fund Drive under the overall chairmanship of Louis Kaufman, and I was being groomed for the general chairmanship. All I had to do to reach this prestigious position was to tone down my rhetoric and become more yielding. But my upbringing in Serei, the yeshiva, and Vilna would not permit compromises in questions of principle—neither did the problems nor the times—and I never regretted my conduct.

A lasting achievement of the CJCC was the establishment of the American Jewish Archives under the editorship of Professor Jacob R. Marcus of HUC. In his own inimitable style, this project was being pushed by Yosef Gootman in session after session for a number of years, but every time he mentioned the need of a "pinkas" (or minutes of the kehila), it met with laughter and derision—largely because the sound of the word "pinkas" struck the others as very funny. Fortunately, Dr. Marcus recognized the importance of the project, and with his help and influence, the American Jewish Archives was established as a national project.

At one time I had to recruit help from outside the Council to carry a point. The allocations committee, which was to distribute $15,000 to the defense organizations, voted to divide the money between the American Jewish Committee and the Anti-Defamation League of B'nai B'rith and to leave out the American Jewish Congress. I decided to take up this matter privately with my influential friend and distant relative Sol Luckman. I spent an entire evening with Sol explaining the differences between the three defense organizations. He asked searching questions which I was able to answer to his satisfaction and, as a result, he went to bat for us and won a share of the allocation for the Congress.

During one of the meetings of the CJCC, as I was presenting the position of the American Jewish Congress in favor of open combat against anti-Semitism through mass demonstrations and a vigorous campaign in the press and in the courts, Mr. Carl Rauh became so exercised over my rhetoric that he demonstratively left the room, slamming the door behind him. I regretted this incident since I had a high regard for this gentleman, who was the scion of a distinguished Cincinnati German-Jewish family and a brother of Dr. Louise Rauh, a colleague and classmate. Mr. Rauh was the owner of a large firm manufacturing national brand shirts and I was his plant physician. Mr. Rauh had never expressed himself at the CJCC on any issue and my rhetoric must have hurt him deeply. Yet, as far I knew, he did not hold it against me.

To occupy the center stage as the scapegoat for the world's ills is a frightening experience and American Jews felt it deeply. The period between the two World Wars, when a vicious anti-Semitism raged and was about to engulf us, was most traumatic, but it also had its salutary effects on the local scene—it helped bring about a truce of sorts between the competing factions. We became more tolerant towards opposing points of view and we got to know each other a little better. The Cincinnati Jewish Community Council, which was in its heyday during this period, served this purpose admirably well. With all the demagoguery and bombastic talk which often characterizes such forums, a great many beneficial results were achieved in addition to the raising and distribution of funds. With the unveiling of the great tragedy of the Holocaust and the emergence of the State of Israel, the need for funds quadrupled and the free-swinging Community Council was viewed by some of the large contributors as an impediment. So when my friend Philip M. Meyers, the newly-elected president of the CJCC, announced that in order to better serve the increased philanthropic needs of the community he was merging the CJCC with the Welfare Fund, it was met with stony silence by a shocked assembly and the Council died a natural death. "The Moor has done his work, the Moor may go."

Another important activity in which I became involved at this time was the American Jewish Congress. The Cincinnati branch of the Congress had ceased to exist in 1920 at the end of World War I. In 1933, I received a letter from Rabbi Stephen S. Wise, the President of the American Jewish Congress and the foremost leader of American Jewry, asking me to re-establish a branch of the Congress in Cincinnati. With the deepening of the Depression and the spreading of a vicious anti-Semitism, discrimination against Jews in employment and other areas of endeavor became widespread and was deeply felt. The American Jewish Congress intensified its fight against anti-Semitism and launched a militant program to combat economic discrimination. The hush-hush methods of the American Jewish Committee were never too effective, and with the wave of anti-Semitism which was being orchestrated by the Nazis, the German-American Jews suffered a severe blow to their pride. They reacted to the gathering storm with painful restraint. I felt that there was a great deal that could be done on the local level, but that we could not employ in Cincinnati the methods that might well be effective in New York. I communicated my thoughts to Rabbi Wise and received a free hand to organize a local chapter of the Congress—substantially on my own terms. Since I felt that economic discrimination was the most important problem at that time, I decided to concentrate most of my efforts in this area.

With the aims fairly fixed, I invited every Jewish organization in the community to appoint two representatives to a founding meeting of a Cincinnati branch of the Congress. The response was overwhelming and the assembly resembled the CJCC in size and representation. The gathering approved the national program of the Congress and my own approach to the problems, and it constituted itself as the Cincinnati branch of the Congress. I was elected President by acclamation and was authorized to proceed with the implementation of the program. The enthusiastic community response to my call indicated a deep-felt concern and readiness for action.

I recognized that in order to combat economic discrimination effectively, it was essential to have a united community behind the effort. In Cincinnati that meant the support of the Federation of Jewish Charities—where the German-Jewish leadership was concentrated. I therefore met with my friend Maurice Sievers, who was the director of the Federation, and solicited his views on how best to approach the Federation about combatting discrimination against Jews in employment. Mr. Sievers promised to think about it, and at a subsequent meeting he expressed his doubts that the Federation would be interested in dealing with unemployment of Jews when there was such widespread general unemployment. The Federation, he continued, "is primarily interested in charity, and if they ever become interested in unemployment they will surely prefer to do it on their own." Despite his discouragement, I prevailed upon him to present my ideas to the Federation formally or informally, as he deemed best. After consulting with the leadership of the Federation, Mr. Sievers informed me that "not only will the Federation reject your proposal, but they will use every means at their disposal to combat it as dangerous to the welfare of the Jewish community and as a divisive activity."

I reported the discouraging developments at a special meeting of the Congress and recommended that we should formally request the Federation to join the Congress in establishing a vocational bureau to deal with discrimination against Jews in employment and related economic problems. I also suggested that the Federation be informed that if they chose not to join we would proceed on our own. After a lengthy discussion, both suggestions were adopted and I dispatched a carefully couched letter to the Cincinnati Federation of Jewish Charities to that effect. My letter hit them like a ton of bricks as they found themselves in a no-win situation—they were afraid of the possible adverse effect of the project on Jewish-Gentile relations, but they were also afraid that if they did not join they would lose any restraining influence they might otherwise be able to exert. After considerable soul-searching, the Federation decided to accept our proposal in principle and to negotiate the mechanics and the details.

The Federation did their best to dilute the program and to make the proposed vocational bureau an integral part of the Federation with a measure of control for myself and the American Jewish Congress. I pointed out that since they served primarily the poor and the indigent, the new organization would be stigmatized and avoided by the rest of the community. I also reminded them of their habit of absorbing and liquidating joint ventures. The mutual mistrust was deep and it required some fifty meetings and dozens of memoranda to hammer out a mutually acceptable agreement. It was my dogged perseverance, the urgency of the cause, and the help of Mr. Sievers that combined to overcome the difficulties. In the end, the Jewish Vocational Bureau of Cincinnati was established as an independent agency with a governing board to be appointed jointly by the Congress and the Federation. We also agreed that Mr. Carl Pritz of the Federation was to become its first president and that I would serve as chairman of a semi-independent committee to deal with discrimination against Jews in employment. A committee on vocational training, testing, and counseling was added to the program of the Vocational Bureau and the Federation agreed to assume the cost of the project. By mutual consent, Mr. George Newburger, a professional social worker, was chosen as the director of the Bureau.

Due to the outstanding qualities of the new director and the dedication of the board, the Jewish Vocational Bureau of Cincinnati became a phenomenal success and it served as a model to other communities and to the United States Government. In later years, the program was modified to accommodate to changing needs and circumstances and a sheltered workshop was added, which also became a model. Eventually the B'nai B'rith asked to be represented on the board by virtue of their special interest in anti-discrimination and the structure of the agency was modified to accommodate their interest. The Jewish Vocational Bureau of Cincinnati is still functioning in a robust fashion and is regarded as one of the most successful public service agencies in Cincinnati. After World War II, the Cincinnati branch of the Congress concentrated for a while on legal activities and then ceased to exist, while the Federation of Jewish Charities became a federation of semi-independent agencies known as the Federation of Jewish Services. With the aid of time, Eastern European Jews began to play a prominent role in the Federation and the Vocational Bureau (now called the Jewish Vocational Service) has remained one of its affiliated semi-autonomous agencies.

The Committee to Combat Discrimination against Jews in Employment became the most dynamic and the most controversial part of the Vocational Bureau. In a preliminary survey, we learned that discrimination against Jews in employment was more widespread than we had expected. One of the surprising findings was that even Jewish employers were discriminating against Jews. Their stated reasons were that their Jewish employees would expect special treatment or excessive familiarity, that their business practices or financial position would be broadcast or compromised, or that they would be training potential competitors. To deal with this type of prejudice, we embarked on an educational campaign with the aid of the Jewish press and the help of the Rabbis and influential members of our board. To combat discrimination in the general community, we decided to tackle one large concern or industry at a time—in Cincinnati it meant the Procter & Gamble Company.

The decision caused an explosion of tempers at a meeting among myself, as chairman of the committee on discrimination, the director George Newburger, the president of the Bureau, Carl Pritz, and the president of the Federation, William Schroeder. Pritz and Schroeder considered it an offense to Mr. Dupree, the Chairman of the Board of Procter & Gamble, who was a personal friend of theirs, an occasional golf partner, and allegedly a very nice person. Mr. Newburger and I pointed out that anti-Semitism and discrimination against Jews had become institutionalized and it was quite possible that Mr. Dupree might be unaware of the existence of overt discrimination against Jews in his vast enterprise and that, in all likelihood, he might even be unaware of the very existence of the problem. We finally agreed to let Mr. Schroeder approach Mr. Dupree as discreetly as he wished and report back to us. Within a week, Mr. Schroeder reported that Mr. Dupree was unaware of any discrimination and that he suggested that we take up this matter with the personnel department of P & G. When Mr. Newburger met with the personnel director of P & G, he learned that the company was not only discriminating against Jews but also against Catholics and other religious groups. Unbelievable as it may seem, it turned out that their employees were almost exclusively Presbyterians. There were one or two Jews among five thousand employees in Cincinnati. One of these was Rabbi Mordechai Schiff, who was in charge of supervising the Kashrut of Crisco and other edible products. The only Jews that the company was employing in significant numbers were salesmen in New York City and in several other major cities with large Jewish populations. All our efforts to remedy the situation proved fruitless. Their bottom line was that employment at Procter & Gamble was done upon recommendation from the heads of departments and that it was only natural that the heads of the departments should choose people who were members of their own church of their own denomination and that these were, naturally, the people in whom they had confidence.

I reported the situation to Rabbi Stephen S. Wise and he exploded with a threat to organize a national boycott against the firm. When P & G learned about the possibility of a boycott, they began to backtrack and promised favorable consideration of Jewish applicants in the future. A few Jews were hired but there were not too many applicants for the menial jobs that were offered. The outbreak of World War II brought an end to the Depression and to major unemployment, yet we felt that our efforts had a permanent salutary effect on the employment policies of this important company.

Our next study was discrimination against the employment of Jews in accounting. Discrimination in this field was a double-edged sword since a period of employment by a public accountant's firm was a prior requirement for certification by the State of Ohio. There was not a single Jewish public accounting firm in Cincinnati and not a single Gentile accounting firm would hire a Jewish applicant. The national accounting firms doing business in Cincinnati admitted discrimination against Jewish applicants but pleaded that they were forced into the practice because Jewish as well as Gentile firms distrusted Jewish accountants. We decided to call their bluff and extracted a promise from several accounting firms that they would consider Jewish applicants if their clients did not object. When we reported our findings to our board, there was an outcry of anguish and disbelief by many of the members who were themselves important clients of these accounting firms. A deluge of calls from our board members to their accountants brought quick results.

We next decided to study possible discrimination against Jewish applicants by the Cincinnati College of Medicine and the State of Ohio School of Dentistry. In both of these institutions there were undisguised restrictive quotas against Jewish applicants. To our surprise, we found that the smallest number of admissions to the Cincinnati College of Medicine occurred during the tenure of the Jewish dean, Dr. Alfred Friedlander. Since the same, allegedly unfriendly, chairman of admissions, Dr. David Tucker, had been in charge over more than three decades, we could only speculate as to the cause of this aberration. Was it a bending backwards by the Jewish dean afraid to be accused of favoring his co-religionists? Or were there other reasons? Dr. Friedlander's embarrassment over these disclosures produced salutary results. At the Ohio State School of Dentistry only three Jewish students were admitted in a class of 150 in the year of our study. This evidence of discrimination was so startling that it was promptly corrected by political action. After fifteen years as chairman of my committee, I retired in the late 1940s from the Board of the Jewish Vocational Service when I began to withdraw from all public activities in order to devote more time to the practice of medicine and the study of accidents.

Among the most interesting and informative activities in which I participated were the meetings of the Cincinnati Jewish Public Relations Committee (JPRC). For the most part, these meetings were round-table luncheon gatherings of an elite representative group that made decisions about various approaches to anti-Semitic incidents and other public relations matters. Out of respect for the greater experience of the more established leaders, I was not very vocal at these meetings. I was often amazed, though, at their extreme sensitivity over the slightest aspersion against Jews in the press by individuals or by groups. On such occasions, I sometimes wondered whether their hypersensitivity was due to their heightened expectations or whether my feelings were dulled by prolonged exposure to hostility and insults in Europe. On the whole, though, I admired the work of the JPRC for it was done with a great deal of tact, dignity, and skill.

During the mid-Thirties, as the entire world turned against us, American Jews began to strengthen their institutions. One such effort was the founding of the Friends of Hebrew Culture (FHC) to coordinate the educational and cultural activities in the country on a non-partisan basis. I was among the founders of the Cincinnati chapter of this organization and I remained its presiding officer for several decades, later becoming its honorary president. The FHC raised funds to help with the publication of Jewish books, arranged lectures and forums by outstanding national figures, and brought to Cincinnati theatrical groups and concert programs in Yiddish and in Hebrew. It was a true community effort and the society still exists, on a reduced scale, under the aegis of the Bureau of Jewish Education.

An incident which caused me great embarrassment occurred at a luncheon meeting of the executive committee of the FHC which was held at the Cincinnati Club under my chairmanship. One of the participants, a well-known Reform Rabbi and a national Zionist leader, ordered a serving of Virginia ham with raisins. While some of the members merely glanced at each other, it threw me into a panic for I expected momentarily the arrival of the venerable Rabbi Louis Feinberg, who was strictly observant. Throughout the luncheon my eyes were glued to the open door and the elevator. I was ready to jump to my feet the moment Rabbi Feinberg arrived so as to detain him until the table was cleared. Fortunately, Rabbi Feinberg was late and we were spared further embarrassment. I have often wondered how I managed to engage in the customary polite dinner table conversation with this "sword of Damocles" hanging over my head!

During this period, the Poale Zion emerged as the dominant Zionist organization in America, if not in numbers at least in vitality and influence. But the organization was handicapped by its socialist program—repugnant to most American Jews. To provide a roof organization for those who sympathized with the Poale Zion program in Eretz Yisroel but had no stomach for their socialist orientation in American politics, it was decided to found the Friends of the Histadrut. The main activity of this organization was to raise funds in support of the mushrooming activities of the Histadrut—the pioneering workers organization of Eretz Yisroel founded by Ben Gurion, Ben Zvi, Zalman Shazar, Golda Meir, etc. I became one of the founders of the local chapter of the Histadrut and remained its presiding officer for several decades until I was succeeded by Maurice Chase. As an outgrowth of my activities for the Histadrut, I participated, together with Rabbi Samuel Wohl of Wise Temple, in founding the labor Zionist Anglo-American monthly *The Jewish*

Frontier. Under the editorship of Chaim Greenberg, the revered ideologue of the Poale Zion, *The Jewish Frontier* became and remained the clarion voice of American Liberal Zionist opinion. The Histadrut fund-raising campaign has remained one of the major activities of this organization.

In addition to my presiding over seven organizations and serving on many boards, numerous organizations and causes were constantly seeking my active or moral support. This period was, without doubt, the busiest time in my life. As a result, my name was constantly on the pages of Cincinnati's two Anglo-Jewish weeklies, *The American Israelite* and *Every Friday*, and I felt embarrassed for myself and my family over the constant barrage of publicity. To casual observers it undoubtedly appeared as if I were running for public office or were deriving some other kind of personal benefit out of it, whereas in actuality it brought me untold harm in my professional career. It remained an unsolved mystery where I found the time and the energy to engage in so many activities and yet spend sixty to seventy hours a week in the pursuit of a lucrative medical practice and an active social life. Part of the answer lies, perhaps, in the old adage, "If you want to get things done, find a busy man." I frequently felt twinges of conscience for not spending more time with my family, yet Pupi did not complain and seemed to encourage my activities.

Another explanation for my unusual involvement in community activities may be found in a family tradition in which leisure was considered the time for doing something really useful such as reading, studying, teaching, or engaging in public service. My grandfather, Moshe Simcho Schulzinger, and my father were seldom seen without a book in their hands or a volume of the Talmud in front of them. My cousin Rabbi Yitzhak Schulzinger—a Rabbi, author, adult teacher, and community worker in Haifa, Israel—his son, Rabbi Moshe Mordechai Schulzinger—a non-practicing Rabbi in B'nai Brak, Israel—and others of my family have all followed in the same tradition. In my generation and in generations past, the wasting of time was considered as sinful as the wasting of anything else that was useful or valuable.

One of my cherished rewards was getting to know numerous persons of achievement and stature. One of these was Mr. Sol Luckman, who was a successful ladies' coat manufacturer in New York who moved to Cincinnati in the early Thirties. Sol and I became close friends and we spent many an evening at each others' homes. His wife, Ann (Levin-Sereisky), was a good-looking woman with a ready wit and an alert mind, and she became a prominent civic leader in Cincinnati. She would probe and challenge me into lengthy discussions on Zionism and other Jewish and general topics. Sol remained an interested listener for many years, seldom offering a comment. A number of years later he began to take an interest in Jewish community affairs and he eventually held every position of leadership in the Isaac M. Wise Temple and in the Jewish community at large. After the emergence of the State of Israel, he became a prominent leader in support of Israel and in fund-raising efforts on the local and national scenes. He served with distinction on the cabinet of the United Jewish Appeal and he became a fiery and stimulating speaker in great demand. He literally used up his deep-feeling heart in the service of Israel, despite warnings of his physicians that his great zeal was devouring him. Sol never failed to credit me for getting him involved in Israel and in Jewish community affairs.

Another distinguished gentleman with whom I established a close relationship was Adolph Rosenberg, the proprietor of exclusive ladies' wear shops. Mr. Rosenberg was a well-read and highly cultured person and former president of Rockdale Temple. He was close in his views on Jewish matters to his mentor, Rabbi Philipson, one of the most radical Reformers and anti-Zionists in the country. Mr. Rosenberg took a liking to me and we met frequently to exchange views on community problems. In committee meetings he would frequently compliment me for my intellectual honesty and idealism even though we did not see eye to eye, and occasionally he would upbraid me mildly for my naivete. I often wondered about the meaning of our close rapport in view of our divergent backgrounds and positions, until I learned that he was a native of Mariyampole and had come to the U.S. as a child. To paraphrase an old adage, one may leave Mariyampole or Serei, but one's origins will never leave him. Adolph Rosenberg's son Lee is a prominent radiologist who follows his father's interest in community affairs.

Another gentleman I was fond of was Mr. Jacob Mack, who was a wise and friendly person and a pillar of strength for Zionism, Jewish education, and every constructive Jewish activity. Mr. Mack was a manufacturer of national-brand shirts (the Mack Shirt Company) and I was his plant physician for decades. His son Richard inherited his father's traits and followed in his father's footsteps. The Mack family were among the few Zionists among German and Reform Jews when such sentiments were highly unpopular in Cincinnati.

Another person with whom I established a close personal relationship and shared many activities was Rabbi Samuel Wohl of Isaac M. Wise Temple. Rabbi Wohl was a product of European yeshivoth who came to the U.S. as a teenager and taught in a Cleveland Hebrew school before he moved to Cincinnati to enroll at HUC. After he was ordained as a Rabbi in 1927, he became the spiritual leader of the Reading Road Temple (Frum Shul) until it was merged with Wise Temple in 1931. Rabbi Wohl was a dynamic leader and a great innovator and he made himself greatly felt in the community. Some of his innovations which were adopted nationally by other Reform congregations included the consecration of young children on entering religious school, expanded educational programs for children and adults, a series of annual forums by outstanding national figures, colorful graduation and confirmation ceremonies, and many others. Rabbi Wohl was a compassionate and charitable person and very much dedicated to his congregation. At the same time, he was an ardent Labor Zionist, a Hebraist, a generous supporter of many cultural causes, and an able representative in the Christian community. During the early years of his ministry, when Zionism was still unpopular and Labor Zionism was anathema, Rabbi Wohl supported these causes quietly through a very narrow circle of special friends. After the birth of the State of Israel, he also became active on the national scene. I met Rabbi Wohl and his wife Belle soon after they came to Cincinnati and our families were neighbors and friends for many years.

On the national scene, I admired and revered Rabbi Stephen S. Wise, who was a proud and fierce fighter for Zionism and Jewish rights and a towering figure physically and intellectually. He was the greatest orator of his time and was close to President Wilson and, to a lesser extent, to President Franklin D. Roosevelt. He was also a close collaborator of Supreme Court Justice Louis D. Brandeis. I had a chance to observe Rabbi Wise at close range in committee meetings during conferences of the American Jewish Congress. Like many gifted people of his caliber, he was impatient with details or opposing views, but his greatness overshadowed his shortcomings. Rabbi Wise came from a long line of distinguished Rabbis in Budapest, Hungary and was brought to the U.S. as a child. He was the founder and Rabbi of the Free Synagogue in New York and the Jewish Institute of Religion, which subsequently merged with Hebrew Union College. One of his favorite activities was interpreting Judaism to Christian denominations and Christian clergy. These activities sometimes brought him censure from non-Reform Jewish groups when he overstepped the bounds of propriety on sensitive subjects.

Another outstanding personality was Dr. Nahum Goldman, whom I met at a national conference of the Congress and who subsequently was our house guest on numerous occasions. Dr. Goldman was a dynamic public speaker in several languages and a very talented political analyst. I chaired most of his appearances in Cincinnati at public events of the Congress and the Friends of Hebrew Culture. His contributions to Zionism and to Jewish rights in the Diaspora are numerous. He served as President of the American Jewish Congress, the World Jewish Congress, and the World Zionist Organization, and he was the chief negotiator with Chancellor Adenauer of the West German Republic for reparations to the victims of the Holocaust. As a Jewish world leader, Dr. Goldman was received at all the important chancelleries of the world where he played the role of a shtadlan (special pleader or negotiator). Goldman was a catalyst or an opportunistic headline-grabber, depending on whether one was with him or against him. After the emergence of the State of Israel, he became more controversial than ever, primarily as a result of his long-standing feuds with the leaders on the left and the right of the Zionist spectrum—especially after his influence diminished. Goldman was a colorful and, for the most part, constructive personality whose stature was diminished by his excessive pride, arrogance, and lack of the common touch. Dr. Goldman was born in northern Lithuania, where his father was a teacher, and he emigrated with his parents to Munich, Germany as a child of eight. He received a thorough German schooling, including a doctorate in jurisprudence from a German university, and he made a small fortune in business. When Hitler came to power, Goldman emigrated to the U.S., and after the war he divided his residence between the U.S., France and Israel. Dr. Goldman was very sensitive about his origins and he was never able to shed the acquired trait of being at one's neck or one's feet.

Other Jewish leaders I got to know were Mr. Louis Lipsky and Dr. Samuel Margoshes, both of whom were gifted writers and pillars of strength in Zionism, the American Jewish Congress, and Jewish educational and cultural causes. Other personalities who contributed to American Jewish letters, thought, and leadership and who have influenced my life were Chaim A. Friedlander, poet and educator of Cleveland; Rabbi Solomon B. Freehoff of Chicago and Pittsburgh; Rabbi Solomon Goldman of Cleveland and Chicago; Rabbi Julius Gordon of St. Louis, and many of the scholars and teachers of HUC. Most of these came to the U.S. from Europe as children, were educated in yeshivoth, and were our house guests on occasion.

By the end of World War I, American Jews were polarized into two main groups—the majority were of the middle class while a strong minority were proletarians. The workers were mainly concentrated in the large Eastern industrial centers, especially in New York, while the others were spread out all over the country. The proletarian Jews were fiercely class-conscious and they developed large institutions of their own which included powerful unions, a vibrant daily Yiddish press, an elaborate parochial school network, teacher seminaries, and adult education programs. They also established banks, insurance companies, trade schools, fraternal lodges, burial associations, and a complete cultural milieu of their own. While their economic institutions were built on solid foundations, their political orientation was a carry-over from their European experiences that had little bearing on the American scene. Their strongest political arm was the Arbeiter Ring (Workers Circle), a descendant of the revolutionary European progenitor the Bund (union). In their national commitments, most of them were anti-Zionist, anti-religious, and anti-Hebrew "Yiddishists" with an assimilationist orientation.

To some extent, "Yiddishism" took on a life of its own for them, akin to a new religion or cult. They argued that the struggle against anti-Semitism and persecution should be fought as part of the classencampf (class struggle) with the aid of strong labor unions and support from the Gentile socialist political parties. They detested Hebrew as the language of the Jewish "clerics," and religion they called the opium of the people. It is ironical that for at least a thousand years Hebrew and Yiddish co-existed peacefully side by side without any problems—Yiddish was used in the home, in business, and in translating the religious literature, while Hebrew was the language of the synagogue and the Rabbis, who used the holy tongue in marriage or divorce contracts and in Biblical or Talmudic exegesis. Both modern Hebrew and modern Yiddish emerged in the 18th century in the wake of the "Haskala" movement which aimed at introducing "Enlightenment" or world culture to Jewish life. The great classical writers of Yiddish literature—Mendele Mocher Sforim (Abromowitz), Sholem Aleichem (Rabinowitz), and I.L. Peretz—wrote in Hebrew as well as in Yiddish and in their later works they advocated a return to traditional Judaism. When those giants chastized they did so with the intent of correcting evils, not destroying. It never occurred to them that the master-pieces they created and the language they enriched would be perverted into a transmission belt for Communist or revolutionary propaganda.

In their defiance of traditional Judaism, the "Bundists" often displayed juvenile spite, extremely bad manners, and a lack of self-respect—as when they held well-publicized balls on Yom Kippur Night during the very hours when most Jews were assembled in synagogues and praying as supplicants in reverence and in awe, or when they arranged Yom Kippur banquets—stuffing themselves with pork and even tallow while thundering insults at observant Jews. In the course of time their causes vanished along with most of their institutions and adherents, and they merged into the mainstream of American Jewish life. Yet even today the attenuated sense of identity of their offspring can be traced back to the anti-religious assimilationist background of their forebears.

Aside from the Zionist and proletarian struggles, the enormous pent-up energies of the Jewish immigrants were directed toward getting rooted economically and most clung to their Judaism through mere inertia, with some help from anti-Semitism. Judaism was reduced to the mere giving of tz'doka (charity), attendance at the synagogue or temple on Rosh Hashanah and Yom Kippur, and the ceremonials at birth, marriage, and death. The attrition was by way of total assimilation, intermarriage, or by leaving the fold as non-practicing Jews or members of the Unitarian Church. Leading the parade were some of the affluent German Jews and those who lived in small communities and in the South. But even the observant synagogue-going Jews did not emerge from this period unscathed, and many were frankly pessimistic about their children or grandchildren remaining Jews. Eventually, most of the differences between the various Jewish factions softened and out of this divergent hodge-podge emerged the proud and powerful American Jewry of today—not uniform, but fairly united in matters related to Jewish survival. But the question of viability has re-emerged.

When Hitler came to power he succeeded in stirring up the latent anti-Semitism all over the world to a point where Jews felt physically threatened and without a ray of hope. The unprecedented world-wide Depression made Jews an easy target for the hate-mongers, the bullies, and the unwary masses. Again, the great European powers—England and France, which had staked their hopes for retaining world dominion on a war between Communism and Fascism—were indifferent to the rising anti-Semitism in their countries. Jews were especially shocked when the Communists and the Nazis signed a friend-ship treaty in 1939 which increased the danger to European Jewry and menaced the peace of the world. This also caused a great deal of confusion and divided counsel in the Jewish defense organizations on how best to combat the menace. The American Jewish Congress, under the able and courageous leadership of Rabbi Stephen S. Wise, thundered defiance against the Nazis and warned about the mortal danger facing the Jews, the U.S., and the Free World. As president of the Cincinnati branch of the Congress and as a member of the JPRC and the Community Council, I was party to all of the raging controversies on the local and national scenes. The Cincinnati JPRC became fearful and insecure and was often governed by the age old "Ma yomru hagoyim?—What will the Gentiles say?" They counseled quiet diplomacy and restraint and were opposed to public demonstrations or boycotts. When I received instructions from Rabbi Wise to arrange a mass demonstration or a public outcry against some particular outrage, the Poale Zion and most members of the community were always with us, while the Public Relations Committee usually had to be coaxed and placated one way or another.

During the 1930s and 1940s, I participated in many conferences as the representative of the organizations in which I was active. The net effect of these experiences was disillusionment with most of the leadership and with some of the approaches. While I still believed in the ideal of the "faithful public servant," I found a disturbing level of petty self-interest and hypocrisy in the highest quarters. I was, perhaps, expecting too much or was still too close to the ideals of Serei and Vilna and not sufficiently attuned to the ways of the world; but it made me very unhappy. The weaknesses of the national Jewish leadership and the divided counsel were exploited by powerful anti-Semitic functionaries in Washington, and in the crunch the Jewish leadership was misinformed, misled, and shamefully deceived until it was too late.

CHAPTER FIVE

The Great Depression

> "The only thing we have to fear
> is fear itself."
> (Franklin D. Roosevelt)

Several months before the Crash on Wall Street, my colleagues were tantalizing each other in the doctor's lounge of the Jewish Hospital with the great fortunes they were amassing in the stock market. Several months after the Crash, when they had recovered from their initial shock, they were talking with equal gusto about the great fortunes they had lost on Wall Street and how they were wiped out clean. From the way they were talking I was never quite sure which experience they enjoyed the most.

One day Dr. Louis Ransohoff, a senior surgeon, said to me, "Schulze, how did the Depression hit you?" "Well, Lou," I said, "I really cannot tell you for I do not know how it was before." Since I had started in the practice of medicine at the onset of the Depression and never knew great riches, I was content with the small pickings that came my way.

Another illustration of the times is the story of a colleague and classmate of mine. After several years of additional training he considered himself lucky when he landed a job with an insurance company at seventy-five dollars a week. Four years later, in the midst of the Depression, he felt crushed when he was laid off for lack of work. During the entire period of satisfactory and faithful service he had never received a raise.

Individual experiences during the Depression varied from complete annihilation to the tolerable. A few even prospered for, despite the massive unemployment, most Americans continued to work. What made the Great Depression such a shattering experience for everybody was the endless uncertainty and the haunting fear of every tomorrow. In this sense, few in the country remained unaffected. It may be difficult for anyone who has not lived through the tragic years of the Great Depression to comprehend the depth of the gloom and despair that enveloped the nation and the world. Overnight, great fortunes were lost, the life savings of many were wiped out, and there were numerous cases of suicide, bankruptcies, bank closures, unemployment, starvation, and other tragedies on an unprecedented scale. Despite the heroic efforts of President Roosevelt and a frightened Congress, the Great Depression did not abate until it was overtaken by World War II. The Great Depression had its roots in World War I and led directly to World War II. In effect, the turbulent Twenties and Thirties were a mere uneasy truce between the two World Wars—the stories of all three are thus intertwined.

Europe emerged from World War I in ruins—ravaged physically, morally, socially, politically, and economically. Violent revolutions toppled the long-reigning monarchies of Russia, Germany, Austria-Hungary and Turkey while England and France, despite winning the war, were faint shadows of their former selves. Before long galloping inflation, unemployment, and currency devaluations led to economic collapse and Europe was on its way towards Fascism, Nazism, combative Communism, class and race hatreds, World War II, and the Holocaust.

The United States came out of World War I with enhanced prestige as the world's dominant military power and as the world's greatest market, producer, and banker—a bastion of capitalism. Unaccustomed to the wielding of such awesome power and torn internally between the forces of isolationism and internationalism, the U.S. fumbled and stumbled on such crucial issues as war reparations, tariffs, foreign trade, fiscal policies, and foreign affairs until the economy of the U.S. collapsed along with the economies of Europe and the world was plunged into the Great Depression.

While the war was won in the trenches at Verdun, the peace was lost at the Palace of Versailles, where greed and myopia triumphed over reason and magnanimity. The Treaty of Versailles not only humiliated a badly defeated enemy but imposed on him such astronomically high reparations as to virtually guarantee the collapse of the world economy. The humiliation of Versailles was the seed that nurtured a new war of revenge and "national honor" twenty years later, while the impossible financial burden imposed on Germany could only be satisfied by a country that lay in ruins through huge American loans and the flooding of world markets with cheap German goods. When the American loans dried up and when Great Britain and France began to realize that the German reparations were causing massive unemployment in their own countries, the entire system collapsed and upheaval beckoned.

As the conquering American heroes were being received back home with great fanfare and exuberance, few people realized that the innocent youths who had leaped into battle to "save the world for democracy" were returning home as brutalized men, and that there were staggering bills to be paid. Also, while the country was busy fighting and winning a war, two Constitutional amendments were adopted which changed the face of America. Before the Income Tax Amendment was passed, the Federal Government played only a peripheral role in the life of its citizens—except in times of war. With this tapping of a seemingly inexhaustible source of revenue, an ever-expanding Government began to exert profound social and economic changes. Of a different nature, but equally troublesome, was the Prohibition Amendment, which led (before it was repealed) to a widespread contempt for law, political corruption, and to the rise of major crime syndicates.

The enthusiasm and good feeling that followed the end of the war was soon overcome by sobering realities. The demobilization of the armed forces and the end of war production led to massive unemployment and the resulting dissatisfaction created a field day for union busters, the KKK, and other hate-mongering groups. The mini-Depression in the wake of the demobilization was followed in fairly rapid succession by a real estate boom, financial excesses, inflation, wild speculation on Wall Street, and ultimately a collapse of the entire economy.

The economic boom of the Twenties was triggered by a shortage in housing, the mass production of automobiles, and the unheard-of high wages of Henry Ford. Pretty soon large amounts of money were chasing inadequate supplies of goods, and the fevers of speculative excesses and high inflation affected large segments of the country. A story circulating at that time told of a man who was sold a pair of matching cats for $20,000 upon arrival in Miami and who sold them, sight unseen, for $40,000 before he had time to check in at the hotel. "And what did he do with the money?" asked an inquisitive listener. "He bought a pair of dogs for $50,000!" was the answer.

When the speculative and inflationary bubbles burst, a total collapse of the economy ensued. It was a shattering fall and what made the situation worse was the lack of any institutions in place to cushion the fall. Most of the arts, higher education, research, and charitable agencies that served the poor were financed through private philanthropy. When their resources dried up as a result of the Crash those dependent on them were the first to suffer. There was no unemployment insurance and no entitlement funds to help the rapidly swelling army of unemployed. A few unions made an effort to come to the rescue of their members, but their meager resources shrank with the rest of the economy. It was heart-breaking to see once proud and well-dressed men panhandling apples in the street to eke out a meager existence for their families. Marriage and birth rates dropped sharply and the sharing of one apartment by two or three families was common. Unemployment reached twenty-five percent and many of those who did work were on a part-time schedule at low pay. Conditions finally reached such an impasse that the war veterans organized a march on Washington to demand redress, and President Hoover found it necessary to call out the Army to prevent riots and bloodshed. In 1932, a disillusioned electorate voted President Hoover out of office. He was a disgraced and dispirited man.

President Hoover was basically a good man but his sense of timing and his understanding of the market forces and of mass psychology were as faulty as could be. Every time President Hoover proclaimed that "prosperity is just around the corner," the stock market plunged, the economy worsened, and bankruptcies skyrocketed. He undoubtedly meant well and tried hard to ameliorate the steadily worsening conditions, but everything he did turned sour. There were other players at fault. Thus a proposal by Senator Philip La Follette, Sr. of Wisconsin at the beginning of the Depression that Congress appropriate five billion dollars to fight the Depression by "priming the pump" was met with derision and was voted down. At a time when the annual budget of the U.S. Government was around one billion dollars, Senator La Follette's proposal appeared daring and reckless. Another reason for the defeat of the Senator's far-reaching idea was the belief, within and without the Administration, that the Depression was a self-limited disease and, given a little time, the natural recuperative powers would assert themselves and the economy would emerge stronger than ever. But the hoped-for miracle did not happen and the Depression and the great tragedy that was enveloping the nation and the world rapidly deepened without a ray of hope in sight.

As if all these calamities were not enough, nature conspired to make matters even worse. During the Thirties, dust storms converted large parts of the farmland of the Midwest into desert and many of the farmers packed their families into their trucks and jalopies and headed off to distant states in search of non-existent jobs. At times the migrants would stop on the road to beg, "appropriate," or work short stints to enable them to continue on their aimless trek. The plight of the migrant farmers swelling the ranks of the migrant city workers touched the heart of America and eventually led to numerous reforms.

Among the evils which led to the economic collapse were the laissez-faire attitude of Government toward business, the lack of Government concern about social welfare, and the predominance of property rights over human rights. The total lack of restraints on business frequently led to the cornering of markets for the benefit of a few speculators, economic ruin for much of the rest of the population, and repeated and disastrous financial "panics." The "boom and bust" economy of 19th century agricultural America obviously was no longer tenable in 20th century industrial America.

In the Twenties there were also violent clashes between industry and labor with "goon squads" frequently being imported by management from neighboring cities to help win labor disputes or to prevent unionization, and local governments usually intervening on the side of management. The Federal Government under Presidents Harding, Coolidge, and Hoover was strongly on the side of capital and it stressed the paramount importance of free enterprise. President Coolidge expressed this philosophy succinctly when he said, "The less government the better government," or, "The business of government is business." Twenty-five years later Charles Wilson, President of General Motors, echoed it with, "What is good for General Motors is good for the country." While this philosophy is now again gaining credence under President Reagan, fifty or sixty years ago it meant condoning child labor, unsafe and unsanitary working conditions, starvation wages, and abject poverty. At the same time, any effort to effect reform was denounced as "un-American," alien and even treasonous.

As a by-product of the social and economic turmoil, bigotry and race and class hatreds raised their ugly heads and the purveyors of hate and discord had a field day. Lynchings in the South were frequent occurrences "to keep the 'Niggers' in their place"—and so were cross-burnings on mountain tops by the KKK to intimidate Jews, Catholics, Masons, liberals, or any other group that disagreed with these "paragons of virtue." A great shock to American Jews was the anti-Semitic campaign waged by Henry Ford on the pages of his *Dearborn Independent*. For several years he published the anti-Semitic Russian forgeries known as "The Protocols of the Elders of Zion" and other inflammatory, scurrilous material. Ultimately, Ford apologized publicly for his anti-Semitic tirades, pleading that he was duped into the campaign by misguided advisors. He made a complete retraction and paid indemnity, but there is no redress that could possibly equal the offense—the poison he instilled could not be withdrawn.

Symbolic of the bigotry of the decade was the trial and execution of the two

Italian anarchist immigrants Sacco and Vanzetti for an alleged bank robbery which brought in its wake a storm of protests from all over the world. In the same vein, the passage of the highly restrictive immigration laws of 1921 and 1924, which closed a glorious chapter in American history as a haven of refuge for the oppressed and the downtrodden of the world, was also largely motivated by hatred. The insults of the special exclusion clause, which was aimed mainly at the Chinese and Japanese, left a festering sore for which deferred payment was to be made in blood two decades later. As a comic relief to these serious goings-on, the Twenties were also known as the decade of the speakeasy, moonshine, booze, and the flapper.

Along with millions of other Americans, the financial position of my parents deteriorated rapidly and they were forced to move out of the suburban Jewish neighborhood of Avondale to a slum building they owned in Mount Auburn. This was a crushing blow for they were deeply religious and they suffered from the lack of a synagogue, a kosher butcher shop, and the company of their friends. My parents' situation depressed me no end, but they were too proud to tell me of their plight and I learned of their move only after the fact. I set aside a weekly allowance for them from my meager resources and we all hoped that the bad times would soon end. My father was sixty-five when I learned that his financial situation was hopeless. Whatever he had earned and saved over a period of twenty years had gone down the drain in his real estate investments, and he suffered the fate of most other owners of rental property with mortgage payments to meet and an inadequate declining income.

The real-estate boom of the early Twenties began with the explosion of marriages and new families at the end of the war and the influx of large numbers of people from the farms and the South who came to the cities in search of a better life and better job opportunities. An acute shortage in housing developed and the value of rental property increased by leaps and bounds and speculation in real estate became rampant. With widespread stories of great fortunes being made "overnight" in "sure-fire" transactions, many people jumped on the bandwagon and they were sucked into the mad scramble for profits. My father was one of this group, but by the time he became involved prices had gotten out of hand. The only things he could afford to buy were dilapidated tenements, and even these were beyond his means without first and second mortgages. By 1931 my father had used up nearly all he had saved or could borrow in an effort to stay afloat. One day he said to me that he was too old and too tired to keep up the struggle and that he would like to retire and spend his remaining years in Eretz Yisroel. The decision was contingent on the premise that I would agree to contribute to their support and liquidate their debts. I undertook both obligations with the knowledge that the task would be difficult and burdensome.

My parents left Cincinnati for their new home in Eretz Yisroel in the summer of 1931. On their way to the Holy Land they stopped off in Serei to see my sister Rivka, her husband, Yitzhak Hirsh, and their young granddaughter, Chana. They had hoped to persuade them to emigrate to Israel with them, but after two months in Serei they left alone to join their other daughter Sheine and her husband, Avram Ber, in Tel Aviv. Eretz Yisroel was the land of their hopes, dreams, and prayers. The Jewish population of Palestine was only some sixty-five thousand at that time; my parents thus became pioneers in their old age and they were made happy by the "privilege" of helping to build the land of Israel amidst their own brothers and family. My parents lived happily in the land of their fathers for another thirty years and these were the happiest years of their lives.

Soon after I began to manage my parents' property, I discovered that I had undertaken an impossible task. The Depression was deepening, unemployment was rampant, vacancies abounded, and the income was insufficient to cover maintenance—let alone debt charges. In desperation I began to do my own repairs, maintenance, and rent collections. I saw hunger, extreme poverty, hopelessness, and human degradation at close range. People would hide at the sight of the rent collector and I felt deeply ashamed and frustrated by the experience. I struggled for a while, trying to meet mortgage payments with the earnings from my medical practice but, despite all of my efforts, I succeeded only in getting deeper in debt without a glimmer of hope in sight. In desperation, I transferred all of my father's properties to the mortgagers and arranged for a legal settlement, using up all of my savings in the process. Another twenty years passed before rental real estate regained a semblance of solvency, and as late as 1951 banks and building and loan companies were ready to sell their rental properties for the asking to anyone willing to make minimum repairs and token payments.

The breakdown of the economies of the U.S. and Europe led to the rise of Fascism, Nazism, and other radical movements to the right and the left of the social spectrum—and once again led to a vicious rise of anti-Semitism. The Jews were held responsible for all of the world's ills and they suffered both as Jews and as citizens of their respective countries. The Communists confiscated their businesses and persecuted them as capitalists, while in the capitalist countries they were persecuted as Communists. The tin-horn dictatorships that sprang up all over Europe at the end of World War I ruined the Jews economically through oppressive, discriminatory laws and politically through coercion, terror, and subversion of their own legal systems. The war, the revolutions, the political instability, and the economic chaos tore the fabric of Jewish life to shreds and led to secularism, factionalism, and fragmentation of the Jewish community. Only the inherent strength of tradition and the accumulated great cultural wealth saved Eastern European Jewry from total disintegration prior to its destruction by the Holocaust.

When the American economy collapsed, it was the coup de grace that plunged the entire world into a social and economic morass. The rise of German Nazism on the heels of Italian Fascism was made possible by a sense of hopelessness in these countries and a loss of the will to resist in the Free World. Other factors were the economic chaos, the Communist menace, and the perceived need of the Germans to purge themselves of the humiliating defeat in World War I. The Nazi myth that "Germany lost the war because it was betrayed by the Jews" became a convenient alibi and a plausible Nazi battle cry. In the ensuing chaos, the Nazis were able to recruit all of the malcontents—the hungry, the unemployed, the anti-Communists, the Jew-haters, the "professional" patriots, the Fascists, the ethnic hate groups, and the lunatic fringe. They then proceeded to mobilize in every country outside Germany the ethnic Germans and every hate group they could coax, buy, or coerce into what became known as the "fifth column" in support of German aggression. Faced by a demoralized Germany and an indifferent world, the aged and tired German President Hindenburg handed over the governmental powers to a contemptuous, demented leader in charge of a blood-thirsty mob, even though the Nazis had never received more than one-third of the German popular vote.

For American Jews, the Twenties and Thirties were the most traumatic period in American Jewish history—an era of disillusionment, frustration, and great pain. It seemed that all the hopes and dreams of a better world free of hatred, persecution, and suffering were about to collapse. Few of the immigrants had succeeded in amassing sufficient reserves to withstand the sudden onslaught of the Depression. For many, their businesses were shoe-string operations that collapsed like houses of cards, but worst of all was the daily abuse and the howling menace of the hate-mongers which reminded the immigrants of Bogdan Chmelnitzky (who slaughtered two-thirds of Polish Jewry in the seventeenth century) and the Czar's hordes. The more immediate menace of Hitler was too awesome to contemplate. Although there had always been anti-Semitism in America below the surface, it was shocking to find it so easily aroused on American soil on such a menacing scale.

While the Nazis were consolidating their political and military strength in preparation for war, they simultaneously launched a campaign to poison the minds of the world against the Jews. It was conducted with daily tirades against Jews on the air waves, in the churches, and in the press. Every malcontent, every anti-Semite, and the entire lunatic fringe were mobilized and it seemed as if the world's best hope, American democracy, was also about to succumb to the vicious Nazi campaign. The entire world was ready to engulf us in a sea of hatred. Among Hitler's most prominent allies in the U.S. in this mad drive were the German-American Bund, the America-Firsters, the KKK, Gerald L.K. Smith, and Father Coughlin. Others who served the Nazi cause were Colonel Lindberg, the expatriate poet Ezra Pound, and the anti-British crowd. We felt helpless and shocked beyond belief when boatloads of Jews who were fleeing from certain death in Germany were refused landing anywhere in the world, including the U.S.A. The fact that the country was paralyzed and badly divided between pro-British and pro-German factions, was a poor alibi and offered little comfort. Only when Germany emerged openly as the enemy of the U.S. after the Japanese attack on Pearl Harbor did Jews get a measure of relief from the anti-Semitic nightmare. But even during the war a great deal of apprehension persisted because of concern about the fate of our families in Europe and Palestine and the constant fear of the unthinkable—that the war might be lost. Only after the war ended in victory were Jews able to feel that the fury of hatred had subsided, but it was the kind of solace immortalized by Sholem Aleichem "Mir is gut, ich bin a yosem." "I am happy," says the lonely orphan, "everybody is so nice to me."

CHAPTER SIX

War and Holocaust

> *"Eicha yashva badad ha'ir rabati am*—How solitary lies the city once so full of people."
> (Lamentations)

As soon as Hitler and his cohorts became the Government of Germany in 1933, he embarked on a two-pronged program—preparation for war and persecution of Jews. He proceeded at first gingerly and later with accelerated intensity and fury as his powerful neighbors and intended victims looked on as if mesmerized and failed to act. Pursuing what became known as "salami tactics," he violated one relatively minor provision of the Versailles Treaty after another, and his appetite and daring grew with the vacillation and sophistry of his adversaries. Instead of stopping or toppling him when it could have been done easily, they let him build up a powerful army, navy, and air force and occupy the Rhineland, Austria, and the Sudetenland. The restrained or pro-forma protestations of the Allies towards Hitler's military buildup and his vicious campaigns against the Jewish people signified a serious malaise of will and spirit. By the time the Allies awoke to the danger it was too late.

Hitler's campaign against the German Jews began with a reign of terror which included vicious mob attacks, mass arrests, murder, burning of synagogues, and the looting of Jewish stores. It soon extended to the confiscation of property, revocation of citizenship, loss of human rights, deportation to concentration camps, and later to the use of extermination camps. American Jews fought against these brutalities with every means at their disposal, including the sponsorship of a world boycott against Germany. But, given a hostile world and the lack of even a semblance of physical strength of their own, it was a losing battle from the start.

To achieve their goals, the Nazis built the most elaborate propaganda machine the world had ever known, based principally on the Big Lie and every kind of fraud and deceit. Their deceptive tactics included temporary compromises to confuse their perceived enemies or to lull them into complacency until they felt strong enough to violate their solemn covenants. Among the deceptive compacts were the Munich Treaty with England and France in 1937, which gave the Nazis a free hand in Czechoslovakia and hegemony over Eastern Europe, and the treaty of 1938 with Communist Russia, which divided Poland between them and delineated spheres of influence for each country in other parts of Europe. There were also agreements to allow German Jews to emigrate in exchange for money and political consideration. In the end everybody miscalculated and everybody lost—the Western Allies, who had hoped that the Nazis and the Russians would destroy each other in a mutually debilitating war; the Russians, who had hoped to save themselves from the Teutonic fury by throwing Poland to the wolves; Hitler, who was convinced that the Western Allies would not fight over the rape of Poland; and the Jews, who failed to heed Hitler's published blueprint for their destruction. Thus was the world thrown into the savage bloodbath of World War II, in which forty million people died, and the Holocaust, in which one-third of the Jewish people perished.

With their preparations for war completed, the Germans used flimsy pretexts to attack Poland on September 1, 1939, and World War II was on when England and France honored their commitment to defend Poland. While the Nazis were ravaging and occupying southern Poland in blitzkrieg fashion, the Russians advanced from the north in accordance with the Russo-German (Ribbentrop-Molotov) Treaty of 1938. The arrogant Poles, in their dress uniforms, were no match for the brutal but efficient German war machine and independent Poland came to an end in three weeks. The murderous subjugation of Poland also caused the loss of tens of thousands of Jewish fighters, and more than one hundred Jewish communities were destroyed. The fiercely nationalistic and anti-Semitic Poles were now on the horns of a dilemma—they could not decide whom to hate more, the Germans or the Jews. To any one familiar with the violent persecution of the Jews in pre-war Poland, it was no surprise when the Poles joined the Nazis in their campaign of extermination against the Jews. The fact that the Poles were second only to the Jews on the Nazi extermination list indicated the depth of their hatred for the Jews. The three million Polish Jews were thus caught in a crossfire between two powerful enemies. Even the Jewish freedom fighters in the underground were in constant fear of exposure by their Polish counterparts. During the heroic Warsaw Ghetto uprising in April 1943, when a few hundred poorly armed Jewish youngsters engaged the might of the German army for nearly two months, the only help they received from the outside world came from Polish Socialists—and very grudgingly at that.

Some Jews took advantage of the lull before the war began and escaped, but most thought they would somehow weather the storm or were simply trapped because they lacked the means to escape. In the final analysis, the European Jews were doomed when the world closed their gates to them. The Nazis viewed this closing of the gates as a signal that the world had succumbed to their blackmail and did not care what happened to the Jews. As the deepening hatred and carnage engulfed the world, the fate of the Jews of Europe became even more irrelevant to the belligerents. Should the Nazis win the war, the Allies argued, the entire world would be subjugated and the Jewish people would be wiped off the face of the earth; to win the war was thus the paramount goal and any special wrongs done to the Jewish people should be considered later. Pleadings by Jewish leaders for diplomatic or military measures to help the European Jews were rejected as detrimental to the war effort and as divisive in the ongoing life-and-death struggle. An anti-Semitic State Department and an equally prejudiced British Foreign Office conspired to keep the Jewish leaders in the dark about the true situation of their brethren and to lull them into believing that the rumored atrocities against Jews were grossly exaggerated. Weak and helpless, the American Jewish leadership accepted the specious reasoning and assurance at face value, at least during the early years of the war, and they dedicated all of their energies to winning the war.

Eventually, as the maddening stories about the extermination camps began to appear in full page ads in the *New York Times*—by Peter Bergson, Ben Hecht, Samuel Merlin—American Jews poured out into the streets in mass protest demonstrations. This forced President Roosevelt to issue strongly worded condemnations and warnings to the Nazis of dire consequences. He also called the Evion Conference on refugees and established the War Refugee Board, headed by the Secretaries of the Treasury, State, and War—with Henry Morgenthau, Secretary of the Treasury, as chairman. But each of these efforts was watered down or sabotaged by the State Department and the net effect was minimal. Not until the victorious Allied Forces entered the exter minating camps was the full horror of the German savagery revealed to the world.

When Hitler and Stalin began the division of Poland, the Polish Jews ran helter-skelter in every direction—some to the forests, some to the West or to Palestine, and many to Lithuania, which was then considered a safe haven. Among the latter were about four thousand Talmudic students and their teachers. The impoverished Lithuanian Jews opened their homes, their synagogues, and their purses to feed, clothe, and house the refugees and they appealed to American Jews for help. An immediate response came from Cincinnati's Rabbi Eliezer Silver, the dynamic and erudite leader of America's Orthodox Jewry, who organized the Vaad Hahatzalah (Rescue Committee) to raise and distribute funds and to affect rescue. This committee continued to function effectively, despite limited means, throughout the war and for several years thereafter.

Even before any appreciable sums of money were raised, the Vaad Hahatzalah borrowed and cabled funds to Lithuania and dispatched a special representative by way of Sweden to organize the rescue effort on the spot. The choice of the emissary, in the person of Samuel M. Schmidt of Cincinnati, was most fortunate since Mr. Schmidt was a professonal social worker who had come to the U.S. from Kovno as a young boy and was deeply involved in Jewish activities and problems. Sam was a friendly, deeply feeling, compassionate man who had lost his left arm as a factory worker soon after he came to the U.S. He subsequently graduated as a sanitary engineer from M.I.T., served during World War I as a sanitation officer for Hadassah in Palestine, and after the war was a social worker in Cincinnati under the pioneering tutelage of Boris Bogen. Sam was a member of the Poale Zion and had been fired from his position for supporting a strike of Jewish workers in a Cincinnati sweatshop. He subsequently became the editor and publisher of an Anglo-Jewish weekly in Cincinnati, the *Every Friday*, with a Zionist and traditional orientation, which he continued to publish the rest of his life. There was a great deal of affinity between Mr. Schmidt and Rabbi Silver even though Sam was a Labor Zionist and only partly observant, which jarred Rabbi Silver's sensibilities.

Mr. Schmidt remained in Lithuania several months in the fall of 1939 during which time he visited many Jewish communities and organized support for the refugees on a systematic basis. Sam benefited in these efforts from the full cooperation of the heads of the yeshivoth (academies), the local community leaders, and the spiritual leader of traditional World Jewry— Rabbi Ozer Grodzensky (the Chofetz Chaim) of Vilna. Of equal importance to his help for the refugees was the succor he brought to the Jews of Lithuania who were languishing under an oppressive, violently anti-Semitic, Fascist regime with the threat of death hanging over them. By his very presence and his dignified bearing, Schmidt managed to raise the prestige of the Jewish community among the government officials and to soften their rhetoric.

On his way back home Sam had some harrowing experiences. For security reasons he arranged his return trip by way of Italy and, although he was traveling on an American diplomatic passport, found it a frightening experience to travel through the length of Germany in wartime with carloads of bloodthirsty, uniformed Nazis ready to pounce on any Jew at a moment's notice. The real horror came, however, two days after he had sailed from Italy, when a Nazi U-boat ordered all passengers to abandon ship prior to its being torpedoed. For some reason the Germans changed their minds, but the several hours in a lifeboat in the open winter sea was a terrifying experience. His close encounter with death, the impact of the saintly personality of the Rabbi of Vilna, and the dedication to Torah of the Talmudic students of Poland in the face of persecution, deprivation, and tragedy changed Sam into a fully observant Orthodox Jew.

Sam's exploits in Europe were published in the Cincinnati press and in his own paper. A touching experience that moved him to tears was finding his grandfather's name engraved on a lectern in an old synagogue in Slabodka where Sam used to pray as a child. While in Kovno, Sam delivered our greetings to Pupi's family and brought back their love and some interesting impressions. It seems that Pupi's uncles, who were important industrialists, had almost convinced Sam that Lithuania was one of the safest places in Europe to wait out the war. When the war ended, Sam returned once more to Europe to give succor to the survivors of the Holocaust in the concentration camps. Sam, his angelic wife Ida, and our families were lifelong friends and in a sense we were like members of an extended family. The Jewish community of Cincinnati was shocked and saddened when Sam suffered a fatal heart attack on his eightieth birthday at a banquet in his honor.

In the early months of the war, during the so-called "Phony War" period when the Western Allies were enjoying the air-conditioning and other comforts of the "impregnable" Maginot Line and the Nazis were preparing for their knockout blow against France, some interesting things were happening in Lithuania. As part of a calculated plan, the Russians returned Vilna to Lithuania and demanded in return the stationing of a Soviet garrison in Lithuania for "mutual" protection. As a result of an ultimatum, the Fascist Lithuanian Government escaped to Berlin and the local Communists took over. During the negotiating period between Russia and Lithuania, the Vaad Hahatzalah succeeded in removing most of the Talmudic academies from

Lithuania to Shanghai, China by way of Siberia. With ongoing help from the Vaad Hahatzalah and other organizations, their students spent the war years under the protection of Japan. After the war, most of them went to Israel and some went to the United States. One of these students, Shmuel Eli Orlansky, married my niece Naomi Ravad, and they raised a fine family of five children in B'nai Brak, Israel.

Among those who escaped from Kovno a month before Lithuania fell behind the Iron Curtain was Pupi's younger sister Leah (Lisa), her husband Nahum, and their two young sons, Joseph and Reuben Marmet, who were seven and three years old. In the prevailing turmoil, they took advantage of the affidavits I had sent them in 1937 when I urged them to leave Europe before it was too late, and they left for America. They were greatly helped in this effort by Mr. Starkus, who was a high official in the government's passport office and a member of a prestigious family of just Gentiles. Mr. Starkus expedited all the exit papers they needed, including transit visas through war-time Germany and Italy and entry visas to the United States. They arrived in Cincinnati in the spring of 1940 and the two Marmet boys are now physicians in Los Angeles.

With the takeover of Lithuania by Communist Russia, trainloads of Lithuanian fascists, the wealthy, and many Jewish and non-Jewish political leaders were exiled to Siberia; among these was Mr. Starkus, who died in Siberia. Some Jews, who were destined for exile to Siberia, succeeded in avoiding deportation through payoffs or influence and many of these were killed within a year when the Nazis entered Lithuania on June 21, 1941 as part of their attack on Russia. In order to avoid deportation to far-off Siberia, Pupi's rich uncles used great influence and shed every vestige of wealth by shredding and flushing down the sewers full bags of securities, bank notes, and cash and by disposing of most of their other valuables. They were among the first to die when the Nazis came in. Hershel Gurvitz, a rich cousin who was exiled to Siberia together with his family, is still alive, but he has struggled all his life as a janitor and has suffered great deprivation.

The German attack on Russia caught Stalin by surprise and found Russia in an extremely weakened and vulnerable military position. As part of their strategy, the Nazis convinced Stalin that his best generals and many high-placed Communists were conspiring to overthrow him. A bloody purge of the Army and the Communist Party ensued and when the war came Russia was weak, disorganized, and totally unprepared. Even more astounding is the fact that the British, and even his own espionage agents, had warned Stalin that the Nazis were preparing to strike against him. But, though he was equally ruthless, Stalin preferred to trust Hitler's assurances to the bitter end. The

Nazi war machine and its "fifth columns" in White Russia, Lithuania, Poland, and the Ukraine worked like a charm and within six months the Germans were at the gates of Moscow, Leningrad, and Stalingrad. But as the winter approached, the Nazis ran into Napoleon's old problems while Stalin, in desperation, turned to the proven elixirs of patriotism—the Orthodox Church and the love of Mother Russia. Before long things began to change and Russia was on the move again.

During the first two years of the war in Europe, the Germans won one victory after another and all of Europe came under their control. Wherever the Nazis came the Jews were their first and greatest victims, usually in collaboration with the native anti-Semites and hooligans. During this period, some two million Jews were killed in Eastern Europe at or near their homes in the most brutal manner. Within a few months after the United States entered the war, a decisive turn took place in favor of the Allies when the Russians soundly defeated the Germans at Stalingrad in February 1942. The Germans lost hundreds of thousands of their best troops on the battlefield and as prisoners of war, and thereafter they suffered one defeat after another. Although the war lasted another three years, during which time tens of millions of people died, the handwriting on the wall was clearly seen at Stalingrad.

The devastating surprise attack of the Japanese at Pearl Harbor on December 7, 1941 galvanized American determination to strike back on the side of Great Britain, Free France, and Russia. Thus was an uneasy alliance born out of necessity and America's plants began to hum again to turn out war material at breakneck speed for ourselves and our allies. The rapid, full mobilization of the Armed Forces and the full deployment of America's productive capacity bolstered the morale and determination of our allies, brought consternation to our enemies, and effectively ended the twelve-year old Great Depression. Women soon began to appear in the workplace in large numbers, volunteer efforts and self-sacrifice became evident on all sides, and the country was united for the war effort as never before in American history. Despite a shaky beginning, there was now some light at the end of the tunnel.

In the later stages of the war the Germans pursued two projects with special zeal—to build an atomic weapon that would snatch victory out of defeat and to disrupt the British-American alliance with Russia. The effort to split the Alliance began with the flight of Hitler's deputy, Rudolph Hess, to England in 1942. During their slow retreat from North Africa, Italy, Russia and the rest of occupied Europe, the Nazis accelerated their attempts to bring about a separate peace with the U.S. and Britain at the expense of Russia. In fact, the Russians became quite paranoid on the subject. There were also several unsuccessful attempts to assassinate or depose Hitler. What kept the Nazis going in the face of certain defeat was their hope of developing an atomic weapon, the certainty of vengeful retribution for their onerous crimes, and above all their insane hatred of the Jews. With defeat nearing, Hitler accelerated the killing of Jews—lest his aim elude him—and two-thirds of the victims of the Holocaust perished during the last two years of the war. The Allied landing in France during the summer of 1944 marked the beginning of the end of World War II.

Throughout the war espionage and other contacts between the warring enemies continued in Switzerland, Turkey, Sweden, and other places. European and American Jews also made contacts with the Nazis in an attempt to ameliorate the fate of their brethren. The American Jewish Committee (AJC) and the Joint Distribution Committee (JDC) had a special representative in Geneva, a prominent Swiss Jew with good Nazi connections, and they also worked through the U.S. ambassadors in Switzerland, Turkey, and Sweden. The Vaad Hahatzalah negotiated with the Nazis through a Mr. Musi, who was a former president of Switzerland and a former head of the Anti-Communist Committee of Switzerland. Musi had easy access to Himmler, who was Hitler's chief of security and in charge of the extermination program. The Vaad Hahatzalah also worked through Rabbi Weismandel of Bratislava, Slovakia, who was able to transmit coded messages to New York by way of Switzerland. Rabbi Weismandel's exploits were made possible through the bribery of high-placed Nazi officials—especially Dieter von Vislizeni, who was Himmler's confidential advisor and who also served, on occasion, as deputy to Adolph Eichmann, Hitler's chief executioner. With the help of Vislizeni, several thousand Jews fled to Switzerland and several deportations were delayed for extended periods of time.

Rabbi Weismandel also succeeded in saving the Jews of Bratislava from deportation to extermination camps by paying a bribe of one million dollars which he obtained from the Budapest Jewish community before its destruction. The Vaad Hahatzalah had earlier borrowed the same amount of money from the JDC for this purpose, but they were not allowed to transfer it to the Nazis on orders from the War Refugee Board. On this occasion, as on many others, Rabbi Weismandel sent a cable to New York calling the Vaad Hahatzalah callous murderers and madmen indifferent to the fate of their brethren. The intelligence received by the Vaad Hahatzalah included detailed maps of extermination camps, strategic bridges, the number and the frequency of trains, etc., and all of the information was shared with the U.S. Government. Rabbi Weismandel once planned to blow up a railroad bridge with explosives attached to his body; the intended purpose was to delay trainloads of Jews from reaching extermination camps for several days. The plan was abandoned when his elders convinced him that such an action would make the fate of the remaining Slovakian Jews even more hopeless. Those who feel that American Jews could have done more to save the lives of European Jews may very well ponder Rabbi Weismandel's dilemmas.

As the end of the war neared, the Nazis became very anxious to "trade Jews for money." The most publicized of these offers was to trade one million Hungarian Jews for ten thousand trucks. This offer was made through a Hungarian Jew by the name of Brand who was flown by the Nazis to Turkey to contact British and Jewish leaders. When the offer was turned down by the British as inconsistent with the war effort and Brand was arrested as an enemy agent, the Nazis reduced the ante and were willing to accept coffee, money, or even token payments for releasing Jews—providing the Western Allies would stress German humaneness. The high-placed Nazis who were involved in these negotiations were variously motivated by greed, by a need of funds to escape underground after the war, by the hope of establishing alibis for themselves or gaining Allied favor as anti-Hitlerites, and—in the case of Himmler himself— by the hope of gaining Allied consideration as a possible replacement for a deposed Hitler. Some of the Nazis were hoping until the very end that they would win a separate peace with the Western Allies through these negotiations.

The U.S. Government, through the War Refugee Board, encouraged these negotiations and even tantalized the Nazis by permitting the JDC to deposit $5,000,000 in a Swiss bank to indicate serious intent. At the same time the negotiators were instructed to drag out the bargaining indefinitely by haggling over minor details. During the early part of the war, I once asked Rabbi Silver how he could negotiate with the enemy in war time without the approval of the U.S. Government, to which he replied that he had tacit approval through Senator Robert Taft, Sr., who was a great admirer of the Rabbi and was himself variously involved in the Vaad Hahatzalah rescue efforts. Later on, when I asked Rabbi Silver what he knew about the Jews in Europe he answered, "S'iz nit gut, men arget Yiden—It is bad, they are killing Jews." Conversations on the subject with Samuel Schmidt were not any more revealing. Despite the alarming stories in the Yiddish and English press of large-scale killings, forced labor camps, ghettos, and brutalities, no one could possibly conceive of the orgy of organized mass murder and degradation as it ultimately revealed itself. The only ones who knew from the outset and remained silent were the natives, the Vatican, and the world chancelleries. This conspiracy of silence is one of the most disturbing aspects of the Holocaust tragedy.

As the enormity of the Jewish tragedy came to light and the details began to trickle out, the effect was stupifying and numbing. We eventually learned the bitter truth that among the victims of the Nazis were my sister Rivka, her husband Yitzhak Hirsh, their son Avram, and the entire Jewish community of Serei. On the eve of Rosh Hashanah 1941, three months after the Germans entered Lithuania, the Jews of Serei were assembled in the marketplace, where they were forced to strip naked, and were driven through Lange Gass, accompanied by the jeers and laughter of their Gentile neighbors, until they reached the lake on the outskirts where we used to bathe in the summer. There, the entire Jewish community of Serei—men, women, and children—were machine-gunned into a common grave which the martyrs were forced to dig in advance. Simultaneous killings took place all over the villages and small towns of Lithuania and but a few survived to tell the tale.

Many of Pupi's family were killed by Lithuanian hooligans under the supervision of the Nazis only a few days after the Germans entered Kovno. Several thousand of the most prominent Jews of Kovno were rounded up, then tortured and machine-gunned in cold blood during this first major "action" against the Jews of Lithuania. The massacre lasted several days and took place at the ninth fort on the outskirts of the city. A wave of terror of unbelievable cruelty began as soon as the Russians left, and Jews were tortured or killed in the streets on sight and even in their own homes. When the Nazis decreed that all Jews were to move to a ghetto, a stampede ensued to get into this "safe haven" as soon as possible. Within a month, fifty thousand people moved to Slabodka, one of the poorest suburbs of Kovno, where five thousand Jews already lived. The Nazis also decreed that the Jews must establish a five-man Altestenrath (Council of Elders) to help carry out their orders. Every single member of the Kovno Jewish community council refused to accept the onerous task of heading up this council. Finally, the Revered Rabbi Shapiro appealed to Dr. Elchanan Elkes in terms the physician could not refuse. They could not have chosen more wisely for Dr. Elkes was a man of sterling character and great wisdom and was highly respected by Jews and Gentiles alike. Dr. Elkes had received a thorough education in Germany and had earned an enviable reputation as a physician in great demand in the diplomatic corps and in top government and social circles. Had he chosen to do so, Dr. Elkes could have saved himself, but he preferred to stay and share the fate of his people.

For over three years the mild-mannered doctor struggled heroically to save as many Jews as possible, to ease life in the ghetto as much as possible, and to carry out the heart-rending responsibilities as fairly as possible. His duties involved organizing work battalions, housing, sanitation, food distribution, medical facilities, schooling, the ghetto police, the husbandry of financial resources, bribery; the acquisition of clandestine food supplies, drugs, and other necessities; intelligence about Nazi extermination or deportation plans; communication with the ghettos of Shavel and Vilna and with the underground fighters, and promoting discreet resistance. An entire underground economy was developed, including the barter of valuables, clothing, and food.

Of the seventy-five thousand Jews of Kovno, about twenty thousand were killed outright during the first few months. Most of the others died of disease or starvation in the ghetto or during the repeated "actions" in which the Germans would round up a given quota of children, the aged, the weak, and the sick and transport them to the ninth fort to be shot. Some able-bodied men and women were deported to various labor camps where most died. In the end, only about five thousand Jews survived in the Kovno ghetto, about a thousand in bunkers or in hiding among Gentiles, and some four thousand were taken by the retreating Germans to Dachau and other concentration camps. Of these, many died of starvation, exhaustion, or disease, and Dr. Elkes was among them. His connections were so good that, with the aid of a Nazi functionary, he was able to correspond with his two sons who were in England studying medicine.

The war in Lithuania began suddenly with devastating air attacks on June 21, 1941 and as soon as the attack started a stampede to escape ensued. Foremost in the mad rush to leave were the Russian civilian and military administrators of Lithuania and their families, but there were also many young Jewish people and local Communists of every nationality. Every form of transportation was pressed into service and many ran on foot. The trains were preempted by the Russians and they functioned poorly; civilian refugees were often dumped from their autos or wagons, the narrow roads became clogged with the heavy, uncontrolled traffic, and few civilians managed to get very far. Those who were on foot or on bicycle often fared the best. Many of those who tried to escape were wounded or killed by strafing from the air or by rifle shots from ambush by Lithuanian Fascist partisans. Many who did reach the Russian border were turned back by the Russians as undesirables or possible spies, and those who were admitted were soon exiled to Siberia or drafted into the Russian Army. Most of the Jewish refugees who were denied entry at the Russian border had no choice but to return to Kovno and seek the haven of the ghetto. A few became partisans or guerrillas and roamed the forests with little hope of finding support among the hostile Lithuanians.

Pupi's youngest sister, Olga, was among those who tried to escape to Russia and failed. For three days and nights she ran on foot and hitchhiked and endured all the dangers and hardships of the desperate situation. For a while she was helped by a Russian soldier who was driving a military truck. When the soldier was shot through both of his hands during the strafing and became disabled, he told her to jump off the vehicle and run for her life. Like many other refugees, Olga had destroyed her identification papers for fear of being overtaken by the advancing Germans or ambushed and killed by Lithuanian partisans. Without papers she had a chance to pass as a native. But when Olga reached the Russian border and could not identify herself, she was turned back as a possible German spy.

Olga was a beautiful young girl with long black braids who had graduated from dental college a year earlier and was practicing dentistry when the Nazis occupied Lithuania. With all hope of escape gone, Olga roamed the forests for six weeks, during which time she fought starvation, the elements, and filth. Finally, in desperation, with her clothing in tatters, she approached a German army camp and threw herself on the mercy of a group of officers. From amidst the merriment and indecent banter of the drunken group, there emerged a young officer who arranged her escape and under the guise of darkness took her back to Kovno in an army jeep.

On the way to the city the officer suggested that she seek shelter with some of her Gentile friends. Not fully convinced of the officer's good intentions and afraid of endangering her friends, Olga hesitated until she became convinced that he meant to help her. She then let him take her to the home of one of her Lithuanian girlfriends. Olga's girlfriend became terrified at her appearance in the company of a German officer, but the officer managed to assure her and her parents of his good intentions. To remove all doubt he returned with a supply of food for all of them. The officer came back with supplies of food on several other occasions, but Olga did not see him again until after the war.

For several months Olga was shuffled around from one hiding-place to another, seldom seeing the light of day and in constant fear of inadvertent betrayal by children or unfriendly Gentiles, or of being discovered during one of the frequent, random block raids. When this form of hiding became untenable she sought shelter in the ghetto for several months. Finally, her Gentile girlfriends found a permanent haven for her on the country estate of the wealthy Lithuanian sculptor Joseph Rimshis, where she worked as a milkmaid until the end of the war. During her two and one-half years on the farm, Olga went under the assumed name of Steputi, attended church with the family and employees of her patron, and sang in the church choir.

On one occasion, Olga was called upon to help serve a group of Germans who were being entertained by her host. In the course of the evening, she overheard a description of the cruelties perpetrated by the Nazi extermination groups against Jewish children and adults in various communities. Unable to withstand the strain, she collapsed. Her disguise was saved only by the quick wit and resourcefulness of her patron. Olga survived the Holocaust with the help of a group of Gentile friends who endangered their own lives in the process. They were mostly her girlfriends and teachers and they were all compassionate individuals and broad-minded liberals. Among these just Gentiles, most of whom subsequently emigrated to the U.S., were Dr. Antanas Starkus, a professor of pathology; his brother, Father Yonas Starkus; the sculptor Joseph Rimshis, and her girlfriends Marita Zelcius (Holecek) and Dr. Valia Karvelis. Olga and her girlfriends all live in Chicago now and they have continued their lifelong friendship.

Olga's mother Beile was killed in one of the Nazi "actions" about a year and a half after she entered the ghetto. Her younger brother Hirsh survived in the ghetto with the help of a ready wit, a quick orientation, and the help of two Lithuanian sisters and their brother. Hirsh worked most of the time in a road-construction battalion and, whenever he learned through the grapevine that the Germans were planning a deportation or extermination "action," he would sneak out of the ghetto and find refuge among his Gentile friends. On three occasions he found himself in a lineup for deportation, but each time he managed to escape. In the summer of 1944, when the Germans began to liquidate the Kovno ghetto in advance of their retreat, they sent the four thousand survivors to the Dachau Concentration Camp, where Dr. Elkes died in July 1944. A few found shelter during the last few weeks among Gentiles, while Hirsh and several hundred other survivors of the Kovno ghetto went into hiding in bunkers. When the Germans set the ghetto on fire to flush out those who were in hiding, most perished—but Hirsh and Rabbi Oshri calmly walked out of the burning ghetto, which was surrounded by Germans and bloodhounds, and ran for their lives to safety.

There were thirty-six members in Olga's immediate family in Lithuania at the beginning of the war. Of these, twenty-five were killed in the Kovno ghetto or in the concentration camps of Auschwitz, Dachau, and Treblinka. One, Osie Rutshtein, was killed while serving in the Russian Army. Of the eight survivors (besides Olga and Hirsh) one, Yocheved Rutshtein, survived as an underground fighter in Poland and the others in the concentration camps. Of the eight family groups among Olga's relations, the Gefen family of four left no survivors and the others had only one or two survivors each.

During the entire period of the Nazi nightmare, Olga and Hirsh did not know of each other's whereabouts. This arrangement was for their own safety and the safety of their patrons. As soon as the Germans left, Olga and Hirsh returned to Kovno and began to look for each other and for other family survivors. It took several weeks of knocking on doors from house to house before they were finally reunited; it took even longer before they felt safe

Olga Gurvitz (Horwitz); Kovno, 1940.

enough to appear outdoors in daytime. On one such occasion, they ran into Mr. Goldstein, an old friend who had survived by masquerading as a Gentile deaf-mute. When he continued to communicate with them in his homespun sign language, Hirsh finally shouted, "Goldstein! It is safe now. Start talking!"

Almost a year elapsed between the liberation of Lithuania from the Nazis and their final capitulation to the Allies in May 1945. During this period, Olga and Hirsh tried to recover from their ordeal and to manage the best they could in the poisoned, guilt-ridden, hostile, post-war Lithuania. They remained in Communist Lithuania for a year and a half, during which time Olga worked at the university and Hirsh in the highway department. When they made up their minds to leave they had to sneak out illegally at great risk. They decided to escape from oppressive Communist Lithuania to the displaced persons (D.P.) camps in Germany in hope of finding some surviving members of their family and starting life all over again in the United States. It took a long time after the war ended before we learned that Olga and Hirsh had miraculously survived. This waiting period was a frightening experience for us and with every passing day our fears grew that none of our families had survived. The delay in reaching the D.P. camps was largely due to the unfriendly attitude of the Russians towards the Jewish survivors of the Holocaust. In order to flee from Communist-occupied Lithuania into friendlier parts of liberated Europe, Olga and Hirsh had to use various disguises, travel with false documents, and cross numerous hostile borders where the danger of death lurked on all sides. They were able to overcome all the difficulties and reach the safe haven of a D.P. camp in Germany only with the aid of trained trouble shooters from Israel who had infiltrated the liberated areas in search of survivors.

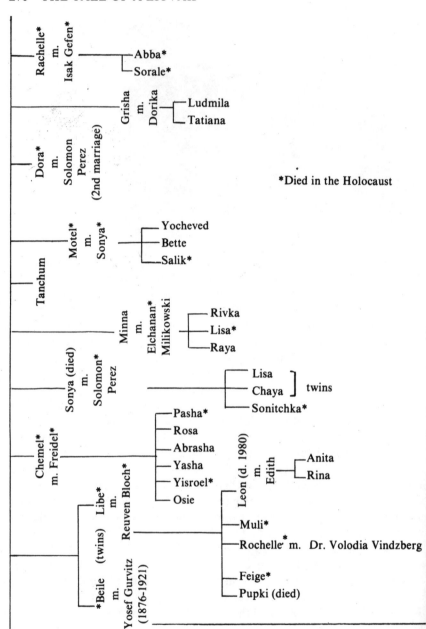

*Died in the Holocaust

Moshe Rutshtein m. Iti Gerstein

Tanchum

Rachelle*
m.
Isak Gefen*
— Abba*
— Sorale*

Grisha
m.
Dorika
— Ludmila
— Tatiana

Dora*
m.
Solomon
Perez
(2nd marriage)

Motel*
m.
Sonya*
— Yocheved
— Bette
— Salik*

Minna
m.
Elchanan*
Milikowski
— Rivka
— Lisa*
— Raya

Sonya (died)
m.
Solomon*
Perez
— Lisa
— Chaya] twins
— Sonitchka*

Chemel*
m. Freidel*

Pasha*
Rosa
Abrasha
Yasha
Yisroel*
Osie

Leon (d. 1980)
m.
Edith
— Anita
— Rina

Libe*
m.
Reuven Bloch*

Muli*
Rochelle* m. Dr. Volodia Vindzberg
Feige*
Pupki (died)

*Beile   (twins)
m.
Yosef Gurvitz
(1876-1921)

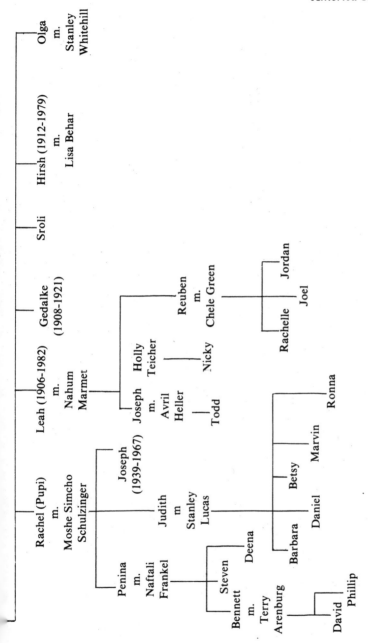

When they arrived in the D.P. camp on the outskirts of Munich, they found there four cousins and one relative by marriage who had survived in concentration camps—Leon Bloch, Dr. Volodia Vindzberg, twin sisters Chaya and Lisa Perez, and Raya Milikowsky. Leon survived largely due to the help he received from his brother-in-law Dr. Vindzberg, who served in the camp's hospital, and he was the sole survivor of his immediate family. Leon's parents, three siblings, and his young wife had all perished. The Perez twins and Raya had each lost their parents and a sister. Soon after their arrival in Munich, Olga and Hirsh were visited by my friends Rabbi Eliezer Silver and Samuel Schmidt, who gave them our love, some money and clothing, and everything else they needed. Rabbi Silver, who came to the camp in a U.S. Army officer's uniform at the invitation of General Eisenhower, was most effective in passing out small sums of money for the asking, in helping to unite families, and in bringing a measure of comfort to the bereaved "walking shadows" of the camps.

Before coming to the U.S., Olga decided to complete her education at the University of Munich. She remained there for over two years and earned a doctorate in oral pathology. Hirsh, who was extremely devoted to his sister, remained with her. During Olga's sojourn in the D.P. camp, she was surprised by a visitor from Vienna who was none other than the German officer who had saved her from his fellow officers in the forest of Lithuania and started her on the road to survival. He had searched for her in several D.P. camps before he found her. He came with his mother and sister to meet Olga and to present her with gifts. The entire family apologized to Olga for the Holocaust, for the tragedies in her family, and for her personal suffering, and he asked her to marry him. It seems that the officer, who was an artist by profession and an anti-Nazi, had fallen in love with Olga at first sight. He brought his diary, which he had kept over the years, to prove it. Olga thanked him for his decency and humaneness, but after what the Germans had done to her family and her people she could never marry a German.

Among those who helped save Jews were some grateful domestics who sheltered the children of their employers. There were also some simple people, peasants, liberals, and priests who tried to save Jews out of compassion or Christian charity. A number of Jews survived in the underground resistance movement and a few by payments to mercenaries—except that the latter often denounced them when the payments stopped. The only problem with these benefactors is that there were so few of them. The countries that acquitted themselves the best were Denmark and Holland. The worst peoples were the Poles, Lithuanians, Ukrainians, the Greeks, and the French. In Italy, Rumania, Slovakia, and Hungary, deportation of Jews was at times resisted by their governments out of political and financial considerations. In the case of Hungary, it was also because large numbers of Jews had entered high society and the governing structure of the country through assimilation and intermarriage. Several thousand Jews were also saved by Franco Spain and in Portugal, in an effort to correct historical wrongs in their countries.

Olga and Hirsh arrived in New York by boat from Munich in the winter of 1948 and Pupi and I went to meet them at the 34th Street pier. We became somewhat uneasy because of the long delay before the boat was allowed to dock. The delay in landing was due to a decision by New York's Mayor William O'Dwyer to make a media event of the arrival of this particular group of displacd persons. During the interval we met Professor Starkus, Olga's former teacher, who also came to the pier to meet her.

With the arrival of the survivors of the Holocaust the Cincinnati Jewish Vocational Service assumed a new role—to help place the survivors and to facilitate their adjustment to the new environment. In 1947, Pupi's cousin Leon Bloch came to live with us in Cincinnati. Leon was a graduate of the University of Manchester, England in textile engineering with experience in his field in England and in Kovno, and he was extremely anxious to find employment in the textile field. We sent out letters to a number of Jewish vocational offices in neighboring states and found an ideal spot for him with the Kentucky Loom Company in Louisville, of which he subsequently became part owner and general manager. Leon married in 1951. His wife Edith is also a survivor of the Holocaust. They raised two lovely daughters, Rina and Anita, and established a fine reputation in their community. Leon succumbed in 1980 to a heart attack, but Edith is still a practicing psychologist. Rina is a physician and Anita is doing post-graduate work in business management.

When Olga and Hirsh arrived in Cincinnati in 1948, the Jewish Vocational Service found a good position for Hirsh with the Keilson Company which he retained until his retirement in 1978. Hirsh was a very kind, self-effacing man who had survived in Kovno with the help of Lithuanian friends, ingenious strategems, and good luck. Although he came from a wealthy family he had no interest in money beyond his modest needs and he found great pleasure in making other people happy. Hirsh married late in life to a lovely Egyptian Jewish girl, Lisa Behar, and succumbed to cardiopulmonary disease in July 1979 after a two-year retirement in Miami Beach, Florida.

While in the D.P. camp, Olga met Mr. Paul Felix Warburg, chairman of the JDC, and Mr. Joseph Schwartz, its executive director, who volunteered to help her when she came to the United States. After Olga rested in Cincinnati for several weeks, she decided to go to New York to call on both Warburg and Schwartz and solicit their help to continue in her profession. An aide, to whom she was referred, told Olga that the laws of the U.S. were highly restrictive in the dental field and that she would have to start all over again in a dental school—if she was lucky enough to be admitted. Even then, she was told, she could not practice dentistry until she became a U.S. citizen. Considering these difficulties, they advised her to adjust to the reality and seek a suitable job outside the dental profession. She should start, temporarily, with a factory job which they offered to obtain for her.

Crushed in spirit and very depressed, Olga returned to Cincinnati. After I discussed the matter with George Newburger, director of the Jewish Vocational Service, he obtained a list of Jewish professors of dentistry in the U.S. and sent out a resume about Olga's qualifications to every dental school in the country with a view to obtaining admission. Most of those who responded were very pessimistic about her prospects, except for one. Within a week we received a letter from Dr. Isaac Shauer, the head of the Department of Pathology and later the Dean of the Dental School of the University of Illinois, who invited Olga for an interview. With Dr. Shauer's help, Olga was admitted to the school as a special student and was awarded her degree in dentistry after sixteen months. The requirement of citizenship was suspended by a special act of the legislature of Illinois and Olga was once again launched on her beloved profession. She has remained as a teacher with the Dental School of Illinois and has become one of their most beloved and honored professors. Olga has also established an enviable reputation for herself as a practicing dentist with many distinguished citizens of Chicago among her patients. In 1970 Olga married Dr. Stanley Whitehill, an excellent dentist and a fine person of Hungarian Jewish descent. In 1980 she was honored by her dental fraternity, Alpha Omega, and the Bonds for Israel Organization. Also, in a survey in Chicago, Olga was named as one of the very few "caring dentists in the city." Recently, she told part of her story on a televised interview program, together with her girlfriend Marita, who had played a major role in her survival. Their moving saga was repeated on the air by popular request. The burden of their message was to stress decency, tolerance, and brotherly love.

In 1978, Olga was asked to come to New York to the funeral of Professor Antanas Starkus, who had helped save her life in Kovno. In the hushed silence of the church and in the presence of a bishop, many priests, and distinguished Lithuanian lay emigrees, Olga was called to the pulpit to eulogize the deceased. In a literate Lithuanian, Olga described the exemplary human qualities of the deceased and she related how Dr. Starkus had endangered his life and the lives of his family to save the life of another human being who happened to be a Jewish girl. She then pointed her finger at the church dignitaries who were seated in the front row before her and said, "The same could have been done by you...and you...and you." The services ended in deep silence. There was some audible crying. Olga's extemporaneous eulogy was later published in several Lithuanian newspapers in Chicago. While Olga was relating her odyssey, a Jewish survivor in the audience who had converted and married her benefactor collapsed.

There are many unanswered questions about the Holocaust. Why didn't the Allied powers blast the gas chambers to pieces or destroy the bridges and railroad systems over which trainloads of Jews were being transported daily like sheep to slaughter? Why was the Jewish leadership of the Free World so helpless while these unspeakable events transpired? What role did Stalin's violent hatred for Jews play in preventing help from arriving? What role did anti-Semitism among top leaders of the Free World play in all of this? And would the Allied Powers have remained passive if the lives of six million, six thousand, or even six hundred Englishmen or Americans were at stake?

The indifference of the world towards the Jewish tragedy has made the entire world a partner to Hitler's extermination of six million Jews, and the Sign of Cain, which the world thus fashioned on its forehead, will undoubtedly pursue it. Can a Holocaust happen again? On the basis of past history and the human condition the answer is, unfortunately, yes. Our best hope for the future is to remember the Holocaust. At the dawn of our history we were admonished to remember the Amalekites (the evil powers). "For there is an eternal struggle between God and the Amalekites."

CHAPTER SEVEN

The Education of a Doctor

> "Life is a ticket to the greatest
> show on earth. As a doctor you
> will have a front-row seat."
> (Martin Fischer)

In the fall of 1921, I walked up the broad stairway of the Clifton Street entrance of McMicken Hall to register in the College of Liberal Arts of the University of Cincinnati. As I entered the building, tears welled up in my eyes and I cried unabashedly. These were tears of joy and I was full of gratitude towards the country which enabled me to fulfill my childhood dreams for a higher education. I recalled Serei and oppressive Russia and I was happy over the geographic and psychological distances I had put behind me, and over the anti-Semitism which I no longer had to endure. Seven months in the U.S. had made me feel ecstatic over the degree of tolerance of opposing or minority views, the prevailing decency, and the spirit of helpfulness towards total strangers. It reminded me of the familiar Biblical injunction "V'ahavta et ha'ger—Thou shalt love the stranger in thy midst." It aroused within me a feeling of love and admiration for the United States, a feeling I had never known towards the country of my birth. I was amazed at the sensitivity of the American political system for the common people and marveled at the forbearance of the aggrieved. My only concern was about some of the new immigrants who carried the virus of hate in their blood, but I trusted that in time the melting pot would digest or purge the destructive elements and that the American democratic ideal would prevail.

My first experience at the University was most fortunate. I met Dr. Ernest Lynn Talbert, the Director of Admissions, who took me gently in hand and guided me through my four years of undergraduate studies. Dr. Talbert was a quiet, self-effacing man who, in addition to his administrative duties, was a professor of sociology and psychology and was active in student affairs and in the International House. Dr. Talbert became my advisor on course selection and he helped me get advanced standing for college-level work I had done in Mariyampole. I was overwhelmed by Dr. Talbert's modesty and kindness and by the feeling that I had found a friend to whom I could turn in times of need.

During the four years at the University, I concentrated in four major areas of study—biology, chemistry, English, and history, with enough courses in chemistry and English to qualify as majors. The first year was the most difficult for me, mainly because of the language barrier. I also became overly concerned about my thick accent and I developed a paralyzing fear of being laughed at, which reduced my class participation. Worst of all, my mind often went blank when I attempted to write an English composition, and sometimes during tests. An added handicap was my being a slow and plodding reader. It was largely through the understanding and kindness of my teachers that I was able to complete my first year in school with passing grades.

The head of the Department of Chemistry was Dr. Shipley Fry, a short, graying, and friendly man and an excellent teacher. In preparation for the first test in inorganic chemistry, I worked very hard and learned the table of atomic weights by heart. I received a zero for my efforts because the questions in the test dealt with altogether different matters. During a brief conference that followed, Dr. Fry discovered the root of my problem and I learned how to study more effectively. This was also my first experience in a mammoth class of some three hundred students. The other chemistry teachers whom I remember were Miss Neufer—a charming, graying, middle-aged lady who was my teacher in organic and advanced chemistry, and Dr. Oesper—a friendly, crew-cut, Prussian-type of a man who was my teacher in qualitative and quantitative chemistry. At a dinner party for graduate students and chemistry majors, Dr. Fry passed out ballots on which we were to state our reasons for choosing chemistry as a career. There were diverse motives and mine was an interest in research. I was surprised to learn that Dr. Fry chose chemistry by accident. "I could have done equally well in any other field," said Dr. Fry. I was shocked, but the lesson sunk in.

In English I received a great deal of help from an HUC student, Akiba Shulman, who later became a prominent Rabbi. I do not remember any of my

English teachers since there were too many of them and I had too difficult a time with most of my English studies. I do remember my teacher of modern poetry, Mr. Bauer, perhaps because he seemed to be partial to a classmate, Libby Holman, who later gained national prominence as an actress and torch singer.

The best teacher I ever had was Miss Miriam Urban, one of the few Jewish teachers on the U.C. staff at that time. Miss Urban taught European history with a clarity and effectiveness which made the subject exhilarating and the characters come alive. Her dramatizations of Napoleon, Josephine, the leaders of the French Revolution, and the reigning heads of Europe at the time were unforgettable, exciting experiences and I eagerly anticipated her lectures. Miss Urban invited me several times to her office for private talks to learn of my experiences in Russia and details about the Bolshevik Revolution. The importance of this world-shattering event was still unclear at that time and I helped clarify for her the difference between the Bolshevik and Menshevik programs in the Russian Revolution. Miss Urban was an attractive, intellectual woman in her thirties with a Mediterranean complexion, fiery eyes, and a well-proportioned figure.

The head of the Department of History was Dr. Beverly Bond, Jr., who taught American history. Despite my deep interest in the subject it turned out to be one of the most boring courses I had to endure. Two pearls of wisdom from Dr. Bond remain with me to this day. His first words to the large, compulsory class were, "In my classes I will not tolerate lipstick, rouge, or mascara. Anyone using these will be sent out of the classroom." While discussing the administration of President Coolidge he pointed with his finger for emphasis and said, "Mark my words! President Calvin Coolidge will go down in history as the greatest President America has ever had!" Perhaps some day a spirit of nostalgia for "the good old days" may make this rash prediction plausible. So far, this story has seldom failed to evoke laughter.

The professor of physics was Dr. Louis Trenchard Moore, a tall, gaunt, friendly, aristocratic-looking gentleman who wore a winged rubber collar and was always neatly dressed. He was the head of the Department of Physics at U.C. from 1900 to 1940 and he was an excellent teacher. Physics was one of the subjects I did not fully grasp and I failed the course during my first attempt. This was a devastating blow as it almost ruined my chances for admission to medical school, which I had begun to contemplate in my junior year. Fortunately I earned an A on repeating the course during the summer. Dr. Moore's remarks about Albert Einstein's Theory of Relativity remain unforgettable. "Gentlemen," said Dr. Moore, "the Theory of Relativity has never been tested. It is contrary to Newton's theories, which are universally accepted as valid, and I doubt that Einstein's theory will ever be confirmed. It seems to me that Einstein is some kind of charlatan." It is true that in 1924 Einstein's theory had not been fully confirmed as yet, and there were quite a few other skeptics about its validity.

The requirements for admission to the University of Cincinnati College of Medicine were a B overall average and a C average in the sciences. I had no problem qualifying on both scores, but there remained one more hurdle— acceptance by the admissions committee, which in reality meant the approval of the chairman, Dr. David Tucker. The chairman was a practicing physician on the staff of Christ Hospital with an alleged reputation of being prejudiced against Jewish applicants. During my interview with Dr. Tucker, I found nothing wrong with him and he found nothing wrong with me. I may have been helped by the fact that I earned A's in most of the critical subjects and that I brought excellent letters of recommendation testifying that I was a serious student of promise. Another factor in my favor was that, since I was a foreign student, it would help to give the school an international flavor.

Acceptance by the admissions committee of the medical school was a major achievement, but there remained three more hurdles to be overcome and all carried the imprint of Dr. Knorr, who was an avowed Jew-hater and taught three critical subjects. Dr. Knorr was the head of the Department of Anatomy and Histology and he also taught the difficult pre-medical subject of embryology. Dr. Knorr delighted in flunking Jewish students in any one of these subjects at his whim, and his decision was irrevocable. There were numerous complaints about this man but no one could do anything about it until 1924 when he showed up in his anatomy class wearing a yarmulke trying to make fun of a Rabbi and embarrass his Jewish students. One of the students in my pre-medical class was the son of a prominent Cincinnati Jewish physician with a great deal of influence in the community. When he heard of this incident he hit the ceiling and Dr. Knorr was forced to resign in the middle of the term. Dr. Knorr's successor was his young assistant, Dr. Oscar Vivian Batson, a burly Texan and an excellent teacher with a pleasant disposition. He appointed Mr. Snyder, a graduate student from the Zoology Department, to fill the vacated post in embryology and the course was a breeze. No one flunked embryology and there was little subsequent attrition in my class of sixty-seven.

The first year in medical school was difficult and involved an inordinate amount of effort. The "no-fail" system had not arrived as yet and we were tested and graded at frequent intervals like undergraduates. The first year was especially trying for some students because of the emphasis on a thorough grounding in anatomy, histology, neuroanatomy, and biochemistry—four major subjects. Failure to get at least a C average and a passing grade in every one of these subjects could mean expulsion. To compound my own difficulties, my command of English still left much to be desired and I was strictly a "loner." I was unaware of the advantages that fraternities offered by way of the availability of previous test questions, intelligence on probable forthcoming test questions, and the benefits of tutoring and mutual testing. I overcame all my handicaps with an insatiable thirst for knowledge and incredibly long hours of study. Another aid was a newly discovered talent to dissect anatomical material with great fidelity. This competence delighted Dr. Batson and he frequently used my dissections as teaching material for the class and interested visitors. My eye for detail and the reputation I earned in anatomy also helped me with histology and other basic subjects. Of considerable help was my anatomy partner, David Joseph Weintraub, who was a brilliant student with a photographic and penetrating mind. We developed an affinity for each other and have remained lifelong friends.

I spent the summer of 1925 at the University of Michigan in Ann Arbor studying neuroanatomy from one of the greatest American teachers of this subject, who was also the author of a major textbook in neuroanatomy. I worked hard during this summer and learned a great deal. Getting this subject out of the way gave me more time to pursue the other basic subjects during my sophomore year. In 1925 Ann Arbor was a small rural community and I boarded in a private home on Church Street, within walking distance of the school. When I visited Ann Arbor twenty-five years later in connection with the publication of my book *The Accident Syndrome*, the campus of the university had absorbed everything within sight and the town and the campus were beyond recognition.

Having majored in chemistry as an undergraduate, I found biochemistry fascinating and easy. The professor of biochemistry, Dr. William P. Mathews, was an excellent teacher, a fine English gentleman, and the author of our textbook on the subject. I enjoyed Dr. Mathew's deportment as much as his teaching, but I established a special relationship with his associate, Dr. Shiro Tashiro, who was in charge of the laboratory. Dr. Tashiro was a noted Japanese-American scientist who had gained international renown through his measurement of carbon dioxide in spinal fluid metabolism. Towards the end of my first year in medical school, Dr. Tashiro asked me if I would like to undertake research under his tutelage. I was only too glad to accept the invitation and I earned a master's degree in biochemistry at the end of my junior year in medical school with research on bile salts. The research was done on weekends, during the summers, and whenever I could spare time from my medical studies. At Dr. Tashiro's suggestion, I undertook to isolate bile salts in crystalline form from steer's blood. I obtained twelve gallons of blood from Kahn's slaughterhouse and began to evaporate it over a low flame. At a certain point the bile salts were to be extracted with various solvents, but within a few days a foul smell began to spread throughout the medical school. Before long it developed into an overpowering stench and the project had to be abandoned. Fortunately, it was summertime and the building was not in great use; but it did take many weeks to rid the school of the lingering odor of decay. I subsequently wrote an exhaustive thesis on the chemistry and biochemistry of bile salt and was complimented by the faculty on my thoroughness.

Dr. Tashiro was a fine teacher and a very patient man. Despite his crowded calendar, he was always available for advice and he gave me a great deal of support. Besides our common interest in biochemistry, we also shared our foreign backgrounds and mutilation of the English language. Dr. Tashiro's Japanese English sounded even more atrocious than my Yiddish English—he dropped the L's and the R's while I dropped the H's and mispronounced most of the vowels. Dr. Tashiro made frequent visits to Japan and he suffered stoically the indignities of the prevailing anti-foreigner environment and the jingoistic Japanese Exclusion Act of 1924.

My class was privileged to have had a group of other outstanding teachers. Dr. William B. Wherry, professor of bacteriology, Dr. Richard Austin, professor of pathology, and Dr. H.G. Foot, associate professor of pathology were all dedicated and lucid teachers and they introduced us to their respective disciplines with consummate skill. Dr. Hiram B. Weiss, who taught physical diagnosis at the bedsides of the General Hospital, gave us an inspired introduction to clinical medicine in a clear and concise manner. He was gentle and considerate and he exemplified superb bedside manners. Dr. Weiss had a large following and he practiced internal medicine into his nineties.

Dr. Dennis Jackson, professor of pharmacology, was a very kind, self-effacing man who gave unstintingly of himself in the lecture room and in the laboratory. He was an ingenious experimenter and he gave us an excellent grounding in the effects of various drugs on experimental animals. He took a personal interest in each student and he made his subject interesting and entertaining. He loved to act out important points as a contrarian, to keep the class relaxed and in good humor. To illustrate the contracting effect of a drug on muscles he would move his hands further and further apart, while to demonstrate an expanding effect he would bring his outstretched hands closer and closer together until they met with a clap. Dr. Jackson retired at the compulsory retirement age of sixty-five and reached a ripe old age of 103. He retained his sense of humor and the sparkle in his eyes, and he kept himself busy painting landscapes and tinkering in his workshop.

Our course in physiology was a never-to-be-forgotten experience. Dr.

Martin Fischer, our professor of physiology, was a philosopher-teacher of German descent and liberal views. His physiology was largely unorthodox and he left the teaching of current principles of physiology to his assistants and assigned readings. Dr. Fischer was primarily interested in teaching us a philosophy of life, medical ethics, and the exalted position of the healer in society. His asides, quotes, and aphorisms were collected by his pupils and were published in 1930 by one of his students, Dr. Howard Fabing, in a booklet called *Fischerisms*. Dr. Fischer challenged "accepted truths" and he tried to stimulate us to become thinking persons. The following are a few examples of his utterances:

"Observation, reason, human understanding, courage; these make the physician."

"Of course, I teach you only the truth—but that shouldn't make you believe it."

"Think any way you please, but know why."

"The great man is he who sees the mundane with uncommon eyes and imagination."

We didn't learn much physiology from Dr. Fischer and the theories he espoused were obsolete or irrelevant, yet he kept us spellbound and no one would dream of missing any of his classes. To dramatize the importance of observation in medicine, Dr. Fischer would resort to a hoax. "Now, gentlemen," he would say, "all that is necessary to determine the presence of glucose in urine is to taste it." With that he would dip a finger in a specimen of urine and touch it to his lips. "You have all noticed, of course," he would continue with a chuckle, "that there was a switch between the cup and the lip." We were so enraptured by his utterances, and he did this so deftly, that few noticed his slight of hand—but we got the point and enjoyed the joke at our expense. Dr. Fischer stressed the importance of upholding the dignity of the patient and the dignity of the profession. "Be a god to your patients," was a frequent saying. He was impatient with mediocrity and he repeatedly exhorted us to aim for the stars and to avoid the trifling, the commonplace, and the vulgar. He stressed wholesome food for the body, especially proteins, and aesthetic and intellectual nourishment for the soul. He was always immaculately dressed in tight-fitting clothes with a fresh flower adorning his lapel and a white kerchief in his upper left pocket. He told us of the great minds in history and of the great achievements by the young. The walls of his classroom were decorated with works of art, including his own paintings, and photographs of great philosophers and teachers.

Dr. Fischer was fond of stressing that body tissues and fluids were in reality a soup made up of water, salts, acids, and minerals in colloidal suspension. He was enamoured with colloid chemistry. "Colloidal chemistry," he would say, "is the twilight between chemistry and physics, but that is where God has chosen to reveal himself." He also stressed a then-popular theory that many diseases were due to foci of infection which were frequently located in the tonsils or teeth, and that these must be removed to effect a cure. Many teeth and tonsils were sacrificed to the new Moloch, although Dr. Fischer warned us to be skeptical of all dogma—including his own—and most of us were. Dr. Fischer cultivated writers and painters and he spent much of his free time in the company of the portrait painter John Weis and his wife Sallie. An inscription on one of his books reads: "To Sallie and John Weis, who have gladdened the world so often with laughter."

The physiology laboratory was headed by two brilliant young instructors of German descent who became famous in their own right. At the head was Dr. Robert E. Kehoe, who did pioneering work in lead poisoning and later founded the Cincinnati Postgraduate School of Occupational Medicine and the Kettering Laboratories. Dr. Kehoe was a friendly, no-nonsense scientist, full of vitality and scientific curiosity. He remained at the head of his school for over four decades, he lived into his nineties, and he established an international reputation for the school.

The other instructor in physiology was Dr. Gustav Eckstein. He was in his own right as exhilarating and inspiring as Dr. Fischer. Dr. Eckstein came to physiology by way of a dental practice, medical school, and a brief, unhappy marriage. He was totally dedicated to his experiments and studies and he lived for some time in his laboratory with canaries and experimental animals as intimate companions. What the famous French physiologist Claude Bernard was to Fischer, the Russian physiologist Ivan Petrovich Pavlov was to Eckstein. Dr. Eckstein finally found his true niche as the author of a dozen or so fascinating books, the most popular of which were *Noguchi, Canari, The Pet Shop*, and *The Body Has a Head*. All of these books made physiology and experimentation exhilarating and readily understood. Dr. Eckstein dreamed of writing a biography of Pavlov and he made several trips to Leningrad to this end, but was frustrated by lack of cooperation from the Russian authorities. He was one of the most sought-after guest speakers to enliven medical or literary gatherings; his buoyant enthusiasm, diminutive size, and high-pitched voice created an aura of perpetual youthfulness and somehow added to his stature as an intellectual giant. Dr. Eckstein died in his nineties and to the very end was able to kindle a fire with a few apt words or an incomplete short phrase.

The third and fourth years in medical school were a sharp transition from the "certainties" of the basic medical sciences to the uncertainties of clinical medicine. After years of preparation we were finally confronted with the harsh realities of the bedside and began to apply what we had learned. During the last two years the teaching was done in the clinical-pathological amphitheater or on the wards of the General Hospital. Our teachers were now the heads of clinical departments who also served as consultants to the medical practitioners of the community, as well as many private physicians who volunteered as lecturers or clinical instructors.

The professor of medicine, Dr. Roger Morris, was a kind and competent clinician and a fine teacher. We were taught the symptoms, the clinical course and the treatment of diseases, and the differential diagnosis when the symptoms overlapped. The professor of pediatrics, Dr. Graham Mitchell, was a witty man, a fine clinician, and an excellent teacher. In surgery, Doctors Heuer and Reid were the self-proclaimed gods who ruled over their department with an iron hand. They were the disciples of Dr. Halstead of Johns Hopkins University and the entire department reeked of anti-Semitism. Over a period of five decades, the department of surgery had only two Jewish senior residents—one of whom they could not have turned down because of powerful family connections and the other who was backed by a powerful non-Jewish pressure group. The five surgeons who succeeded Dr. Heuer were all (with one exception) like peas in a pod—competent, arrogant, and anti-Semitic. The irony is that the Johns Hopkins group was preceded by Dr. Joseph Ransohoff, a member of a prominent Cincinnati German Jewish family, and was followed by an Eastern European Orthodox Jew.

The other clinical departments were headed by private physicians, a considerable number of whom were German Jews. Outstanding among these were Doctors Elmore B. Tauber, Samuel Iglauer, Henry W. Bettman, and Albert Freiberg. Dr. Tauber conducted a well-organized dermatology clinic and was neatly dressed with an aristocratic bearing, but was aloof and snobbish. Dr. Iglauer, who taught ear, nose and throat, was an outstanding teacher and a very kind and considerate man; Dr. H.W. Bettman, who taught gastroenterology, was also an excellent teacher and his nobility of character emanated from his every word and gesture; Dr. Albert Freiberg, who taught orthopedic surgery, was an excellent teacher and surgeon but was somewhat overbearing.

There were very few Jewish physicians of Eastern European origin in

Cincinnati during the Twenties and, with the exception of Dr. Hiram B. Weiss, none did any teaching. Neurology was taught by Dr. Herman Hoppe; psychiatry was a six-hour course in the department of neurology and was taught by Dr. Emerson A. North, a very refined gentleman; obstetrics was taught by H.L. Woodward; gynecology by Dr. Charles Bonefield; and ophthalmology was taught by Dr. Victor Ray, a well-groomed man who gave a well-organized course.

The Cincinnati General Hospital, where I spent four years, was a sprawling institution of some twenty multi-story buildings connected by underground tunnels and ground-level covered walks. The hospital had three thousand beds and the wards were scattered over numerous buildings and many acres of land, with the intention of minimizing the spread of disease. Physicians and other personnel lost a great deal of time negotiating the great distances, and the maintenance turned out to be costly. Even before the advent of antibiotics it was obvious that the concept was faulty and the project became known as a "white elephant." Over the years other expensive facilities were added to the hospital, including a high-rise hospital building, a new surgical pavilion, and a magnificent new medical school complex. But faulty planning is like chronic disease—it can be improved but never cured.

On the wards of the General Hospital I came face to face with the joys of birth and the tragedies of death. Many of the intimate histories I was privileged to learn were sad and pathetic. There was a great deal of human interest and drama in many of these and I often pondered over the purpose and meaning of some of those lives. Despite my youth and inexperience, these people looked up to me for help and a ray of hope. It was at the bedsides of the General Hospital that I began to understand the meaning of Dr. Fischer's comment, "As a doctor you will have a front row seat to the greatest show on earth."

At the end of my junior year I began to think about internship, residency, and beyond. I applied for an internship at the Cincinnati General Hospital and hoped for a favorable reply; it was a prestigious teaching hospital and only ten places were reserved for graduates of the Cincinnati College of Medicine. Although I was among the top ten students gradewise, there were other considerations and an appointment was by no means certain. I therefore applied also to the Cincinnati Jewish Hospital and the Mount Sinai and Beth Israel hospitals in New York. In New York I brought letters of recommendation to Dr. Bella Schick, the famed pediatrician and discoverer of the Schick Test; I also had letters of recommendation to a prominent surgeon and to an influential internist at Mount Sinai. I was well received by all—they invited me to their offices, they were generous with their time, and I learned something of value from each of these successful physicians. The bottom line, however, was not to rely too much on a place in their hospital since the competition was too fierce from top-notch graduates of the Ivy League schools. Advice at Beth Israel hospital was on the same order.

While in New York, I was entertained by my cousin Jules Levy and his wife Mae. She introduced me to her father, Dr. Arnold Wolf, who was a successful gynecologist-obstetrician and the head of the gynecology department at three hospitals. He took me around to all of his hospitals and he offered me an internship in any of these. I was also assured of an association in his lucrative practice if I remained in New York. I appreciated Dr. Wolf's kindness but his hospitals lacked scientific standing and I was still contemplating a career in research. I therefore thanked Dr. Wolf and took a "rain-check"—just in case. Towards the end of December, I received an internship appointment from the Cincinnati Jewish Hospital and the next day the hoped-for letter arrived from the General Hospital. I promptly accepted the General Hospital appointment and sent a letter of regret to the Jewish Hospital.

The Jewish Hospital was a small, seventy-five-bed, private facility dominated by three physicians—Dr. Albert Freiberg, Dr. Louis Ransohoff, and Dr. Sigmund Stark—while the rest of the small medical staff had little to say about the operations of the hospital. The laboratory consisted of one man, Dr. Mortimer Hertzberg, the X-ray department consisted of Dr. Samuel Brown, and the anesthesiology department consisted of Dr. Mose Salzman. There was little for an intern to learn in a small private hospital since he was only permitted to write a history and, at that, only with the permission of the patient's physician and the patient. Another dubious pleasure was to serve as lackey to self-proclaimed "greats." Internships in small hospitals were therefore accepted only as a last resort. Even though the Jewish Hospital was paying its interns twenty-five dollars a month (a respectable sum in those days) in addition to food, quarters, and a chance of outside earnings or a junior partnership, the hospital had great difficulty getting its minimum quota of interns.

When Dr. Freiberg saw my letter of regret he came running across the street to the General Hospital and insisted that my appointment be revoked. Dr. Arthur Bachmeyer, who was the superintendent of the General Hospital and the dean of the medical school, advised me that it gave him great pleasure to tell Dr. Freiberg that I was a mature man and that if I chose to intern at the General Hospital it was my business. Dr. Freiberg never forgave me my audacity and he made certain that I would not be admitted to the staff of the Jewish Hospital until he went the way of all flesh. Fortunately, my plans for the future did not depend on the Jewish Hospital.

There were sixty-seven students in my class at the time of graduation, four of whom were women, four foreigners, and eleven Jewish. These three groups and two Gentile fraternities constituted the social structure of the class and each group kept pretty much to itself. There were no overt animosities, but neither were there any close intergroup friendships. Real camaraderie existed only in the two fraternities. Two classmates, Robert (Bob) Rothenberg and Louise Rauh, were able to cross the religious barrier to a degree, by virtue of their social position. As expected, this was only superficial but it helped the other Jewish students to deal more successfully with the strong anti-Jewish bias that was palpable under the surface. Bob Rothenberg gave an annual party for the entire class at the home of his parents, Dr. and Mrs. Samuel Rothenberg. During the four-year period at school our class president was James Howles, who was a friendly, athletic young man and a football hero. Regretfully, he was among the first of our class to die.

My other Jewish classmates were David Joseph Weintraub, Douglas Goldman, Edward Friedman, Simon (Si) Rosen, Rudolph Zodikoff, David Miller, Solomon (Sol) Bruson, and Bernard Robbins (Rabinowitz). Bob Rothenberg, who was elected on graduation as class president for life, was as charming and as ingratiating as his father. He became an internist and a member of the faculty, but he retired early from active practice and continued teaching psychosomatic medicine. Louise Rauh became a pediatrician and dedicated herself to public service at Children's Hospital and at the Cincinnati Milk Fund. My best friend, Dave Weintraub, specialized in ophthalmalogy and attracted a large following. Immediately after graduation he spent five years teaching anatomy at the University of Pennsylvania under Dr. Batson. During World War II, Dave served in the navy and became an observant Jew; he retired young and devoted his time to Hebrew scholarship and other studies. Douglas Goldman has had a varied and active career, at first in laboratory medicine, then as chief clinician and medical director of Longview Psychiatric Hospital, and later in the private practice of psychiatry. He began to emphasize the value of psychotropic drugs in the treatment of mental illness considerably ahead of other psychiatrists and he contributed extensively to the psychiatric literature. Edward Friedman practiced obstetrics-gynecology and succumbed to heart disease just before the fiftieth anniversary of his graduation from medical school. Si Rosen became a pediatrician and retired after four decades of practice in Hamilton, Ohio; he remained a quiet and friendly man and a devotee of his favorite game of bridge. Rudolph Zodikoff practiced internal medicine in Mariemont for four decades before he retired to medical administrative work. Dave Miller, who was a son of a great Cincinnati Talmudist, moved to the West Coast to practice and teach proctology;

Sol Bruson practiced ear, nose, and throat in Los Angeles; and Bernard Robbins (Rabinowitz) practiced psychiatry in New York. Bernie braved a sound razzing from the entire class when he showed up at the beginning of the junior year with his abbreviated name.

Among the Gentile students whom I remember well are William Bruggeman, John Dawson, John Phair, Herbert Conway, George Heidelman, and James Patterson. William Bruggeman was always considerate and friendly with a ready smile and a hearty laugh. He entered the private practice of medicine in Westwood in the middle of the Depression and continued there until his retirement; his son is on the staff of Christ Hospital, specializing in obstructive lung diseases. John Dawson, a native of Newport, Kentucky, has practiced general medicine in Northern Kentucky since graduation. He was always cheerful and I considered him a friend. Dawson became a student of Shakespeare and the Bible and he made it a lifetime practice to read a portion of each daily. John Phair, the hardiest consumer of alcohol as a student, became a public health officer and later Professor and head of the Department of Public Health at the University of Kentucky—and ultimately at his alma mater, the Cincinnati College of Medicine. We became close friends during his teaching years in Cincinnati.

One of the most distinguished careers of our class was made by Herbert Conway, who went to the Presbyterian Hospital in New York as a favorite student of Dr. Heuer. Conway became a celebrated, wealthy New York plastic surgeon and a well-known teacher in his field; he was not known as a brilliant student but he excelled in his ability to get on the good side of people that count. Conway exhibited no interest in his classmates or class functions and, like his teacher, was allegedly full of prejudice. George Heidelman was a handsome young man of slight build. He was a native Cincinnatian of German descent and he became a successful ophthalmalogist. He had a pleasant demeanor but displayed a palpable arrogance, and his prejudice towards Jews was ill-concealed. He died relatively young. James Patterson became a successful pathologist in Florida and he is the co-owner of several pathologic laboratories. At our fiftieth anniversary in 1978, more than half of our class was still alive; at our fifty-fifth class reunion in 1983 only twenty-four remained.

On a sunny afternoon in June, the day after graduation, the entire class assembled on the steps of the medical school for a class picture. During the social hour that preceded the event, nearly everybody drank to excess and a few of the young doctors were stone drunk. I was still allergic to alcohol from my sad experience with the stuff in Serei and, being the only one sober, I felt totally out of place amidst the shouting and screaming and the boisterous

Pupi and the author at the 55th reunion of his medical school class, June 1983.

"hoopla" all around me. The photographer had a hard time lining up the rowdy bunch and I hid whenever he tried, ashamed, behind the head of a tall colleague who chanced to stand in front of me. Thus, after seven and one-half years in the United States I had become a full-fledged doctor but was not yet fully "Americanized." I remembered a saying of Shakespeare, "O God, that men should put an enemy in their mouths to steal away their brains." But I had not yet learned the value of good-natured banter as a means of releasing pent-up emotions and tensions. While acquiring erudition in Shakespeare and the art of healing, I had forgotten an earlier teaching that on the Feast of Purim (celebrating the triumph over Haman) it is laudatory to imbibe intoxicants "until one is oblivious of the difference between 'cursed be Haman and blessed be Mordechai.'" I do not recall ever seeing a copy of this class picture.

My internship at the Cincinnati General Hospital extended without interruption from July 1, 1928 to July 1, 1929. It was a good "rotating" internship with two months on each of the six major "services" and an abundance of clinical experience on each service. The clinical benefits derived depended in a large measure on the teaching abilities and attitudes of the resident physicians under whom we served. There were daily clinical bedside rounds by the respective chiefs of staff, accompanied by their associates, residents, and nurses. There were also weekly clinical-pathological conferences where clinical impressions and diagnoses faced the moment of truth as revealed in the autopsy findings. With due allowance for the benefits, the internship was akin to slave labor. We were on call twenty-four hours a day, seven days a week, for twelve consecutive months—without pay, with horrible food, and we even had to pay for the laundering of our white uniforms. We did have fairly decent private sleeping quarters on the second and the third floors of the administrative building, and we were occasionally permitted a few hours "off-duty"—providing we secured a replacement. Our duties were to meet the patients upon their arrival on the ward and to do detailed histories, physical examinations, all of the on-ward laboratory tests, make a definitive or provisional diagnosis, prescribe orders for treatment, request needed laboratory tests or special consultations, and consult with the supervising residents.

By November 1928 I had served on the medical and surgical wards and was beginning to serve in obstetrics-gynecology. By the end of the month I had delivered one hundred twenty babies, including a fifteen-pound infant from a diabetic mother with a history of nine previous oversized babies. Anticipating problems, I put in a call for the resident and the chief of staff when the patient went suddenly into premature labor. Being forced to do the best on my own, I pulled and manipulated and sweated blood and, surprisingly, managed to deliver the oversized infant by the time the senior staff arrived. Aside from a temporary slight weakness of one arm, the fifteen-pound infant did remarkably well.

I was not quite sure at the time which branch of medicine to choose, but I was perfectly satisfied that it would not be obstetrics or gynecology. When I learned that an intern on the emergency ward was anxious to effect a trade in services, I grabbed the opportunity—not realizing what a momentous decision I had made. During the month of December on the emergency and receiving ward, I worked long hours day and night receiving, referring, or treating between one hundred to one hundred fifty patients a day. I loved the excitement, the kaleidoscopic nature of the clinical entities, and the unusual amount of experience I was getting. For me it was without doubt the best part of my internship. By the very nature of the emergency service, I was forced to make prompt decisions and I learned to act with dispatch. I was especially impressed by the enormity of the alcoholism and accident problems.

In 1928 there were no emergency facilities to speak of in any of the private hospitals to care for alcoholic or accident patients, and even at the General Hospital the staff doctors tended to avoid the untidy or dirty work involved in the care of these patients. Alcoholism was still thought to be a nasty habit leading to perdition, and the treatment often consisted of incarceration until sobriety, while accidents were judged to be fortuitous events or due to "care lessness." Not until several decades later did the profession begin to think of these conditions as disease entities. I perceived that the prevailing attitude towards these afflictions was wrong and attempted to treat them with the same respect and deference as other afflictions. I enjoyed the experience and was stimulated to think about remedial measures, which ultimately led me to emergency medicine as a career.

While serving on the receiving ward, I was surprised by a call from Professor Roger Morris, the Director of Medical Services at the General Hospital. I was even more surprised when Dr. Morris asked me if I would like to do research in experimental medicine after my internship. I told him that I would like it very much but being married and poor I could not afford it. He then advised me that I had been awarded the Holden Research Fellowship in Experimental Medicine, the highest fellowship being awarded by the University of Cincinnati. I accepted the award with deep thanks for the confidence and the opportunity. Dr. Morris congratulated me, wished me good luck, and then advised me to contact Dr. Clarence Mills—the Director of Experimental Medicine—for further details. I did not know then, nor did I ever learn, who was responsible for this pleasant surprise. In any event, it was a great boost to my morale and I began to give serious consideration to making a career in academic medicine and medical research. Feeling more secure now, I found the remaining six months of my internship even more enjoyable and meaningful, and I began to see Pupi more often on weekends at home or in my hospital quarters.

Dr. Clarence Mills was a young medical scientist with a reputation for his work on blood clotting. I first met him in the biochemistry laboratory where he was an assistant to Dr. Shiro Tashiro. When I came to see Dr. Mills in his laboratory on the fourth floor of the medical ward about my project, he seemed friendly and outgoing despite an ill-concealed reserve. After due congratulations and an exchange of pleasantries, Dr. Mills suggested that I investigate the mechanism and treatment of surgical shock. During World War I, many of the battle casualties succumbed to shock rather than to their injuries. Some work had already been done on this problem through perfusion of shock victims with acacia and other viscid fluids, but a great deal more remained to be learned. The experimental animal was to be the rabbit because it is so easily shocked, and shock was to be produced by scalding with hot water. I was to measure the viscosity of the rabbits' blood before and after shock and was to use a variety of perfusion fluids to determine the most effective means of getting the rabbits out of shock. I was advised that my appointment was from July 1929 to July 1930 and that I should register as a candidate for a Ph.D. in Experimental Medicine, which I did.

I began my work promptly, full of hope and enthusiasm with expectations of significant achievements. I was ready to dedicate myself fully to the project and to give it all I had. A number of flaws soon appeared which dampened my enthusiasm. Dr. Mills was primarily interested in studying the effects of environment on human physiology and behavior. To this end he built, on the research floor, two hermetically sealed rooms with controlled environments in respect to temperature, humidity, and barometric pressure. Beside his being engrossed in his own experiments, he did a great deal of traveling to remote areas of the world and was away most of the time. Dr. Mills was a true pioneer in environmental research but he had very little time for me and my project and, since I was all alone in the huge laboratory with no one to turn to for advice, it did not augur well for my efforts. I needed a preceptor to learn from and to work with since there was little in my previous experience to prepare me for independent research.

In the course of my experiments on shock I learned that by cooling and centrifuging parenteral fluids over short periods of time, I could distinguish between degrees of viscosity. This became known around the wards and before long Dr. Leon Schiff, the Chief Medical Resident, and other residents of other services began to bring up specimens to differentiate between exudates and transudates. If I had the necessary technical and financial aid to quantitate the test, it would have been known as the Schulzinger Test rather than the Gravity Test!

I was halfway into my research project when the Great Depression struck and I realized that there would not be any funds to continue in research, especially since many senior members of the teaching and research staffs were receiving severance notices. In the meanwhile, my financial situation became more precarious as Pupi and I were expecting our first child and my parents, on whose support I still depended, were becoming impoverished as a result of the Depression. Providentially, I met Mr. Sidney Rose, the president of the Cleveland Wrecking Company, who offered me a job as company physician. Mr. Rose was a towering, dynamic figure, my own age, who had recently come to Cincinnati from Minneapolis by way of Cleveland. He had just landed a demolition contract which was to last over a year to raze some four hundred buildings in the West End of Cincinnati, and I was to open an office in the vicinity of the project to provide care for the injured. The assured income it provided was just what I needed and Mr. Rose remained a lifelong friend. His company became one of the largest demolition contractors in the United States.

Despite the Depression, I was busy from the very first and my practice kept increasing as time went on. This was contrary to the general trend when many physicians did not earn enough to meet office expenses. I also found my work interesting and I pursued it with enthusiasm. Every accident told a story and I was fascinated by the state of mind of the injured before and immediately after the accident. As time went on I became ever more satisfied with my decision to enter the field of emergency medicine and to concentrate on the study of accidents. This decision required considerable soul-searching because the field lacked acceptance and it even carried a stigma. My decision was strengthened by a conviction that I was exploring a new frontier and that there were hidden truths to be discovered. Ultimately, no less than six distinct, highly respected specialties evolved from the new field of medicine on which I embarked in 1930 with so much fear and trepidation.

In addition to my office near the demolition project, I also hung up a shingle at the entrance to my first home on Reading Road and Rockdale in Avondale, but few people came knocking at the door. Before the demolition project ended, I opened an emergency clinic in a new building on the corner of Reading Road and Broadway because there was an abundance of small and medium-sized factories and business establishments in the area and there were no convenient facilities for the care of the injured. I have remained in the same quarters for fifty-five years, although the area has changed beyond recognition in the last two decades. The ten-unit building where I opened my emergency clinic was vacant for three years before I moved in and two more years elapsed before another tenant appeared. The new tenant was the pharmacist Isadore Fleischman, who also hailed from Serei. He was a friendly and compassionate man and was well liked by my patients and by all who knew him. I was happy to see him prosper and he remained my friend and neighbor until his death in 1980.

To open my clinic I needed two hundred dollars to pay for rent and equipment. A dentist friend whom I approached for a short-term loan refused to lend me the money. I then turned to Dr. Samuel Brown, whom I had recently met, and it restored my faith in humanity when he promptly took the money from his wallet and handed it to me. "You will repay me when you have it," said Dr. Brown with a broad smile as if to thank me for the opportunity to do a good deed. A few months later when I repaid the loan, he looked at me in disbelief and said, "You know, Morris, it is the first time I have been repaid a free loan." Dr. Brown, who was an excellent pioneering radiologist, remained a lifelong friend and I never forgot his gracious help nor failed to admire his outgoing personality and his true compassion for the needy.

With the two hundred borrowed dollars, I paid sixty-five dollars for a month's rent and used the rest to put up partitions, paint the offices, and make down payments on the purchase of used office furniture and equipment. I did all the necessary carpentry and painting by myself with the help of a junior medical student, Hyman Helfman, who became a successful physician in Middletown, Ohio. When Helfman came to my rescue he too was desperately in need of funds and he welcomed the seventy-five cents an hour I paid him for his help. My emergency clinic proved an immediate and continuing success and it fully justified my faith in the need for the services I was providing. A bonus reward was the abundance of clinical material which enabled me to study the accident phenomenon in great depth. I reported my findings in the medical literature and in a book I authored in 1956 which deals with the causes and prevention of accidents. The next chapter deals with my trials and tribulations as a would-be author, and the acclaim it brought me.

In 1978 my medical class celebrated its fiftieth graduation anniversary and a dozen or so classmates and their wives showed up for the festivities. Our invited guests were our former teachers, Doctors Gustav Eckstein and Hiram B. Weiss, both of whom were in their late eighties. On this landmark occasion, we reminisced about the giant strides that medicine had made in our lifetime, the transition from leeches to laser, from cupping to computerized tomography, and from diagnosis by clinical acumen and our five senses to the daily use of a vast array of highly sophisticated diagnostic tools. Numerous new clinical entities have been uncovered, many diseases have been conquered, most epidemic diseases have been brought under control, the life span has nearly doubled, and infant mortality has been reduced to insignificance. From hit-or-miss gunshot prescriptions we have advanced to precise organ-directed or even cell-directed therapeutic agents. New advances are crowding out old teaching at such a rapid pace that the best medical education has a half-life of only five years. Medical publications have so proliferated that it is now impossible for anyone to keep up with them, and over thirty new specialties have emerged to keep pace with the new discoveries.

The introduction of antibiotics in the Forties and the psychotropic drugs in the Sixties have revolutionized the practice of medicine beyond recognition. In Cincinnati alone this revolution has led to the razing of a two-thousand-bed tuberculosis sanitarium and six wards for the treatment of other contagious diseases, and resulted in the virtual emptying of the psychiatric hospitals. While these diseases have declined as the most important cause of morbidity and mortality, the degenerative diseases have taken their place and now have become the new frontier in medicine.

The phenomenal progress of the past half century has not been without cost. A steady deterioration has taken place in the warm, personal relationship that once existed between physicians and patients. Many physicians have become scientists, highly-trained technicians, or business administrators instead of healers, while the patients have come to expect instant or impossible cures. As a by-product of these changes, medicine has become aggressive in an effort to meet some of the exaggerated expectations and to avoid malpractice suits. Also, medical care has become too costly and an adversary relationship has crept in between doctors and patients. The intrusion of government and other third parties has further aggravated these conditions. The highly trained modern physician feels intimidated when he is subjected to a variety of clerical chores and to a vast array of nuisances, irritants, and political chicanery; yet, with it all, physicians are engaged in one of the most trusted professions, ministering daily to sacred human needs.

Projecting the present rate of advances into the future, it is not unreasonable to expect that in the next half century cancer will be conquered, organ replacement will become commonplace, the aging process will be slowed, and the life span will be further increased. But another doubling of the world population and the menace of nuclear war that is facing us will confront the world with staggering problems. While our knowledge has made it possible to peer into the remotest corners of the universe and into the tiniest threads of life, our wisdom—the wisdom distilled from the Hebrew Prophets and the Greek philosophers—has not kept up with our knowledge. Yet, as a Jew—the eternal optimist—I prefer to believe that in the end wisdom will re-emerge and triumph.

1979 was the year of my harvest when I received the Fifty-Year Award in the practice of medicine from the Cincinnati Academy of Medicine, the Ohio State Medical Association, and the American Association of Family Physicians. The same year I was elected to life membership in the American Medical Association, the American Association of Occupational Medicine, and the American Association of Family Practice. After a medical banquet at which two classmates and myself were presented with awards, I wrote a poem which fairly expresses the mood of the occasion. My colleagues liked what I wrote and caused its publication in the *Ohio Journal for Family Physicians*.

Reflections—On an Award

Plaudits, trophies, photoflashes,
Faces full of admiration,
Survivors of a thousand battles—
Hailed by thunderous ovation.

Friendly strangers, festive mood,
Spring and fall commingled,

Is it really meant for us
Or hope vicarial—in the applause?

A myriad thoughts surge to fore
Of instant past and of yore—
Struggles won and lost,
Problems posed—embraced.

Two faces at my side
Clearly tell the toll of time,
Unwilling to admit, I know,
The same (to them) is mine.

Devoted, privileged observers,
By their followers revered,
These heirs of Aesculapius profess—
Hopeful, fervent prayer,
Humility, and gentleness.

8-10-79

CHAPTER EIGHT

The Accident Syndrome

> "Chance is a word void of sense.
> Nothing can exist without a cause."
> (Voltaire)

In the fall of 1947 I decided to go to Israel to see my parents, whom I had not seen since 1931. During the seven weeks I was away from home I had time to reflect about the future. My emergency clinic had been a great success, it was open seven days a week, around the clock, and I was treating one hundred or more patients daily, working from ten to twelve hours a day with the help of six assistants and several doctors on a part-time basis. At times, when I contracted to do pre-employment examinations, the daily number of patients exceeded two hundred. With ample time on my hands, a luxury I had not known for nearly three decades, I began to think about possible alternatives for the future. Should I expand my clinic still further through the employment of full-time physicians and the addition of hospital facilities, or should I retreat to a more relaxed type of practice with more time for family, study, and perhaps research?

I was still ambivalent about the future when I returned home, so I consulted with Lester Jaffee, a partner in the prestigious law firm of Paxton and Seasongood, about the problems involved in founding and operating a small hospital. I also consulted with Dr. I. Arthur Mirsky, the director of the May Research Institute of the Cincinnati Jewish Hospital, about a suitable research project. Lester Jaffee was a tall, presentable, and brilliant Harvard lawyer with an active interest in community affairs. We had met often at community board meetings and had developed a friendly relationship. Dr. Mirsky was an illustrious author and medical researcher in the fields of diabetes, endocrinology, and psychiatry who had an abrasive personality. I had known him only casually. After several meetings with each of these men, Mr. Jaffe talked me out of extending my practice or entering the hospital field and Dr. Mirsky encouraged me to undertake a serious study of my records for the causes and prevention of accidents. On a deeper level, my advisers helped me resolve a dilemma which had troubled me for some time—whether to continue on the road to riches or return to the path of study. With due credit to my advisers, it was the quiet voice of Serei that triumphed.

Once the decision was made, I withdrew from active community work and took a number of steps to reduce the workload in my practice. I then began a study of the literature and my own records to learn what I could about the accident phenomenon. Little did I know at that time that I was embarking on a research project that would keep me busy for twenty-five years. The intensity of my drive being what it was, I threw myself into my studies with the same all-consuming passion I had shown in community work and in my practice—again at the expense of my loving Pupi and the children.

In 1947 most accidents were considered chance occurrences and prevention or "safety" consisted of mechanical restraints, machine guards, clever slogans and safety campaigns. Some psychological insight into the causes of accidents was given by the psychiatrist Dr. Flanders Dunbar, who observed during World War II that eighty-five percent of all accidents in army camps involved fifteen percent of the population. With the gain in popularity of Freudian psychology, the concept that most accidents were caused by an odd group of people gained rapid and widespread acceptance. These people became known as the "accident-prone" and a campaign was in progress to identify and treat the culprits. Although I approached my study with an open mind, I knew from my eighteen years' experience that the concept was faulty. When I began to review my records I discovered what a mammoth job I had undertaken since it ultimately entailed the study of more than forty thousand cases. As a result of the teachings of Dr. Fischer and my own penchant for details, my records proved to be a veritable gold mine of exciting information, although in the absence of computers the process of sorting out the data was tedious and time consuming. When I began to analyze the raw data it proved what I had suspected—that the theory of accident-proneness was a misconception born of a methodological flaw in Dr. Dunbar's studies.

My records proved, beyond a shadow of a doubt, that when accidents are observed beyond Dr. Dunbar's one-year period of study that "the fifteen percent of the population who cause eighty-five percent of the accidents" are not the same people, and that new victims constantly enter and leave the small group that had been dubbed the accident-prone. I further concluded that susceptibility to accidents was, in the main, a passing phenomenon and was due to a combination of environmental hazards and such human factors as age, sex, tension, aggression, maladjustment, the consumption of alcohol or drugs, exposure to a variety of toxins (such as carbon monoxide), or other disease processes. I also theorized that a suitable trigger mechanism in the presence of the above factors describes a diagnostic syndrome that could be useful in predicting and preventing accidents, and I called it the accident syndrome.

During the two years I spent studying my records, and for several years thereafter, I attended weekly seminars at the departments of psychiatry of the Cincinnati College of Medicine, under the direction of Dr. Maurice Levine, and the Cincinnati Postgraduate School for Industrial Medicine, under the direction of Dr. Robert Kehoe. I learned new insights from each of these departments and was given consultative access to Dr. Donald Ross, Associate Professor of Psychiatry, and to Dr. Frank Princi, Associate Professor of Industrial Medicine—both of whom became interested in my work. As I was preparing my findings for publication, I learned that there were formidable barriers for the publication of work done by unknown, non-academic researchers. I had condensed my thesis from three hundred pages of tables, graphs, and interpretations into a thirty-five-page monograph and submitted it to Dr. Kehoe for review. Dr. Kehoe praised my work and volunteered to send it to several editors of medical publications. I waited about four months before I approached Dr. Kehoe again about the fate of the monograph. Dr. Kehoe advised me that he had sent my material to four editors and that they had all turned it down for the same reason—my studies were interesting but "since the conclusions are contrary to all accepted opinion, there must be something wrong with the material or its method of treatment." It seemed incredible to me that new information would not be given a chance to be heard. When I expressed my dismay to Dr. Kehoe, he let me read the letters after deleting the identities of the writers.

Several months after the disheartening conversation with Dr. Kehoe, I was approached by Dr. Frank Princi about getting my material published. To my great surprise, he advised me to reduce my conclusions to a one-page paper and to leave out all of the supporting evidence. I was shocked by what seemed to me an impossible task, but promised to try. When I showed him my one-page paper he jumped up with visible excitement. "Excellent!" he said. "It

At the American Medical Association scientific exhibit in San Francisco in 1954, which launched the author's book on the accident syndrome.

will get published." The paper was published in the April 1954 issue of *Industrial Medicine and Surgery*, four years after I had completed my studies, and it made quite a splash. Dr. Princi also advised me to prepare a scientific exhibit for the 1954 Annual Meeting of the American Medical Association in San Francisco and to make an effort to present a scientific paper at the same meeting. I applied for both the exhibit and the presentation and was promptly accepted. The graphic and technical material for the exhibit was prepared at the University of Michigan with the help of Dr. Carey P. McCord, a consultant in industrial medicine and an editor of *Industrial Medicine and Surgery*. Pupi accompanied me on my trip to San Francisco and I was full of hope and trepidation. The results were beyond my expectations.

I set up my exhibit in the scientific section of the AMA, in the San Francisco Convention Hall, on the weekend preceding the meeting. On the first day of the meeting I presented my paper to a small audience and spent the rest of the day in my booth explaining my exhibit to casual visitors. Little did I know that before the day was over my work would be acclaimed around the world. The San Francisco evening papers featured my presentation on the front page under banner headlines and my findings were proclaimed as the outstanding scientific event of the prestigious AMA annual meeting of 1954. The next day all hell broke loose as my exhibit was swamped with visitors, many of whom were speaking foreign languages and were dressed in their multicolored national garb. During the next three days some fifteen hundred guests passed through my booth and over twelve hundred signed their names in the visitor's book. I was interviewed at length by the three international news services and, despite my efforts to keep the enthusiasm within bounds, my findings were sensationalized on the front pages of most newspapers in this country and overseas. Among the prestigious Cincinnati physicians who came to see my exhibit and sing my praises were Doctors Hiram B. Weiss, Cecil Striker, Julian Benjamin, Ralph Carothers, Frank Mayfield, Elsie Asbury, Frank Princi, and others. A few weeks later Dr. Howard Rusk, the science editor of *The New York Times*, described my findings and their implications in a four-column spread in the July 4th edition of the *Times.* A graphic description was published in the *Journal of the AMA* and my exhibit was published in the *Archives of Occupational Medicine.* There were editorials and feature stories in nearly all medical journals around the world, including two editorials and two stories in the prestigious British medical journal *The Lancet.* The reverberations, including requests for reprints, continued for two decades.

When I awoke Tuesday morning I felt pleased and vindicated, accepting my success with a strange equanimity. It seems that the adrenalin flows placidly in my blood—no great excitement in moments of triumph and no great despondency in times of despair. I sometimes envy those whose emotions are capable of greater flights, but placidity also has its reward— endurance. My basic work was subsequently published and republished in professional and lay periodicals by a host of writers and I was invited to speak to may groups and to publish papers in various magazines. I was also asked to show my exhibit at half a dozen universities and before the actuarial staffs of some large insurance companies. The insurance industry subsequently used my findings to change the insurance premiums of certain classes of drivers penalizing the young males, and those with other predisposing conditions. The flood of publicity that came my way soon translated itself into a heavy flow of new patients to my emergency clinic and before long I was busier than ever. Thus, the fame and fortune which I tried to escape a few years earlier returned with a bang!

Soon after my San Francisco triumph, I was approached by Mr. A.D. Cloud of Chicago, the publisher of *Industrial Medicine and Surgery* and an author in his own right, who commissioned me to write a series of papers for his journal. Later on, when he sensed that there was more to the story than my papers had revealed, he invited himself to Cincinnati for an in-depth interview. It was a beautiful summer day when he came to our home on Red Bud Avenue for the interview. We seated ourselves outside on the shady terrace, sipping refreshments. Then in response to a few searching questions, I began a discourse that lasted for several hours. When I finished, Mr. Cloud said to me, "You know, Dr. Schulzinger, what you have just told me is extremely valuable and is enough to fill a book." I looked at him in disbelief for the thought had never occurred to me. As I expressed my reluctance to undertake such an awesome project, he said to me, "Why don't you repeat what you have just told me on a recorder and I will talk to my editor, Dr. Cary McCord, to see if he will undertake to edit your book." Mr. Cloud planted the seed which two years later resulted in the publication of *The Accident Syndrome*, published by Charles C. Thomas. Dr. McCord, who edited my book, was a legendary figure in industrial medicine and a true pioneer in his field. He was a tall, gaunt man with a dry sense of humor and was a veteran of many struggles. In semi-retirement, he served as consultant to General Motors and as professor at the University of Michigan. He invited me to his home in Ann Arbor for a weekend of discussions and socializing in which he also displayed considerable talent in the culinary arts. He was a charming, sensitive person of slight build, in his late sixties when we met. We became close friends and he helped me in many ways.

The Accident Syndrome was not a best seller, but it was used extensively in medical postgraduate teaching, by safety societies, insurance companies, and by safety personnel. The director of the National Safety Council wrote to me that they were using my book like the Bible and it remained in circulation for two decades. It was reviewed all over the world and I received many letters of commendation. In 1958 I was invited by President Dwight D. Eisenhower to the White House for a conference on accident prevention; I was also chosen to represent the United States at the Second World Congress on accident prevention of the World Health Organization. The meeting was held in Brussels, Belgium and I participated in the discussions and read three short papers. I was particularly intrigued by the interest in my work by the representatives from Russia, Romania, Yugoslavia, China, and the Scandinavian countries.

Over the years I made several additional attempts to advance accident prevention. At the height of the popularity of my studies, I attempted to undertake a new research project to refine the diagnostic criteria of the accident syndrome. I obtained the cooperation of the departments of medicine and psychiatry of the University of Cincinnati and the out-patient departments of the General and Jewish Hospitals. The Jewish Hospital assured me of ample quarters for the project. I prepared a detailed research protocol and applied for a three-year grant from the National Research Foundation in which I volunteered my own time and asked for a modest sum of money to pay for the services of a clinician, a psychiatrist, a physiologist, an engineer, a social worker, and auxiliary personnel. Doctors McCord and Princi warned me that the likelihood of receiving a grant was not too good because of the chronic shortage of funds, the tendency to favor institutional applications, and the practice of those in charge to favor each other. When the predicted denial arrived I was disappointed, but was at least forewarned. Similar attempts to advance accident prevention through research in accordance with my principles were made several years later by a group of California researchers and a South African group, but their efforts to obtain the necessary funds were no more successful than mine.

My last effort was made in 1973 in Israel. I had lectured to physicians and safety groups in Israel on many occasions under the auspices of the Ministries of health and labor, my work had been published in the *Israel Medical Journal,* and I was well known to government leaders. Israel had, at that time, one of the worst records of automobile accidents in the world. The high accident rate was due to some extent to the aged condition of the vehicles and to the congestion and hazardous conditions of the roads, but to an even larger extent it was due to the inexperience, the excitability, the impatience, and the stressful conditions of the drivers. It seemed to me that a disciplined group like Israel's Citizen Army could provide an ideal population for a scientific study of accident prevention.

On my initiative, the Israeli Government arranged in the spring of 1973 for a two-day seminar at the Technion in Haifa, where I presented my program to a group of university specialists and Government functionaries. The program I offered was in essence an adaptation of the reseach project I had previously proposed to the National Research Foundation of the United States. I suggested that by pooling the medical records of Israel's Armed Forces into a computerized bank and adding psychological profiles as indicated, an effective accident prevention program would evolve that would save many lives and even improve military efficiency.

Prior to my scheduled visit to Israel I wrote to Moshe Dayan, who was the Defense Minister in Golda Meir's Cabinet, and asked for an appointment to discuss my ideas on accident prevention since the accident rate in the armed services was numerically high. I received a prompt reply that he was referring the matter to the Army Chief-of-Staff, who would make the necessary arrangements. When I called the A.C.S. I was told that I had an appointment with the Chief Physician of the Army.

The meetings at the Technion went very well. There were questions and answers and serious discussions and I had a chance to elaborate and clarify my ideas while an official stenographer recorded the proceedings. Throughout the two days of the seminar I sensed an invisible veil between me and the Israeli experts which I could not penetrate. The veil was lifted when one of the Technion experts, who was driving me back to Herzliya, told me that the medical records of the armed services were worthless because the physical examinations were perfunctory. He also expressed grave doubt that there would be enough cooperation from the physicians, the military personnel, or the Government to conduct a worthwhile study. He suggested instead that my program be tested in a small town or a large industrial establishment. I began to see the light and lost all interest in meeting with the Chief Physician of the Army, whom I was supposed to contact.

A few years after the publication of my studies, I began to encounter verbatim passages of mine in the literature without reference to the source. I was quite incensed about it until Mr. Cloud pointed out to me that my ideas had gained such wide acceptance that they were already a kind of folklore. Gradually people quit viewing accidents as purely fortuitous events or as mishaps caused by a small, odd group of "accident-prones" and began to pay attention to a broad range of identifiable human factors. The schools, the press, and the safety organizations helped a great deal with periodic campaigns of public education. As a result, it is now widely known that anger, tension, alcohol or drugs, etc. in an adolescent or young adult male will almost inevitably cause an accident, even in the quiet of the home—let alone behind the wheel of such a lethal weapon as a motor vehicle or with some other trigger mechanism. These and other recognizable human factors are a certain recipe for destruction by way of impaired judgment, faulty coordination, uncontrollable speed, and other resulting deficits. Physicians can play an important role in accident prevention, if they will, by recognizing and alerting their patients to the dangers of the accident syndrome—and some do.

There are, however, distinct limitations to the effectiveness of any accident-prevention program. Aside from the fortuitous nature of some accidents and the unavoidable hazards involved in others, there is the rebelliousness of the human spirit against fetters of any kind to contend with. It is commonly known that most of the fifty thousand annual casualties on the highways of the U.S. could be prevented through the avoidance of alcohol, reduced speed, and the use of seat belts. Yet this largely remains a pious wish. Many laws have been enacted to facilitate and encourage the noble aims of accident prevention, but all legal measures—weak, strong, or prudent—have been equally defeated by poor compliance, equivocal public support, and impossible enforcement problems. Accidents are not the only conditions in which beneficial remedies are frustrated by public indifference or reluctance. The best examples are smoking, alcohol or drug abuse, and overeating—which also shorten human life. Is there a self-destructive principle involved as some psychoanalysts contend—or are the tempo and tension of modern life simply too great for normal adaptation?

CHAPTER NINE

Beth Hatanach

"And let them make me a sanctuary
that I may dwell among them."
(Exodus 25:8)

Early in 1976 I met Professor Chaim Gevaryahu, who came to Cincinnati to deliver the Ephraimson Lectures at HUC. He delivered a discourse on *The Religious Philosophy* and *The History of Israel's Faith* by Yehezkel Kaufman. Despite the disorganized nature of his lecture series, Dr. Gevaryahu made a deep impression on me by his personal warmth, his sincerity, and his dedication to the Bible, so that by the end of his week's stay in Cincinnati we had become great friends. Dr. Gevaryahu is president of the Israel and the World Bible Societies and he is also the founder and moving spirit behind the Bible seminars held tri-weekly in the Beth Hanasi (the President's Palace) or at the homes of the Prime Ministers of Israel; he also leads the bi-annual World Bible contests in Jerusalem. The World Bible Society publishes the quarterly magazines *M'dor L'dor* in English and *Beth Mikrah* in Hebrew, which are dedicated to Bible studies, and it also publishes periodically original books on Biblical themes under the editorship of the Bible scholar Dr. Ben Zion Luria. The societies which Dr. Gevaryahu heads are co-sponsored by the World Zionist Organization, the World Jewish Congress, and the Jewish Agency.

312

Unknown to me, Dr. Gevaryahu had come to Cincinnati with my name and address and with special designs on me. After one of his lectures, he invited me to his quarters for "a serious talk," the upshot of which was that he wanted me to undertake a fund-raising campaign to build an imposing Beth Hatanach (Bible House) in Jerusalem. This edifice was to be built on an eight-acre plot of land which the Keren Kayemeth L'Yisroel (Jewish National Fund) had deeded for this purpose. I was told that David Ben Gurion, the first Prime Minister of Israel, was the initiator of the idea, that all the architectural plans were ready, and that the Knesset had voted an operating budget for this great enterprise. In essence, the project was meant to combine a major Bible library, a Biblical museum, and a center for Bible study and research with special facilities for scholars, students, and the lay public. Major gifts of great historical value, I was told, were offered to Ben Gurion by two European governments and by a number of individual collections. I was not told that several people had already tried and failed to achieve this aim. Among those who tried were none other than Ben Gurion himself, the late Finance Minister of Israel, Pinchas Sapir, and the former Supreme Court Justice of the U.S., Arthur Goldberg.

I was intrigued and flattered by the suggestion that I undertake such a grandiose project, but begged off because of my advanced age and long retirement from public activities. Single-minded men like Dr. Gevaryahu do not accept no for an answer and he succeeded in exacting a promise that I would give the matter further consideration. Since the Bible had played such an important part in the formative years of my life, I did not have to be convinced of the merits of the project—especially when Bible study among Jews had fallen on bad times in the current century. In my mind's eye I could see an imposing Jewish World Bible Center in Jerusalem as an effective instrument for shoring up Jewish values, restoring the "Book of Books" to the "People of the Book," and stemming the tide of rampant assimilation and the loss of Jewish identity.

The more I thought about it the more I was intrigued by the challenge and I gave Dr. Gevaryahu a tentative commitment to see what could be done. Dr. Gevaryahu was happy to learn of my decision and he approved the plans I outlined in a series of communications. Before making my final commitment, I visited Israel to see for myself what was involved and whom I could count on. I visited many of the Biblical sites in Jerusalem and Samaria with Dr. Gevaryahu and Ben Zion Luria. With Bible in hand, I had an inspiring tour and many of the Biblical events came to life under their expert guidance. The site where the Beth Hatanach was to be erected had a magnificent view of the Kidron Valley and the Monuments of Absalom and the Prophet Zeharyahu. I was received by President Ephraim Katzir and Golda Meir, both of whom assured me of their interest in the Beth Hatanach project and promised every possible help. The more I saw of the people involved whom I was to work with, the better I liked it, and I returned to Cincinnati determined to proceed.

I plunged into the Beth Hatanach project with all of my former vigor and began with calls on a number of local dignitaries to win support for the project. Rabbi Fishel J. Goldfeder, the spiritual leader of Adath Israel Synagogue, and my son-in-law Dr. Stanley J. Lucas gave their unqualified approval. The most important among the others was Philip M. Meyers, Sr., a highly successful businessman and a former president of the Jewish Community Council, the Jewish Welfare Fund, the University of Cincinnati, and the Jewish Hospital—and an important contributor to many other important civic and Jewish activities. As I described the Beth Hatanach project to him he listened with unusual interest and then enthusiastically endorsed it and agreed to become a founder and treasurer of the contemplated organization. He was subsequently generous with his counsel as well as his financial support. I had known Phil Meyers since he started on his road to success and was even closer to his father, Mitchell Meyers, who was an old-time maskil (adherent of Enlightenment), a good friend, and a patient of mine. After these preliminaries, I proceeded to found "The American Friends of the World Bible Center Jerusalem" with myself as president, Rabbi Goldfeder vice-president, Philip M. Meyers, Sr., treasurer, and Dr. Stanley Lucas secretary. It was a tightly knit group with myself in complete control and my officers ready to render active support as needed. We then obtained an Ohio charter and incorporated as a tax-exempt organization.

As soon as the architectural drawings arrived from Jerusalem I conferred with Charles Messer, president of the prestigious Messer Construction Company, and was floored when his engineers estimated the cost of the project at a minimum of twenty-five million dollars—about ten times the Israeli estimate. In the meanwhile, I contacted leading Rabbis, Judaic scholars, major Jewish organizations, and community leaders in the U.S. and abroad to obtain their support, and received the enthusiastic endorsement of over three hundred founders. Among the Israelies who endorsed the project were: Ministers of State Moshe Dayan, Shimon Peres, Abba Eban, Dr. Joseph Burg, (president) Chaim Herzog, former Prime Minister Golda Meir and Prime Minister Menachem Begin, Presidents Ephraim Katzir and Itzhak Navon, and many of the leading Bible scholars of Israel. With such an illustrious sponsorship gracing our stationery, I launched a campaign to reach the three thousand Rabbis of the U.S. and every congregation and every Jewish and non-Jewish foundation that might have an interest in the project. For two years my office staff and I did all the work and I covered most of the expenses. In response to

Family group at the Beth Hatanach dinner, 1978.
Seated left to right: Chana Rosen, Nahum Marmet, Leah Marmet, Dr. Joseph Marmet, Dr. Stanley Whitehill, Dr. Olga Horwitz (Whitehill) and cousin Dorika Rutshtein (visiting from Moscow).
Standing: Dr. Stanley Lucas, Dr. Irvin Dunsky, Abe Dunsky, Penina Frankel, Naftali Frankel, Judy Lucas and Label (Leon) Block.

our appeals for financial support, we received small and moderate contributions from over six hundred Rabbis and congregations, but the total sum raised was insufficient to engage a professional director and fund-raiser.

Early in 1978, during a visit of Dr. Gevaryahu to the U.S., we made a major effort to gain support for the Beth Hatanach with visits to Chicago, Los Angeles, Miami, and New York—again without significant results. In July 1978 we did manage to engage an executive director, Rabbi Joel Goor of San Diego, California and Plantation, Florida, who undertook to organize a major fund-raising drive. He raised enough money to cover his salary and office expenses but not the millions of dollars that were needed.

In the summer of 1978 Rabbi Goldfeder met with Dr. Gevaryahu and his executive committee in Jerusalem and they decided to launch a formal fund-raising campaign with a testimonial dinner in my honor. Having grown publicity-shy over the years, I declined the honor in a letter to Jerusalem, but later yielded to persuasive arguments by Rabbi Goldfeder that a major public gathering might produce the necessary momentum. The testimonial dinner was held in Cincinnati at the Adath Israel Synagogue on Sunday, November 5, 1978. It was a beautiful affair with nearly three hundred guests consisting of family, friends and sympathizers in attendance. Rabbi Gunther W. Plaut of Toronto was the guest speaker; among the other speakers were Rabbi Goldfeder, Rabbi Goor, and myself. Rabbi Albert Goldman gave the invocation, Rabbi Donald Splansky gave the benediction, and Dr. Lou Witten, professor of physics at the University of Cincinnati, was master of ceremonies. Cantor Paul Kowarsky rendered appropriate musical selections. From Jerusalem came Dr. Gevaryahu, who spoke in Hebrew, and Chaim Finkelstein, former head of the cultural department of the Jewish Agency in Jerusalem and an orator of note, who spoke in a beautiful classical Yiddish. As usual, our sincere efforts to keep the program within reasonable bounds was only partly successful. A fair amount of money came in response to this affair, but nothing big. My daughers, Penina and Judy, and a group of friends outdid themselves in arranging the affair; so did Rabbi Goldfeder and his staff. From my long experience I knew that those who did not need convincing were greatly impressed while the others were probably bored.

In our communications with the Rabbis we sought their help in reaching some of their most affluent members and an increased effort to promote serious Bible studies in their congregations and communities. I was dismayed to learn that whatever influence the Rabbis had with their wealthy members they needed to keep their own establishments going. With regard to promoting Bible studies, a few Rabbis reported successful innovations, a few opposed any joint effort, and most were mute. To ascertain the nature of the difficulties first hand, I called on the Cincinnati Rabbis and on a number of professors at HUC to help with a local Bible study project. Although promises were readily given, Dr. Jacob Marcus, distinguished professor of history at HUC, expressed skepticism about the commitments. In due course, an elite city-wide Bible study group was launched at the home of Nachum and Sham Eden, but the Cincinnati Bible Society died a natural death after a dozen or so monthly meetings due to steadily declining interest. From this experience I learned that it required unusual special talent to keep such groups going. From my contacts with the Rabbis of the country I learned that there were a few Jewish Bible societies in existence that were on their last legs. But more hopefully, some attempts were being made to form small congenial study groups (havurot) with a fair promise of success.

During the visit to Cincinnati of our Israeli guests, Rabbi Goldfeder, Rabbi

Goor, and myself held several meetings with them at which we pondered over how to advance the Beth Hatanach project and our overall program. The guests from Jerusalem advocated the founding of Bible societies around the country under the auspices of a new roof organization, and Rabbi Goor tended to agree with them. On the basis of our local experience and my soundings around the country, I saw little promise in this approach and suggested that a concerted effort be made to reach the large contributors, and if the effort failed to draw the necessary conclusions. I also urged that in the interim a greater effort be made in Israel itself and to send emissaries to the larger European cities as well as to South Africa, Argentina, Mexico, and Canada. All of these efforts were made but nothing substantial resulted. I, for one, was not interested in adding one more struggling society to the already overcrowded arena of contesting Jewish organizations, and our activities were suspended until a more opportune time.

Rabbi Fishel Goldfeder was of great help to me throughout all of these efforts with his counsel, his encouragement, and his readiness to perform many practical tasks. Rabbi Goldfeder had come to Cincinnati after World War II as an assistant to Rabbi Louis Feinberg, the spiritual leader of the Conservative Adath Israel congregation. Rabbi Feinberg was a quiet, genteel person with artistic and intellectual qualities, and he achieved wonders considering the polyglot Polish-Lithuanian immigrant group he was molding. When the revered Rabbi Feinberg died within a few years after the arrival of his assistant, Rabbi Goldfeder was chosen to succeed him. The young Rabbi was full of new ideas and youthful vigor and, being American born, he became a magnet for the young Orthodox Jews of Cincinnati who were eager for new leadership. During the thirty-five years of his ministry, Rabbi Goldfeder remained dynamic, compassionate, and forthcoming, and it seemed as if he was born for his exalted calling. Rabbi Goldfeder had come from an Orthodox home in New York where he attended Yeshivoth and absorbed a love of Torah. He then spent three years studying in the famous Mirer Yeshiva of pre-war Poland and graduated with honors from the Jewish Theological Seminary of New York. He died suddenly in Jerusalem in February 1981, two months after his retirement. He had lived up to the highest expectations of his calling, serving his congregation and the community in admirable fashion. In accordance with his wishes, he was buried in his beloved Jerusalem, to which he was dedicated with his entire being.

In recent years an increased interest in Judaic and Bible studies has developed in the U.S. and in Israel. This interest is shared by the lay public and by some of the established Jewish organizations which should have evinced more concern about the problem a long time ago. The Government of Israel has also come forth with help for a modest interim Beth Hatanach in Jerusalem. The favorable sentiments which so many Jewish leaders have expressed towards our program augur well for the future, and a grandiose Bible edifice in Jerusalem will undoubtedly be erected in due course.

PART THREE

ISRAEL

CHAPTER ONE

Israel

> "And I shall give you the land
> for thy inheritance."
>
> (Genesis)

In the fall of 1947 I went to Israel (Eretz Yisroel) to see my aging parents and tour the land of my dreams. Two years after the end of the war, transatlantic travel was still erratic and the waiting list was up to twelve months. There were no direct flights to Palestine but with the help of a friend I was able to secure a round-trip TWA flight to Cairo. Because of the difficulties of travel and the terror that raged in Palestine, Pupi and I decided I should go alone. Remembering my European experiences, I secured a letter from John W. Bricker, the Governor of Ohio, which stated that "any courtesy shown him on his travels abroad will be appreciated by the Governor and the State of Ohio." With the Gold Seal of the State of Ohio and the bright blue ribbon, it made a very impressive document and it proved priceless when the need for it arose in the course of the trip.

Full of excitement about seeing my parents and the land I had loved since my earliest childhood, I started out for New York after elaborate preparations at home. On arriving in New York on a September Monday morning, I checked in at the Commodore Hotel and learned from the newspapers that a pilots' strike was in the offing. Early that evening I was advised by TWA that the flight had been postponed until Tuesday morning. Later that morning the strike became official and all flights were canceled. Since I had engaged a physician to take care of my practice during my absence, I had no choice but to wait it out. After some hesitation I called Mr. L. Fry, the President of TWA, and asked his help to get me on another airline. Mr. Fry was very understanding and suggested that I inquire at the British Airways, which were scheduled to fly to Cairo in a few days. If the British were unable to accommodate me, Mr. Fry continued, he would try to put me on a chartered KLM flight which was to return a Saudi-Arabian delegation to Cairo—providing the Saudis did not object. I thanked Mr. Fry for his kindness and promptly proceeded to the offices of British Airways. The British were unnecessarily rude in denying me a seat, probably reflecting the tense situation in Palestine. I communicated my disappointment to Mr. Fry's office and was advised to keep them informed of my whereabouts in case there was a sudden break in the strike or a favorable reply from the Saudis.

With nothing but time on my hands, I telephoned my cousin Jules Levy. My call had to go through four secretaries, but when I finally reached him he was very friendly and invited me to his home for a drink and to go out on the town for dinner and nightclubbing. Everything about Jules was large-sized. He was six-foot-three, broad-shouldered, full-faced and of heavy build, every inch of him the high-powered executive he was—except that his speech was measured and his words were few. Both Jules and his beautiful wife Mae, a tall, slender, middle-aged blonde, greeted me with open arms and we sat down for a few drinks and some socializing. I was amazed by the unusual size of the rooms of their plush Riverside Drive apartment and by the tremendous bar which extended the entire length of the wall with hundreds of bottles of whiskey, brandy, and liqueurs in full display. After two rounds of drinks we started out on the town by taxi. On the way to a famous French restaurant we stopped in a Romanian bar for a few more drinks. I was flabbergasted by their capacity for hard drinking but, unwilling to be a "spoil-sport," I did not do too badly myself. We finally reached our restaurant and, being quite hungry, I ate heartily of the delicious food that was being served while my cousins and their lady guest just nibbled. The conversation was amiable and we all seemed to have a good time. Around midnight we ended up at a Hungarian night club for their floor show. I do not remember too much about the show except that I thoroughly enjoyed myself. The marathon of eating, drinking, and merry-making was a unique experience for me, but it reminded me in a way of the farewell party in Serei a quarter of a century earlier.

On Wednesday I had lunch with my gymnasium classmates Julius Kushner and Frieda Mecklenburg, and late that night I was the "house guest" at the famous 21 Club, where I tasted a fantastic variety of gourmet dishes, was given a V.I.P. tour of the entire establishment—including their storied wine cellers, and was introduced to several celebrities. I owed this unexpected pleasure, which lasted until 2 A.M., to my Cincinnati friends Dr. Louis and Katie Kreindler, who were cousins of the owners and were visiting New York.

I slept late the next morning and since there were no new developments I decided to take in a Broadway show, which turned out to be *Annie Get Your Gun* with Ethel Merman in the starring role. I arranged to be called at the theater if TWA called, and left for the theater. It was a magnificent performance but during intermission I had some foreboding and decided to call the hotel. I was astonished to learn that TWA had been trying to reach me for several hours and that the theater refused to transmit the message. I hurriedly phoned TWA and was advised that the Saudis had agreed to let me fly with them and that the KLM flight was scheduled to leave at seven o'clock in the morning. If I wished to go on this flight, TWA continued, I would have to come to their office to get a transfer ticket, then obtain a visa at the Dutch consulate and pick up my plane ticket at the KLM offices. The exciting news turned to panic when I realized that I had left my passport at the hotel, that it was 4:30 P.M., and that I most certainly could not accomplish all of these tasks before these offices closed—and in the midst of the New York rush hour at that!

Yet, with the help of some decent people and quick thinking, I did accomplish the seemingly impossible. I phoned the Dutch consulate and the KLM offices and both agreed to wait for me. I then rushed to the Commodore Hotel at breakneck speed and bribed the taxi driver to wait until I picked up my passport and take me to the TWA office. At TWA I was stunned to learn that all the TWA personnel were tied up at a meeting with representatives of the striking pilots and that they could not be disturbed. Upon hearing the bad news with such a tone of finality, I told the receptionist, with equal firmness, that if she could not get my transfer ticket for me I would walk into the conference room and get it myself. Somewhat shaken, she went into the room and returned with an official who handed me the transfer ticket. It was after six o'clock by then and I again phoned the Dutch consulate and the KLM offices to tell them that I would arrive shortly. The Dutch consul, who was friendly and outgoing, overlooked the regulation photograph requirement and accepted a small snapshot of Pupi and myself. He even called the KLM offices and asked them to wait for me. It was a full hour past the regular office hours when I walked out of the KLM office with ticket in hand—a tired but very happy man. Only three years later, when *Annie Get Your Gun* played in

Cincinnati, did I realize that I had missed seeing the second half of the show in New York.

On boarding the KLM plane, I learned that there was another passenger who was not a Saudi. My travel companion, Mr. J. Johnson, had served as a representative of the Standard Oil Company of New Jersey in the Middle East for fifteen years before the war, and he was now returning to his former post in Beirut. The Saudi delegation of about thirty consisted of the Minister of Finance, his advisors, valets, and chefs. The Saudis occupied the front part of the small plane and they prepared and served their own food while Mr. Johnson and I shared the customary fare with the flight crew. The Saudis kept strictly to themselves and, in accordance with their cultural and religious practices, there were no females aboard. The flight took some forty-eight hours with an overnight stopover in an Amsterdam hotel and refueling stops in Gander, Paris, Rome, and Athens. There were photographers and newsmen to greet the V.I.P.s on boarding in New York, on landing in Cairo, and at every stop in between. The Saudis carried with them numerous American products including bicycles, radios, household appliances, and a variety of toys and gifts for chldren. They seemed oblivious to the presence of the two "infidels" in their midst and neither side engaged the other in conversation.

Mr. Johnson proved a most engaging travel companion. He filled me in on the cultural patterns of the Middle East and about the hidden wealth that was rumored to be beneath the desert sands. During World War II Mr. Johnson, who was an engineer by profession, was in charge of surveying the floor of the English Channel and of laying down the oil pipes that were to provide the British and American forces with fuel on D-Day and for several days thereafter. The Channel floor was so jagged with sharp rocks that five parallel lines had to be laid down a day or so before the invasion with the hope that one or two lines would survive the inhospitable environment.

During one of our conversations, Mr. Johnson said to me, "Doctor, beware of the dragomen (guides) in Cairo. Before you know it they will take you to the bazaar and there you will really be taken! If you want to buy Egyptian presents for your wife and children you would do better if you stopped at the Egyptian department at Macy's in New York on your way home. You will find them well stocked with reliable merchandise and you can return or exchange anything your wife does not like. If you do find yourself in the bazaar I would like to give you a few words of advice which you may find helpful.... There are no set prices in the Middle East. The people like to engage in a very intricate process of bargaining, and if you pay the asked price the merchant will consider you a fool and will also feel unhappy about being denied the pleasure of haggling—notwithstanding the excessive profit he has made. So if you do go to the bazaar and the merchant asks $100 for an item, you should offer him fifty cents. He will start screaming at the top of his voice that you are killing him and that it is an insult to Allah and his Prophet, but this is merely a charade. He will end by saying that since you are his first customer and he desperately needs the money, he will come down to fifty dollars. After some leisurely deliberation you should offer him one dollar. The merchant will repeat the same verbal tirade as before and end by reducing the price again in half. You will increase your offer by another small amount and in the end you will buy the hundred-dollar item for four or five dollars, and at that price you may have overpaid!"

After resting in Cairo overnight at the Shepherd Hotel, I took the daily morning flight of the Mizrah airline to the Lod Airport in Palestine. The plane was a rickety biplane of ancient vintage with the wings and doors reinforced with bailing wire. One look at this unbelievable decrepit flying machine and my heart sank, but I had no choice in the matter. I was the only passenger and I had to climb inside the plane through an open window and sit on a crate with another crate supporting my back. During the flight, as I was looking down on the desert sand dunes, I wondered whether it would be a soft landing if we were forced down. Fortunately, the pilot was a skillful war veteran and we landed safely at Lod after a smooth one-hour flight.

I found my parents unusually alert, in excellent health and thoroughly satisfied and happy with their lives in the Holy Land. My parents' home on Hadar Street in Herzliya was a small, one-floor structure which was enlarged and divided to accommodate my sister Sheine, her husband, Avram Ber, and their three small children. The house was situated in the midst of a young orange grove. The fragrance was intoxicating and fresh oranges and grapefruit were plucked from the trees before each meal and served fresh all year round. They also had their own chickens, fresh eggs, and a small vegetable garden yielding a variety of greens in three or four crops annually. My parents had dedicated part of their home as a synagogue and there were three daily services for the devout. During the Sabbath Morning Services I was called up for the reading of the Torah and I recited the customary benediction of "Hagomel"—the prayer of thanksgiving for having safely completed a dangerous journey. After the services there was a reception for the worshippers and Mother and Sheine served cakes and cookies which they had busily prepared for the occasion, as well as Israeli wines and liqueurs. The entire congregation was like one happy family and there was a great deal of jubilation, greetings, toasts, and well-wishing. The congregation represented a kaleidoscope of people from many parts of the world and many vocations. There were farmers, laborers, craftsmen, businessmen, clerks, and artists, and professionals. Their easy and open relationship with one another reminded me of Serei. Even the more reserved Germans and other Western Europeans, who were in the minority, joined in the uninhibited way of celebrating. I could see that spiritually my parents had achieved their heaven on earth and, even though the State of Israel was yet to be, for them the "Galut"—or the two thousand years of exile—had ended.

For the Sabbath meal we transferred to my sister's quarters. My mother and my sister, both of whom were excellent cooks, had each prepared a variety of dishes from those I had liked best in Serei, along with some adaptations from Cincinnati and Israel. It was a Herculean task to consume even a small fraction of all they had prepared and I was at my wits' end not to displease my dear ones by sampling at least part of what each served—regardless of taste or appetite. Among the dishes they prepared were petcha (jellied calf's foot with garlic and other condiments), sliced radishes with chicken fat, chopped liver, gribines (fried chicken skin with onions), chicken soup, cholnt (a twelve-hour stew of potatoes, beans, meat, fat, and flour), gefilte fish, tzimmes (grated carrots with sweet potatoes, white potatoes, and prunes), kishke (stuffed derma), and several varieties of meat—including boiled chicken and tzimmes meat, with carmel wine and several brands of liqueur at suitable intervals and hot tea with several kinds of cake at the end of the banquet. Most of the dishes were delicious and I was being watched by my mother and my sister for clues of approval, which they judged by the quantities I consumed. My greatest problem turned out to be the petcha which I loved as a child and which Mother prepared specially for this occasion as the piece de resistance—but after twenty-seven years in America this dish was no longer palatable. Although every morsel was a torture, I had to consume a full portion and pretend that it was delicious. Between each course there were the customary Sabbath songs, or z'miroth, and some learned discourses by my father and my brother-in-law. It was a three-hour banquet, we were all in good spirits, and it set the tone for the rest of my first visit to Israel.

My brother-in-law Avram Ber, whom I had never met before, was an unusually handsome, refined, and good-natured man. To meet him was to love him and he was admired by all. He was also a great Talmudic scholar and I found his company stimulating. My sister Sheine, whom I had not seen since I was a teenager in Serei, was a pious, good-hearted soul who was completely devoted to raising her children and to pioneering the land. In her rhetoric she was somewhat philosophical and rigid and she tended to adhere to some of the best and the worst of Serei. Father was the same old self—quiet, retiring, and forever absorbed in his studies. His queries were limited to the bare essentials about people, friends, and conditions in Cincinnati and about the children,

Pupi, and the family. Mother, on the other hand, had carved out a rather busy life for herself. She managed their properties in Tel Aviv on Yona Hanavi Street and on Almoni Court off King George Street. She also attended to the cultivation and the harvesting of the orange grove and garden. Above all, however, she was very active socially and in charitable work. She helped found a home for the aged and a children's home in Tel Aviv and she was an active member on both boards. She also conducted an active correspondence with family and friends in many parts of the world and she was the recipient of charitable contributions for a variety of causes. My parents also founded a free loan fund with their own money which Mother managed. I noticed that some of the people who came to see my parents would ask for a "gemilas hesed" (a small loan) which Mother would give without asking any questions, making any entries, or requiring any receipt. When I asked Mother how she kept track of her loans, she seemed surprised at my question and said, "These are all honest people in need. If they have the money they will repay it so that others can be helped, and if they do not have it there is no need of making them feel worse when they already feel bad at being unable to repay a gemilas hesed."

During the ten days I remained in Herzliya, I enjoyed being with my parents and conversing about the happenings of these many years. The loss of my sister Rivka and her family came up frequently, often with heart-rending crying. We also talked a great deal about the calamity that befell our people. From time to time survivors of the Holocaust came to my parents' home and they were greeted as if they had returned from among the dead. I spent a great deal of time meeting friends of my parents who came to congratulate them and to meet their important guest. Although they were total strangers to me I welcomed the opportunity of meeting my parents' friends and getting to know these old-young idealists who had come to Israel in the Twenties and Thirties to rebuild the country of their dreams, hopes, and prayers.

There was also a parade of cousins on my father's side whom I had never met before. These were the children of Uncle Eli Dovid of Petach Tikva who came to Eretz Yisroel from Semyatich, Poland in 1921 together with his wife and eleven children. By this time they were all married with large families of their own. One son, Yitzhak, was a Rabbi in Haifa; two daughters were married to Rabbis and one daughter was a member of the socialist Kibbutz Nahalal, where Moshe Dayan grew up. There were also my three cousins from Suchovolia whom I had not seen in twenty-nine years. Chana Druyan came with her husband, Dr. Avram Druyan, who was a practicing dermatologist in Jerusalem, while Chana was a nurse and the chief aide to the director of the X-ray department of the Hadassah Hospital. Chanele, who was a gifted free-lance writer, came with her husband Yitzhak Steinberg, a skilled iron worker in Tel Aviv. And Chanele's sister Valia, who was also a nurse, came, together with her husband, Moshe Yanovsky, who worked for a movie theater. There were also landsleit from Serei, schoolmates from Mariyampole, and Yankele Bernstein and his wife, who were old friends of Pupi from Balbirishok. Yankele was the head of the sanitation department of the Herzliya district. They were a charming couple and a fine example of the early hard-working pioneers from the time when the country was infested with malaria. This was the same Yankele to whom Pupi sent my beautiful riding boots when my equestrian activities ended around 1940.

Before I set out to see the country, I decided to return every weekend to Herzliya to spend the Sabbaths with my parents. After ten days in Herzliya, I began to travel around the country, which was then in the grips of the British terror and the Jewish counter-terror. The Israeli freedom-fighters consisted of the Irgun Zvai Leumi headed by Menachem Begin, the former Prime Minister who hails from Brest-Litovsk; the Sternists, headed by Avram Stern who hailed from Suvalk, and the official para-military organization of Eretz Yisroel, the Haganah, which was under the control of the Histadrut and the Vaad Leumi, the National Assembly. Avram Stern, who led the most militant group, had organized in his youth an effective defense against Czarist pogroms in his home district in Poland. Menachem Begin, a disciple of Vladimir Zhabotinsky, had a long history of resistance-fighting in his native Poland before he became the commander of the Irgun in 1944. After Israel declared its independence in 1948, Begin converted his guerrilla organization into the Herut political party. As a lifelong member of the Histadrut, I supported the official defense force of Israel, the Haganah, and shuddered at some of the atrocities perpetrated by the extremists. In retrospect, however, I believe that the extremists were nearly right and that the Haganah was too timid in the struggle. This change in viewpoint appears to me to be justified by the provocative atrocities of the British, their arming of the Arabs, their betrayal of the mandate, and their cruelty in preventing the victims of the Holocaust from entering Israel.

As I began to tour the country, I was shocked to see all public buildings surrounded with barbed wire and machinegun nests and to find checkpoints with bayonet-wielding soldiers at all strategic crossroads, bridges, and highways. Some of the atrocities were of recent vintage. A wing of the King David Hotel was blown up by the Irgun, killing many British officials; there were public floggings of British soldiers by the Sternists in retaliation for similar acts against Jewish freedom fighters; and there was the arrest of the entire Jewish leadership. In the end, it was the terror of the extremists against the

British and the sense of shame that the behavior of their administration evoked at home that prompted the British Government to surrender its mandate and to throw the fate of the country into the lap of the United Nations. After several months of debating and a bitter struggle, the U.N. ultimately created the State of Israel on May 14, 1948.

The Jewish population of Israel numbered some 650,000 in 1947 and a little more than half of these pioneers lived in the three major cities of Tel Aviv, Haifa, and Jerusalem, while the rest were scattered in communal agricultural settlements (kibbutzim and moshavim), villages, and hamlets. Herzliya consisted of one long street extending from the Tel Aviv-Haifa road to Hadar Street at the eastern end of town. All the side streets were short, narrow, unpaved alleys of deep, fine sand. On a Saturday afternoon Avram Ber took me to the outskirts of Herzliya where newly arrived Yemenite Jews lived in tents or in temporary shacks (tzrifim). It was an exhilarating experience to behold these long-lost brethren with their charming simplicity, their abiding faith, and the sing-song of their Sephardic Hebrew dialect which sounded like an enchanting melody. We arrived to find the menfolk assembled in the makeshift synagogue, seated on rough wooden benches or standing wrapped in their taleisim (prayer shawls) reciting Psalms responsively. The scene took us back thousands of years to ancient Israel as if time had stood still and nothing had happened in between. We also made courtesy calls on the Mayor of Herzliya, Mr. Michaeli, a Histadrut functionary, and the Rabbi of the community—both of whom brought me up to date on local developments.

On my visit to Tel Aviv I was excited to see the first all-Jewish city in action. At that time, it was less than forty years old. The main avenue and the center of all major activities was Allenby Street, which ran from the Petach Tikva Road due west to the Mediterranean; all of the major Histadrut, public, cultural, and commercial activities were clustered on this street. The second major avenue, Ben Yehuda Street, branched off Allenby near King George Street and ran due north parallel to the Yarkon Rivulet. There were elections being held to the National Assembly, the Vaad Leumi, and I was amazed to see thirty parties with full lists of candidates competing for this precursor of the Knesset (Parliament). The walls of many buildings were plastered with the emblems, slogans, and platforms of the respective parties, there were graffiti on every available space, and handbills littered the sidewalks.

When I was invited to meet Yosef Sprinzak, the leader of the Histadrut and later the first Speaker of the Knesset, he asked me—with evident pride— what I thought of Tel Aviv. After telling him of the deep emotions which the first Jewish city stirred in me, I could not refrain from asking why it was necessary to mar the beauty of the city with all of the electioneering claptrap.

With a twinkle in his eye this great Labor Zionist leader who was famous for his wit replied, "Chaver (comrade) Dr. Schulzinger, Tel Aviv is more than a city—it is an adventure (Tel Aviv zu lo eer, ze hu mif'al)." In that sense he was, of course, right. As a large, all-Jewish, self-governing city, it stood for the embryonic State of Israel—the emerging Jewish commonwealth.

Wherever I went I ran into one exciting experience after another—the young children at play innocently creating a new Hebrew vocabulary; the classical Hebrew theater, the Habima, with its first-class repertoire and actors speaking their lines in a flawless Hebrew to a Hebrew-speaking audience; and the street corners bearing the proud names of the Prophets, Kings, and Jewish leaders of old or the names of modern Hebrew and Yiddish writers, poets, or Zionist leaders. A Jewish policeman directing traffic in the holy tongue became an unforgettable experience for me. The people on the street, though total strangers, appeared to me like one extended family—all being pioneers, builders of a home for the common weal, and oblivious of self-interest. I was also impressed by the open doors that were seldom locked, even at night, and the near absence of inequity or crime. With all of their high-handedness, the British had the good sense not to show themselves in Tel Aviv.

In Tel Aviv there were dinners and receptions given by our cousins to which my family from Herzliya was invited. At these gatherings we had the pleasure of meeting many other relatives and friends and we were liberally informed as well as entertained. In Jerusalem I stayed with my cousins Chana and Avram Druyan, who arranged a gala party to which my parents and sister and many of Jerusalem's prominent physicians and Zionist leaders were invited. This was a most interesting group of people, many with historic achievements to their credit, and some lively and stimulating discussions ensued.

The approach to Jerusalem, which was surrounded by barren, steep mountains, deep gorges, and twisting roads, was breathtaking. The desolate surroundings were broken here and there by patches of green, new saplings, or trees planted by the Jewish National Fund in an effort to reforest the denuded land and to cover the nakedness that resulted from centuries of neglect and abuse. The city itself was small and clustered around the western approach to the Old Walled City of Jerusalem.

The first sight of the holy Western Wall of the Temple stirred me to the quick and brought tears to my eyes. Chana was my guide to the Wall, which could only be reached through narrow winding alleys full of filth and overpowering smells. Only a small part of the Wall was visible. Most of it was hidden by small Arab dwellings which were attached to it on either side, while the space in front of the Wall was a mere two yards wide. As soon as we reached the Wall a shammes (sexton) suggested the lighting of a candle. He then recited the "el molei rahamim" (prayer for the souls of the deceased) and, after the payment of a small offering, we were left to ourselves to behold this magnificent and tragic reminder of our ancient glory and to reflect in deep silence. Also impressive was the ancient Hurvah Shul, which was entered near the far end of the Wall while crouching down sunken steps. It was full of marvelous carvings and the Aron Hakodesh (holy ark) and the large bimah (podium) in the center were in the oriental style—a reminder of the architecture of the Middle Ages. The Hurvah Shul and the Jewish Quarter of the Old City of Jerusalem were destroyed in 1948 during the War of Independence and the entire area was occupied by the Jordanians until it was liberated in the Six-Day War of 1967.

Another Jerusalem landmark was the Keren Hayesod Building, which was the nerve center of all Zionist activities. It was also the headquarters of the Vaad Leumi (National Assembly) and the Keren Kayemeth (Jewish National Fund). In this building was a replica of Theodore Herzl's study with all of the original furnishings and mementoes as they existed in his lifetime in Vienna. It was a moving experience to look at the work desk, the writings, and the library of the founder of the Zionist organization—the modern-day prophet who foretold the rebirth of Israel as a Jewish state almost to the day. I was proud to affix my name in the Golden Book of the JNF among the other visitors to this hallowed shrine.

An exciting experience was a visit to ancient Jericho and a V.I.P. tour of the Dead Sea Salt Works, which was then situated at the northern end of the sea. The forty-mile trip from Jerusalem to Jericho was through the barren Judean Hills with a clear view of the Dead Sea all the way down to the lowest spot on earth. Jericho itself is an oasis with fine stone houses nestled amidst luscious orchards and gardens. Chana Druyan traveled with me and she introduced me to the manager of the Dead Sea Works, who was a friend of hers. He was a charming host and he guided us through the intricacies of the plant as well as the huge outdoor basins which were flooded with the waters of the Dead Sea and then permitted to evaporate in the sun—the dried residue of which was then separated into table salt, bromides, phosphates, and other chemicals and minerals. We were treated to a delicious lunch and early in the afternoon we enjoyed bathing in the sea. The heavy mineral content of the water keeps the body afloat in any position, which was a godsend for an indifferent swimmer like myself. The salt water has an astringent and bracing effect with a slight stinging and burning sensation. The rapid changes in temperature seemed incredible to me—bracing cool in the morning, suffocating heat at noon, comfortably warm in the early afternoon, and chilling cold after 4 P.M.

The next adventure was a three-week tour of the pioneer settlements of the country as the guest of the JNF. My traveling companion was the Secretary-General of the JNF, who was on an inspection tour to check on the crops and the economic and financial needs of the settlements. We spent about three hours in each place during which time there was an exchange of information while inspecting the fields, orchards, livestock, barns, water tanks, agricultural equipment, etc. The tour always ended with a delicious meal in the public dining hall which usually consisted of dairy products and fresh vegetables from the garden. It reminded me of the delicious fresh dairy and vegetable meals I enjoyed in Serei, with the added thrill that these tasty fresh foods were the products of Jewish pioneers in our ancestral land. Among the settlements we visited on this tour were several that were only a few weeks old. They consisted of a large, prefabricated community hall, a barn, a water tower, and a barbed-wire fence with a few sandbagged guard posts. These settlements were among the eleven that were set up in the dark of night at the end of Yom Kippur of 1947, by members of neighboring kibbutzim. The stealth was dictated by the British ban against establishing new settlements. Under Ottoman law, which was the law of the land, the British could not intervene once a viable settlement was in place.

Before leaving for Eretz Yisroel, Dr. Helen Glueck, a prominent Cincinnati physician and researcher, had given me a letter and photographic material for her husband, Dr. Nelson Glueck, who was on a tour of duty in Jerusalem. Dr. Glueck had made important archeological discoveries in the Negev and in Transjordan before the war and had done classified intelligence work for the American Government during the war. He was now serving as head of the Rockefeller Archeological Museum in Jerusalem and was continuing his efforts to cultivate friendly relations with important Arab leaders. Since regular mail had not been re-established as yet, Dr. Glueck was very happy with the letter and the supplies I delivered and was glad to get filled in on news from Cincinnati and about mutual friends. He took me on a tour of the museum, pointing out some of their more valuable possessions, after which we sat down for tea and a discussion of the political climate.

Like most teachers at HUC at that time, Dr. Glueck was lukewarm towards Zionism and was strongly opposed to the creation of a Jewish state. He was an active member of Brith Shalom, an organization of intellectuals headed by Rabbi Judah L. Magnes, the Chancellor of the Hebrew University and formerly of New York, which advocated the establishment of a bi-national Arab-Jewish state on the model of Austria-Hungary before World War I. Their arguments were that the Arabs would never agree to the creation of a Jewish state, that the creation of a Jewish state would lead to endless wars, and that the Jewish people were bound to lose out in the end because of the disproportionate numerical strength of the Arabs and their eventual economic and strategic superiority. The Arab world was then in a state of flux with only a few weak Arab states in existence and the leader of the Palestinian Arabs, the Grand Mufti of Jerusalem, in exile as Hitler's confidant and as one of the chief architects of the Holocaust.

I pointed out to Dr. Glueck that most Zionists and the vast majority of all Jews were opposed to his group's views because of a conviction that a dual state of hostile peoples would not be viable, that the superior birthrate of the Arabs would engulf a shrinking Jewish minority, and that if Jews ever needed a place they could call their own surely this was the time. After the lesson of World War II, I continued, when country after country refused Jews even a temporary haven, an independent state would be worthwhile even if its viability was ultimately threatened. The discussion lasted for several hours and became quite heated at times. There were no winners or losers and we parted amicably. Dr. Glueck later served with distinction as president of HUC and was instrumental in founding the HUC campus in Jerusalem and the Nelson Glueck School of Archeology. He was the scion of a long line of Lithuanian Rabbis and his grandfather, Rabbi Nachum Feivel Zvi Revel, was the Rabbi of Pren, a shtetl fifty miles north of Serei. His cousin, Rabbi Bernard Revel, was the founder and president of Yeshiva College, the first Orthodox Rabbinic seminary in the U.S., which later evolved into Yeshiva University.

Dr. Glueck offered to drive me to the home of Yitzhak Ben Zvi, the head of the Vaad Leumi and later the second President of Israel, which I gratefully accepted. Mr. Ben Zvi was a quiet, scholarly man with expertise on the Falashas (Ethiopian Jews) and he had been entertained at our home on several occasions in connection with his visits to Cincinnati. Ben Zvi had aged considerably since I had last seen him and, as he appeared to be under the weather, we did not stay very long.

Another memorable experience was a visit to the Hebrew University on Mount Scopus. It was a clear day and from the height of Mount Scopus one could see the Mediterranean Sea to the west and the Dead Sea to the east. The view of Jerusalem and its immediate environs was breathtaking from this vista, especially when seen from the amphitheater. Chana took me on a tour of the Hadassah Hospital, where she worked, and I was introduced to more people than I could remember. On the way to Mount Scopus I had an interesting experience with a local Arab taxi driver. As I paid the fare he noticed that I had given him all the money I had on me. "It is not good to be left without money in a strange city," the taxi driver said. With that he quickly returned part of the fare and drove off in a hurry. He was an intelligent, young,

Hebrew-speaking Arab and we had a pleasant conversation on the way from the city.

Because of the uncertainties of overseas travel, I had obtained a round-robin letter from Mr. Fry to all TWA representatives abroad asking them to facilitate my return home. After four weeks in Eretz Yisroel and with no end to the TWA strike in sight, I began to worry about my return flight. From the TWA representative in Jerusalem I learned that a group of Zionist leaders was arranging a charter flight to the United States by way of Brazil. With some difficulty I obtained a seat on this flight even though it was on a small military plane and the itinerary was considerably out of the way. A few days before the departure to Brazil the TWA strike ended and I was advised to be in Cairo in three days. Now that I had two tickets and could use only one, I wanted to cancel the Brazil flight but met with considerable resistance. Although my case was not too strong, the problem was quietly solved by a high-placed friend. The next day I returned to Cairo by train as I had no stomach for the hazardous flight via the Mizrah airline. The entire family came to the Lod railroad station to see me off. It was a sad and tearful parting.

The train to Cairo was of old European vintage with a narrow corridor along the length of the car and narrow doors leading to small compartments seating six passengers. There was only one other traveler in my compartment, a Jewish man from Minneapolis who was returning home on the same TWA flight from Cairo. Within an hour after boarding the train, as we were approaching Gaza, an Egyptian customs official entered the compartment to check our documents. Prior to this my companion had managed to tell me that, because of the transportation difficulties, his planned three-month visit with his sister in Eretz Yisroel had extended to six months. Although he was worried about his business, he had enjoyed the visit and was ecstatic over the beauty of the country and the prospects for a Jewish homeland. He also told me that he was overloaded with presents for his family and friends in Minneapolis.

When the customs official asked for our passports, I fumbled in my pockets and my companion got his out first. After examining the passport, the official asked my friend whether he was carrying gifts and what their value was. His straightforward answer was that the gifts he was carrying were mostly presents and they could not have cost more than seventy-five dollars. The official then asked whether he had an Egyptian import license. My heart sank at this question since I was carrying as many gifts as my friend, if not more. But the worst was yet to come when the official told my companion that he would have to get off in Gaza because he lacked an Egyptian entry visa. The pleading of the hapless man that Cook's Tours had made all the arrangements for his trip and that he assumed that everything was in order was to no avail. Neither was his pleading that missing the scheduled TWA flight would mean a delay of several months before he could return home.

When my turn came I was ready. I handed the official my V.I.P. letter from Governor Bricker together with the passport. He read the letter very attentively and was visibly impressed. He then turned to me and said, "You know, Doctor, I am a graduate of the American University in Beirut." "Oh," I said. "The American University in Beirut is a fine university and we are very proud of it." The customs official then engaged me for several minutes in a friendly conversation, which he closed by saying, "You don't have anything to declare, do you?" I replied in the negative and heaved a sigh of relief as he left my compartment with a handshake and a sincere wish for a safe return home.

The trip to Cairo was a long overnight journey on a slow, lumbering, wood-burning train through the Sinai Desert by way of El Arish, Kuneitra, and across the Suez Canal. Although the compartments had snugly fitting double-glass windows and doors, the fine grains of desert sand filtered in and covered everything in sight; they also entered my nose, mouth, and throat and penetrated through my garments to the bare skin. As there was no water or any other kind of refreshment to be obtained, the arrival in Cairo was a true deliverance. Cairo, with its minaretes, the legendary Nile River, and the lush gardens, made a fine impression on emerging from the desert on a cool, sunlit morning.

I was driven to the Shepherd Hotel in a horse-drawn taxi and was shown to my room by a seven-foot black Sudanese wearing a one-piece, ankle-length white gown and carrying a foot-long door key that could pass for a lethal weapon. My room turned out to be a suite of three oversized rooms with fourteen-foot ceilings and a fine balcony with an intricate iron-grill design. The furnishings were comfortable, luxurious, and Victorian in style but, as was frequently the case in the Near East, there was only one lavatory and bathroom to a floor and mine was at the far end of a long, wide corridor. The Shepherd Hotel was built by the British at the height of their power to impress the natives with the wealth and might of the Empire. The show of affluence, the daring architecture, and the rich decor were best seen in the main dining hall. It was a huge room with massive pillars and equally massive crystal chandeliers hung from an extremely high ceiling. The most unusual features of the dining hall were the inlays that covered all of the walls, pillars, and ceilings and displayed a fantastic blend of variegated woods and stones of many colors with a rich admixture of gold. The floor was of inlaid wood in intricate geometric designs, which complemented the rest of the magnificent museum-quality hall.

During the two days before departure I decided to see as much of Cairo as I possibly could. My first destination was a former professor of antiquity at the

University of Cairo to whom I had a letter of introduction from his brother in Tel Aviv. This was a time of great nationalistic fervor and turbulence in Egypt as revolutionaries were trying to overthrow the regime of King Farouk, who was reigning under British tutelage. The professor had lost his teaching post of long standing because he was Jewish and he was not allowed to work, even as a guide. But I was told he could help me in a private capacity. I intended to fetch a taxi to get me to the professor's home, but as soon as I passed the doorstep of the hotel I was surrounded by a swarm of guides (dragomen) in multicolored flowing robes who were shouting and screaming, competing to be hired by me. Finding myself surrounded and trapped, unable to move or be heard, I picked the neatest of the lot, who spoke a passable English, and the others retreated. I explained to the guide that all I wanted was to fetch a taxi to take me to my destination. He pointed out that there were no taxis in sight but that since the addressee lived within walking distance he would take me there. The guide was a pleasant-looking man so I agreed to his suggestion. But this was merely a ruse for he never intended to find the addressee, and before long I found myself in the bazaar amidst screaming and shouting merchants proclaiming their wares. My protestations that I did not wish to buy anything were of no avail. Each merchant offered a thimbleful of Turkish coffee as a token of hospitality which, according to my guide, I dared not refuse—although the strong, bitter taste of it was most unpalatable to me. I remembered Mr. Johnson's warning about avoiding the bazaar and how to bargain with these merchants, but when I offered pennies for their inflated prices they uttered bloodcurdling, piercing shrieks which frightened me into submission. I pleaded in vain with my guide to take me out of there but felt compelled to buy some things—things which I did not need and which Pupi did not like and on which I wasted some good money in the bargain. While walking with my guide through the streets of Cairo, we passed areas of unbelievable filth and squalor with sex for sale, both male and female, at every step of the way.

Tired of the fruitless search for the professor, I readily accepted my guide's suggestion to see the Pyramids. He fetched a taxi and off we went to the Cheops Pyramid of Giza. The sight of this Seventh Wonder of the World was overwhelming. Like many other tourists, I marveled how the huge boulders were lifted into place with primitive means and how they were fitted in perfect alignment according to plan. It is difficult to comprehend the total effect of this massive man-made mountain until one stands in its shadow. The surrounding desert only adds to the grandeur. The fact that it was built with the sweat and blood of my ancestors, that it was the focal point of the rebellion of the Hebrew slaves, that it was here that the Hebrew-Egyptian Prince Moses emerged as the emancipator and law-giver of his people and the fountainhead of three world religions—made me reflect and ponder. My guide related that he had seven children, that some of them were attending the University of Cairo, and that he had a fine home in the suburbs. Before parting, he warned me not to wander too far from the main streets, to wear subdued clothing, and to act in a restrained manner. "The young students are hostile towards anyone in Western dress and you may be attacked." Within the year after my visit to Cairo, the Shepherd Hotel was burned down to the ground during one of the student riots against foreign rule.

Next day my guide took me to the Cairo Museum, the old Jewish quarter, the Ancient Synagogue where Maimonedes worshipped, and to the famous Al Saladin Mosque. At the museum I spent most of the time viewing the Tutankhamen treasures, which were spread out over an entire wing. Besides the mummy itself, I was fascinated by the detailed drawings of his burial grounds, his toys as a child, the symbols and retinue of his court, the grainery with seven compartments and the different grain still intact, the sealed perfume bottles from which the contents had evaporated, and some of the magnificent jewelry, statues, and artifacts. On the whole, however, the museum bore evidence of neglect. The Al Saladin Mosque was in the usual Arabic style, but its walls of solid goldleaf and the rich Persian carpets enhanced the beauty of this historic mosque.

The Jewish quarter of Cairo was rebuilt as a shrine by the Cairo Jewish community and the residents of the quarter were being subsidized to retain the ancient atmosphere. I found the Maimonedes synagogue most attractive in its antiquity, especially the carved wooden Aron Hakodesh (Holy Ark). I tried to visualize Maimonedes at prayer in the synagogue and as he was rushing from the small synagogue, which faced the Pyramid of Giza, to the Caliph's Palace to attend to his royal patients. There were all kinds of Hebrew carvings on the lectern and ancient prayer and study books were strewn all over the place. Well-preserved pages of ancient books and whole manuscripts dating back some two thousand years were discovered in the eighteenth century in a section of the synagogue and were rediscovered in the early part of the current century by Rabbi Solomon Schechter. This discovery, known as the Cairo "Genizah," has provided scholars with research material for many decades past and will continue to do so for many decades to come.

In the evening I went to see a show where the foremost belly dancer of Egypt was the main attraction. Since I was a good student of anatomy, it gave me a thrill to see in action every muscle that I knew so well by name, origin, insertion, and function. The dancer was a first-rate artist and she totally captivated her male audience, which became part of the act by joining in with singing and hand-clapping at appropriate junctures. In a performance that lasted well over an hour, this scantily clad and heavily bejeweled artist did not display any vulgarities or erotic nuances. Perhaps it is because of my first exposure to this art form that I remember it so well.

The next day I was on my way home by way of Athens, Rome, Paris, Shannon, and New York. The flight was uneventful except that it was delayed in Paris for several days because of a storm over the Atlantic. We were put up at a first-class hotel and were encouraged to enjoy the sights. Despite the lapse of thirty months since the end of the war, many of its ravages were still in evidence. The hotel rooms were cold, the bathrooms were without soap, towels, toilet paper, or hot water, and the meals were frugal. Many of the famous buildings looked bleak and dilapidated and some of the tourist attractions were still inaccessible. The walls of the Louvre were bare and the only painting on display was that of the Madonna, which was placed on an easel at the top of the main staircase. The only other works of art were the heavy sculptures which were apparently left in place when the Germans occupied Paris.

An unusual experience was a performance at the Folies Bergere. It was a variety show of song, dance, and pantomime in thirty-seven scenes and it lasted over three hours with one brief intermission. Although there was a great deal of nudity and I did not understand French too well, the artistry was so superb as to keep me totally enraptured. As a result, I never missed seeing the Folies on my subsequent visits to Paris, but the quality of these shows seemed to deteriorate with time and the first performance was undoubtedly the best. After three days in Paris, the flight was resumed and we returned to New York after a refueling stopover in Shannon, Ireland. An overnight sixteen-hour train ride by pullman brought me back to Cincinnati, tired but happy to be home.

My second visit to Israel came in 1951 in response to an invitation from Golda Meir, then Labor Minister in Ben Gurion's Cabinet, to advise the Israeli Government on industrial hygiene and safety. Pupi was happy to join me on this trip, as was our twelve-year-old son Joseph. On reaching our cabin on the *Queen Mary*, we found a gorgeous bouquet of flowers and a telegram wishing us a happy voyage from Mr. and Mrs. George Rosenthal of the Rosenthal Printing Company. We were favored by unusually fine weather and, as the skies were clear and the ocean relatively calm, we spent most of our time on deck playing shuffleboard and other games as well as reading and socializing. The meals were like banquets, we met many interesting people, the ship's entertainment was excellent, and the crossing was made in four and one-half fun-filled days. At times I could not help but think of my previous crossing thirty years earlier aboard *The Cedric* when mid-winter thirty-foot waves pounded the converted troop ship and for fourteen days I was seasick, miserable, and alone.

On Friday night during the crossing, we went to the ship's chapel for Sabbath services and Pupi was thrilled to meet the Solomons, a couple from Toronto who were friends of my cousin Belle James. During the Sabbath Morning services I was called up to the reading of the Torah for an "aliya" and was surprised when the next worshipper to be called was none other than Mr. Herbert Lehman, the former Governor of New York and confidant of Franklin Delano Roosevelt. Although Mr. Lehman was now a private citizen, he was the recognized leader of the American Jewish community and a member of the Lehman Brothers banking house. The *Queen Mary* docked in Cherbourg, France and we took a train to Paris. There was an immediate rush to the dining salon on the train and we were thrilled to see the Governor being seated at our table. We had a long and interesting conversation and the Governor was genuinely pleased to learn of our commitment to Israel and about my mission. Joseph was excited by the presence of such an illustrious person at our table and he was made very happy when the Governor gave him his autograph. Europe had now partly recovered from the ravages of the war and we spent three days each in Paris, Zurich, and Rome visiting museums, taking in the sights, and seeing some shows.

In Israel we were greeted at the airport by the entire family and from then until we left it was an endless succession of dinners, receptions, get-togethers, and touring the country from Dan to Beersheva. We made our headquarters at the Dan Hotel in Tel Aviv, which had just opened for business, and it was at this hotel that we received a stream of relatives and friends, many of whom had only recently arrived in Israel. Some of the guests were members of Pupi's family who had survived the Holocaust and we were all happy to see each other and to exchange information about family matters and about other survivors. Among the family members and friends we saw were Pupi's cousins Betty Ushpitz, Raya Milikowsky, Yocheved Bronshtein in Tel Aviv; her school friends Chaya Hendelman in Raanana and Miriam Epstein Harpaz in Jerusalem, and my cousins Chanele Steinberg and Valia Yanovsky in Tel Aviv. In Jerusalem we stayed with our cousins Chana and Avram Druyan, who lived on the corner of Jaffa Road and King George Street. While there Joseph struck up a close friendship with Zvi Druyan, Chana's son, and the two spent a great deal of time together. During this visit to Israel we did not stay with my parents in Herzliya for lack of facilities, but we did see them frequently—between visits to other parts of the country and on Sabbath weekends. As in 1947, the Sabbath services and the Sabbath meals turned out to be memorable events and they were made even more poignant by Israel's newly-won independence. Pupi and Joseph, to whom this was a new experience, were also greatly impressed. The festive mood of the Sabbath was magnified by the presence of many guests—our neice Chana Slavita who was living in Tel Aviv, Chana Druyan from Jerusalem, my brother-in-law's sister and her husband from Rehovot, and other invited guests.

It was an exhilarating experience to see Israel as an independent state even though the ravages of the two-year War of Independence were still in evidence. Especially noticeable were the burned-out hulks of motor vehicles along the roadside. Another jarring experience was the sight of the "no-man's land" in the middle of Jerusalem separating Israel from Jordan just beyond the King David Hotel. Similarly depressing was the sight of the barbed-wire barricades at the Mandelbaum Gate, Mea Shearim, and other prominent border places in the center of the divided city. Access to the holy Western Wall was closed.

Soon after we arrived in Jerusalem we called on Golda Meir, whose ministry was then housed in the Russian compound. She received us with open arms and extended to us every possible courtesy throughout our stay in Israel. After she inquired about mutual friends in Cincinnati and about our plans for seeing the country, we discussed current events and she told us about some of her experiences as Israel's ambassador to Moscow and her emotional encounter with the Jews of Moscow when she visited the Moscow synagogue on Rosh Hashanah. Golda then introduced me to the Director of the Ministry of Labor, Mr. Zvi Bernson (who later became a Justice of the Supreme Court), and Mr. Bernson called in Mr. Aaronson, the head of the Division of Industrial Hygiene and Safety, and his assistant, Chaim Pomerantz, both of whom were engineers. We discussed various technical problems and then agreed on an itinerary which consisted of a two-week guided tour of Israeli plants and workshops with Mr. Pomerantz as my guide. I was also to conduct a series of seminars in Tel Aviv, Haifa, and Jerusalem for groups of physicians and safety engineers. At the end of the tour we were to meet again and I was to give my impressions and make recommendations.

There were only three major plants in Israel at that time—the Ruthenberg Electric Station in Tel Aviv, and the Imperial Chemical Works and the Nesher Cement Factory in Haifa. There was also one large construction company in the country, the Solel Bone Co-operative of the Histadrut. The rest of Israel's productive capacity consisted of small and primitive workshops. There was only one industrial physician in the country and he was employed on a part-time basis by the Nesher Cement Company. We discussed various problems as we went along and Mr. Pomerantz took voluminous notes.

My seminars were well attended and a great many questions were asked, especially in the area of accident prevention. At the end of my tour I met again with Golda Meir and her chief aides and I made a number of recommendations which I later incorporated in a twenty-page report. Foremost among my suggestions was to concentrate new plants and workshops in industrial compounds with well-staffed clinics to identify and eliminate hazards, to prevent accidents, and to provide emergency care for the injured. Industrial compounds were non-existent at the time, even in the U.S., but since Israel was beginning from scratch I thought that a concentration of facilities would be most opportune. I also recommended that a physician and an engineer be sent to the U.S. for a year to study modern safety methods, occupational hygiene, and toxicology, and that these trained persons should then form the nucleus of a department of occupational safety and health at one of the Israeli universities. Another recommendation was to install "scrubbers" or electrostatic precipitators in the smokestacks of all major plants, especially in Haifa, where the air was grossly polluted from the Nesher Cement works.

Before I left for Israel I had prepared a lengthy paper on the causes and prevention of accidents for delivery before the Israel Medical Association. This paper was published in full in the medical journal of the Israel Medical Association and it was the first publication of my researches. Seeing it in print in the Hebrew language in the land of my dreams greatly enhanced the pleasure of my visit to Israel. Before delivering this paper I showed it to Dr. Rubenstein of Herzliya, who was the town's foremost physician and who revered my parents. Besides his great erudition in medicine, Dr. Rubenstein was a distinguished philologist and a linguist well versed in Latin, Greek, Arabic, ancient and modern Hebrew, and other Semitic languages. Dr. Rubenstein was the son of the famous Rabbi Rubenstein of Vilna whom I knew during World War I; he was also the author of a ten-volume encyclopedia of Hebrew medical nomenclature. As he was reading my paper he kept jumping out of his chair. When I asked him if my Hebrew was adequate and to correct any linguistic errors, he exclaimed with his customary impatience, "There are no errors and those ignoramuses do not possess one tenth of your knowledge of Hebrew." He did suggest a few minor changes but on the whole he made me very happy. When I asked Dr. Rubenstein why he called his ten volume encyclopedia an abridged dictionary, he replied, "Because I abridged it from twenty volumes." By contrast, Dr. Goldstein of Tel Aviv called his small two-volume medical dictionary "The Great Encyclopedia of Hebrew Medical Nomenclature." It all seemingly depends on the point of view. Dr. Goldstein was a practicing internist in Tel Aviv and the founder of the Israel Magen David Adom—the equivalent of the Red Cross—and I spent a pleasant afternoon with him covering a variety of topical subjects.

One of the most revered physicians in Israel was Dr. S. Sherman, an E.N.T. specialist in Tel Aviv who was the founder and lifetime president of the Israel

Medical Association. I was introduced to this gentle man by my cousin, Dr. Avram Druyan, who practiced dermatology in Jerusalem and was the lifetime secretary of the Israel Medical Association. Israeli medicine was largely under the control of the Kupat Holim (Sick Fund) and Israeli physicians found themselves overburdened by excessive record keeping, inadequate compensation, and numerous petty bureaucratic annoyances. Doctors Sherman and Druyan poured out a litany of grievances and they asked me to intervene on behalf of Israel's physicians with Kupat Holim and the Israeli Government. Israel was still a very small country and my close relationship with Golda, the Israeli Government, and the Labor Party which controlled it was well known. I met with Dr. Toibe Berman, the head of Kupat Holim and a close friend of Golda Meir, and discussed with her the just complaints of the Israeli physicians. She promised to take them up with her executive board and the problems were subsequently adjusted to everybody's satisfaction. I performed the same task as unofficial intermediary between the Israel Medical Association and Kupat Holim during my subsequent visits to Israel in 1954 and 1958. On these occasions I was invited to sit in at meeting of the Vaad Hapoel (the Executive Board) of the Kupat Holim and to present my views directly to the governing body. Later on, as the Government grew and became more bureaucratic and the problems became more complex, they were no longer amenable to informal mediation and Israeli physicians had to resort to strikes to redress their grievances.

On one occasion, Doctors Sherman and Druyan urged me to undertake the organization of American physicians as an auxiliary of the Israel Medical Association. Having contributed my fair share to Jewish public service and being in the midst of my accident researches, I begged off for lack of time. They declared me the first foreign member of the Israel Medical Association and turned to Dr. Glaser of Boston to undertake the task. He is still the secretary of this organization, which has proved useful and viable.

In 1951 Israel was still in the grip of an economic crisis and there were shortages of many household necessities and most appliances. After we returned home I sent a refrigerator, an electric stove, and an electric washing machine for my parents and a Ford van for my brother-in-law. My parents were unable to use the appliances for several years because of a shortage of electricity. The washing machine they never used in the normal way because they lacked confidence in its cleaning capacity, but to please me they used it for a final rinsing. My brother-in-law, however, made good use of the van for a long time. Hitherto he used to distribute dairy products to retail stores on the back of a small donkey. The van enabled him to expand his business, to be relieved of a great deal of drudgery, and to earn a good living with enhanced self-respect. In each of Israel's wars the van was mobilized together with my brother-in-law in a transportation pool and upon his retirement two decades later, he sold it at a decent price. For Pupi's girlfriend Miriam Epstein Harpaz, whom we saw on every one of our visits to Israel, we sent a set of new tires for their small car and they were very grateful for our thoughtfulness. Mr. Harpaz was an old pioneer who became a building contractor. At one time, we were told, Mr. Harpaz met King Hussein's grandfather King Abdullah in connection with a building contract which he had undertaken in Jordan. Miriam Harpaz served as a nurse in the first-aid station of the Israeli Knesset and died in 1980. Of their three sons, one is a colonel in the Israeli Army, one is in international agricultural banking, and the third lives on a kibbutz.

Shortly after we returned to Cincinnati, I received a letter from Dr. Claus Dror of Haifa, a 1936 emigré from Germany, that he would like me to help him come to Cincinnati to enroll in our Postgraduate School of Industrial Medicine. I felt gratified by the prompt response to one of my recommendations, but there were major obstacles to overcome. Dr. Dror was married with two small children and he had no funds with which to support himself in the U.S. for a year; he also had to be released from his Army duties and his obligations to Kupat Holim. Another problem was getting him admitted to the Postgraduate School and obtaining an entry visa to the U.S. I immediately contacted Dr. Robert Kehoe, the dean of the school, and Dr. Dror was admitted even though the school was already three weeks in session. A call to the office of Senator Robert Taft in Washington produced an assurance that he would expedite an entrance visa for Dr. Dror's behalf with the Israeli Army and the Kupat Holim. He obtained a prompt release and within three weeks after I received Dr. Dror's letter he was in Cincinnati attending school and living in one of the spare rooms in my clinic. My clinic was still on a twenty-four hour-schedule and, by covering for me during off hours, Dr. Dror earned the necessary funds while receiving a rounded education in occupational medicine.

Dr. Dror proved to be an ideal choice for the task. Upon returning to Israel he established a department of occupational medicine in Kupat Holim and several decades later, upon his retirement, he established a department of occupational medicine at the Tel Aviv University. Engineer Pomerantz also sought my help for admission to the Graduate School of Hygiene and Safety in New York, which I gladly provided. Upon his return to Israel, Mr. Pomerantz helped develop the section of hygiene and safety in the Israeli Labor Ministry. Mr. Aaronson, a charming person and an able administrator, remained the head of the section of hygiene and safety for several decades until his retirement. Also, some industrial compounds were built in Israel with considerable success. The only one of my recommendations that was not acted upon was pollution—it seems that the economics of the problem was too great of a hurdle to overcome.

During our 1954 visit to Israel, as on previous occasions, we toured the country and spent a great deal of time with friends and relatives, and I conducted seminars. A special feature this time was the pleasure of taking my parents for a tour of the southern part of Israel, which they had never seen. As we passed luscious orchards, new settlements, or Biblical sites, my parents expressed their thanks to God for his miracles and wonders with appropriate benedictions. At noon we stopped in Beersheva for refreshments and to rest. Beersheva was still a small Arab village with a few Jewish settlers on the outskirts. We parked in front of an Arab inn and found room around a small table in the ancient stone structure in which the inn was housed. The place was crowded and noisy with Arabs and Jews conducting business in loud voices and with lively gesticulations while treating each other to Turkish coffee or cold drinks. Mother and my sister Sheine spread out the kosher food they had brought with them, which consisted of hard-boiled eggs, cheeses, and oranges, and we all ate heartily after washing and saying grace. After reciting aloud the Birhat Hamazon (Grace after Meals), Father expressed a desire to see the desert, which was some ten miles south of Beersheva past Abraham's Well and the camel market. On reaching the edge of the desert, we stopped and Father looked around and again recited a benediction. After driving a few miles into the sameness of sand dunes, stunted plants, and blazing sun, we turned back towards Herzliya. About midway we stopped in Rehovot for a rest and, after attending to our personal comforts, we recited the mincha prayers in an open clearing and returned to Herzliya at about 6 P.M., somewhat tired but very happy. After resting for a while, Pupi and I began to dress for a dinner party in Tel Aviv and we were surprised when Mother insisted on joining us despite the fact that she was in her mid-eighties and had just completed a twelve-hour, grueling journey. It was a family gathering which she did not want to miss and she proved herself up to the challenge. When we returned to Herzliya at 1 A.M., Mother was beaming and felt less tired than we did.

During this visit, my father accepted our invitation to go with us to see a movie. Father was now approximately ninety and it was the first and only time that he had gone to a theater. He marveled at the miracle before his very eyes, but maintained that it was a waste of valuable time and a possible cause of iniquity. One day, Father took me aside "for a serious talk." He told me that he had prepared a manuscript consisting of Talmudic excerpts and commentaries and that he would like me to publish it. Father's manuscript was written on the margins and unused pages of his customers' peddler ledger that he had brought with him from Cincinnati. Without hesitation I promised him that it would get published, and I could see that I had made him very happy.

When I returned from Israel with Father's manuscript, I sought the advice of Rabbi Eliezer Silver about its publication. "I will let you know in two weeks," said Rabbi Silver. When I met him again in his study at the appointed time, Rabbi Silver offered three "good reasons" why the manuscript should be published: "The first reason is 'kibud av v'eim (thou shouldst honor thy father and mother)'; the second reason is that your father's selections from the vast ocean that is the Talmud are a mirror of the man and the book is therefore of importance to you and your family; and the third reason is 'es iz nit shlecht (it is not bad)' "—which, in the Rabbi's way of speaking, meant that it was pretty good. Rabbi Silver edited the book, wrote a laudatory haskama (approval), and made all the necessary arrangements for its publication. I greatly appreciated his efforts and was only too happy to defray the expenses, which were not excessive. I was especially grateful when Rabbi Silver ordained my nonagenarian father as a "Rabbi"—knowing what it meant to my father. The book, *Likutei Chaim*, was published in New York and Father was excited and rejuvenated when I brought him four advance copies of the book on my visit to Israel in 1958. He read the book from cover to cover and before I left he handed me a list of corrections for the final printing.

Rabbi Silver, who was known as the "Gaon Hador" (the most erudite Talmudic scholar of his generation) was the Chief Orthodox Rabbi of Cincinnati and the U.S. for forty years and the most dynamic leader American Orthodox Jewry had produced. He was the lifetime president of the Agudat Harabonim (the organization of Orthodox Rabbis) and he wielded great influence. He divided his time between New York and Cincinnati and achieved wonders in bringing order out of chaos in the religious, educational, and philanthropic institutions of his constituency. His greatest achievement was perhaps as head of the Vaad Hahatzalah, the rescue committee which saved many thousands of Rabbis, Talmudic students, and other Jews from Nazi extermination and brought help and comfort to the survivors of the Holocaust. Rabbi Silver was a brilliant young Rabbi and the descendant of a long line of prominent Lithuanian Rabbis when he came to the U.S. in 1907 at the age of eighteen. Within a decade he was well known among Orthodox Jews in the U.S. and he became a force to be reckoned with. Despite his impatience and his dogmatic manner with those who deviated from Orthodoxy, he befriended many of the non-observant, especially the Cincinnati Labor Zionists, the Poale Zion. Rabbi Silver spent many hours on innumerable happy occasions at our home, celebrating and singing Hebrew and Yiddish songs with Hassidic exuberance. "Anyone who works for the upbuilding of Israel fulfills most of the commandments of the Torah," said Rabbi Silver—this from a man who was, for many years, president of Agudath Yisroel, a non-Zionist Orthodox organization. His attitude towards the Jewish causes I espoused and to me personally can be seen from his introduction to my father's book:

"During the past twenty-seven years in Cincinnati I have come to know my friend Dr. Moshe Simcho Schulzinger intimately as an outstanding physician, as a man of great learning and as a dedicated community leader who is interested in everything that is good and useful. I have seen him in his home, in his succah, at his office, and at public meetings, and have observed his love for Torah, Jewish education, our people, and our land. He is a man full of enthusiasm and has great admiration for his nonagenarian father...."

In 1958, while conducting a seminar on accident causes and prevention in Tel Aviv, I was surprised to learn that some of my listeners had advanced copies of my talk. Upon inquiry, I learned that they had received reprints of several papers I was to read before the World Health Organization in Brussels two weeks hence. I was also surprised when some of the physicians in my audience began instantly translating my Hebrew remarks into Polish. When I stopped to ask how many did not understand Hebrew more than half raised their hands. I then continued in English, which nearly all understood. Many of the physicians in my audience had arrived in Israel a year earlier from Poland, during the mass exodus of 1957. The language factor represented a veritable Tower of Babel during the early years of Israel's statehood. This problem was eventually overcome, but with a deleterious effect on the purity of the Hebrew language.

On our way home from Israel, after I was through with my offical business at the W.H.O. Congress in Brussels, I contacted a classmate of mine from the gymnasium (and a former suitor of Pupi's sister Leah) who entertained us at his home and took us on a two-day tour of Belgium. Lazar Burak studied engineering in Belgium and married a Belgian girl. He became a successful businessman in forest products and survived the Holocaust with the help of his wife's family. Although he became totally assimilated, he heartily participated in a review of the Hebrew and Yiddish songs we used to sing. I was also told that he supported Israeli causes liberally, though anonymously. His only son was not aware of his father's Jewish origin.

Pupi and I subsequently visited Israel ten more times, sometimes in consecutive years and at other times after considerable lapses of time. Although some details remain vivid, most have fused into an overall impression. The tempo of building new towns, villages, and agricultural settlements was so great during the Fifties and Sixties that important landmarks faded out of sight year after year. The twisting, narrow roads eventually gave way to modern expressways; Jerusalem was transformed from a small, ancient town to a beautiful, modern metropolis; a dozen important universities were founded; a major high-technology industry came into being; and the per-capita publication and reading of books became the highest in the world. One of the greatest achievements of the State of Israel is undoubtedly the absorption of three million immigrants by 650,000 Israelis, and molding them into a functioning democracy in the short period of three decades. These achievements are even more remarkable considering that most of the new arrivals were poverty-stricken and unskilled, that many came from the hell of Hitler's Germany, and many others came from the Arab world where time had stood still for a thousand years—and all of this despite five full-scale wars.

Two of my visits to Israel were in connection with the publication of scholarly works. In 1972 I learned from Rabbi Gershon Winer that an Israeli scholar, Yehuda Even Shmuel (Dr. Kaufman), had worked forty years to produce a scholarly translation of *The Kuzari* in modern Hebrew, but that its publication was being thwarted by a lack of funds. I volunteered to have the volume published at my expense and authorized Rabbi Winer to negotiate the details. In a few weeks I was advised that the President of Israel, Zalman Shazar, would like to join me in this effort. I was elated over this development for I knew that the President and the author were lifelong friends and that the President's endorsement would enhance the public acceptance of the book. Even Shmuel's *Sefer Hakuzari* has remained on the best-seller list in Israel since its publication, and the author was awarded the highest literary prize of Israel.

The story of the Khazars had a great influence on me as a child. At a time when beleaguered Judaism was in very low esteem and the Jewish people were in danger of extinction, the pagan King of the Khazars converted to Judaism and his people followed suit. For a period of four hundred years, from the eighth to the eleventh centuries, this powerful empire thrived in Central Asia astride the main caravan routes from China and India until it was defeated by Slavic warlords, the early ancestors of the Russian people. The story was depicted by the great Torah sage and poet of the Middle Ages Rabbi Yehuda Halevi (1095-1150) in his philosophical treatise known as the *Sefer Hakuzari*. It deals with the fundamental concepts of the Jewish faith, revelation, and ethics, and embraces all of the lofty spiritual values of mankind. It was written in Arabic so as to reach the widest possible audience, especially the assimilated

348 THE TALE OF A LITVAK

Jews of the period, and also because some of the philosophical concepts and terms were then better conveyed in Arabic, the chief language of many Jews at that time. The book was written in the form of a dialogue between the King of the Khazars and a Rabbi whose wisdom the King admired. Halevi presents a profound and masterly defense of Judaism against Militant Christianity and Islam, which were threatening Judaism from without, and against the Aristotelian rationalists and the anti-Rabbinic Karaites, which were threatening Judaism from within.

As an impressionable youngster I was carried away by this fascinating story. It bolstered my morale, it stimulated my Jewish pride, and it was the subject of many enchanted dreams. One of the early practitioners of the art of translation, Yehuda Ibn Tibbon, rendered *The Kuzari* into Hebrew, but his stilted rendition made the volume unreadable. During our visit to Israel in the spring of 1973, we were entertained several times by Even Shmuel at his home and he presented us with an appropriately inscribed copy of his *Sefer Hakuzari* in which he stated that he too had been haunted by the story of the Khazars from his early youth. He also presented us with copies of his other works. Although in his eighties, he was working long hours to complete six other studies in a race against time. Even Shmuel, who died a few years later, was a witty, gracious, and entertaining host. Among the guests he invited to meet us were the former Mayor of Jerusalem and his wife, Mr. & Mrs. Shragai; his daughter, Mrs. Harris, a noted mathematician and a former secretary to Albert Einstein at Princeton; and his son-in-law, Dr. Hyman Harris, a musicologist, who presented us with a copy of his book on the history of Hebrew liturgical music from ancient until modern times.

In 1974 Pupi and I went to Israel as guests of the Board of Governors of the HUC. Other guests from Cincinnati were Mayor Theodore Berry and newsman Al Schottelkotte, who covered the tour for television. It was a well-organized and most enjoyable gala affair throughout. We spent one Sabbath in Rome, where we attended services at the Rome synagogue and enjoyed a kiddush and a sumptuous Sabbath meal at the Flora Villa Hotel, and on Saturday night we attended a reception at Israel's embassy, where we met Israeli diplomats and some of Rome's Jewish leaders. We also viewed an impressive collection of Japanese art from the ambassador's private collection. The unusually tight security at the embassy was impressive and revealing.

This tour of Israel was studded with many unusual events. There was a visit to the farthest military outpost in the Golan Heights, where I was surprised to see an Israeli soldier studying the Talmud in an army camp-synagogue between tours of duty in the trenches; another learning experience was a visit to a military workshop where massive quantities of captured Russian tanks and other heavy equipment were being reconditioned for future use. We also enjoyed the Sabbath service in the chapel of the Jerusalem campus of HUC on Saturday morning. Amidst a profusion of taleisim (prayer shawls) and yarmulkas (skull caps), we were treated to a three-hour service in Hebrew which was accompanied by a fine choir and was followed by a kiddush and reception that lasted another hour. Pupi and I were thrilled by this rich and beautiful experience, but I said to myself, "Im kein, ma ohilu hahamim b'takantam—If so, where is the reform?"

A most impressive event was the banquet in the Knesset, which was richly decorated for the occasion with the finest of Israel's flowers. The hall was jammed with important members of Israeli society, leaders of thought, and representatives of the Knesset, the Government, the military, and labor. During the cocktail hour we socialized with some old and new friends and everyone was in a happy mood. At the dinner table we were seated between former Ambassador to France Eitan and the president of Israel's Reform Movement, an industrialist from Haifa of German descent, while at the table ahead of us was seated Rabbi Mordechai Kaplan, the well-known dean of American Rabbis and founder of the Reconstructionist Movement. I looked at this nonagenarian and marveled at his impressive appearance and agility.

The speeches were all in good taste, well-proportioned, and to the point, but for some reason I remember only the remarks of Mayor Berry, who quoted, in a correct Hebrew, the famous passage from Micah—

"It has been told thee, O Man, what is good, and what the Lord does require of thee: only to do justly and to love mercy, and to walk humbly with God."

It seemed to me that this non-Jewish, black gentleman neatly summed up what the others meant to say.

During the two weeks of the tour, we got to know one of the finest groups of people we had ever met—all of whom were men of distinction in their respective fields, and I marveled at their sincerity and their dedication to the cause of Reform Judaism. We spent most of our off hours with our fellow Cincinnatians Mr. and Mrs. Robert Goldman and Mr. and Mrs. Richard Mack, and we enjoyed return private visits to the National Museum with them. The tour was under the able leadership of the President of HUC, Rabbi Alfred Gottschalk, who performed his task flawlessly. The Nelson Glueck School of Archeology was launched on this occasion.

The second book which I helped publish was written by a Siberian author, M. Eliuveani (Meir Kantorovich), and deals with researches in Ecclesiastes and Proverbs. The author was a former Zionist leader and Bible scholar in Kovno who was exiled by the Russians to Siberia in 1940. The work was written secretly in a woodshed, from memory, without the benefit of reference books. Eventually some of Eliuveani's writings began to reach the World Bible Center in Jerusalem and a few books were smuggled to the author by underground means. The request that I subsidize the publication of this book came from the former President of Israel Zalman Shazar, who was on his death bed, and it was one of the last letters he wrote. Zalman Shazar (Rubashov) was a poet, publicist, dedicated Labor Zionist leader, fiery orator, and a very warm human being. He had visited our home on many occasions during the pre-State period. Reminding me of our successful joint ventures in the publication of *The Kuzari*, he urged me to "facilitate the publication of this important volume that is being edited by Dr. Ben Zion Luria." It was an heroic task on the part of the editor for the manuscript was written on poor-quality tissue paper and was virtually unreadable, parts were lost in the Russian mail and had to be retrieved, and some of the author's expressions were archaic and they had to be clarified by mail at considerable risk to the author. This volume is of great historical and scholarly interest, but it did not become a best seller.

During our last visit to Israel in 1976, we were received by President Ephraim Katzir in the Beth Hanasi (President's House), where we presented him with a copy of the book by Eliuveani. In the course of the visit, on which we were accompanied by Dr. Gevaryahu and Dr. Luria, we discussed the author and the contents of the new publication as well as the Beth Hatanach project in which I had become interested. President Katzir showed great interest in all of these as well as in my personal and professional background. The leisurely visit ended with tea and picture-taking.

Earlier the same day we spent nearly two hours with Golda Meir in her home at 8 Baron Hirsh Street in Tel Aviv. It was an emotional get-together and Golda and Pupi embraced and cried. We had not seen Golda at close range for about fifteen years after a close, personal friendship dating back to 1922. For a period of about twenty-five years Golda had come annually to Cincinnati on behalf of the Histadrut and the Moetzat Hapoalot (Women's Council). After her lectures she would come to our home or to the home of my cousin Ben Zion Doll for an intimate discussion of topical Zionist subjects. These ad-lib conversations would often last one or two hours past midnight and Golda would occasionally remain with us overnight. Golda's presentations were always distinguished by clarity and simplicity. She had the remarkable gift of making the most complex subject easily understood and self-evident while winning the admiration of her friends and the attention of the skeptics. Yet, despite her personal charm and her many superior qualities, she attracted only a very narrow following before the emergence of the State of Israel. Golda's greatness is perhaps best revealed in the fact that she remained the same inspiring, unassuming, and loveable person after she had achieved world fame as before. During the first decade of the State, we never failed to call on Golda at her Government office and she would often share with us some of her experiences. As her responsibilities grew she became less accessible and we began to abstain from this pleasure and privilege so as not to overburden her.

Nineteen seventy-six was the year after Entebbe and before Egyptian President Sadat's visit to Jerusalem, and Golda filled us in with some details about both. She showed us a photograph of a British bishop on his knees being humiliated by Idi Amin. Sadat, she said, was "oif groise tzores (in great trouble)"—referring to the great poverty and the mind-boggling economic and social problems facing Egypt. Golda was a folk socialist all her life with only a marginal interest in religion, yet she displayed a deep interest in the Beth Hatanach project and she promised her support if I needed sponsorship help to influence interested philanthropists. Her interest in the matter was heightened by Ben Gurion's sponsorship of the project. She also told us that she was trying to raise funds to build a conservatory of music in Tel Aviv, in

In 1976 Pupi and the author visited with Golda Meir in her home in Tel Aviv. Their personal friendship dated back to 1922.

which her son was interested. I presented Golda with a copy of *Researches in Ecclesiastes and Proverbs*, which she accepted with thanks. She asked many questions about the author. She served us tea and cookies which she had baked in her famous two-by-four kitchen, and we had many candid pictures taken by my nephew Rami Ravad. Golda invited her sister, Mrs. Stern of Connecticut, to come and meet her "charming old friends from Cincinnati" and she remained standing in the doorway of her home until we entered our taxi and departed. To the end of her days she continued her chain-smoking habits and denied her terminal illness. Except for some puffiness of the face and swelling of the ankle, she was alert and witty and looked like her charming old self. When I asked her about her health she told us of a recent recovery from a painful attack of the shingles (herpes zoster) and joked about the numerous suggestions she received from well-wishers on how to get rid of the scourge.

Our taxi driver, who had waited in front of Golda's home for two hours to take us to Jerusalem, was so moved by "the great honor of transporting guests whom Golda so singularly honored" that he refused to accept payment for the waiting time. I did not argue but made it up to him later. My nephew Rami, whom Golda had called in from outside to take the pictures, was also deeply impressed—especially when Golda asked him about his studies in the yeshiva and whether he intended to serve in the Armed Forces or claim exemption as a divinity student. Golda was pleased when Rami told her that he was a member of B'nai Akiba, which considers it a duty to serve in the defense of Israel.

Within a year after our visit with Golda we were saddened, along with the rest of the world, by the news of her death from lymphatic leukemia, from which she had suffered during the last fifteen years of her life. This mother in Israel had attained some of the greatest achievements of her glorious career during the years of her affliction. Throughout her life she remained the same honest, compassionate, and dedicated worker for Israel and nothing could sway her from it. I remember a fund-raising visit to Cincinnati when she was Foreign Minister. She had invited herself to our home for the Sabbath. The word spread and many people came to our house to greet her. During the social hour that followed the Sabbath meal, she suffered an attack of cholecystitis (inflamation of the gall bladder) and she remained with us for two days. Yet, while still in her sickbed, she made telephone calls to neighboring communities in fulfillment of her mission.

I administered morphine to her several times to relieve the pain, and on Sunday I took her to the train for St. Louis; the fact that she still had fever did not deter her. Golda's phenomenal impact has generally been attributed to her great personal charm and her God-given abilities as a political leader, diplomat, and statesman. Although she possessed all of these attributes in full measure, she captivated people mainly because she was uniquely natural, genuine, and true.

President Ephraim Katzir and the author; Israel, 1976.

Epilogue

While the fire is out the embers are still burning. Thanks to Providence, a fortunate ancestry, and a loving family, I enjoy good health, am still engaged in my beloved profession, and remain attuned to unfolding events. My admiration for the United States is unabated, my love and great hopes for Israel and the Jewish people continue high, and my faith in a better world is undiminished. I firmly believe that despite inherent difficulties, humanity will eventually emerge triumphant and will establish a peaceful and just society. "In days to come," says Micah, "nation shall not lift up sword against nation.... Each man shall dwell under his own vine and under his own fig tree undisturbed.... Let all the peoples walk, each one in the name of his God."

INDEX